Managing Business Projects

Managing Business Projects: The Essentials differs from many other project management textbooks. Foremost, it is about *business* projects as opposed to construction or engineering projects. Although many techniques, like schedule management, apply to both, they are usually applied differently. As its title conveys, the book explains the essential techniques and perspectives needed for business projects to be successful. The focus is on small- and medium-sized projects, up to $20 million, but often below $1 million. Some literature favors large and mega-projects, but for every mega-project, there are many thousands of smaller projects that are vital to the organization and could involve considerable complexity and risk. Nevertheless, the techniques outlined here also apply to mega-projects and their many subprojects; they even apply to some aspects of construction or engineering projects.

This book does not aim to cover all project management techniques. In real life, there is simply no time for sophisticated 'should-dos'. Rather, it covers the essentials that apply to almost all business projects; these are unlikely to change in the future even as technology and methodologies advance. The driving idea, which is stated repeatedly, is to do the essentials and to do them consistently and well.

Strong emphasis is placed on things that happen before, around, and after the project itself. So, while the basic disciplines like engaging with stakeholders, managing scope, schedules, costs, risks, issues, changes, and communication, are thoroughly explained, other important aspects are covered. These include: governance of a project and of a portfolio of projects, project selection with its financial and non-financial aspects, effective use of the business case through to benefits realization, procurement, outsourcing, and partnership, and also the agile mindset that is valuable beyond Agile projects.

Besides project managers and sponsors, this book is intended for people who are working in business or government, at any level, or for MBA students. It offers perspectives that enable them to learn more from their everyday experience. It is not aimed at undergraduate students, although many would benefit from the contents.

Managing Business Projects

The Essentials

Frank Einhorn

CRC Press
Taylor & Francis Group
Boca Raton London New York

CRC Press is an imprint of the
Taylor & Francis Group, an informa business
AN AUERBACH BOOK

First edition published 2023
by CRC Press
6000 Broken Sound Parkway NW, Suite 300, Boca Raton, FL 33487-2742

and by CRC Press
4 Park Square, Milton Park, Abingdon, Oxon, OX14 4RN

CRC Press is an imprint of Taylor & Francis Group, LLC

Library of Congress Cataloging-in-Publication Data
Names: Einhorn, Frank, author.
Title: Essential project management for business / Frank Einhorn.
Description: First edition. | Boca Raton : CRC Press, 2022. | Includes bibliographical references and index.
Identifiers: LCCN 2022024511 (print) | LCCN 2022024512 (ebook) | ISBN 9781032342320 (hardback) | ISBN 9781032276021 (paperback) | ISBN 9781003321101 (ebook)
Subjects: LCSH: Project management.
Classification: LCC HD69.P75 E45 2022 (print) | LCC HD69.P75 (ebook) | DDC 658.4/04--dc23/eng/20220610
LC record available at https://lccn.loc.gov/2022024511
LC ebook record available at https://lccn.loc.gov/2022024512

ISBN: 978-1-032-34232-0 (hbk)
ISBN: 978-1-032-27602-1 (pbk)
ISBN: 978-1-003-32110-1 (ebk)

DOI: 10.1201/9781003321101

Typeset in Garamond
by SPi Technologies India Pvt Ltd (Straive)

Contents

Preface

Scope and Objectives

This book is intended to be of practical help for all those involved in small- and medium-sized business projects, typically $1 million or less, but up to, say, $20 million. Business projects are needed in both government and in the private sector. In the book, I share concepts that seem obvious to me now, but took years of reflection for me to understand. For example, it took time to recognize the considerable differences between business projects and construction or engineering ones, which are discussed in Chapter 1.

Much of the content covers the project life cycle, which begins when the project is formally started and ends with closeout, by which time the project deliverables have been handed over to the business stakeholders. However, important things like evaluating the justification for the project and benefits realization usually occur before and after the life cycle. Hence the project 'lifetime' concept is used; the lifetime starts when the project is first conceived and ends when the planned benefits have been substantially realized. Thus the project lifetime, during which project governance is done, overarches the project life cycle.

The project sponsor, who may also be the business owner, is involved throughout the project's lifetime, whereas the PM (project manager) may only be involved during the life cycle which ends at project closeout. Both are key players. However, there may be many other important people, like business stakeholders and portfolio management, who would be involved in a broader range of projects.

The book discusses, but does not focus on, portfolio management or program management, which, by definition, deal with multiple projects. Nevertheless, what is covered has considerable relevance for portfolio and program managers. Likewise, the content is relevant for many aspects of construction, engineering, or mega projects, even if these are not specifically addressed.

Because the discipline of project management grew out of engineering and construction projects, many practice guides and textbooks are oriented toward them. In fact, some of the techniques described need to be adjusted, or simply do not work for business projects. The same applies to many project management training courses, some of which use building a house as a sample project. Because the activities involved in building a house are well understood, the ease with which a house project can be planned and tracked gives a false sense of competence. Enthusiastic graduates from such courses may be disappointed that the learning is difficult to apply on a business project, where, even if the goals and deliverables are understood, the activities to achieve them may not be, and evolve over time. This early ambiguity affects everything, including resourcing, scheduling, cost tracking, and communication.

More on Background and Philosophies

Most textbooks and software packages are comprehensive and cover sophisticated techniques. My recommendation to people involved in projects is to develop a broad understanding of project management, but to avoid sophistication and to do the essentials thoroughly. This book covers these essential disciplines which I have applied over many years. They will still be relevant in future in our evolving world of Agile approaches and collaboration technology.

Stakeholders, which include the project team, are key to business projects. Without their willing cooperation, business projects are unlikely to succeed. Listening to them, taking advice, and winning their respect and trust are vital. But this does not mean acceding to their every request. Sound governance contributes greatly to the success of business projects. Governance starts with the project sponsor, the executive who is accountable for the project meeting its objectives. It covers things outside of the project that support or affect the project. Through governance, even the most turbulent project environments can be managed. The PM is the link between governance and the project.

Documentation structures need to be as simple as possible. Templates are fine, but they should be flexible and lightweight. Most documents will be text (such as MS Word), and spreadsheets (such as Excel). A managed documentation repository, whether local or 'in the cloud', to which stakeholders have ready access, is essential.

Technology is helpful, but, contrary to what advertising suggests, there are no products or techniques that will manage the project for you. They are merely tools that enable you to work effectively. There needs to be a balance between becoming an expert at a tool, and shunning technology or being unwilling to adopt new ways of doing things. That said, I recommend focusing on the people and the project rather than getting side-tracked by new tools, techniques, or 'flavors of the month'.

Because communication is such a big part of the PM's job, using well-understood terminology is important. This applies not only to project management terms, but also to business terms, where each organization will have some unique terms or acronyms. Therefore, a glossary for this book is given in Appendix 1; it is simply a list of terms and what they mean.

The PM benefits from a thorough understanding of the justification for the project – the business case. The attitude of "I'm just here to execute the project, so I don't need to understand its rationale" is usually inadequate. To be motivated, the project team and other stakeholders want to know that they are working on something that is important to the organization. If the PM does not communicate the importance, morale may flag. When a project experiences its first serious issue, someone will ask "why are we doing this project in the first place?" The PM needs to provide good answers. Moreover, if there is any concern that the project will not meet expectations, the PM should engage with the sponsor to review the business case, which could even result in the sponsor terminating the project.

Openness and honesty are already alluded to above. If things are not going well and the success of the project is threatened, the sponsor and other key stakeholders must be informed in good time. Naturally, the PM may need time to explore what can be done about it, and to have alternatives and a recommendation when approaching the sponsor. But a lengthy delay, or worse-still saying nothing, would be unacceptable. Executives do not like to be caught off-guard, and delays prevent them from taking timely decisions. Honesty also applies to estimates. Adding unexplained 'fat' to estimates is likely to erode trust between sponsor and PM. On the other hand, outlining the risks and suggesting that an appropriate contingency amount be set aside, is totally acceptable and indeed, necessary. So, while practical techniques will be covered in some detail, building understanding and perspective are also goals.

Applicability and Use of the Book

This book is based on my experience over many years. Most of that experience was in South Africa, where organizations operate similarly to those in North America and Europe. Therefore, the content certainly applies in the 'Western world', but most of it would apply universally. The writing style is informal and almost 'chatty', as though I'm talking to participants on a project management education program. However, sometimes more structured tables or checklists are used.

The book can be used in a number of ways, some of which are: (i) For reading and to contrast the contents with what you already know and use. (ii) To provide a simple project methodology. (iii) To give you a comprehensive course in business project management, and allow you to test yourself using quizzes and case studies. (iv) To offer courses to others, referencing concepts and material. Any manager or PM can benefit from the book, and no specific pre-requisite training is needed. However, without several years of general business experience, some of the concepts may be difficult to assimilate.

Acknowledgments

Many people contributed to this book by reviewing chapters and giving feedback, often leading to considerable changes. Each chapter was reviewed by at least one person, sometimes selected for having specialized knowledge in a particular field. Therefore, I would like to express my thanks and appreciation to the following people who assisted me in this way:

Dr. Giles Austen	Rory Burke
Gareth Coats	Andrew Einhorn
Bronwen Einhorn	Gillian Einhorn
Dr. Clive Enoch	Dr. Geoff G. Garrett
Daléne Grobler	Zubair 'Shoop' Hassen
Dr. Geoff Heald	Rob Jackson
David Merand	Prof. Jack Meredith
Dr. Elizabeth Mkoba	Thabo Mophiring
Dr. Lunga Msengana	Peter Ochse
Mark Peters	T.W. 'Bill' Pierce
Dr. 'Sunny' Ravu	Michael Reynders
Patricia Robinson	V-Adm. Robert Simpson-Anderson
Dr. Peter Tobin	Linda Turner
Thabang Thaoge	Anton van Dalsen
Linky van der Merwe	Dr. Robert Venter
Amanda Versveld	Louise Worsley

I would also like to thank my wife Carolyn who supported me during my project management career. She patiently accepted the hours spent at my desk while doing a PhD, and then several years later, while writing this book.

Another person who deserves special mention is Eric Glover. He was the one, in IBM, who persuaded me to leave sales and to join his project management team. As my manager, he guided me during my years of learning and ensured that there were challenging projects on which to apply the disciplines. He was always a sounding board and friend. Over the years there were many other colleagues and clients that have broadened my understanding of project management.

In 2010, Mark Peters invited me to fill a gap in the executive education team at Wits Business School. He guided me during the first years with the result that I still convene programs and facilitate on them. In 2014, Prof. Carl Marnewick (University of Johannesburg) accepted me as a PhD student and was my supervisor. Then Prof. Jack Meredith (Wake Forest University NC) joined us and together we produced three journal papers which shaped my thinking in a number of areas. During the writing of this book, Dr. John Wyzalek of Taylor & Francis Group gave me valuable advice on aspects like structure and layout, and on what readers will expect to find in the book.

Finally, I would like to recognize the delegates who attended our executive education programmes over the past 12 years. They are from varied organizations and business disciplines. Through discussion, both informal and in class, they greatly enriched our perspectives as a facilitating team.

About the Author

After my school and undergraduate education in Cape Town and being in the provincial gymnastics team for 6 years, I graduated as an electrical engineer in 1966. Then, following on from national service as a naval officer and working as an engineer in the UK and Canada, returned to do an MBA at the University of Cape Town in 1970.

Thereafter, I started 'at the bottom' in IBM South Africa, first as a systems engineer working with customers and later in management roles. A common factor throughout, was the need to manage projects. Even in customer account management roles, the reason customers placed orders with me was that they knew that I would deliver via well-run projects. Realizing that this was what I did best, in 1992, I became a full-time project manager, working on customer projects, on their premises, with staff from their organizations. Although the projects had a large IT content, they were essentially business projects. There were many successes but also a few failures. Some of the latter were due to factors beyond my control, but whether successful or otherwise, there were always things that I might have done better – lessons to be learned.

Even while at IBM, I started teaching project management, and after taking early retirement after 32 years, did project management work as a contractor, consultant, and teacher; I still convene and teach on programs at a local business school. In 2018, I completed a PhD in applied information systems, focusing on the business case for business/IT projects. The content of this book is based on those 50 years of learning what works and what does not. It also reflects what I teach on business project management programs.

In private life, Carolyn and I have been married for 48 years and have three children in Melbourne, Geneva, and Johannesburg, as well as three grandchildren. I also exercise, garden, do pre-marriage counseling, play guitar, and sing.

Finally, here are a few philosophies and practices that have served me well in the stressful project environment that I would recommend to others. Keep fit and well. Keep learning. Have interests outside of your work. Develop relationships with peers in your own and other organizations that you can use as a sounding board when confronted with tough problems and choices. Be self-critical, but don't blame yourself for everything that goes wrong.

1 OVERVIEW OF THE BOOK AND OF BUSINESS PROJECT MANAGEMENT

Chapter 1 starts by discussing the broad range of people in business that the book is intended for. It explains why it is different from other books with the focus being on business projects. It ends by outlining the structure of the book. Chapter 2 gives an overview of business project management, stating why it is needed and how the various stakeholders are involved. After mentioning the range of skills needed, it invites you, the reader, to do a self-assessment which will serve as a personal guide to the book based on your role and your needs. Methodology is discussed in Chapter 3, showing its strengths and limitations, but emphasizing the benefits of sound documentation. The lifetime of a business project is presented in Chapter 4, showing at what point important documents are produced and used. The role of governance to support project management is stressed throughout.

DOI: 10.1201/9781003321101-1

1 OVERVIEW OF THE BOOK AND OF BUSINESS PROJECT MANAGEMENT

[illegible]

Chapter 1

Introduction to the Book

1.1 Objectives of the Book

The purpose of a business project is to get something important done and the purpose of this book is to help you to get those important things done effectively. Chapter 2 expands on what a project is. Many players are involved in achieving project success which, for business projects, goes beyond producing defined project deliverables. The people involved in making projects successful include the project sponsor, the business owner (who may be the same person), the project manager (abbreviated to 'PM'), team members, business stakeholders, and other stakeholders (Nieto-Rodriguez, 2021). This book is intended for all of them – which probably includes you, the reader. It provides a general understanding of the many facets of business projects and gives detail on the essential disciplines required for them to be successful. The PM is responsible for much of what gets done, but sometimes other stakeholders or the sponsor take the lead. Whatever the project situation, the aim here is to stick to what is essential and avoid unnecessary sophistication. I try to use language that is easily understood, but should you encounter a term whose meaning you are not sure of, it is likely to be found in Appendix 1, the glossary.

Some topics will be of great interest to certain role players who would want to study them in depth; the same topics may only be of general interest to others who could still build their knowledge by reading more superficially. For example, the PM needs a sound knowledge of how to produce and manage a project schedule while a sponsor would just want an overview. Similarly, both sponsors and PMs need a sound understanding of project governance, while for team members, it might just be of interest.

The book is based on my experience on a broad range of business projects. Possibly you have been involved in different types of projects, and certain approaches may not fit your projects or your style. Nevertheless, comparing what is suggested in this book with what you believe works best in your environment will broaden your perspective and give you a better overall grasp of business project management.

DOI: 10.1201/9781003321101-2

1.2 Objectives of This Chapter

This chapter covers:

- How this book differs from other books on project management.
- Why business projects are different from construction or engineering projects.
- Some 'true or false' scene-setting statements to get you thinking.
- The structure of the book.

1.3 How This Book Is Different

This book differs from many other project management textbooks in a number of ways. It is about *business* project management as opposed to construction or engineering project management. Although many techniques, like schedule management, apply to both, they are usually applied differently. Here we cover what is suitable for business projects. The focus is on small- and medium-size business projects, up to say $20 million, but often below $1 million. While some literature favors large and mega-projects, for every mega-project there are many thousands of smaller projects which are vital to the organization and may involve considerable complexity and risk. Having said that, the techniques outlined here may also apply to mega-projects or to the many subprojects that they comprise. The book is intended for people who are working in business at whatever level or for MBA students; it is not aimed at undergraduate students, although many would benefit from the contents.

Increasingly, project management skills are expected of every manager (Nieto-Rodriguez, 2021). Both PMs and other managers have limited time, and need to work with what is essential to get a project done while communicating effectively with a broad variety of stakeholders. Here, a stakeholder is defined as any person that contributes to the project or is affected by it, which of course includes the project team. While in the past, most projects were contained within one department, nowadays projects typically span many departments and locations, making communication even more important.

Project management started in the construction and engineering disciplines. Therefore, not surprisingly, many textbooks go into much detail on things that apply to such projects but which may be inappropriate or need to be adapted and simplified, for use on business projects. This book does not aim to cover all available techniques, even those that apply to business projects. In real life, there is simply no time for all the 'should-do's'. So, it covers the essential things that apply to almost all business projects. The advice that will be given repeatedly is to do the essentials and to do them consistently and well. Certainly, each project will need some approaches specific to that project or type of project, but I do not cover them here. For example, I do not address the many techniques and records required to manage the testing of a large IT development. But of course, many of the basic approaches mentioned above also apply to IT testing.

Before going further, it is important to give more insight into what is meant by a business project, and a good way is to contrast it with a construction or engineering project.

1.4 Business Projects Are Different from Construction or Engineering Projects

The spectrum of projects is broad, so here we shall just contrast a *typical* business project with a *typical* construction (or engineering) project. You will find exceptions because construction projects have business components, and, some business projects have construction elements – there can be no hard-and-fast rules. So, what are the fundamental differences between business and construction projects?

Let's start with the requirements. In a construction project, the requirements are well understood. A great deal of work has been done before the project even starts. There might have been a feasibility study. There must be a design, which would be cost estimated by a quantity surveyor. Changes after the project starts are likely to be minor. With a business project, very often, little is known at the start. Certainly, the broad goals will be known, for example, "we need to streamline our warehouse distribution processes", but up front, stakeholders will seldom be sure of exactly what they need. So project definition is done by making many assumptions as to what the requirements are, and those requirements change as more information is uncovered.

What about the environment, both inside and outside the organization? For a construction project, this changes relatively little. Once contracts are in place, and construction of a bridge has started, environmental factors are unlikely to change the design, so the effect on the deliverables is minimal. For a business project, the environment changes all the time and may change the business case and the project plans. So the plans need regular review, and even the business case should be checked periodically. Scope changes may arise, sometimes from a review, but more often due to ad-hoc requests from stakeholders. Also, the project forms part of a portfolio, and its priority is under constant review. Indeed, its priority may be raised or lowered due to other things that are happening concurrently.

What about project size? A $1 million business project is already medium size, whereas for a construction project, medium might be $20 million. So, the construction project could justify staff to do administration and track costs, whereas for most business projects, the PM does most of this work.

The contractual situations are different. For a construction project, the scope is well understood and can be estimated fairly reliably. Therefore, fixed-price contracts are the norm, and being within budget is vital lest profit be eroded, and being on time may avoid penalties for lateness. By contrast, most business projects are internal and may be initiated with no more than a few emails to confirm understanding. Initially, the scope is uncertain, so any time and cost estimates are known to be unreliable. Where external resources are used, they would typically be paid for by the hour. Regarding outcomes, provided that the expected business benefits can be achieved, the PM would be forgiven for explainable time or cost overruns.

The patterns of communication are not the same. For construction projects, the roles and communication channels are fairly well defined. Before the project starts, there would be liaison between architects, designers, quantity surveyors, and engineers – whatever skills are needed. After the project starts, the PM would work with the supervisors who would manage the people doing the work. Some problems during construction are inevitable, but most of the politics would be over after the design is done and the project approved. For each business project, a different combination of disciplines may be needed. Often the disciplines have different skills, culture, and terminology. Thus good communication does not happen naturally and requires constant effort. Indeed, misunderstandings are a common cause of business project failure. These can be exacerbated by politics or stakeholders having conflicting perceptions and expectations. Although usually not overwhelming, such differences can persist until after project closeout.

Regarding benefits: For a construction project, a deliverable like a road or a building provides benefits by its very existence. For engineering, commissioning would be part of the project and there may be some staff training. On the other hand, for a business project, the deliverables themselves may have little value. For example, IT deliverables on their own do not help until business stakeholders change their processes to take advantage of the deliverables. Often the people-change aspects are considerable, and OCM (organizational change management), covered in Chapter 23, becomes a major component of the project or even a parallel project. Underestimating the OCM requirement is common and can even cause project failure.

Visibility: For a construction project, progress is visible and inspections by management wearing hard hats, or tests by engineers, give useful feedback. For a business project, and especially for an IT project, progress can be difficult to see. The person doing the work may give misleading feedback that is hard to validate. In addition, issues (problems) can arise unexpectedly which require major work or even a re-think of the design. Part of the solution may be to structure the work so that regular demonstrations of output can be given. This both gains feedback, and is motivational for the workers. Indeed, the 'Agile' way of working (Chapter 30) is built on the culture of frequent deliverables that can be demonstrated.

Schedule and cost management, which go hand in hand, are easier for a construction project. The activities are relatively well known and stable, so EVM (earned value management) techniques, covered in Chapter 12, work satisfactorily. For business projects, the schedule activities change regularly as the project unfolds, making 'classical' EVM, as covered in textbooks, difficult or even impossible to apply. To this end, Chapter 12 explains a technique that works well for business projects: PPTR (project progress tracker) honors EVM principles but takes far less effort and accommodates changes easily.

Location and staffing: Construction projects are usually on one main site, with the suppliers being distributed and having to solve the problem of getting their resources on site. Almost all the project resources are dedicated. A business project may have staff in multiple locations, and a matrix structure is common with staff being shared across several initiatives. Hence, the business PM's negotiation around staff may be ongoing.

Skills and management: Construction projects are done by many workers that can be replaced at short notice because there is almost no learning curve. The PM has authority on site and needs to be in charge. However, there could be union and community pressures that impact progress. By contrast, business projects require staff with unique skills. If someone leaves or moves to another project, there will be a learning curve. Attempting to speed up a project close to the deadline by adding more resources seldom works and may actually slow the project unless the added person has exceptional skills. Because of the skill levels, the balance of power is different. The PM needs to negotiate tactfully with the team, rather than dictate what will be done. But, union problems seldom arise.

In summary, business and construction projects differ in many ways. So even though the basic project management disciplines like scope, schedule, cost, and people management are similar, the ways in which they are practiced will almost certainly vary. This book deals with what is needed for business projects.

1.5 Setting the Scene – Some Statements to Get You Thinking

Let's start with some 'true-false' statements about business projects. Rate these statements true or false according to your current perspective and keep a note of your ratings and any reasons that go with them.

- With sound training in project management, anyone can be a good PM.
- If one follows a methodology, project management becomes straightforward.
- The first thing a PM should do is schedule the project from start to finish.
- Risks are a fact of life, so there's no point in bothering about them.
- Project management software allows one to manage projects effortlessly and efficiently.
- If we are behind schedule, it is easy to catch up by having people work overtime.
- If there are problems, the PM should keep them to herself so as not to upset management or threaten team morale.
- Documentation is a waste of time because it does not contribute to getting the project done.
- The PM takes most of the key decisions on the project.
- Once thorough planning has been done, very few issues arise.
- Unless a project is on time and within budget, it is a failure.
- However challenging the project or tight the deadline, a good PM will get it done successfully.
- Project management is no longer necessary. With an Agile approach, the team always does what is most important to produce business value.

In Chapter 33, which is a 'wrap-up' of the entire book, these statements will be discussed. At that point, you can see whether your views have changed after reading the book. I also provide my own true-false ratings of the statements – which are subject to challenge!

1.6 Structure of the Book

The book is structured into the following parts, which start with an introduction:

- Part 1. Overview: This gives a general introduction to business project management and what is required of the PM. It also covers related topics like documentation and emphasizes the importance of the project's sponsor and of governance.
- Part 2. Core elements. These give what I consider to be the essentials which should be done thoroughly and consistently on almost all business projects.

- Part 3. Special topics. These cover things, outside of the essentials, that might be important on a particular project. For example, procurement may form a cornerstone of one business project but may not be needed for another. Topics like project portfolio governance build perspective which is useful to all managers and professionals.
- Part 4. Wrap-up and learning materials:
  - Chapter 33, the 'wrap-up', summarizes what is needed for a project to be successful and discusses the 'true-false' statements given above. In closing, it reiterates the essential disciplines.
  - Chapter 34 is a study guide which suggests ways of using this book allowing for a range of requirements. At the one end, it suggests an approach for any professional or executive to get just the knowledge that they need without reading everything. The self-assessment in Chapter 2 gives guidance on what might meet your needs. At the other end, it outlines a comprehensive program in managing business projects which you can take yourself or can facilitate for others.
  - There are three further chapters: Chapter 35 gives short, multiple-choice quizzes with answers, which are referred to in the study guide. They enable you to check your understanding of the main topics. Chapters 36 and 37 give the cases and answers, respectively. The cases are referred to from most chapters and also from the study guide. Each case could either be an exercise or a short case study. Where the case is an exercise, there is only one correct answer; where it is a case study describing a situation, then a 'possible' answer is provided because different people might adopt different, but equally valid, approaches.
- The appendices. The first one is a glossary for you to look up acronyms or terms used in the book that might be confusing. The second presents the theory of scheduling using precedence diagrams. The third gives two useful templates which are referred to from Chapters 6 and 25, respectively.

In some chapters, I give short anecdotes from my past experience. These are indented and shown in italics. An indent without italics is occasionally used to differentiate something from the normal text.

The book is not intended as a primer for certification examinations because the content is far broader. However, the techniques and the underlying theory that are explained apply to all methodologies. This learning and the perspectives given should help you with your practical involvement in business projects and form a sound base from which to study for any specific certification.

Reference

Nieto-Rodriguez, A. (2021). *Harvard Business Review Project Management Handbook: How to Launch, Lead, and Sponsor Successful Projects*. Harvard Business Review Press, USA.

Chapter 2

Business Projects and Their Management

2.1 Objectives

Here we shall cover:

- What a business project is.
- Terminology that relates to projects.
- Why a project sponsor is essential.
- Why we need project management.
- The role of the PM (project manager).
- The characteristics and skill areas that enable a person to become a capable PM.

Finally, a self-assessment is provided to enable you to get the maximum mileage from this book – whether you are a PM, sponsor, or any other role player on business projects.

2.2 What Is a Business Project?

In business, there are broadly two types of activities: operations and projects.

- An operation is something that is done routinely, following a well-understood process – for example, customer checkout at a supermarket or ordering stock from a main depot.
- A business project is needed whenever anything important needs to change, and business projects are often accompanied by changes to processes – for example, implementing a new system for online customer ordering.

DOI: 10.1201/9781003321101-3

Certainly, there are initiatives that have elements of both. For a business school running courses, each course is like a new project. But the activities may be very similar to those for other courses and the staff would be experienced at managing them. Therefore, simple checklists may be all that is needed, and initiating new courses may be considered normal operations.

Projects vary greatly in size, from tiny ones that can be achieved with one person in a few days to mega-projects requiring thousands of people over several years. Many small initiatives are done without calling them projects, but there is a trend toward organizations managing more work as projects and this trend is referred to as 'projectification' – work that was previously done informally is now defined and done as projects (Nieto-Rodriguez, 2021). In this book, we mainly consider projects requiring 5 or more person-months of effort to accomplish. Below 5 person-months, one might refer to a 'work request' rather than a project, but even work requests might now be managed with some structure. So small projects might be from 5 to 50 person-months and medium might be from 50 to 500 person-months (for the project team and other stakeholders that contribute directly).

Whatever its size, a project is a set of activities that are managed to produce defined deliverables and to support a business goal. Usually, there will be dates specified, and often a budget. Activities need to be assigned to people, and there should be some agreement as to the acceptance criteria for the deliverables. Similar methods are needed, irrespective of size, but more rigor is needed for larger and riskier projects.

Things are not always clear-cut. For example, with our new online ordering system mentioned above: Is the project complete when the system is live and the customers start using it? Or, should a support period be added until any issues have been ironed out? At what point do we expect the new processes to be fully operational and achieving the planned benefits? It is important that such matters be clear up-front, as it affects the planning. Hence, project definition, covered in Chapter 6, is a vitally important topic.

2.3 Terminology That Relates to Projects

Here are some terms that are commonly used in the context of projects, with their meanings. The same terms may have different meanings in other contexts.

- Program: A set of related projects, managed in a coordinated way to achieve a broadly defined goal. The program seldom has an end-date, but the projects that are defined within it should have target end-dates.
- Portfolio: A group of projects and programs that support all, or a significant part, of the organization. Ongoing re-prioritization is done based on the limited resources available.
- Phase: The term can be used in two ways, so it can be confusing. A phase can be part of the project's life cycle like the planning phase, the design phase, the build phase, the testing phase, and the closeout phase. It can also define entire projects. For example, phase 1 is to conduct a pilot in Region A, and phase 2 is to roll out the solution to other regions. Here phase 1 and phase 2 are projects in their own right, but related to each other.

- Stage: This is sometimes used synonymously with 'phase', particularly in the latter context where each project stage is managed like a project in its own right.
- Subproject or work stream: Usually it is a functional element of a project with specific activities and people. Ideally, activities can be done independently of other subprojects, but usually there is interaction. Thus if business analysis were to be a work stream, it would interact with several other work streams.

Managing a project and a program have much in common (purists might disagree with me). Certainly, program management is broader, but an experienced PM should have no difficulty running a program, and indeed, managing a larger project uses many approaches that are also used in programs. Therefore, apart from some further explanation of a program in Chapter 19, I shall not distinguish between the two because the techniques described apply to both.

2.4 The Need for a Sponsor or Business Owner

Although some experts distinguish between the business owner and the sponsor, I use the terms synonymously, and shall, in this book, use the term 'project sponsor' or just 'sponsor'. When asked what the role of the project sponsor is, most will say "it's the person that supplies money to fund the project". This perception arises from sports where a corporate might sponsor a football team by providing money and having their name mentioned in advertising. In the project management context, the term 'sponsor' is used differently. Certainly, in some situations, sponsors may provide the money, but that is not their primary role. By my definition, the sponsor is the executive that has the most to gain from the success of the project, and the most to lose if it fails. An executive that does not care about the project should not be the sponsor, and such a situation can be just as bad as not having a sponsor at all. For a small project, the department head might be the sponsor; for a larger project, the sponsor might be appointed by the CEO (chief executive officer) to promote success.

Sponsors, because of their seniority, are busy people, and delegate running of the project to the PM. However, they cannot be totally hands-off or abdicate their accountability. Indeed, there are many specific ways, that are not time-consuming, in which they need to interact with the PM and support the project. These are detailed in Chapter 17 on project governance.

Having a sponsor is so vital to the success of the project, that, if no suitable sponsor exists, then I believe that the project should not be undertaken. Projects inevitably have problems that are beyond the PM's control, and if there is nobody to turn to for support, then even the best PM might fail. The sponsor will be referred to throughout this book and plays a pivotal role in project governance.

2.5 Why Is Project Management Needed?

Let's consider what happens if a project is initiated without project management. This may be satisfactory if the team is just one or two people. But, if the project is larger, there is likely to be conflict over what the project should deliver, the priorities, and who does what, among other things. Risks may not be addressed, issues that arise may go unresolved, and stakeholders are unlikely to be informed of progress or lack thereof. The initiator of the project, probably the sponsor, might then intervene to sort things out, or else the project might wither and die, with people going back to their normal jobs. In short, without project management, outcomes are at best unpredictable and at worst chaotic.

Therefore, someone needs to do the coordination. The PM role may be part-time and it may be played by a person who is not called a PM. But the role needs to be played by someone. For small projects, a mature group of people might be able to self-manage and keep relevant people informed. But typically without a PM, goals are not met, with the resulting frustration of all stakeholders. There is a cost associated with project management activities which might typically be in the range of 5% to 15% of the project's cost, depending on the project and the role that the PM plays.

2.6 What Role Does the PM Play?

This is much of what this book is about, so here is a brief overview (OGC, 2009; PMI, 2017). Mainly, the PM would:

- Understand the business case or justification for the project.
- Document the definition of the project and ensure that the sponsor and other key stakeholders are in agreement.
- With input from stakeholders (which includes the team), plan all aspects of the project such as the activities, resources, costs, schedule, communication, risks, and how to respond to the risks.
- Manage the day-to-day activities which include handling issues (problems) that arise.
- Track progress, based on the schedule and costs incurred.
- Keep stakeholders informed and report regularly on progress and challenges.
- Facilitate meetings and act as the central point of contact, especially for the project team.
- Maintain documentation related to the project.
- Ensure that the output of the project is produced and handed over to business people or whoever will take the implementation further, before closing the project in an orderly manner.

Naturally, for larger projects, some of this will be delegated, and for small projects, the PM may handle several projects concurrently.

2.7 What Qualities and Skills Does the PM Need?

Many people ask what it takes to be a good PM. Figure 2.1 gives an overview of the characteristics that help to make a PM competent. No doubt, many of the characteristics apply to sponsors and other key stakeholders as well.

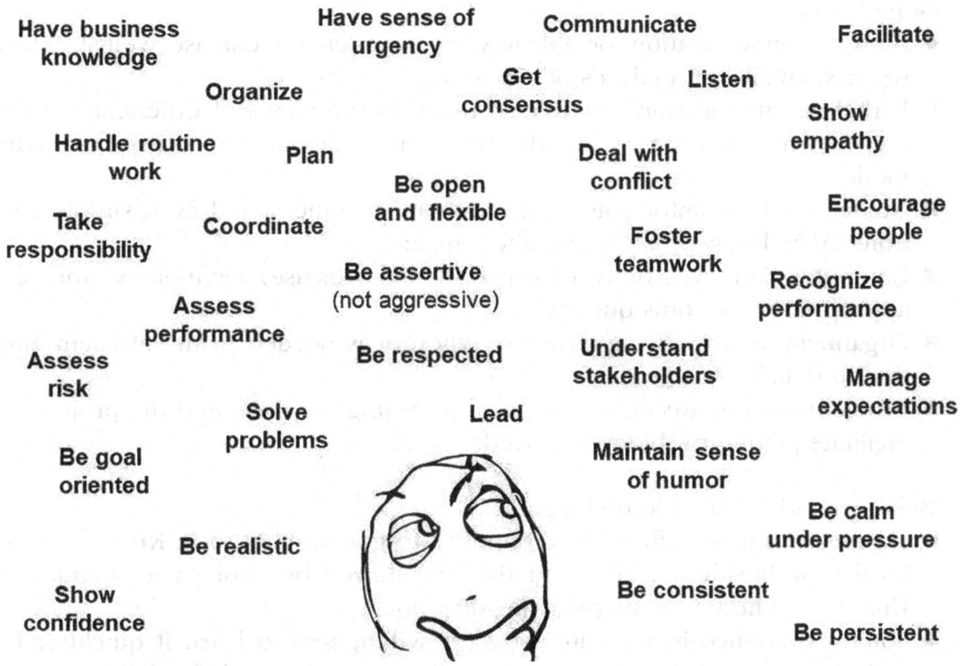

Figure 2.1 Characteristics of the PM.

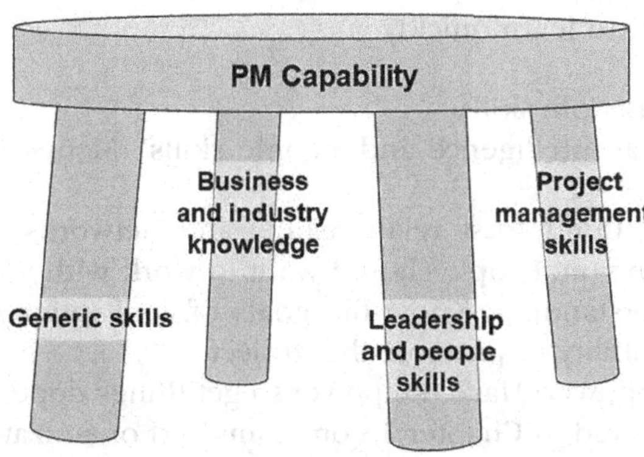

Figure 2.2 The project management capability stool.

For the PM, there is more. Let's consider what it takes to be a competent PM by looking at Figure 2.2 and I suggest that much of what the PM needs is also needed by all managers to varying degrees. I have identified four basic skill/knowledge sets as the four legs of a stool; the characteristics in Figure 2.1 apply to more than one of the legs.

Few PMs are excellent in all four areas, but some ability in each is essential. If any leg is missing or inadequate, the stool would become unstable; it would not be a useful stool.

1. Generic skills:
   - Written communication: Be able to write complete but concise, well-structured reports, emails, or analyses of situations.
   - Verbal communication: Be able to listen to the views of others, and to put one's own views across clearly, whether in discussion or in presentation mode.
   - Numeracy: Be comfortable with numbers, arithmetic and even simple equations. Also, know what the numbers mean.
   - Computer literacy: Ability to use (but not over-use) technology, and learn appropriate new tools quickly.
   - Organizing ability: Bring structure where it is needed, with sufficient attention to detail.
   - Problem solving: Recognize what is impacting the team and the project, and facilitate getting problems resolved.

2. Business and industry knowledge:
   - Business understanding (which applies to government too): Know at a high level how business works and the role played by your own organization. Understand how various projects add value.
   - Some experience in your industry (or willingness to learn it quickly): This includes grasping the culture and terminology used, and also being sensitive to the norms in both the industry and your own organization.
   - Business and technical skills: It helps to have relevant skills that apply to your projects. You can probably get by with a basic understanding provided that you are willing to learn quickly.

3. Leadership and people skills:
   - Have emotional intelligence and 'people skills': Many of these are given in Figure 2.1.
   - Relationships: Build trust relationships and networks of people that will cooperate with you. People should want to work with you.
   - Strategic understanding: Know the goals of, and rationale for, each project and have the ability to promote the project.
   - Influence and power: Have the power to get things done; the PM's sources of power are covered in Chapter 13 on teams and organization.

4. Project management skills:
   - The essentials: Know the project management essentials and carry them out in a disciplined way. Even the building blocks can take time to assimilate, and that is what much of this book is about. The self-assessment items in the next section include these essentials.
   - Experience and practice: Gain skill at the techniques through practice, getting input from peers or mentors, and learning from both success and failure.

You, the reader, as an executive, a manager, a professional, or as a PM, are probably proficient in the first three legs. For PMs, and others that manage projects, the fourth leg is valuable and you may already be well-advanced. Using the disciplines consistently will help you to survive even the most adverse circumstances (that are seldom of your own making). So, enhancing the fourth leg (the right hand leg in the figure) will help you to manage your projects in less time, with less frustration, and with lower risk.

2.8 Self-Assessment on the Project Management Skills

Table 2.1 allows you to assess your knowledge and experience level in the project management skills leg from two points of view: (i) the skill level that you have and (ii) the level that you need, to do your job effectively. A suggested rating scale might be:

1. Little or no understanding,
2. Broad/high-level understanding only,
3. Working knowledge,
4. In-depth knowledge and ability.

Your responses will guide your use of this book. The elements given correspond with the chapters in Part 2 and many of those in Part 3, whose numbers are indicated in the right-hand column.

Table 2.1 Self-Assessment in Skills Related to Project Management

Description of the Project Management Related Skill Area	*Skill Level*	*Need Level*	*Ch.*
Engaging with project stakeholders			5
Project definition and ensuring the alignment of stakeholders			6
Gathering of stakeholder requirements and definition of project scope/exclusions			7
Project estimating using top-down and bottom-up approaches			8
Scheduling and tracking of project activities; meeting tight deadlines			9
Management of the quality of project deliverables			10
Identification and management of project risks			11
Practical progress and cost tracking using earned value principles			12
Project organization structures; building and leading an effective project team			13
Managing project issues (problems) in a structured way			14

(Continued)

Table 2.1 (Continued)

Description of the Project Management Related Skill Area	*Skill Level*	*Need Level*	*Ch.*
Controlling changes to the approved scope, cost, and time; avoiding 'scope creep'			15
Ongoing monitoring of the project and regular communication with stakeholders			16
Governance of a project and the role of the project sponsor			17
Closing the project, reporting the outcomes, and gathering lessons that were learned			18
Managing a portfolio of projects (where resources are always limited)			19
Creation of a business case and its use throughout the project's lifetime			20
Project selection using financial and non-financial criteria			21
Project procurement, outsourcing of work, and partnership with other organizations			22
Organizational change management – the people aspects of change			23
Working with project contracts; how to avoid or manage disputes			24
Project review and checking the health of a project			25
Knowing the project norms of professional conduct and how to adhere to legislation			26
Handling project negotiations – informal and formal, with any stakeholder			27
Managing projects in foreign countries which involve diverse cultures			28
Understanding 'Agile' projects and how they are managed			30

Where the gaps between your skill level and what you need are small, you might want to skim through the chapter and only home in on any sections that might offer new ideas. On the other hand, where the gap is larger, then you might prefer to study the chapter in depth and spend time on the cases before looking at the answers. Should you be a PM then, if there are any gaps, select one or two areas where you plan to apply the suggested techniques in your day-to-day project responsibilities.

2.9 Summary

In this chapter, we have discussed what a business project is and the broad range that it covers. Some of the terminology used in the context of projects has been clarified. We have learned why project sponsorship is essential and why project management is needed. The characteristics and skills needed by the PM, or any other person managing projects, have been outlined, and you have been able to do a self-assessment to enable you to benefit optimally from this book in the time that you have available. Although there are many topics within project management, the emphasis will be on doing only what is essential, because most business projects are complex enough without adding unnecessary sophistication.

References

Nieto-Rodriguez, A. (2021). *Harvard Business Review Project Management Handbook: How to Launch, Lead, and Sponsor Successful Projects*. Brighton, MA: Harvard Business Review.

OGC. (2009). *Managing Successful Projects with PRINCE2*, 5th edition. In A. Murray (Ed.). Norwich: TSO (The Stationery Office) on behalf of Office of Government Commerce.

PMI. (2017). *PMBOK - Guide to the Project Management Body of Knowledge*, 6th edition: Pennsylvania, USA: Project Management Institute.

Chapter 3

Methodology from Unusual Angles

3.1 Introduction and Objectives

In this chapter, we critically examine project management methodology from a number of angles. Methodology can bring enormous benefits, but there are also some limitations and misconceptions to watch out for. So, the objectives are to:

- Know what a project management methodology is and whether it will ensure success.
- Know where project management methodologies come from and some of their strengths and limitations.
- Consider the merits of certification.
- Know the value of producing the documentation required by a methodology.
- Understand the benefits of being able to access the right information quickly.
- Be able to master terminology – project management, organization, or industry.
- See how technology supports or inhibits methodology.
- Gain insights on how methodologies are evolving and the effect on your role.

3.2 What Is a Project Management Methodology? Will It Ensure Success?

What exactly is a project management methodology? In simple terms, it is: (i) a defined set of steps that one follows and (ii) documentation that one creates and maintains.

I sometimes ask course participants: "Can I give you a methodology, or a 'cookbook recipe', that will ensure project success if you follow it?" Quite a number respond "yes", but in fact, my answer is "no, I cannot". To follow a cookbook recipe: one has all the ingredients before one starts; the activities are mostly done one at a

DOI: 10.1201/9781003321101-4

time – beat eggs, add milk, add flour, etc., and the activities are quite straightforward; after all, anyone can beat an egg. A project is different. As PM, you seldom have what you need up-front. You may not even know exactly what is required and you need to negotiate to get suitable people and other resources. Then, everything is happening concurrently and seems to be interdependent. There are stresses and constant interruptions, so your time must be prioritized. Finally, the activities are far from straightforward. For example, defining scope may be an iterative process and sometimes, the best way of doing something only becomes clear later.

Nevertheless, while a methodology will not *guarantee* success, it can certainly prevent critical things from being overlooked, and it enables one to explain what was done and the reasons. I would not like to overlook something, and invite the comment "surely an experienced PM should have taken care of that?" Under pressure, it's easy to overlook things, so I always follow a simple methodology to ensure that the essential things get done.

3.3 More About Methodologies

3.3.1 Who Offers Them?

There are many organizations that foster project management disciplines and support methodologies. The following mentions just a few of the ones that operate internationally (Hartney, 2018; OGC, 2009; PMI, 2021):

- APM (Association for Project Management) in the UK has links to the PRINCE2 methodology.
- IPMA (International Project Management Association) is based in the Netherlands.
- PMI (Project Management Institute) in the USA has a handbook called 'PMBOK' or more fully the Guide to the Project Management Body of Knowledge. Although not a methodology itself, many methodologies are based on it and use its terminology.

These, and many other organizations, put out excellent literature and training material, and offer qualifications and certifications. Unless mandated by your organization, it is not essential to belong to any one of them, but they can help you to stay abreast of current thinking. It falls to you to use whatever material is provided with discretion. Prioritize what you read and then decide what applies to any particular project. The same goes for methodologies of which there are many in use. Not only are they being updated, but new ones emerge. Before the year 2000, most were 'traditional'. Then, in the early 2000s, Agile methodologies emerged which adopt a different philosophy that applies to specific types of project. The distinction between traditional (or 'waterfall') and Agile is explained in Chapter 30.

Some organizations have their own methodology supported by templates that are recommended or even mandatory. All methodologies have much in common because project management is fairly generic and similar things need to be done.

3.3.2 Project Methodologies – Their Strengths and Limitations

Most methodologies have strengths and limitations and here are some of them:

Strengths:

- They capture the learning of experienced people gained over many years.
- They provide sound literature, training material, and education. If one is selective, one can learn much from studying a methodology.
- If everyone in an organization is working with common methods and templates, communication is easier and people can more easily move between projects.

Limitations:

- Methodologies try to be comprehensive and cover all situations. However, what the PM needs is the things that are essential for a specific project. As PM, if you try to do everything you will be swamped and are likely to end up with half-done and useless documentation. In organizations where standards have too many mandatory requirements, I have observed PMs drowning in the rigor, abandoning the methodology, and doing everything intuitively with minimal documentation.
- Methodologies cannot cover everything, and some exclude aspects that I would consider important.

So in this book, I shall provide an essential set of processes and documents, that if used in a disciplined way, will generally lead to success, or, if there are insurmountable obstacles, will help you to anticipate the problems and explain them to management. I have yet to find an organization where I could not adapt my simple approach to their standards.

3.3.3 Certification in a Methodology – Essential or a Waste of Time?

Most certifications relate to a guide or methodology. I have mixed feelings about certification because there could be the mistaken assumption that, certification ensures that a person is competent to run a project. In fact, all that certification does is confirm that the holder has some experience, and has an understanding of a particular framework or methodology. Nevertheless, for the PM, there are advantages to being certified by a credible organization:

- Most employer organizations expect certification – for example, in IBM where I spent many years, PMI's PMP (Project Management Professional) certification was a requirement. Many job adverts specify a particular certification – PMP and 'PRINCE2 Practitioner' being typical ones.
- Ongoing learning is encouraged as most certifications expire unless ongoing project-related learning can be demonstrated.

However, really important are the skills described in Chapter 2 via the 'four legs of the stool' metaphor, namely: (i) generic skills like communication and problem solving, (ii) business and industry knowledge, (iii) leadership and people skills, and (iv) project management skills. So while certification expects something in all the legs, it mainly addresses the fourth leg – project management skills.

3.4 Effective Use of Documentation

All methodologies require documentation. They specify which documents are required and give guidance as to the contents and frequency. They are not specific as to how or where the documents should be stored, but the implication is clear: Unless the documents are being produced, the methodology is not being followed. Therefore, I would like to expand on things that the methodologies say very little about.

3.4.1 The Value of Documentation

Whether you are a PM or any other key stakeholder, the greatest value of a document is the thinking that goes into creating it. It is difficult to put something down 'in writing' if you do not understand it. Therefore, while creating a document new ideas will spring to mind and often you will need to find something out from people or from some other source. Most documents used on projects are short. A great deal of thinking can go onto less than a page.

The documents that you create mean that you do not have to remember all the facts; you merely need to know where to find them. Your documentation helps you to communicate, whether you actually send a document or just talk to people. When talking to people, the thought process that you have gone through helps you to put ideas across well and with confidence. This gives you credibility and influence. Also, as will be shown in Chapter 27 on negotiation, having sound facts enables you to negotiate more effectively. There are further purposes for maintaining a variety of documentation items. When dealing with other organizations, the contracts or service level agreements often require them. Should your project be reviewed, you will probably be asked to provide essential documents – which are covered in the next part of this book. No doubt, these are some of the reasons why methodologies specify what documentation needs to be created or maintained.

Finally, your documentation enables you to protect yourself under adverse circumstances. This is a by-product and should never be the primary purpose of documentation. When under attack, for example, when choices you have made do not work out, you may need to defend your reasoning or demonstrate that things have happened that were beyond your control. I jokingly refer to it as CYA – 'cover your assets'. Even though I cannot remember when last I used documentation for this purpose, knowing that I have such evidence gives me confidence when the going gets rough.

3.4.2 Some Guidance on the Document Itself

Fortunately, documents seldom need to be printed out because they are stored and circulated electronically. Even so, here are some suggested guidelines:

- Every document should have at the top of the first page:
  - the document title,
  - the name of the author(s), and
  - a date (sometimes also that of the last update).

  Several times on projects, I have found useful-looking documents that lacked both an author and a date; it was difficult to tell whether it was current and there was no indication as to whom to ask.
- Avoid unnecessary pages, like header pages, circulation list pages, revision number pages, or contents pages. Contents are hardly necessary for documents of less than eight pages, and most project documents are short (often only one page). Short documents are more likely to be read, but this does not mean that important detail should be omitted to save pages.
- Avoid over-structured documents that invite a box-ticking mentality. Keep templates simple and flexible. Suggested headings give useful guidance. Documents need to be functional rather than good looking. Clearly, standards should be adhered to, but, hopefully, your standard templates are not over-structured.

3.4.3 Making Documents Accessible to Yourself and Others

Once created, and possibly circulated, documents need to be in a place where you and others can find them quickly if they are needed. This can be challenging because, during a project, many documents of different types are created by a variety of people. So, documents are best stored in a repository where they are easily accessible by stakeholders, and are backed up regularly. This could be on shared folders or 'in the cloud'. I generally allow updates and additions by anyone, and have never experienced deliberate sabotage. In fact, involved people seldom access such shared information, but take comfort from the fact that they can if they wish to. There will be some confidential documents, like people appraisals or sensitive procurement information, which might be held in a password-protected folder or container.

The repository needs to be structured for ease of access. Having sub-folders with names like project definition, schedules, cost tracking, minutes, reports, risks, issues, etc., that are standardized within your organization, certainly helps. Within the folders, some documents need to be versioned; one approach for doing this is to append a date to the document's name for every new version. If there is a search facility, then standard names and tags will support it. Always bear in mind that all relevant documentation must be easy to archive for future reference, after project closeout. Project folders might be copied to the 'closed projects' repository. PPM (project portfolio management) software might do this by merely changing the project's status to 'closed'.

Finally, allow a place for general project documentation like specifications and equipment lists, which are not necessarily project management documentation, but are nevertheless important. As a PM, I encouraged people to copy me, so that I could save such documents with meaningful names, ensuring that date and author information were available. It was amazing how often I was able to add value by retrieving a document that team members had mislaid.

3.5 Get to Know the Terminology

To be guided by a methodology, it helps to understand the terminology that it uses. Some terms are specific to a methodology, but most are generally accepted and widely used. In this book, I generally use PMI's terminology and have put many of the words or acronyms into the glossary in Appendix 1. So, if you encounter a term whose meaning you are not sure of, try the glossary first and if that does not help, then search for it on the web.

Organization and industry terminology are equally important and PMs are recommended to create their own glossary.

> *When working in a sophisticated life insurance organization, I accumulated six pages of glossary to help me with their jargon. It had nothing to do with project management, but it was a great help with communication at all levels.*

In summary, terminology can be confusing and can lead to misunderstandings which affect one's credibility and waste time.

3.6 Will Technology Replace Methodology?

What about technology? There is a plethora of software out there with more being released every month, so will it replace project management and its methods?

> *I once had a course participant mention a new smartphone messaging app and say "surely this means that we no longer need project management?"*

Unfortunately not. No tool can replace the people interaction and thinking that the PM does. All it can do is make one's job a bit easier. Generally tools cannot manage people, resolve issues, and deal with politics and conflict. As PM, *you* can, and using a sound methodology helps you to do that. A new tool's promotion might leave the impression that it can make your life easy by taking over your routine project management tasks like communicating or reporting. But no tool has yet replaced a PM's insights and ability to prioritize what is most relevant. There are some excellent tools around and many organizations make wise decisions as to which to use and then support them through a PMO (project management office). Having determined what software is standard in your organization, it pays to choose a subset that suits the methods that you are using. There is a danger that a PM suffers from 'goal displacement' by becoming so enamored with tools, that becoming an expert at the tool becomes more important than the project and the people involved. By all means, stay up to date with technology, but don't expect it to do your job for you – project management using sound methods remains essential.

Here we have looked at technology from the PM's point of view; Chapter 31 considers it more from an organizational perspective.

3.7 Some Conclusions on Methodology

We have discussed what methodologies are and who offers them, trains on them, and certifies practitioners. We are also aware that methodologies rely on sound documentation and terminology that everyone understands. We have seen that they are supported by, but not replaced by, technology. A final concern might be that the methodology being used might be superseded by newer ones. It's true that most methodologies are updated periodically and new ones have arisen for specific types of project like those associated with Agile (see Chapter 30). One of the findings discussed in Chapter 32, on trends in business project management, supports this view but finds that the use of methodologies will need to be more flexible. No longer will it be possible to rigidly apply a single methodology for all types of project. One may need more than one, and any that one does use, need to be adapted to the project at hand. The essential disciplines will be needed in most situations. Indeed, that is what this book is about, learning those essential disciplines, most of which will always apply. Likewise, in the chapters that follow, it will become apparent that nothing will replace the role that you play, whether as a PM, sponsor, portfolio manager, or any other stakeholder.

References

Hartney, J. (2018). *Overview of the IPMA Methodology*. Retrieved from 18 Aug 21 https://www.projectengineer.net/overview-of-the-ipma-methodology/

OGC. (2009). *Managing Successful Projects with PRINCE2*, 5th edition. In A. Murray (Ed.). Norwich: TSO (The Stationery Office) on behalf of Office of Government Commerce.

PMI. (2021). *PMBOK - Guide to the Project Management Body of Knowledge*, 7th edition: Pennsylvania, USA: Project Management Institute.

Chapter 4

The Business Project Environment

4.1 Introduction and Objectives

This chapter discusses, at a high level, the project environment and the stages that a business project goes through. The aim is to give a broad understanding. Detail of techniques and documents are given in subsequent chapters. The objectives are to:

- Learn how projects might arise and how the organization selects which ones to do.
- Get an introduction to governance of a project and of a portfolio of projects.
- Understand how the business project's life cycle relates to the project's lifetime.
- Have an overview of the lifetime stages – before, during, and after the project.
- Know the key documents needed for governance and for the project itself.
- Understand the importance of a business case and the PDD (project definition document) – and how they are related.

4.2 How Do Business Projects Arise?

There are three, and maybe more, ways that projects can arise (Larson & Gray, 2018):

- Strategy: Projects arise from corporate strategy (government or private sector). Executives decide on the direction in which the organization needs to move, and inevitably this results in projects to do new things or to change things.
- Operational: Projects arise from operational needs. For example, when technology becomes available that will be cheaper to maintain and offers new benefits, a transition from the old to the new technology could become one or more projects.
- Legislation: Almost all industries are controlled by legislation of some kind. For example, the protection of personal information results in projects in most organizations.

DOI: 10.1201/9781003321101-5

Where projects are within a department (or part of the organization), it is clear who is responsible. However, where projects cut across departmental boundaries, responsibilities would need to be assigned by an executive or an executive committee.

4.3 How Does the Organization Decide Which Projects to Do?

Inevitably there are more proposed projects than there are resources (people and money) to do them, so prioritization is needed. Within a department, the department head normally decides what needs to be done. But, where projects are larger, and require resources from multiple departments, then senior executives would become involved. Some organizations take decisions based on executive judgment at individual or group level, others have a more structured approach involving portfolio governance.

The mission of the portfolio manager is to achieve the optimum set of projects to pursue. The portfolio function does not necessarily take the decisions in this regard. Rather their role is one of facilitation. They gather the information that will allow executives to take well-informed decisions. The information needed includes lists of proposed and active projects, agreed budgets by project, and skills availability. They may also have business cases for projects. Choosing which projects to do is often referred to as 'project selection' (covered in Chapter 21) and facilitating project selection is a key portfolio role. New initiatives are constantly proposed, and it may sometimes be necessary to put a well-justified project on hold, to free up resources for something that is critical or even just higher priority.

4.4 Why Do We Need Governance and Structure?

What has just been covered happens outside of the project and forms part of governance. Indeed, governance is so important that Chapters 17 and 19 are devoted to it and, as will become apparent, the PM plays a vital role in governance. Broadly, governance can be described as a 'set of principles and processes to improve the management of projects in the organization'. Although governance goes beyond the project, there are many interfaces between projects and governance. Governance can be considered as the organization 'wrapped around' the project. It is not there to hinder the PM, but rather to provide support and reduce risk. Where a project is attempted in isolation and things go wrong, there is nobody for the PM to turn to.

Project governance happens at two levels. Governance of a portfolio of projects includes project selection, tracking of all projects, and managing resources across the entire portfolio. Governance of a single project ensures that the business case is sound at the start, remains sound throughout the project, and that its proposed benefits are realized.

Much project governance is done between the sponsor and the PM. A typical governance structure in a larger organization is illustrated in Figure 4.1.

The top management determines strategies and the senior management oversees carrying them out. The sponsor for a large or business-critical project would normally be at this level. Business management would be the main stakeholders in

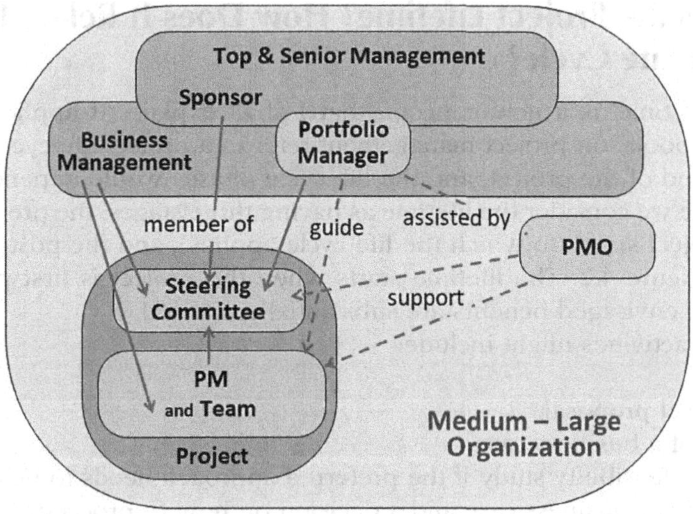

Figure 4.1 Project governance structure.

determining what the deliverables of the project are, and would be involved in the justification (business case) for the project. A portfolio manager would work with all levels of management to ensure that the right projects are done and that they are appropriately prioritized. The portfolio function might be supported by one or more PMOs (project management offices). PMOs generally support many projects and their responsibilities vary over time and across organizations. Their likely roles are covered in Chapter 19, but some of the things that they might do are: collate project-related information for management, hire and train PMs, and set project management standards. The PMOs' interests should be aligned with those of the portfolio manager and the organization. Each project might be headed by a PM who would, for the purpose of the project at hand, have a reporting line to the sponsor. The sponsor might chair a steering committee (or project board) which would comprise senior management with a direct interest in the project. Key roles would include the sponsor, the business person for whom the project is being done, and a person that provides, or influences the allocation of, project resources. But, the same person might fill different roles, and there might be multiple people playing similar roles – it all depends on the project and how the steering committee is set up.

The PM would be part of any steering committee and would provide up-to-date project information and answer queries. Sometimes the PM also plays an administrative role by minuting meetings – seldom does a secretarial person have sufficient appreciation of the project to produce meaningful minutes. Overall the sponsor, the steering committee, the PM, the portfolio manager (who might also be part of the committee), and the PMO should have objectives that are roughly aligned and mutually supportive. In practice, this does not always happen due to politics and other factors that are mostly beyond the control of the PM.

In smaller organizations, things would usually be done far more informally, but governance concepts still apply – the PM should not work in isolation.

4.5 What Is the Project Lifetime? How Does It Relate to the Project Life Cycle?

The project 'lifetime' is a new concept, that I shall explain. It applies to business projects. Most books on project management refer to a project life cycle, which runs from start to end of the project, and the life cycle phases would depend on the type of project. Here we consider the lifetime as having three stages: the pre-project stage, the during-project stage (to which the life cycle applies), and the post-project stage, as shown in Figure 4.2. The lifetime starts when the project is first proposed and ends when the envisaged benefits are substantially realized.

Pre-project activities might include:

- A high-level proposal.
- Creation of a business case.
- Possibly, a feasibility study if the preferred approach needs to be determined.
- Review of the business case and a decision on how to proceed.
- Prioritization of the project against other projects.
- Appointing a PM and identifying key resources.
- Agreeing a start date.

During-project activities might follow life-cycle phases, depending on the project:

- Project definition is one of the first activities (more about this in Chapter 6).
- A traditional (Waterfall) project might have planning, execution, and closing phases.
- An Agile project would have its scope refined and prioritized during execution.
- Activities to align groups of stakeholders to the project's objectives might be part of the project or might be done in parallel with the project. This is known as OCM (organizational change management) and is covered in Chapter 23.
- Handover of deliverables is usually toward the end, and closeout would be done at the end of the defined project.
- Some benefits may already be realized during the project.

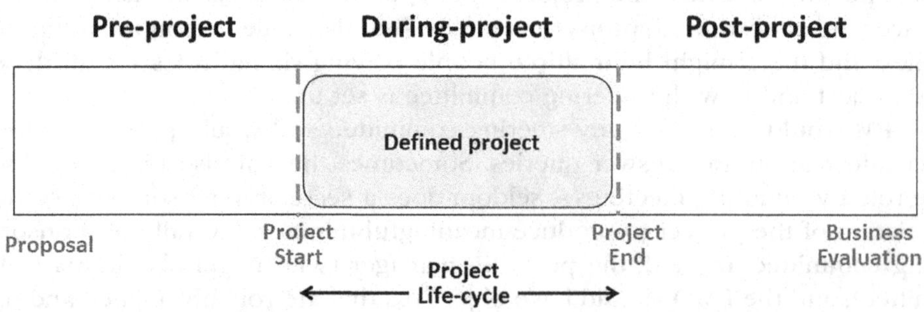

Figure 4.2 Project lifetime stages.

Post-project activities are done to ensure that planned benefits are realized and measured.

- Many of these activities are business-process related and have much to do with realizing benefits.
- OCM activities, involving the people that will use the changed processes, might continue under the supervision of business people.
- Business activities, to realize the benefits outlined in the business case, need to be tracked, and decisions taken if problems arise.
- Evaluation of the outcomes can usually only be done after several months, by which time any new processes should have settled down.

Theoretically, the PM is appointed just before the start of the project and moves on at the end of the project after closeout is done. In practice, the PM may be involved much earlier and might participate in creating the business case. The PM might also be involved after the project to handle follow-on activities and problems that arise. This could happen where the PM *is* a business stakeholder, in which case the during- and post-project activities might merge. Whatever the situation, the PM needs to understand and communicate the rationale for the project to stakeholders. If at any time the PM has doubts about whether the project is worth doing, then it needs to be discussed with the sponsor.

4.6 The Project Lifetime and the Documents That Support Project Governance

The value of project documents was covered in Chapter 3 but some aspects are worth repeating: While the document itself has some value for reference and review, the greatest value is to the person that produces the document. It is almost impossible to write about something that one does not understand, so the act of documenting forces one to gather facts and think through the issues. Then, the document structure and logical sequence need to be such that a reader will understand it – which requires further thought. So, assuming that the PM is the author and has done a thorough job, she will have an excellent grasp of the content on completion. As will be discussed in future chapters, the same applies to minutes, reports, issue records, and more. On a larger project, where there are subprojects, many documents are produced by team members, but it's best if the PM does the project-level ones and reviews the others.

Figure 4.3 is conceptual and not to scale. It shows some of the key documents that *may* be created during the project's lifetime (OGC, 2009; PMI, 2017). Many projects will omit some of the documents or add others. Some of the earlier ones may be produced by people other than the PM, but from the project charter to the closeout report, it is generally the PM. So, the figure, and the notes that follow it, give an 'ideal' progression in a structured organization. What happens in practice might be different and a lack of these documents may contribute to challenged or failed projects.

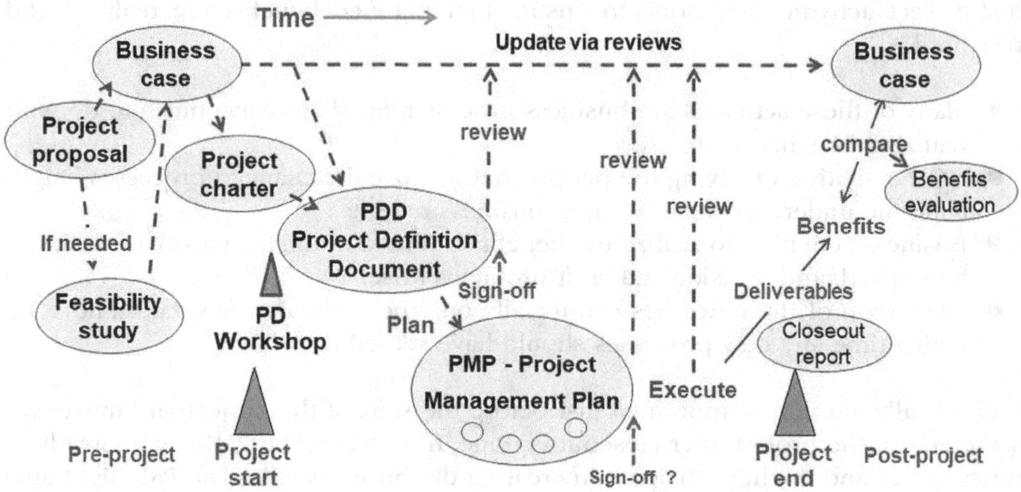

Figure 4.3 Key documents throughout the lifetime (not to scale).

4.6.1 Pre-project

The project lifetime starts with a concept which might be contained in a project proposal (typically 1 to 3 pages) including business drivers, goals, broad scope, benefits, costs, and possibly risks. It would be discussed between business and management, and, if given the 'green light', a person or persons would be assigned to produce a business case, which would be an expansion of the proposal. Where the solution is fairly clear, one can proceed with the business case, but in a few situations, it might be necessary to do a feasibility study first, whose main output would be to arrive at a preferred solution. This is needed because it is difficult to estimate costs and risks if the solution is undefined.

The business case (more detail in Chapter 20) would include the benefits, costs, and risks and might be between 1 and 10 pages. It should have the support of key stakeholders and contain enough information for executives to make a decision. Such a decision might be to go ahead (subject to prioritization), to reject the project, to make changes to the project, or to gather more information. The sponsor 'owns' the business case which is one of the few 'living documents' on the project. As such, it should be reviewed periodically, and updated when anything important changes.

> For living documents, I suggest that after each major change, a new version be created with the date in 'yymmdd' format as part of the name. Thus '220610' would supersede '220318', and, if sorted by name, the latest version sorts to the bottom.

Assuming that a go-ahead decision is taken and prioritization has been done (sometimes immediately and sometimes many months after business case approval), a project charter is needed. The charter is a mandate from the sponsor to the PM to do the project. It would spell out the broad scope, timeframe, and budget, all of which might be drawn from the business case. In practice, I have *never* received a charter – few sponsors have time to produce one. What generally happens is that, once the PM has been appointed, there is a discussion between sponsor and PM, possibly with some related documentation being handed over. A wise PM would then document the understanding, and email it to the sponsor for review. When agreed, that would constitute the charter. PRINCE2 uses the term 'project mandate' which has a similar meaning.

This would be a good time to do Case 1 on Endura, which gives a situation where the PM will meet with a likely sponsor and needs to find out as much as possible.

4.6.2 During-project

Figure 4.4 shows the phases of a traditional life cycle during the project.

Just a word of caution: the term 'initiation' may be ambiguous. In PMBOK, it can start when the project is first proposed and continue after the project has started. In PRINCE2, 'Initiation' is a defined stage that includes some planning activities.

The charter and any business case would be used to start the project. The descriptions that follow refer to the phases which almost always overlap for a business project. Thus execution might start even before initiation is complete, and closing activities start well before execution is complete. Planning activities are most intense early in the project, but continue throughout. An Agile project would have a different life cycle and is covered in Chapter 30. PMBOK uses a similar model with initiating processes, planning processes, etc. It refers to tracking as 'monitoring and controlling' processes.

Having received the charter or mandate, the PM needs to get the project started. Even if the PM knows the stakeholders, an early activity is to engage with them and confirm how they perceive the project, what their roles will be, and what their expectations are. It is rare that stakeholder expectations are aligned, and often they have *very* different understandings of what the project will deliver. Addressing this is one of the main reasons for producing the PDD (project definition document).

The PDD should be produced by the PM. The business case is an important input because it has much information needed for the PDD. The main difference is the purpose. The purpose of the business case is to determine whether the project is or

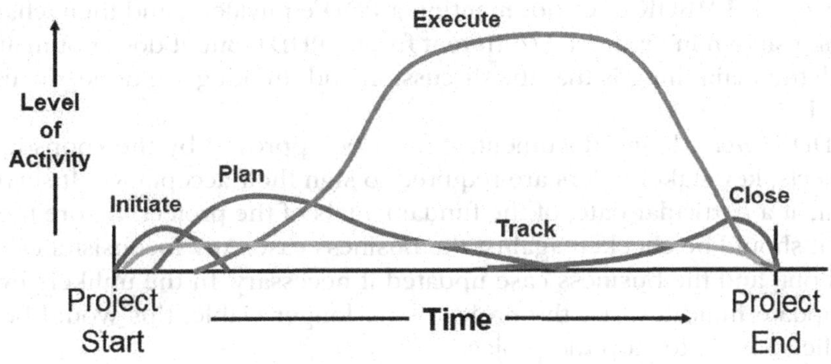

Figure 4.4 Phases in the traditional project life cycle.

remains justified. The main purpose of the PDD is to spell out what must be done and by whom, and also to outline the deliverables and the timeframe. So a clear high-level scope of work is an essential component.

> *Often I have started projects without any business case and in such situations I ensured that the PDD contained a business case which could later be extracted for ongoing review.*

Another vital purpose of the PDD is to ensure that key stakeholders' expectations are aligned. It should not be a long document – typically 3 to 12 pages and taking 1 to 4 weeks to assemble. The PDD must be easy to absorb else the stakeholders are unlikely to read and understand it.

Stakeholder input is vital. There are two broad approaches to gathering input: hold a PDW (project definition workshop) with stakeholders, or engage with them individually. Where everyone is available at the same time, it is best to hold a PDW (details in Chapter 6) which might last for an hour or two for a small project and up to a day for a larger one. It could be run by an external facilitator, but as a PM, my preference is to run it myself. If a PDW is not possible for logistical reasons, then the PM would talk to each key stakeholder and understand their views. Either way, the PM would assemble the PDD. Doing it by individual discussion might be iterative, involving going back to stakeholders where there appears to be disagreement; where such disagreements cannot easily be resolved, the sponsor is the final arbiter.

> *The PDD is one of the most important documents in the entire project, and for over 20 years I have never proceeded with planning without one. Back in the late 1990s we started a large project without a PDD only to find, three months down the track, that a common understanding was lacking. So we held a PDW, did a PDD, and things went better after that – lesson learned!*

The PDD also ensures that the PM has a really good grasp. Without it, PMs might be trying to run projects that they do not understand.

Two items worthy of note: (i) Few organizations use the term 'PDD'; similar documents may be referred to as a 'project charter', a 'project brief' (PRINCE2), or 'terms of reference'. (ii) PMBOK does not mention a PDD equivalent, and their 'charter' has the meaning shown in Figure 4.3 (different from a PDD). But, it does not matter what it is called; the main thing is that the discussion and thinking are done, documented, and agreed.

The PDD is *not* a living document. It must be approved by the sponsor, and on some projects, key stakeholders are required to sign their acceptance. It serves as an agreement, at a particular date, of the fundamentals of the project. Before the PDD is finalized, it should be checked against the business case. Any inconsistencies should be ironed out, and the business case updated if necessary. In the unlikely event that such an update indicates that the project is no longer viable, this would be a good time for the sponsor to stop the project.

Once the PDD is agreed, planning continues, going into more detail, the aim being to produce the 'project management plan' (PMBOK) or 'project initiation documents' (PRINCE2). So while the PDD is a single document (usually MS Word), the full plan is multiple documents each based on one or more sections of the PDD. For example, the scope statement would be input to a WBS (work breakdown structure) and the risk list would move to a risk register. Based on estimates of time and cost, an initial schedule (timeline) would be set up, and a budget produced. Project meetings and tracking would start early in the planning phase. Project execution might start in parallel with planning. Indeed, planning is likely to continue well into execution. For a business project, it may be impossible to plan everything in detail up front, as there are often many unknowns. For example, one of the early activities might be to do an investigation, do a design, or run a procurement cycle, with later activities only becoming known when the earlier activities are complete. The output is the project management plan (the PMP in Figure 4.3). The circles within the plan illustrate that it comprises many separate documents. Most literature says that the plan must be signed off, at least by the sponsor. In my experience, this is seldom practical or even necessary. An executive is unlikely to have time to look at such detail, and would probably not understand it all. When the plan is substantially done, it is far more important for the PM to schedule a business case review (including the sponsor) and to check that the key parameters like expected benefits, costs, risks, and assumptions are still realistic. Once again, if the project is no longer viable, the sponsor would want to make changes, or in the extreme, terminate the project. Taking such actions would not indicate failure on the part of either the PM or the sponsor. On the contrary, it would be a sign of effective governance. Too many projects continue after it is clear that they are no longer viable, causing wasted expenditure and lost opportunities elsewhere.

As shown in Figure 4.4 execution is the biggest consumer of resources. For a business project, there are likely to be changes in requirements along the way. The larger and longer the project, the more are the changes that can be expected. Moreover, things seldom go according to plan. Issues arise along the way that affect schedule, costs, and resources. Some are foreseen as risks; others arise unexpectedly. Sometimes things just take longer, in part because estimating is an 'inexact science'.

All of this might affect the project's justification. Therefore, it is advisable to hold business case reviews every 3 to 6 months, or when a serious concern as to the viability of the project is expressed by any stakeholder. Such reviews should involve at least the sponsor and the PM, and be minuted. Assumptions need to be checked as more information becomes available. For example, are the benefits still realistic? and is their value greater than the remaining cost? For most projects, an hour should be sufficient to confirm that it is still justified. Only if there are grave doubts would more work be needed, but that is still better than applying more resources to an unjustified project.

The project ends when the deliverables are produced and accepted. Chapter 18 covers the many activities required for project closeout. One of them is to produce the closeout report which, as shown in Figure 4.3, is usually only finalized soon after closeout.

4.6.3 Post-project

After project closeout, there is still work to be done. Often the deliverables enable business people to make process changes to derive benefits and to do necessary training. This tends to happen after deliverables have been handed over, especially where the project has a large IT content. Even where business process changes were part of the project, it takes quite a while for the processes to bed down and for problems to be ironed out. It also takes time to measure the effectiveness of the changes and to estimate the value that has been derived.

During this time, it is important to revisit the business case and 'close the loop' by comparing actual benefits with the envisaged benefits. Sometimes benefits are lost sight of and never realized. Other times, it may be more difficult than expected to derive the planned benefits. The latter can often be resolved by adjustments to the processes and with post-project changes to a deliverable. It can even happen that unexpected additional benefits emerge. Again, such business case reviews do not need to be time-consuming. Once the benefits have been substantially realized or it is accepted that further effort will not be made, then a final evaluation of the project can be done (whose conclusions might differ from those in the closeout report).

4.7 Summary

The above lifetime description gives one possible scenario. Each organization and each project is different. Do not be surprised if things are done differently in your organization. The project, as run by the PM, is important. But, from a business point of view, there is more, and much of it is overseen by the sponsor who is accountable and plays a governance role throughout. There is work to be done before the project and work to be done after the project; sound governance ensures that it happens. This contrasts with the construction of a bridge where the benefits usually start as soon as the bridge is complete. For a business project, the business case, used from approval until the end of the project lifetime, acts as a guide to governance and without it much of decision-making is guesswork. The PDD plays a pivotal role in checking that stakeholders have a common understanding and that the PM has a sound grasp of the project. The business case and PDD, as well as many of the items touched on above, are covered in more detail in the ensuing chapters.

References

Larson, E & Gray, C. (2018). *Project Management: The Managerial Process International Edition*. 7th edition. New York: McGraw-Hill Education.

OGC. (2009). *Managing Successful Projects with PRINCE2*, 5th edition. In A. Murray (Ed.). Norwich: TSO (The Stationery Office) on behalf of Office of Government Commerce.

PMI. (2017). *PMBOK - Guide to the Project Management Body of Knowledge*, 6th edition: Pennsylvania, USA: Project Management Institute.

CORE ELEMENTS OF BUSINESS PROJECT MANAGEMENT

2

Part 2 provides the method which I consider the essential minimum needed for most business projects. It is not tightly defined or prescriptive. However, it reminds the PM of the main things that need to be done. Although the method can stand on its own, it can equally integrate into any other methodology. Part 2 is mainly written for the PM. Nevertheless, it should also be of interest to the sponsor and other stakeholders. Here are the main elements of the method and the chapters of Part 2 give 'how-to' guidance.

1. Ensure that you have a sponsor.
   The sponsor should be at the appropriate level, for example, a departmental head for a small project, or a senior executive for a larger one. The sponsor must want the project to be successful and should have much to gain or lose, depending on the outcomes of the project. The PM must agree to the project charter with the sponsor and establish a relationship that makes sparing use of the sponsor's time while enabling urgent matters to be dealt with promptly.
2. Talk regularly to the stakeholders (which includes the project team).
3. Maintain a structured repository for documentation.
   It could be in the cloud or on folders, either of which should be accessible by the stakeholders and especially the project team. From day one, all project documents should be stored in this repository with only the most sensitive ones being stored elsewhere. It must be backed up regularly.
4. Produce a PDD (project definition document).
   If there is a business case, it provides much of the input, if not, your PDD will at least have the benefits, costs, and risks (the main justification elements). Even if the PDD is called something different in your organization, it can ensure that your stakeholders understand the project and are aligned. Equally important, the PDD will ensure that *you* have a solid understanding.

DOI: 10.1201/9781003321101-6

5. Define the scope and the deliverables from the PDD in greater detail.
Having outlined the scope and deliverables, ensure that requirements are agreed with the stakeholders and can be met. For a business project, some activities may not yet be fully understood, but at least it is a starting point for your schedule. Creating a WBS (work breakdown structure) is a possible way of achieving this.
6. Develop and track a simple schedule, noting the milestone events.
It would probably be a Gantt chart, but, for a very small project, it could be an activity list with dates. Once set up, the schedule rather than the WBS holds the scope. Expect the activities and dates to change regularly.
7. Develop a cost budget and track the costs.
The actual costs should be related to what has been achieved. For a small project, this would be at project level; for a larger project, one might track the costs of major subprojects separately.
8. Hold regular, short, team meetings.
They help you to: communicate, track progress, monitor action items, and pick up new risks or issues. Minute meetings immediately afterward and circulate the minutes to stakeholders.
9. Document and manage project risks, issues, and changes.
Facilitate discussion around them and create simple, flexible, documents with necessary detail. Documents should be numbered, dealt with, and stored for reference. They help you to understand the situation and enable you to refer back to them because it's amazing how quickly one forgets.
10. Produce regular one-page reports – usually weekly or fortnightly.
Reports encourage one to reflect on progress while keeping people, and especially the sponsor, informed. They form a vital record and may even trigger useful discussion.
11. Close the project with a report, and review it with the sponsor.
Lessons learned, negative or positive, could be in the same or a separate document.

Some projects need more, and some items may not apply to a particular project. I managed a number of small projects where deadlines were critical, but management was not interested in the costs because the team was fixed. Similar considerations apply to Agile projects where scope change control is not needed because the scope is defined dynamically.

In the chapters that follow, I mention how I approach and document things; no doubt there are other equally valid approaches. However, it is very important that what you produce is done consistently and thoroughly. Part 2 does not include portfolio governance. Nor does it include project management topics that only apply to *some* projects or are of a more general nature. These are covered in Part 3.

Chapter 5

Engaging with Stakeholders

5.1 Introduction and Objectives

Stakeholders are fundamental to any project. Unless their needs are met, the outcomes may be unsatisfactory. So, the objectives are to:

- Know how to identify your project's stakeholders.
- Understand their power, influence, and interest in relation to your project.
- Do a brief analysis and decide on the best approach to engage with them.

5.2 Who Are the Stakeholders?

In the project context, stakeholders are any persons or groups that are actively involved with, or whose interests are affected by, the project itself or the outcomes of the project (PMI, 2017). They can exert influence over the project or a deliverable. Besides the PM, stakeholders include the sponsor, the project team, the business people that will use the output of your project, and other people inside or outside your organization that fit the above definition. When starting a project, one needs to understand, as early as possible, who the stakeholders are. Some of them will provide the business case and charter which may not even be documented. At the outset, you may not know of all the stakeholders. Even your team members may not have been assigned yet.

It is said that PMs spend over 80% of their time communicating, whether verbally, via email, or via any other written document. Almost everyone that the PM would communicate with would be a stakeholder, and PMI deems them to be so important that 'stakeholder management' was added as a new knowledge area in the 2013 edition of the PMBOK guide. PMI's stakeholder processes are to identify the stakeholders, to plan how the project will engage with them, and to manage such engagement (PMI, 2017). The latter includes setting realistic expectations, and ongoing monitoring of the relationships. Most project areas involve stakeholders. For example, leadership

DOI: 10.1201/9781003321101-7

is about influencing stakeholders positively. Risks often relate to stakeholders, and an unengaged stakeholder can even derail a project.

> *I nearly experienced this on a banking project. We discovered, very late, that the credit management function needed to approve our new system. This caused considerable delay because they had some requirements that we were unaware of. We had tried to engage with them during the project without success – we should have tried harder!*

The lesson here is that stakeholders are busy and have other priorities. The PM needs to find out who the important ones are and to persevere until there is adequate engagement (Burke & Barron, 2007). The sponsor can often point out stakeholders that the PM may have overlooked. If you were to list the stakeholders on a typical project, they might include:

- The project sponsor, the Steercom, and members of senior management.
- Customers/clients, users, and sometimes even a community of people.
- The project team including subproject managers and of course, the PM.
- Business partners and contractors.
- Support groups, within your organization, such as Procurement, Legal, and the PMO.
- Functional managers such as Marketing or Engineering.
- Government agencies.

5.3 How Might Stakeholders Affect My Project?

Having listed the stakeholders one needs to prioritize them from an engagement point of view. Some may be very influential and have strong views; others may have little influence and be largely unaffected by the project. There is everything in-between. A useful way to classify stakeholders is to put them onto a grid, as shown in Figure 5.1, called a 'power/interest' grid. The example is about a project to maintain and replace the machinery in a manufacturing plant.

It would probably be done in 15 minutes with paper and pencil, and could involve discussion with a trusted person. Place each stakeholder or group according to their interest in the project and their power (or influence). Where a stakeholder is very positive about the project possibly mark with a '+', and where resistant to the project, a '–'. For example, in the situation illustrated in Figure 5.1:

- The CEO has considerable power, but she may only be moderately interested if this is a non-critical project.
- The designers have a great interest because their current designs are limited by what some of the aging machinery can do.
- Machine operators may have little interest in what solution is developed because they are used to following instructions from their supervisor. They have little say in what will be done, but cannot be totally ignored because they may object to an unsatisfactory solution.

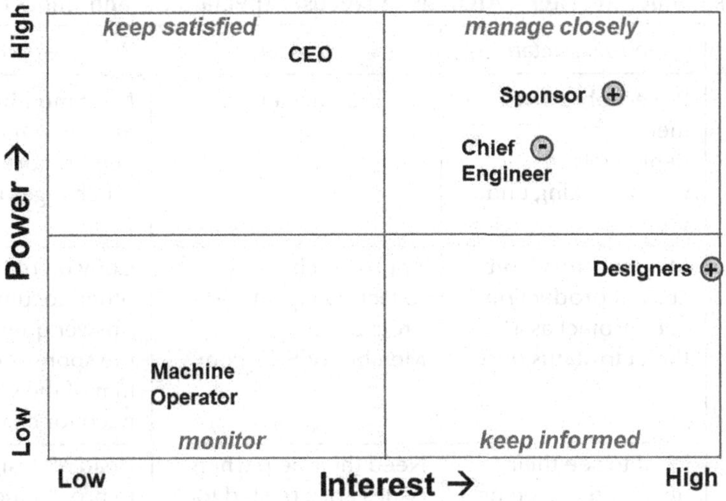

Figure 5.1 Stakeholder power/interest grid.

- The chief engineer is looking forward to going on retirement in 8 months' time. He is negative about the project as the disruption in the plant will be considerable and he is not looking for new challenges. So, he certainly has an interest and is fairly influential (power).

Subsequent engagement might attempt to move influential people (high power) that are negative to at least a neutral stance and those that are neutral to a supportive stance.

5.4 How Should I Engage with the Stakeholders?

Clearly, these examples are hypothetical – each project is different. So, while it is worth knowing where various stakeholders are positioned, the knowledge needs to guide your actions in engaging with them. Suggested strategies are given for each quadrant:

- Top right (high power, high interest): Manage them closely. Communicate regularly and respond to changes that they may propose.
- Top left: Keep them satisfied. Respond only if they raise a concern. It is not necessary to copy them on all important documentation; too much interaction might even irritate them.
- Bottom right: Keep them informed. Send them information and respond if they express opinions, but do not overreact.
- Bottom left: Monitor their views. You will not spend much time communicating with them, and would probably do so through their manager or a representative. But they cannot be ignored.

Table 5.1 Stakeholder Register – Analysis of Needs, Expectations, and Impact

Name/Group	*Needs/Expectations*	*Impact*	*Approach*
Neo Kahle (Sponsor, and marketing executive)	Project objectives met. Kept involved without taking undue time.	Decision maker	Meet monthly in Steercom meetings. Send reports. Involve for changes/issues.
Jack Jones (Chief engineer)	Minimal impact on current production. Sees project as a threat to status quo.	Approves changes to factory layout and procedures. Member of Steercom.	Copy on reports and other documents. Answer queries, but let the sponsor convince him of the strategic need for changes.
Designers	Want to see their new products being manufactured soonest.	Need their help when issues arise related to design. Their supportive attitude influences other groups.	Head of design invited to project meetings. Copy on reports. Consult only when necessary.
Machine operators	Any new production process must be easy to follow with minimum breakdowns.	Any negativity may lead to reduced productivity which will affect the profitability of new products.	OCM principles apply, and must be included in the project plan. Hold info. sessions, and ensure training is in place.

Having gone through this exercise fairly quickly it is worth doing a basic analysis in tabular form as illustrated in Table 5.1 – sometimes called a 'stakeholder register'. The table need not be comprehensive and, here, the CEO is omitted.

Going through this thought process should identify where OCM (organizational change management) activities will be needed as part of the plan (see Chapter 23).

The illustration shows that both rational and emotional needs must be taken into account. Some of the emotional needs may relate to politics which happens to a greater or lesser extent in all organizations (Msengana, 2012). A wise PM will, through talking to people, be aware of the political forces at play but would avoid 'playing politics' or mentioning it in reports. However, where politics threatens the project, the PM might discuss the problem with the sponsor and agree on the best way forward.

The diagrams or documents that you have created are sensitive and might need to be kept (and backed up) in a password-protected folder. After all, nobody would want to be seen as negative – even if they are! The actual documents (or scribbles) may never be referred to again, but the thinking that you put into creating them will be valuable.

5.5 Final Thoughts on Stakeholders

Managing stakeholders is an ongoing PM role, but because it is time-consuming, prioritization is needed. Some of it is best delegated, upward to the sponsor and also to your team, some of whom may already have established relationships with certain stakeholders. Although there are exceptions, an open honest approach will build the trust needed to get things done. Try to identify concerns and seek solutions before they become issues. Where problems arise, give bad news early, but only after giving some thought to what can be done. When solutions, possibly involving scope changes, are agreed among stakeholders always put the understanding in a note or a document, and keep it for future reference. The verbal discussion, backed up by something 'in writing' is sound practice when managing stakeholder expectations.

To consolidate your understanding, I suggest that you do Case 2 which involves implementing a patient records system in Waluma hospital with a variety of stakeholders.

References

Burke, R., & Barron, S. (2007). *Project Management Leadership: Building Creative Teams.* London: Burke Publishing.

Msengana, L. (2012). *The Missing Link in Projects.* Republic of South Africa: Knowres Publishing.

PMI. (2017). *PMBOK – Guide to the Project Management Body of Knowledge*, 6th edition: Pennsylvania, USA: Project Management Institute.

Chapter 6

Project Definition

6.1 Introduction and Objectives

Project definition is done, mainly by the PM, as soon as the project starts. The aim is to ensure a thorough understanding by all stakeholders, of what will be done. The PM, who is also a stakeholder, may only have received a high-level briefing. The objectives of this chapter are to:

- Reinforce what a project definition document (PDD) is, and why we need it.
- Bear in mind the constraints of scope/quality, time, and cost.
- Be able to produce a sound PDD for any business project.
- Explain the importance of aligning the business case with the PDD.
- Show how the content of the PDD feeds into detailed planning.

6.2 Why Do We Need Project Definition?

At the time of taking on a new business project, there is seldom clarity on what must be delivered. It is sometimes not even clear who the sponsor is. Referring back to Figure 4.3 which indicates key documents, I have seldom received a project charter, a business case, or a feasibility report. If any of these or related documents are available, it is a bonus. Assuming no documentation, a project charter (or the equivalent), as described in Subsection 4.6.1 is the first step, but it is unlikely to have enough detail to ensure consensus among the stakeholders. We need to produce a PDD, and one of its main purposes is to get the stakeholders aligned. Certainly, there may be disagreements, which must be resolved during definition, but through the PDD there must be a common understanding of what the project will produce. Although more will be learned as the planning proceeds and the project unfolds, the PDD gives all stakeholders, including the PM and sponsor, a clear initial understanding of the project.

Knowing the importance of a project to the organization motivates stakeholders and especially the project team. The PM can build such motivation by periodically emphasizing the justification for the project – which is embodied in the PDD. It also helps

DOI: 10.1201/9781003321101-8

when there are difficulties, and even projects that are ultimately successful, often go through times of serious problems, where people challenge the need for the project. In such situations, knowledge of the justification from the PDD enables the PM to explain the importance of the project and to maintain the focus on resolving the problems. So, producing the PDD should be one of the PM's top priorities when the project starts.

Some might say that a PDD is not needed for an Agile project (covered in Chapter 30). My belief is that it *is* needed for the reasons given above. However, the content would need adjustment. For example, the scope might be stated at a higher level because it will evolve. Similar considerations would apply to other headings.

6.3 How Do We Produce a PDD?

The approach to producing a PDD is touched on near the start of Subsection 4.6.2, but details of how it is developed and its content are described here. The essential first step is to ensure that it is clear who will act as the sponsor and be accountable for the project. If no sponsor can be confirmed, then the project is best not started – there must be someone in authority that needs the project to happen. All activities to bring definition to the project will be done while keeping the sponsor informed.

One of the main benefits of the PDD is the considerable investigation needed to produce it. This gathering of information about the project will vastly increase the understanding by the PM and stakeholders, and will help to resolve misunderstandings or disagreements. My suggestion is that you, as PM, start writing the PDD from what you already know, and make a list of all the things that you are uncertain about (and there will be lots) even before you engage with stakeholders.

Next, and most important, is engagement with the stakeholders. There are two basic approaches: individual discussions or a workshop. Where most stakeholders are in different cities or not available for a workshop, you need to engage with them individually by meeting or videoconference. Because different requirements and viewpoints will emerge, some iteration is inevitable, particularly to iron out contentious issues. Where most stakeholders are able to attend a workshop, the process is faster. A PDW (project definition workshop) typically lasts for between 2 hours and a whole day, depending on the size and complexity of the project. Having between 6 and 15 attendees, seated in a horseshoe configuration, is ideal. You might bring in a facilitator to run it, but I prefer to run my own PDWs. The sponsor would probably not attend the whole workshop, but might be present at the start to explain the importance of the project. The sponsor might also attend the last half hour to get feedback and understand any issues to be ironed out. An agenda is needed and time must be carefully managed. Often the way the PDW is run sets the tone for the project. The agenda items would correspond closely with the headings in the PDD (detailed below) including a high-level description, goals and objectives, scope, benefits and costs, roles and responsibilities, milestones, risks, and issues. The facilitator might summarize the points made by attendees on a whiteboard which could be photographed as a record. A flip chart can be used to record issues that arise along the way. Issues might be points of disagreement among the stakeholders or information that is missing. While being in the same room always has advantages, nowadays it is possible to hold a PDW by online conference, thus enabling remote people to be included.

A 'kick-off meeting' is often referred to, and potentially it could fulfill much the same purpose as a PDW. However, my concern is that kick-off meetings are often too short to achieve much, and tend not to allow all stakeholders to have their say. Moreover, it is often necessary to define the project when only a few team members are on board, so I would prefer to have a team briefing and discussion a bit later, when most of the team have joined.

The output of the PDW serves as input to the PDD, but it may not be enough, and as PM, you are responsible for producing the final result. If a business case exists, some of the content can be drawn from it, but checking is necessary because much may have changed since the business case was approved.

6.4 The Triple Constraint – What Are Our Priorities?

Before proceeding further, it is useful to clarify the priorities. In most projects there is a trade-off between the:

- Scope and quality delivered.
- Time taken.
- Cost of completing the project.

Ideally, stakeholders would like lots of scope/quality, in little time, and for a low cost. Unfortunately, it is seldom possible to achieve all three desires. If one wants:

- More scope or better quality, the project usually takes longer and costs more.
- The project completed in less time, it is likely to cost more and one may need to reduce the scope.
- Lower cost, the project is likely to produce less scope and may take longer.

These limitations are known as the triple constraint and sometimes called the 'iron triangle'. They are illustrated in Figure 6.1.

The sponsor, guided by the PM, needs to decide on the relative priorities: Are any of the parameters (scope, time, cost) non-negotiable (constrained)? For example, once the date is set for a conference the time becomes constrained. Where a bid has been accepted for a well-documented work, the scope may be constrained. Once the most constrained parameter has been established, the sponsor needs to consider

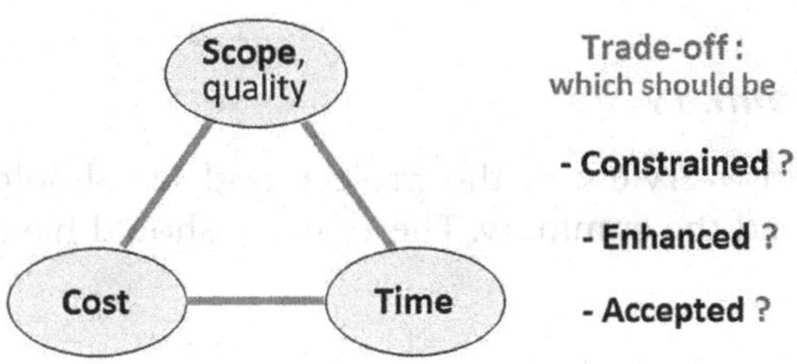

Figure 6.1 The triple constraint and prioritization options.

the other two and decide which is more important, and request that it be enhanced at the expense of the third parameter where it would be accepted if the outcome is not according to plan. For example, for the time-constrained conference, the sponsor may believe that it is important that the event should be affordable by the organization, in which case cost would be enhanced, with the consequence that some scope (or quality) reduction would need to be accepted, for example, a simpler gala dinner or no gifts for attendees. So, the sponsor needs to indicate which triangle parameters in Figure 6.1 are:

- Constrained (plan must be met),
- Enhanced (improve on the plan if possible),
- Accepted (worse than plan will be accepted).

With this approach, each parameter gets one of the above designations, which will be a useful starting point for doing the PDD. To get a better understanding, I suggest that you do Case 3.

6.5 What Should Be in the PDD?

The PDD is one of the main outputs after the project starts. Typically it would be between 3 and 12 pages (1 500 to 6 000 words) depending on the size of the project. Even for a complex project, the PDD should not be more than 15 pages, as stakeholders are unlikely to read more. Senior people will probably only read the executive summary. Further detail could be in separate documents. It is best if the PDD is date versioned until finalized. Late in the process, it might be circulated to selected stakeholders, inside and outside the team, with an invitation to comment. Resolution of such comments would reflect in the final version. When final, I recommend that approval be given by the sponsor and maybe one or two other stakeholders. Gathering a large number of signatures is often counter-productive. If key stakeholders appear reluctant to review the document, they could be invited to a review session, where the PM would lead them through the various sections. If the project was initiated via a contract, then the PDD should be consistent with the contract. After approval, the PDD should no longer be changed. Any subsequent changes should be dealt with via the change process, covered in Chapter 15.

A PDD is a single document whose template is given in Appendix 3. The sections below describe the suggested content. Neither the template nor the guidance needs to be followed slavishly. By all means, make adjustments to suit the project at hand.

6.5.1 Executive Summary

The Summary gives an overview of the project, and we should assume that some executives will only read the summary. Therefore, it should have all the salient facts including:

- A high-level description of the project;
- The main outputs (deliverables) which make it very clear how stakeholders will know that the project is complete;

- The benefits, or the problem that will be solved, which answer the question "why are we doing this?";
- A summary of the costs and any major risks;
- The planned completion date.

6.5.2 Glossary

The glossary explains all acronyms or terms used. It should be near the start, so that reviewers do not struggle to understand the PDD, only to find the glossary when they reach the end. There are two columns.

- Left-hand column: The acronym or words needing explanation.
- Right-hand column: The expansion of the acronym or the explanation of the words.

6.5.3 Business Goals and Project Objectives

The business goals should state the things that would be of interest to executives. For example, in the insurance industry, goals might be to reduce the time taken to assess and pay an insurance claim, or to have a full range of vehicle insurance offerings. The goals would be high-level because more detailed benefits are stated under another heading. Project objectives should be things that indicate what the project team must deliver. For example, the restructured department must be fully operational by 15 June, or the prototype must be demonstrated to marketing by 20 September. One to three goals, and a similar number of objectives, should suffice.

6.5.4 Critical Success Factors (Abbreviated to CSFs)

CSFs state the most important things that must be in place for the project to succeed – not too many as it would be hard to focus on more than five items. Often CSFs relate to people and relationships. For example, a sound relationship with, and skilled resources from, department A. No need to mention funding – if funding is not available, there can be no project. Note that CSFs are not the deliverables of the project. Rather they are the things that are critically needed for the deliverables to be produced. Less-critical items might be placed under the heading of assumptions or dependencies.

6.5.5 Scope

This is a high-level statement of what must be done on the project, whether by the project team or any other party. It is probably the most important part of the PDD because, if we don't understand the work, then we don't understand the project. Starting each item with a verb is a good practice, like 'give training on X to department Y'. Your judgment is required to get the right level of detail. It does not need to be a full work breakdown structure (which is explained in Chapter 7), and it certainly should not be a detailed technical specification. However, it must give a clear picture of the main activities with stated or implied deliverables and, when in doubt, it is better to go into too much detail than too little.

Sometimes it is appropriate to amplify the scope by stating volumes. For example, when referring to training, the rough number of people to be trained should be indicated. Or when an activity involves communicating with clients, the number of clients might be relevant.

6.5.6 Approach and Context Diagram

These items are optional. Where it is not clear how the scope would be done, then an explanation might be needed on the approach to be taken. For example:

- Where procurement activities are needed before later activities can be done, this should be explained.
- Where alternative approaches were considered, it might be explained which one was chosen and the reasons.

It could also help to include a diagram, map, picture, or anything that will give stakeholders a better understanding of the project.

6.5.7 Scope Exclusions and Other Exclusions

Exclusions are important because they help to set the boundaries. Exclusions avoid stakeholders making assumptions that are invalid. For example, if the project scope were to develop and pilot a new business process in one region, then it should be stated that implementing the process in other regions is excluded. If it is not explicitly stated, stakeholders may assume that the project is organization-wide. If something is essential for project success, but will be done outside of the project, then it should be stated as an exclusion with an indication of who will do it. Alternatively, such an item might be stated as an assumption or a dependency. Avoid having it under both headings. Also state anything that will be excluded from the output (deliverables) of the project, for example, 'This new benefit only applies to current employees but not to contractors or retirees'.

6.5.8 Benefits from the Project

This expands on the business goals of the project. If the goal itself spells out the entire benefit, then refer back to it. Even if covered in a business case, benefits should be re-stated in the PDD. Monetary amounts should be used where possible. Supposing that one of the benefits is improved customer satisfaction. Even if it is difficult to put a value on satisfaction, one could 'put a stake in the ground' by proposing that this will have a value of $200 000 per year from increased business and fewer queries. Then the sponsor might agree that it is representative, or might ask for it to be changed. Some executives might prefer not to show a value at all. We need to be flexible.

6.5.9 Costs of Doing the Project

Most costs will be incurred during the life of the project. Operational costs may continue after project completion and could be shown either as ongoing costs or as an offset against the benefits. It may be relevant to categorize costs. For example, costs might be separated according to whether they are internal or from procurement. It is usually important to understand which costs will be charged to your project. For example, check which stakeholders (other than the team) will charge their time to the project. Five to ten line items should suffice for most projects.

For certain types of projects, some organizations require financial estimates like net present value (NPV), or internal rate of return (IRR). These require a time-phased estimate of both benefits and costs. Only give NPV or IRR estimates if they are relevant, and if so, ensure that you understand the organization's method of calculation. It is equally important to round numbers and avoid precision that suggests accuracy because NPV and IRR percentages are especially sensitive to small changes in benefit and cost estimates (refer to Chapter 21 on project selection).

6.5.10 Resources and Stakeholders

People resources are also stakeholders. We must mention the people who will actually do the work, even if they are from an outside company. At the time of doing the PDD, some of the players may not be known, so just put something like 'to be assigned' and the role and responsibilities. By all means, state the interested executives, but avoid having a long list of 'bosses' with grand titles and omit the people that will manage or do the activities. Sometimes it is sufficient to mention resources as a group, for example, change analysts or trainers. Responsibilities should be at a high level, but must be stated where they may not be obvious. Thus, for a PM 'normal PM duties' might suffice, but for a business executive, one might want to state that they will be responsible for supplying people, approving documents, driving changes to business processes or other benefits realization activities. Where a project is being done for a customer organization, it is particularly important to spell out the customers' responsibilities, lest they assume that the project will take care of everything without their involvement.

6.5.11 Milestone Schedule

Schedule details will not be known at this point, so only the main events like completion of an important deliverable should be stated, and always with a target date, which may need to be changed at the end of planning. Stating a month would be too vague as there are about 30 days between start and end. Milestones not only tell stakeholders what to expect but also set shorter-term targets for the team to avoid the "there is still plenty of time" syndrome (student syndrome). Note that activities are not milestones, but the *completion* of an activity might be a milestone event. Milestones should be reasonably spread out over the duration of a project. Only on a very short project would there be more than one milestone per month, so an 8-month project might have about six milestones (including the project end-date).

6.5.12 Risks

Risks are covered in more depth in Chapter 11. They are events that *might* happen, and if they were to happen, would affect the project or its outcome. Here we are mainly interested in risks that could have an *adverse* impact. The question to be answered is "what could go wrong that would materially affect the project or reduce the benefits and hence the project's justification?" However, positive risks like "what if the sales volumes are far greater than expected?", should also be considered.

Risks need to state what the adverse event would be and the impact if it were to happen. One-word risks like 'weather' do not give enough detail. Obvious possibilities, like time or cost overruns, should not be mentioned – they could apply to any project. The PM should also rate the probability, and the impact size, of the event. The rating scale must be stated, and in the template a 1 (low) to 10 (high) scale is used. Usually, response actions can be taken to reduce the probability or impact of the risk event or even to avoid it entirely, and these should be stated.

6.5.13 Issues, Assumptions, Dependencies, and Constraints

Here, these are given reference letters E (issues or exceptions), A, D, and C. They are lumped together because sometimes the same thing could be stated as more than one of them, and we only want it stated once. For example, suppose that the upcoming project depends on statistical analysis support from Department X, and that the manager of Department X has been uncooperative to date, then the PM could enter one of the following:

E (issue): To date, there is no agreement from Dept. X to give statistics support.
A (assumption): Dept. X will provide statistics support for activity Y.
D (dependency): Activity Y depends on statistics support from Dept. X.

Which is appropriate in this instance is up to the PM's judgment.

6.5.14 Management System and Documents for Reference

This describes how the project will be managed. For example:

- Regular minuted meetings that will be held such as project tracking meetings or steering committee (project board) meetings. How often the meetings would be and who should attend.
- Regular communications, like project reports, or financial tracking spreadsheets. To whom they would be circulated and how frequently.

A statement can indicate who needs to approve the PDD for it to be considered final.

Lastly, list any documents currently available that relate to the project. Examples might be, a business case, contracts, product specifications, or procurement documentation.

Now that you have understood the purpose and content of a PDD, I recommend that you do Case 4 to give you practice at completing its sections for the Trandy Inc.'s corporate scholarship project.

6.6 Confirming the Business Case After the PDD Has Been Finalized

While the PDD is now a record of what was initially agreed, planning must continue with increasing detail. Possibly some execution activities may start in parallel with planning. The PDD serves as a starting point and guide for planning, but another important document is needed – the business case. If a business case existed, it would probably need an update to align it to the PDD, and then a short review with the sponsor to confirm the justification. If the business case did *not* exist, now is the time to create it. This should not take long as most of the business case would come directly from the PDD. The following might be added if not already in the PDD:

- An explanation of why the value of the benefits is sufficiently greater than the costs (which includes a contingency for risks).
- The persons responsible for realizing the benefits and how the benefits will be measured.

The assumptions must be included, as their validity needs to be checked at every review. Risks should also remain as they underpin the contingency part of the cost. The following might be removed or reduced as they will become part of the project plan:

- The scope, approach, and scope exclusions.
- Diagrams, unless they directly support the justification.

The business case should be as easy to follow as the PDD, but it would probably be shorter – perhaps 500 to 4 000 words. It needs to be updated and reviewed regularly, always in collaboration with the sponsor who owns the business case. The first such review should take place toward the end of planning, at which time far more will be known about the assumptions and costs. Later, should the project be going well and remain justified, a business case review might only take an hour. However, where there are serious problems, it may be necessary to initiate changes or, in the extreme, to terminate the project – clearly requiring a longer meeting.

6.7 Continuing with Planning

The PDD gives an excellent start, but planning continues. Many elements of the PDD now become separate documents which will be updated as the project unfolds. The scope is expanded and forms the basis for schedule and cost estimation. The costs are detailed and are often broken down by week or by month for tracking. People are brought on board and the schedule is created. The risks move to a risk register. The issues go into the issues log and are documented further. Project tracking meetings and reports will have started because planning also needs to be managed and communicated. It is difficult to say "the plan is now complete" because, for a business project, it evolves all the time.

Chapter 7

Scope Definition

7.1 Introduction and Objectives

In this chapter, we shall discuss the importance of scope definition, including:

- Understanding the relationship between objectives, requirements, and scope.
- How to gather requirements from stakeholders.
- The WBS (work breakdown structure) theory and how to build a WBS.

I shall also explain some practical differences between business projects and construction or engineering ones, and also how to adapt the theory for business projects, where most scope activities are not known up-front and only become clearer as the project unfolds.

7.2 Why Do We Need to Know the Scope in More Detail?

In project management, 'scope' is used in two ways.

- *Product* scope is about the output deliverables with their functions and features.
- *Project* scope is the work or activities that need to be done to produce the required outcomes of the project, which include the deliverables.

Here, we are talking about project scope. The product scope which may be described in specifications remains relevant because it influences the project scope.

Having done the PDD, we should already have a fair understanding of the project scope. But more detail is needed for scheduling and cost management. Our aim is to arrive at a WBS (work breakdown structure) which defines *all* the work needed to complete the project and *only* the work needed to complete the project. The required work is broken down into 'packages' that form the WBS – as described later in this chapter. The packages can then be used for estimating, to support scheduling, and for cost tracking. The progression is broadly: (i) Agree the goals and objectives. (ii) Gather (or collect) the requirements. and (iii) Define the scope with the aid of a

DOI: 10.1201/9781003321101-9

WBS. Some of this will have been done for the PDD, but further investigation and documentation may be needed as planning progresses.

Scope definition for a business project is often difficult. For some projects, the scope is fairly well understood up-front - the Trandy Inc. scholarship scheme in Case 4 is an example. For other projects, at the beginning, one may understand the deliverables at a high level, but one may *not yet* know the activities needed to achieve them. Some of the planning activities may be to investigate and do analysis work which will result in a clearer picture of the approach and activities involved. In such situations, one may have to either settle for high-level activities that will later be broken into detail or attempt to list the activities, knowing that there will be changes as work progresses. For example, for a project to merge two departments, activities relating to premises may be straightforward, while aspects relating to people, skills, processes, and systems only evolve after much discussion. Thus, determining the scope can be iterative. Nevertheless, it is essential to arrive at the best scope statement possible during planning, while knowing that planned activities will change. Approaches such as 'progressive elaboration' or 'rolling wave planning' recognize this difficulty and accept that the plan will evolve as the project unfolds.

Even for these approaches, it is necessary to define the scope as thoroughly as possible for estimating and communication purposes. Probably the commonest cause of underestimation is omitting elements of scope. For example, it is easy to overlook the people-change aspects of a project which are covered in Chapter 23 on OCM (organizational change management). OCM is about getting buy-in from the people who are affected by the project or must develop new skills and change the way they work to achieve the project benefits.

So, adjustments to project scope during execution are almost certain. However, the adjustments are far more easily managed if the scope was appropriately defined in the first place, using good judgment as to its level of detail. Debate about scope during execution is inevitable, but will be minimized through sound definition.

7.3 What Are Requirements and How Do We Gather Them?

Project failure is likely to result if the requirements are not understood or if deliverables are not agreed upon. So, it is particularly important to understand the requirements which usually come from business stakeholders. Stakeholder needs and expectations must be documented, sometimes in the form of a specification or 'spec'. Specifications give complete, precise, and verifiable detail (with relevant numbers) for the output of a project, which could be a process, a product, a service, or a combination. There must be enough information that deliverables can be measured during execution. For example, if a new process will depend on enhanced IT function, then the specification must be in enough detail for the function to be tested. Such requirements form the basis for all scope planning and the activities needed to meet them. Requirements are gathered through communication which could take many forms including:

- Structured interviews.
- Focus groups which are facilitated workshops, with selected groups of people, to understand needs and perceptions in depth.

- Observation of the current situation and asking questions.
- Prototyping, which means building something which could be a model, and getting feedback on it.
- Questionnaires or surveys.

Reviewing the requirements and checking that all of them are covered by the scope helps to reduce scope omissions – referred to as creating traceability (between scope activities and requirements). Getting stakeholder approval for requirements documents helps to confirm understanding and to minimize disputes later.

There is often confusion between objectives, requirements, and scope. I have seen the statement 'uplift the community' under scope. But it says nothing about the work that must be done. At best it might be an objective, and then one might ask "uplift in what way?" In this situation 'build a library' or 'train school leavers on how to seek jobs' would be valid high-level scope items. So I suggest that you do Case 5 which presents statements for you to classify as objectives, requirements, scope, or scope exclusions (things that will not be done - as explained in Chapter 6).

7.4 WBS Theory and How to Create a WBS

The WBS is created by starting with the high-level scope items, referred to as components, and breaking each component down to further levels of detail – sometimes called 'decomposition'. Each level needs to be deliverables oriented with clear completion criteria. For a particular project, there are many ways that it can validly be done, for example, by project phase, by subproject, or by major deliverable. The two common ways of representing the WBS are shown in Figure 7.1.

The outline numbered WBS could be done in an MS Word or Excel document. It is easy to add scope components or to move them between higher-level summary components. I almost always use this approach because it is flexible and quick, but it would not be suitable for presentation to the sponsor. The hierarchical WBS, possibly

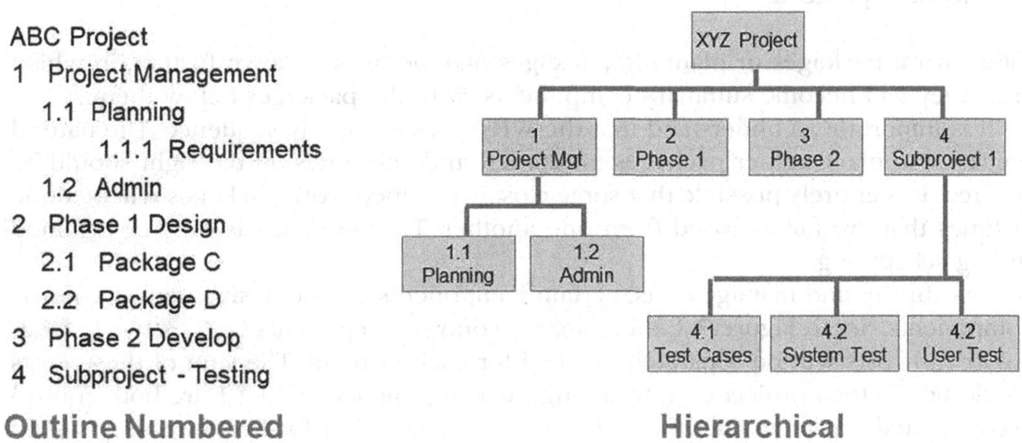

Figure 7.1 WBS representations.

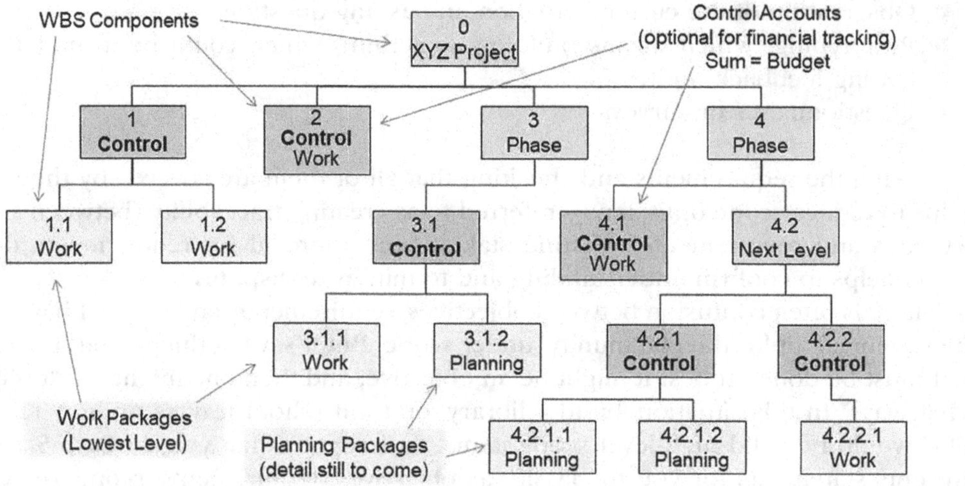

Figure 7.2 WBS components.

done in PowerPoint, is more suitable for explaining the project to stakeholders, but takes more effort, gets less onto a page, and is time-consuming to change.

The theory behind the different components of the WBS is illustrated in Figure 7.2. It shows each component as a rectangle. Only components at the lowest level are called 'packages', the sum of which represent the total work of the project.

The packages can be of two types:

- Work packages. These are used where the deliverables and the work to produce them are well understood. They can be estimated and assigned to resources.
- Planning packages. These are used where it is known that work is required, but where the deliverable may not be fully specified and where the activities to produce it still need to be determined. They are not ready to be assigned for work to proceed.

Either work packages or planning packages may be broken down further, in which case, they will become summary components, with the packages below them.

It is important to understand that the WBS does not imply sequence. The natural tendency to place earlier packages on the left and later ones on the right should be resisted. It is entirely possible that some closely grouped work packages will be done at times that are far removed from one another. The sequence is only determined during scheduling.

To estimate and manage costs, certain components can be designated as 'control' components. So, in Figure 7.2, there are six control components (1, 2, 3.1, 4.1, 4.2.1, 4.2.2) and costs will be separately tracked for each of them. The sum of these costs would be the total project cost. In the figure, components 2 and 4.1 are both control accounts and packages. If they were to be broken down further then they would become control components with the packages below them. Let us now consider the planning packages. As planning packages become better defined through rolling wave planning, they become work packages, or summary components if they are broken down further.

When it comes to scheduling, each work package may result in one schedule activity, or many activities. It is entirely up to you as the PM. Some PMs consider packages as internal if their deliverables, like reporting, are used within the project, or external if the deliverables will go to the customer or sponsor. Once reviewed, many PMs consider that if something is not in a package, then it is not part of the project – in other words, it would be an exclusion.

7.5 Business Projects Use the WBS Differently

That is the theory, and large construction or engineering projects running from $20 million to billions of dollars often closely adhere to it. They have administration and cost control offices, which are needed because they work on tight margins with much money at stake. The activities are usually well understood and they maintain a 'WBS dictionary' of all the packages with their descriptions, completion criteria, resources, estimated costs, and sometimes also the actual costs.

My practice for running business projects is very different. Most business projects are smaller, typically under a million dollars, and I do much of the administration and tracking myself or through an administrator. The WBS is done using MS Word in an outline numbered format, with input from team members and other stakeholders. I avoid having too many levels so as to reduce the number of summary activities. Once done, it goes into a scheduler like MS Project, after which any further breakdown of activities is done in the scheduler. I do not have the time to maintain a WBS as well as a schedule. Costs are tracked at the project level because usually the people are working on several activities concurrently, and asking them to allocate their time to specific activities would be an unnecessary overhead. A few business projects are larger and such projects may be broken down into subprojects or multiple related projects, where more rigor is warranted.

Nevertheless, even for a business project, the WBS concept is valuable. One way that it can be applied is for the project team to work together to produce the WBS, optionally with a facilitator. Participants would write down activities, using a whiteboard marker, on slips of paper (4 by 3 inches is ideal) or on post-it notes. They would be arranged on a surface, starting with high-level activities at the top, and arranging the other slips below them. The surface could be a wall or large table, but not something that will be damaged by having slips stuck onto them. The result is unlikely to be complete as there will probably be some activities that have not been thought of. Nevertheless, the benefit is that participants will have a better understanding of what must be done and will have bonded as a group.

7.6 Summary

It is important that you fully understand the differences between objectives (or goals), requirements (usually from stakeholders) which determine any specifications, and scope which is the things that must be done to produce the required outcomes.

Gathering requirements, if not already done, can be quite a bit of work and might itself be an early scope activity. The WBS would be the output of the early scope planning and would be input to the initial schedule. For a business project, it would probably not be complete, but as the project unfolds, new or changed activities can be added to the schedule; seldom would the WBS be maintained in parallel.

You can now consolidate your understanding by doing Case 6 which is to draw up a WBS for a medical conference. It can be done on your own or in a syndicate group.

Chapter 8

Project Estimating

8.1 Introduction and Objectives

In this chapter, we discuss project estimating, including:

- What an estimate is, and why we need to estimate.
- How estimates are made.
- The times in the project's lifetime that estimates are done.
- 'Top-down' and 'bottom-up' estimating approaches.
- Factors that influence the reliability of estimates.
- Some guidance for sound estimating.

When you have been through this chapter and the cases, you should know when estimates are needed for a particular project, and how you might go about making the estimates.

8.2 What Is an Estimate, and Why Can't It Be Accurate?

First of all, what is an estimate? In project management, an estimate is a forecast of time and/or cost to produce defined deliverables. Next, why can an estimate seldom be accurate? Estimates are inherently uncertain, and the degree of uncertainty varies with the type of project. For well-understood projects, like building a house, estimating is relatively straightforward. Estimating is far more difficult where many of the scope activities are not yet known, and business projects often fall into this category. Estimates are always based on assumptions which should be stated. The less we know about the scope, the more assumptions we shall need to make. Fortunately, there are various approaches to estimating. Some of them need fewer assumptions and can be remarkably valid. I use the word 'valid' rather than accurate because the word 'accurate' implies that the reality will be very close to the estimate. An estimate can be valid, but what happens in practice can be very different. Especially in business projects, much depends on the skill and commitment of the people doing the

DOI: 10.1201/9781003321101-10

work. So, for a valid estimate, an excellent team may do it in half the time and a poor team may take twice as long. And there are many other factors, like changes in priority, that can affect what actually happens. Similar considerations apply to cost.

Another important concept: estimates are not done once only. Some estimates are done before the project starts with scant information. Further estimates are done later with more information. They are done for different reasons and using different approaches. Some approaches are top-down while others are bottom-up. More about this presently.

8.3 Why Do We Need to Estimate?

We have already learned that estimating is difficult, so why bother? Why not just get on with the project? There are several reasons:

- Executives must decide whether to do the project; the business case relies on estimates. Also, decision making continues, always based on things that are already known and estimates of the future.
- From the estimates, the PM needs to schedule activities and confirm milestones. Similarly, costs may need to be planned for tracking purposes.
- Tracking of progress is done based on schedules and budgets. So without valid estimates, tracking is unlikely to be meaningful.
- Stakeholders need information. If their expectations are not set based on valid estimates, there is likely to be dissatisfaction.

However, estimating takes time and comes at a cost. It is always a matter of judgment how much effort to put into estimates.

8.4 When and How Does One Do Estimates?

First of all, there are two fundamentally different approaches to estimating: Top-down and bottom-up (Burke, 2013).

- A top-down estimate involves someone with experience, using limited information to give a preliminary estimate of time and cost. Top-down is usually the only option before the project starts.
- A bottom-up estimate involves breaking the project into packages, estimating each package, and summing the estimates upward, to arrive at an estimate for the entire project. Bottom-up is usually only possible late in the planning phase.

Which gives a better answer? It's hard to say. Bottom-up estimates give quite a bit of detail, but top-down estimates are often remarkably close to the mark. So it is best to do both at different times and compare the results. Looking into why estimates differ can be revealing. For example, suppose that a business project were to have a top-down estimate of $800 000, and later, a bottom-up estimate of $500 000. It would be worth debating the difference with the person (or people) that did the initial top-down estimate. It may turn out that there were different assumptions, but often the reason is that scope is missing. The person who did the top-down estimate might look at the scope used for the bottom-up estimate, and make a comment like "you have not allowed for X, and when we did a similar project a few years ago the X activities took months and added greatly to the cost".

It is also important to give an indication of the range of the estimate. A narrow range indicates a reliable estimate, while a broad range indicates a less reliable one. For example,

- If an estimate of $600 000 were to be made with very little information, it might be communicated as $600 000, plus or minus $300 000 (or plus or minus 50%). In other words, the estimate is anywhere between $300 000 and $900 000. Such an estimate is known as an 'order of magnitude' estimate or a 'rough order of magnitude' estimate.
- A later estimate with more information might be $750 000, with a range from $650 000 to $900 000 (minus 13% to plus 20%).

As illustrated in the second example, it is *not* essential that the minus and the plus are the same percentages. They merely reflect the judgment of the estimator. Note that the estimates are given in rounded numbers. Suppose that the estimate given were $745 820, the reader might assume reliability and accuracy that are simply not there.

8.5 More About Estimating Techniques

Top-down and bottom-up have been mentioned, but actually there is a range of techniques, some having an element of both (PMI, 2017). Although the estimates usually relate to cost, they could equally relate to duration.

8.5.1 Analogous Estimating

Analogous estimating can be done when a similar project has been done in the past and can give a good indication for our project. We use the past project as an analogy.

Let us consider an example. Suppose that a project to train 1 000 people, in 5 different locations, on new operational processes, had been done 3 years ago at a cost of $610 000. If we now have a project to train 1200 people in 8 locations we might use the $610 000 as a starting point and adjust for known differences such as the subject matter is simpler; there have been 3 years of cost escalation; there are more locations and people; some of the training can be done online; etc. Making all these adjustments, and others, we might arrive at a figure of $720 000 (plus or minus 20%) as a cost estimate.

Analogous estimating has its limitations. It only works if there is reliable information about the analogous past project. Also, any comparison factors that have been misunderstood are a source of error. For example: suppose that in the earlier project the training material had already been developed and approved, while in the new project it must still be done as part of the project. If this difference were not allowed for, the new estimate would be less valid.

8.5.2 Expert Opinion

Expert opinion has something in common with analogous estimating because experts (experienced people with sound judgment) will be influenced by past projects. Involving people with solid experience can be quite quick and very beneficial. Often they will point out scope that has been missed, or risks that have not been thought of.

One form of it is called the 'Delphi' method. Here, a project proposal, with as much detail as possible, is sent to more than one expert. They independently arrive at an estimate and submit their rationale in writing. Each estimate goes to all other experts who then have the opportunity to modify their own estimates. If there are still significant differences, the experts can meet (online if necessary) and try to reach some consensus. Whatever the final outcome, much will be learned through the process. In practice, the Delphi method is seldom used, and then only for very important projects. The reasons are that experts are hard to find, and that the process takes time and is expensive.

8.5.3 Parametric Modeling

Parametric modeling works well where similar projects are repeated often. Assembling products to customer specification or running training programs, are examples. It could equally apply to building houses. The approach is best illustrated for building a house. Suppose it is known that an average house costs $1 000 per square meter to build. Then if a client requested an estimate for a 200-square meter house, the answer would be $200 000 (200 × $1 000). One would not even need a spreadsheet. But suppose that one wanted a more definitive estimate, one might create a spreadsheet that asks questions, and factors-in things like the location, the number of bathrooms, the type of roof, etc. These might all influence the estimate.

Parametric models work best when they have been tested over a period of time, with real situations of variable size. Parameters should be reviewed periodically due to cost and other changes in the industry, or whenever an estimate differs considerably from the reality.

8.5.4 Definitive Estimating

Definitive estimating is only possible where the activities and resource costs are known and where there is experience as to the rate at which work is done. Case 7 is an example and gives practice at making this type of estimate.

8.5.5 'Rule of thumb' Estimating

Many rules of thumb are in general use. Here is an accepted one that relates to activity duration estimation (PMI, 2017; Pinto, 2013). For each activity, the optimistic (minimum) time, the likely time, and the pessimistic (maximum) time are estimated. Then it is suggested that a suitable duration estimate is: Planned duration = (pessimistic + 4 × likely + optimistic)/6

So if the estimates are Pessimistic 8 weeks, Likely 4 weeks, and Optimistic 3 weeks, then the planned duration would be = (8 + 4 × 4 + 3)/6 = 27/6 = 4.5 weeks.

This multipoint method, which can also be used for costs, probably works well for stable activities, such as on a construction project. But, to date, I have never used it for a business project where: people work across more than one activity concurrently, there are many subtle dependencies, and the activities change regularly.

8.6 Factors That Influence the Reliability of Estimates

As mentioned above, the main influence on reliability is the type of project, and the estimate ranges given below are illustrative:

- Construction projects with well understood scope, done by experienced, people may be very reliable and have ranges like plus or minus 10%.
- Simple business projects may have ranges of −10% to +20%.
- Business projects, involving IT work, may have ranges of −20% to +35%.
- Projects to develop something totally new may have ranges from −25% to +50% or even more. Complex IT projects might have a similar range of uncertainty.

Other things that influence reliability of estimates are:

- Duration: The longer the project, the less reliable, because unforeseen changes tend to happen.
- People doing the work. The lower their skills and experience, the less reliable.
- History of similar projects. If this can be used, estimates will be more reliable.

The organization's culture is another factor. Estimating 'gamesmanship' is sometimes prevalent. It works like this. When people do estimates they add 'fat' (deliberately inflate their estimates). Executives then, knowing that estimates are inflated, habitually cut the time and costs and set tougher targets. Because the estimators expect this to happen, they feel even more justified in inflating their estimates. And so the vicious circle continues. A healthier culture is where people present their estimates and add a contingency amount based on risk. Then, if executives try to reduce the amounts, the presenters can justify their estimates, and truthfully say that such reductions are only realistic if the scope is reduced as well. Honest estimating is also encouraged where PMs are not unreasonably punished for failing to meet targets. Rather the emphasis should be on how the PM handled project issues that arose, and what can be learned from the adverse experience.

8.7 Some Guidance for Sound Estimating

Some of the following advice has already been alluded to:

- Be very clear about what is included in the estimate.
- Get estimates from the people who will do the work. This helps in other ways too. It gets buy-in and helps communication. However, be aware of people who consistently overestimate or underestimate.

> *One IT developer in my team consistently gave me optimistic estimates. So, I accepted the estimates and set target dates accordingly. But when setting expectations with the sponsor, I used later dates, which almost always turned out to be more realistic.*

Comparing their estimates with what actually happens is good learning for such professionals.

- Get estimates from more than one source, and initiate a discussion where they differ considerably.
- Estimate based on normal work days and allow for leave. Never build in overtime work to give shorter time estimates. Keep overtime for when it is really needed (as a form of contingency).
- Estimate using consistent units like work-days for duration and person-days for effort (or cost). Avoid having some activities in weeks and others in days. Also, avoid confusing elapsed days with work days.
- Keep contingency out of package estimates. It should be added afterward, probably at the project level, based on a documented assessment of the risk.

8.8 Summary

Estimating is difficult and is almost always done with incomplete information. Estimates should be done at different times using different estimating techniques. The reliability of an estimate should be indicated, usually by stating the range of the estimate. Documenting your estimates with assumptions, and stating the source of information, is sound practice in case estimates are queried or need to be revised. Keeping records of past projects, often with a PMO, is of great value for estimating future projects.

I recommend that you now do Case 8 which outlines three different projects. It asks you to state when and how estimates should be done, and to list considerations that need to be discussed and agreed on, before finalizing the estimates.

References

Burke, R. (2013). *Project Management Techniques*, 2nd edition London: Burke Publishing.

Pinto, J. K. (2013). *Project Management, Achieving Competitive Advantage*, 3rd edition. Harlow, Essex, England: Pearson.

PMI. (2021). *PMBOK - Guide to the Project Management Body of Knowledge*, 7th edition: Pennsylvania, USA: Project Management Institute.

Chapter 9

Project Scheduling

9.1 Introduction and Objectives

Peoples' time and project time are valuable assets. Once used or lost they cannot be replaced. So, the aim of this chapter is to give a good understanding of how a schedule can help to plan activities and resources and then track progress. To do this, you need to be able to use certain techniques and know the terminology that goes with them. There are many realities in business projects that textbooks may not cover. For example, often the activities are not fully understood during planning and the schedule evolves after planning. These aspects are discussed and practical approaches suggested. What follows assumes relatively little prior scheduling knowledge, so by all means skip things that you are already familiar with. The main objectives are to:

- Know why schedules are important and the forms that they can take.
- Learn essential terminology for dependencies between activities.
- Learn how to produce a Gantt (bar) chart and determine the critical path.
- Know how to adjust the schedule when resources are applied.
- Be able to handle the uncertainty and ambiguity typical of business projects.
- Shorten the project duration for time-critical projects.

Precedence scheduling, which is valuable for understanding the theory, is covered in Appendix 2. Here, we consider Gantt charts and milestones which are dominant in business projects – and whose tools use precedence theory. Doing exercises (cases) gives useful practice and helps one to grasp the techniques. Several cases are referred to in this chapter, so I suggest that you do them all unless you are already experienced at scheduling.

DOI: 10.1201/9781003321101-11

9.2 Why a Schedule, and What Does It Look Like?

9.2.1 Why Do We Schedule?

A schedule allows you to document, communicate, and track:

- What activities need to be done (the scope).
- Who will do the activities and hence plan resources.
- When activities should start and how long they are expected to take.
- When activities should be complete.
- The milestone events and when they should occur.
- The dependencies between activities, for example, activity B can only start when activity A is complete.
- Progress on the activities and especially the activities that are on the 'critical path' – activities that directly affect the end date for the project.

Much fact-finding, estimating, and discussion go into the schedule, but once done, it gives a view of when certain milestones should be achieved and when the project might end. The progress against the schedule can be tracked regularly with reports being produced to keep stakeholders informed. When issues arise along the way and changes need to be made, one of the first things to do is to assess how the schedule will be impacted. Such changes result in amended or additional activities which are reflected in an updated schedule. In short, without a schedule, the PM will not know what to get on with and it is difficult to know where the project stands. So the schedule is essential for monitoring and controlling the project.

9.2.2 What Does a Schedule Look Like and When Is It Produced?

A schedule can take many forms, some high level and some detailed. Illustrative examples follow:

- A milestone schedule is high level and takes the form shown in Table 9.1. This high-level list of events might be used as part of a business case or as part of a PDD (project definition document). Even during the project, milestones help the team to focus on the next milestone. This engenders a greater sense

Table 9.1 An Illustrative Milestone Schedule

Date	*Milestone Event*
08 Feb 22	Approval given to start the project
08 Apr 22	Design of the new product is approved
15 Jul 22	Prototype of the new product is demonstrated
	Possible additional milestone(s)
14 Oct 22	End project. First production run was successful

Table 9.2 An Illustrative Activity List

Ref.	*Activity Description*	*Start Date*	*End Date*	*Responsible*
12	Survey the requirements of business users	22 Feb 22	04 Mar 22	John Malaba

of urgency than looking at the project end date which causes people to believe that there is still plenty of time.

- A task list or activity list could give the start and end dates, and who will do them. In this book, the terms 'task' and 'activity' are used synonymously. Such a list is illustrated in Table 9.2.
  Although simple, the format is flexible and easy to understand. Columns can be added and removed. It is important that there is agreement among the stakeholders and that the list is reviewed and updated regularly. Use of the reference number ensures that people are talking about the same activity. Completed activities can be archived by moving them down to a 'completed' area with an actual date – entirely up to the PM.

  > *In the past, before scheduling software was available, we used this technique to manage a large organizational restructuring project in a mining company. There were eight subprojects, each with such a task list. Weekly, the subproject leaders met with the PM and executive sponsor to discuss progress and what needed to change. The project was successful mainly because of the involvement of the sponsor and the level of commitment and cooperation between the teams. But the task list certainly helped to keep things on track and focus on activities that needed to be expedited.*

  Agile projects might use such a list to plan and track activity details, while higher-level activities would be monitored on a Kanban board through daily reviews.
- A precedence or network diagram
  Before 1995 when scheduling tools like MSP (Microsoft Project) became readily available, precedence scheduling was used quite often resulting in a network or precedence diagram. 'Precedence' means recognizing which activities precede (come before) which other activities. Such diagrams come in several forms including AOA (activity on arrow) and AON (activity on node). The AON format is illustrated in Figure 9.1. Each block (activity) is a node in the network with letters A to J, and the start and end are also nodes. The arrows show which activities precede (come before) which other activities. Here, for example, activities A and B precede activity C; in other words, C can only start when A *and* B are complete.
  AOA is almost never used nowadays and will not be discussed further. Even AON is seldom used, but it helps to understand the theory underlying MSP and other scheduling tools where the output is usually shown in Gantt chart format. Precedence scheduling using AON is covered in Appendix 2.

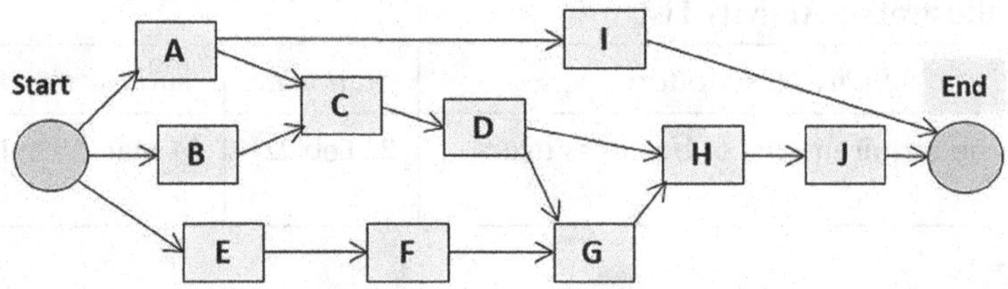

Figure 9.1 AON (activity on node) precedence schedule.

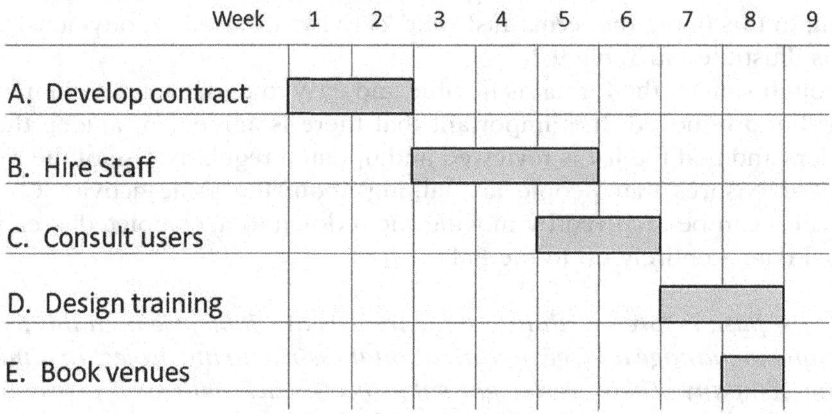

Figure 9.2 Gant (or bar) chart schedule.

- A Gantt or bar chart
  Henry Gantt developed the bar chart concept back in 1910 and hence the chart is called after him. Figure 9.2 illustrates a Gantt chart, where activities are represented as bars.

  Time goes from left to right and Figure 9.2 gives it in weeks from the start of the project. Most of the exercises on Gantt charts will be in weeks. However, in practice activities are usually entered in work days and schedulers show start and end dates. The length of each bar reflects the planned duration of each activity based on estimates. Where the bars are positioned is entirely up to the PM's judgment, but Figure 9.2 suggests that the PM wanted activity A (develop contract) completed (with the contract signed) before hiring staff.

9.2.3 What Happens Before We Produce a Schedule?

A popular misconception is that the first thing a PM should do is schedule the project from start to end. Maybe this would be possible if the project were to build a wall, but business projects are usually considerably more complex and pre-work is needed. So typically the following needs to happen before a schedule can be produced:

- The requirements need to be gathered from various stakeholders.
- The activities to produce the required deliverables must be documented. This is often done in the form of a WBS (work breakdown structure).

- Dependencies between activities need to be noted and activities sequenced to honor the dependencies.
- Resources (usually people) must be planned.
- The duration of activities must be estimated based on the planned resources.

Only when this has been largely done do we have enough information to develop the initial schedule which would also take into account business priorities.

Here I need to emphasize that all of the above are parts of the scheduling process that the PM goes through. The resulting data may go into a scheduling tool (like MSP) but never will the tool replace the hard work that the PM does to produce and maintain the schedule.

9.3 Some Important Scheduling Concepts and Terminology

We have already mentioned dependencies. By far the most common type is 'finish-start' or FS. This is the default and is assumed if no dependency type is specified. Another useful type is 'start-start' of SS. These are illustrated in Figure 9.3. There is an FS relationship between activity A and activity B: when A has finished, B can start, so B depends on A. There is an SS relationship between C and D: as soon as C has started, D can also start, and note that D depends on C. Dependency types can be shown in upper or lower case.

There are two other relationship types, namely start-to-finish and finish-to-finish. In practice, I have never needed to use them, and avoid them in order to keep things simple.

FS and SS are suitable for most dependencies between activities. However, sometimes one needs to make an adjustment, like delaying, or pulling forward, a dependent activity. So two new concepts are needed: lags and leads. The likely situations are illustrated in Figure 9.4, going from left to right with scheduling in weeks:

- FS+2w: The plus sign indicates a lag (or delay). There is an FS relationship between E and F, but, the '+2 weeks' means that after E has finished, we plan to wait 2 weeks before starting on F. There are many situations where the PM might use such a lag. An example is where something is ordered from a supplier (E) and we must wait for the goods to arrive before we can use them (F). Another example is where the first activity is training (E), but we want to allow study time and the writing of an exam, before the dependent activity of exam-marking (F) starts.

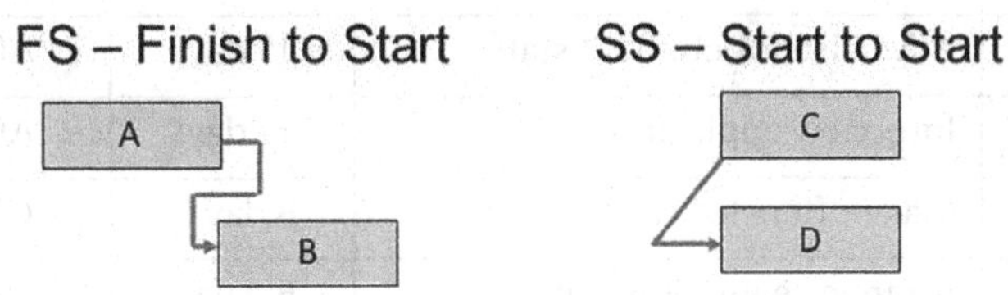

Figure 9.3 Dependencies between activities.

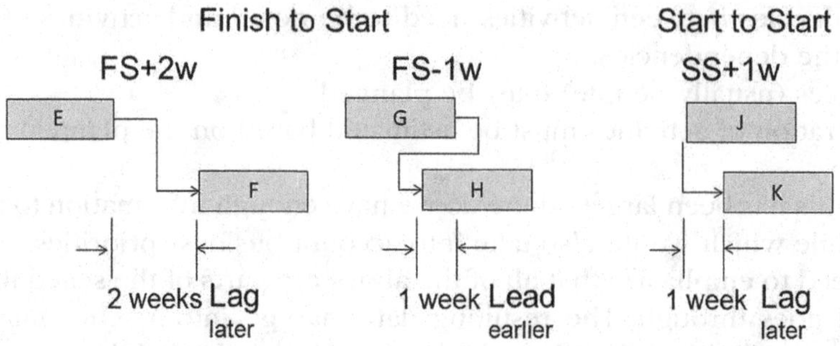

Figure 9.4 Lags and Leads.

- FS-1w. The minus sign indicates a lead (or pull-forward). There is an FS relationship between G and H, but we plan H to start 1 week *before* G has finished. An example is where G is a design activity ending in formal approval, but even before approval is given we shall accept the risk of starting one of the follow-on activities H. This is at the discretion of the PM and may be done due to schedule pressure.
- SS+1w. This is a start-start relationship and the plus sign indicates a lag. This means that after J has *started*, we plan to wait 1 week before starting on K. An example is where, for a conference, J is the recording of conference applications with payment and K is the activity of booking hotel rooms. An SS with a lead (minus sign) is possible but is not used often.

One thing that can cause confusion is the delay between ordering something and it being delivered by the supplier. In procurement terms, this is called the 'lead time', but in scheduling terms, it is a delay and hence a lag.

Prior to actually producing a precedence schedule or a Gantt (bar) chart, the activities are sometimes listed as shown in Table 9.3. This is the format used here for examples and exercises.

Here the duration is given in days and it helps to be consistent. Having some activities in days and others in weeks is likely to cause errors. Because we are scheduling in days, the numbers in the precedence column are also in days. Let us refer to the table. Activity A has no predecessor and can start immediately. B can start 3

Table 9.3 Preparation for a Schedule with Durations and Precedences

Reference	*Activity Description*	*Duration*	*Precedence*
A	Sign client contract	10 days	
B	Advertise for contract staff	15 days	Afs-3
C	Interview applicants	12 days	Afs+5, B
D	Make offers for contract staff	5 days	Cfs+2
E	Arrange seating for staff	6 days	Dss+3

days *before* A has finished (minus 3 means a lead or a pull-forward). Activity C has two dependencies: it may only start 5 days after A has finished, and B must also be finished. Activity D is scheduled to start 2 days after all applicants have been interviewed (C has finished), but we allow 2 days to discuss and prioritize the candidates. Yes, we could have inserted a 2-day activity to prioritize the candidates, but it is omitted to keep the schedule simple – after all discussing, the candidates may only require a 1-hour meeting. E is scheduled to start 3 days after we have *started* making the offers. The same could be achieved by specifying it as Cfs+5, but how it is done is entirely up to the PM.

Note that most schedulers, like MSP, use numbers to reference activities, so if the precedence for activity 3 is '1fs+5d, 2', it means that activity 3 can start: 5 days after activity 1 is complete and immediately after activity 2 is complete.

9.4 Scheduling with a Gantt Chart

If you are unfamiliar with scheduling theory, you may wish to go through Appendix 2 which uses precedence diagrams to illustrate it. Here we shall use the Appendix's example which is given in Table 9.4. It involves designing and building a shed surrounded by a wall.

We show the Gantt chart development in Figure 9.5. First, we insert the activities that have no precedence – A and C.

Table 9.4 Preparation for Our Scheduling Exercise

Reference	*Description*	*Duration*	*Precedence*
A	Design shed	2 weeks	-
B	Build shed	6 weeks	A, C fs-2
C	Build wall	5 weeks	-
D	Paint wall	4 weeks	C fs+1

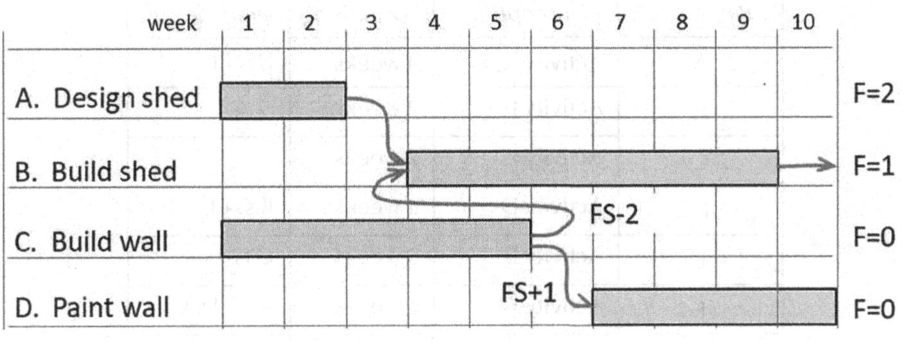

Figure 9.5 Gantt chart from Table 9.4.

Now we can insert B which has an FS dependency on A and an FS-2 dependency on C. Finally, we can insert D which only has an FS+1 dependency on C. This shows that the project can be completed at the end of week 10. This is equivalent to the 'forward pass' shown in Figure A2.4 of Appendix 2.

We now need to determine the critical path – the activities that cannot be delayed without affecting the end date. To do this, we must calculate the float for each activity. Float can be described as the amount that an activity can be delayed without affecting the end date (sometimes referred to as 'total float'). To determine the floats, we work backward starting with D which is the last activity to end. It always has zero float, as any delay will delay completion of the project. Next, we consider what D depends on, i.e. C. The lag of 1 week from C to D is not float, but a lag that must be honored. Therefore, C also gets zero float. Moving upward, B has a float of 1 week as it can be delayed by a week and still finish at the end of week 10. Going back to A, we see that it has a float of 2 weeks. It can be delayed 1 week before it affects B, but as B itself has a float of 1 week, we can add that week to arrive at a float of 2 weeks. In other words, if A were delayed by 2 weeks, it would push B out by a week, but B could still meet the end of week 10. This is equivalent to the 'backward pass' shown in Figure A2.5 of Appendix 2 and produces the same results. Activities C and D form the critical path because they both have zero float.

Table 9.5 gives one more example which uses both FS and SS dependencies, as well as lags and leads. It does not get much more technically complex than this. Maybe you want to try it first, before looking at the solution?

The solution is given in Figure 9.6. When inserting the bars (effectively a forward pass), one starts with activities with no dependencies – in this case, activity B. Only then can we position A, C, and D, which all depend on B.

Proceeding forward, we find that G determines the end of the project as the end of week 9. Therefore, it has zero float. Now we work backward to determine the floats of all other activities. F has a float of 1 as no activities depend on it, but it must be finished by the end of the project. E has a float of 2, as 2 weeks delay pushes F to the end of week 9 (one from F and one between E and F). D is critical with float of zero because G depends on it. D has a SS dependency on B, which makes the *start* of B critical (any delay starting B will push D out). However, the end of B is *not* critical

Table 9.5 Example with FS, SS, Lags, and Lead

Reference	*Description*	*Duration*	*Precedence*
A	Activity A	4 weeks	B fs+1
B	Activity B	2 weeks	-
C	Activity C	2 weeks	B
D	Activity D	4 weeks	B ss+1
E	Activity E	3 weeks	C fs-1
F	Activity F	1 weeks	A, C, D, E
G	Activity G	4 weeks	D

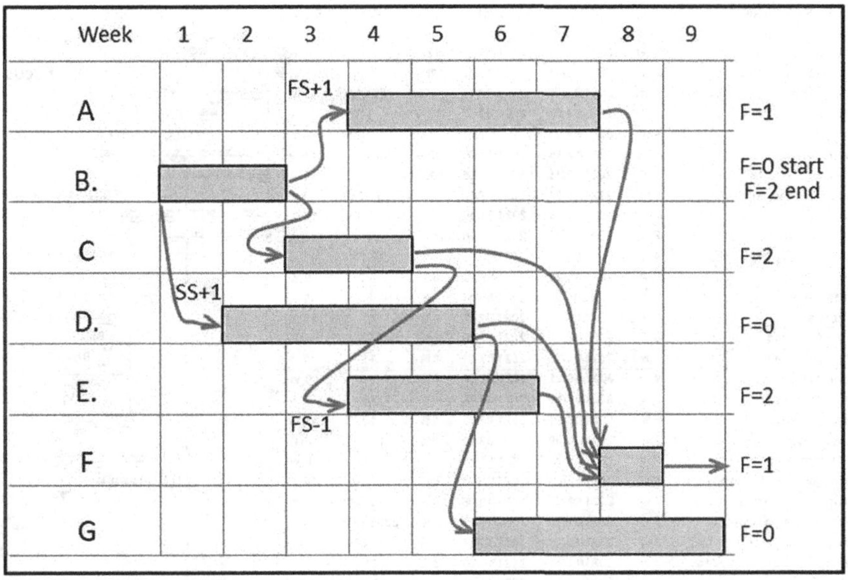

Figure 9.6 Gantt chart from Table 9.5.

as it has a float of 2 from the path through A; this is a slight anomaly that only happens with SS relationships. In an MSP schedule, the float would be taken from the start, and B would be shown as critical (often colored red).

It is now time to get some practice with doing Gantt charts manually, so I suggest you do Case 9 part 2 and Case 10; after each one, check against the answer. When done, you should have a solid understanding of scheduling theory before we move to the practical aspects.

9.5 Use of the Gantt Schedule in Practice

On business projects, the Gantt chart is used far more often than the precedence chart. As an illustration, an extract from a sample project, done in MSP, is given in Figure 9.7. It is a hospital project with building as well as IT elements.

The schedule was copied from MSP into a PowerPoint slide. The vertical line was inserted to show the current date and a 'focus here' note was added just to show that it is easy to annotate such schedules when they are in PowerPoint. All the rest came from the scheduling tool. Each tool will have slight differences, and even within MSP, it was possible for me to make some choices as to how data is presented. The detail given here may be too small to read, so normally I produce it in landscape which allows more width. Here are some points to note:

- MSP refers to 'tasks', whereas this book calls them activities (same thing). Likewise, MSP refers to 'slack' whereas we talk about float (once again, same thing).
- The numbered activities are shown on the left. The activities themselves are indented one level, while the summary activities like Construction, Plumbing,

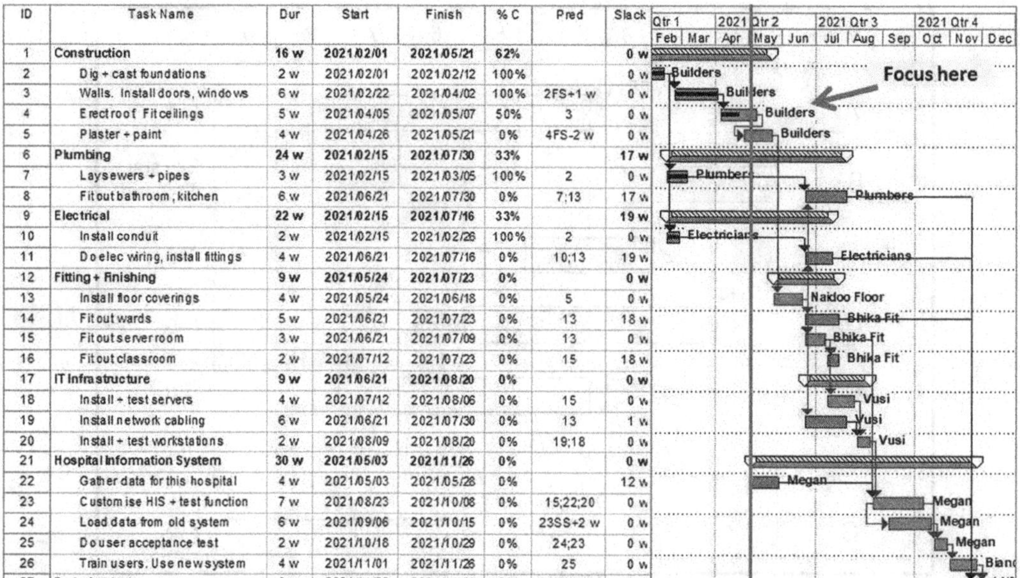

ID	Task Name	Dur	Start	Finish	% C	Pred	Slack
1	**Construction**	**16 w**	**2021/02/01**	**2021/05/21**	**62%**		**0 w**
2	Dig + cast foundations	2 w	2021/02/01	2021/02/12	100%		0 w
3	Walls. Install doors, windows	6 w	2021/02/22	2021/04/02	100%	2FS+1 w	0 w
4	Erect roof Fit ceilings	5 w	2021/04/05	2021/05/07	50%	3	0 w
5	Plaster + paint	4 w	2021/04/26	2021/05/21	0%	4FS-2 w	0 w
6	**Plumbing**	**24 w**	**2021/02/15**	**2021/07/30**	**33%**		**17 w**
7	Lay sewers + pipes	3 w	2021/02/15	2021/03/05	100%	2	0 w
8	Fit out bathroom, kitchen	6 w	2021/06/21	2021/07/30	0%	7;13	17 w
9	**Electrical**	**22 w**	**2021/02/15**	**2021/07/16**	**33%**		**19 w**
10	Install conduit	2 w	2021/02/15	2021/02/26	100%	2	0 w
11	Do elec wiring, install fittings	4 w	2021/06/21	2021/07/16	0%	10;13	19 w
12	**Fitting + Finishing**	**9 w**	**2021/05/24**	**2021/07/23**	**0%**		**0 w**
13	Install floor coverings	4 w	2021/05/24	2021/06/18	0%	5	0 w
14	Fit out wards	5 w	2021/06/21	2021/07/23	0%	13	18 w
15	Fit out server room	3 w	2021/06/21	2021/07/09	0%	13	0 w
16	Fit out classroom	2 w	2021/07/12	2021/07/23	0%	15	18 w
17	**IT Infrastructure**	**9 w**	**2021/06/21**	**2021/08/20**	**0%**		**0 w**
18	Install + test servers	4 w	2021/07/12	2021/08/06	0%	15	0 w
19	Install network cabling	6 w	2021/06/21	2021/07/30	0%	13	1 w
20	Install + test workstations	2 w	2021/08/09	2021/08/20	0%	19;18	0 w
21	**Hospital Information System**	**30 w**	**2021/05/03**	**2021/11/26**	**0%**		**0 w**
22	Gather data for this hospital	4 w	2021/05/03	2021/05/28	0%		12 w
23	Customise HIS + test function	7 w	2021/08/23	2021/10/08	0%	15;22;20	0 w
24	Load data from old system	6 w	2021/09/06	2021/10/15	0%	23SS+2 w	0 w
25	Do user acceptance test	2 w	2021/10/18	2021/10/29	0%	24;23	0 w
26	Train users. Use new system	4 w	2021/11/01	2021/11/26	0%	25	0 w
27	End of project	0 w	2021/11/26	2021/11/26	0%	26;8;11;14	0 w

Figure 9.7 Gantt chart from a scheduling tool.

etc., are not indented and are shown in bold. One can go to many levels, but I avoid doing so for a number of reasons. First, it results in many summary activities which consume rows and make the schedule more difficult to read. Second, each indent takes a bit of horizontal space in the 'task name' column, and I prefer to conserve space and use it for other purposes. It is for that reason that I do not have a project-level summary activity – there are other ways of stating the project title.

- The duration is given in weeks – a setting in the scheduler. It can equally be set to work in days – which is what I normally use.
- Once the start date is set by the PM (01 February 2021 in this example), the scheduler automatically calculates the start and end dates for each activity based on the dependencies entered. Here the dependencies are entered in the 'Pred' (predecessor) column, and you will recognize that some of the dependencies are SS (start-start) and some have lags or leads. MSP uses numbers whereas earlier we used alphabetic references (A, B, C, etc.). Some of the precedence entries are only numbers, in which case the default FS (finish-start) dependency type is assumed. But as soon as there is a lag or lead, one must specify the dependency type.
- The '% C' column gives the estimated percentage completion, and the black bars in the tasks indicate the progress visually. A few activities are shown as fully complete (100%) or partially complete (like 50%). Note that MSP calculates a percentage complete for the summary activities. For various reasons, MSP's estimates of percentage complete for the summary activities can be misleading. For example, if an activity (within the summary activity) is delayed and stretches out, MSP will assume that extra work was done, and credit that work to the percentage complete of the summary activity.

- The 'Slack' column shows the float that MSP has calculated, using the same forward and backward pass algorithms that are explained in Appendix 2. Although not visible in Figure 9.7 which is in grayscale, I usually show the critical (zero float) activities in red.
- To the right of each bar are the resources used. One can use any meaningful name, and here I have sometimes used a generic name like 'plumbers' and sometimes a person's name like 'Megan'. I prefer to use first names rather than initials because most people think of others by their names and not their initials. If two people have the same name then distinguish them by the first letter of their surname, for example, 'JohnM' and 'JohnP'.

Normally I filter out completed activities, and would not show the predecessor or float columns – to keep the chart simple. In a tracking meeting, we are far more interested in how the activities are going. How far are they complete? and more importantly, whether they will meet the planned end date? The discussion that takes place if the answer is "no, we cannot meet that date" is covered later in Chapter 16 on project tracking (or controlling). The following are the reasons why I prefer a Gant chart (to a network chart) for business projects:

- The Gantt chart is more compact and fits more onto a page.
- It visually shows how activities relate to time. Even without the line that I inserted above, one can quickly see which activities should be underway.
- It is easy to show progress, usually with a black bar indicating the percentage complete.
- There is more room for text, for example, the name of the activity and the people that are assigned to it.
- It can easily be filtered so that only the activities that need to be discussed are shown in the chart. Usually, completed activities and those far in the future are filtered out, so that we can focus on the in-progress activities and those due to start soon. For a short tracking meeting, one page is plenty for all the activities that we have time to discuss.
- It is easy to import into a PowerPoint slide (or other common document types) for distribution to stakeholders who may not have the scheduler software.

The Gantt chart honors exactly the same data that one uses for a precedence (network) chart. It requires the same activities, durations, and dependencies. In fact, once the data has been entered into most scheduling tools, one can display the output as a bar chart (Gantt) or as a precedence (network) chart. But, for the above reasons, I always use the Gantt chart or 'timeline' as it is sometimes referred to.

9.6 'Real world' Scheduling Issues

Now that we have covered the background, let's consider the practical aspects.

First of all, where does the data come from? Ideally, we need to know what the activities are, their durations, and the dependencies – possibly in a format similar to

Table 9.5. The activities might be the output of a WBS (work breakdown structure) which would give the activities themselves as well as the summary ones. The durations might be the output of an estimating exercise, or more likely the PM would get them from the people assigned to do the work. Some of the dependencies would be intuitive, but others would come from discussions with the stakeholders – mainly the project team. The dependencies and durations require: listening to people, producing a first-cut schedule, discussing it, and making changes. In other words, it is an iterative process that uses judgment. The process ends when an initial schedule can be produced that the sponsor is satisfied with and that the team believes is feasible. But, it is not worth trying to get it 'perfect' as the schedule is likely to change a great deal before the project is complete.

At this point, I suggest that you do Case 11 which gives practice at deriving dependencies from what stakeholders say.

Another question that comes up a lot: "how detailed should the schedule be?" There is no universal answer, but as a guide activities should be between 2 days and 3 weeks. If an activity were longer, then maybe it should be broken down. You don't want to find out just before a 3-week activity is due, that there are major problems – shorter activities force earlier communication of problems. However, you certainly don't want too much detail.

I was asked to help a PM colleague that appeared to be struggling with a project. One problem was immediately apparent: the Gantt schedule was 14 pages long, and had activities down to one or two hours. This was because the client sponsor believed in fine detail, and the PM was working into the evenings to maintain the schedule. Interestingly, the team (about 10 people) were unaware of the schedule and what they were actually doing, bore little resemblance to it.

The moral of the above story is: Keep the schedule simple and use it as a communication vehicle between you and the team. If the project is large, it needs to be broken down into subprojects, each with its own schedule. Here, using a fancy technical solution to integrate the separate schedules into a 'master' schedule may not be worth the effort. There are often easier ways to get the overall picture. It is true that some activities need detail, but then it is best for the people doing the activity to create task lists and work from them. You do not need to micro-manage their work. Clearly, there are exceptions to everything, and that is where your judgment comes in.

9.7 Thoughts and Tips for Scheduling Business Projects

9.7.1 Thoughts

- When using a WBS as input, you may find that a work package actually breaks down into several activities. Likewise, you may choose to wrap two work packages into one activity. It's entirely up to you as the PM. For business projects, I do not update the WBS after moving the activities into the scheduler – the schedule becomes my WBS. On the other hand, for construction or engineering projects where a lot of detail is stored in the WBS, one is encouraged to maintain the WBS continually.

- How should we handle a situation where, later in the project, there is work to be done but we don't yet know the details? An example from an organizational restructure might be that there is overlap between two departments but there has been no discussion on how it should be handled. Here, one might just put in one activity like 'resolve departmental overlaps' with a duration, as a reminder that it still needs to be addressed and detailed.
- When using a scheduler, it is best to put in the durations and dependencies and let the scheduler position the activities accordingly (using the default 'start as soon as possible' rule). Then, if something changes early on, like an activity taking longer, the scheduler will automatically move dependent activities out. However, if one has put in specific dates for tasks, then, if an early activity takes longer, one would need to manually change the dates of all dependent activities. There may be exceptions, where there are external dependencies. For example, if another party has committed to a deliverable on a certain date, then an activity that depends on the deliverable, would have its start date set to the delivery date.
- At this point, you might have the impression that scheduling is about doing the estimates and then following the scheduling rules. This implies that the schedule drives the project. In fact, the schedule is merely there to help the PM and team. So the PM can make any changes provided that they are reasonable and reflect the realities of the situation. Some of the reasons for flexibility will emerge in the following points.
- Not all dependencies are the same. Some are inherent in the nature of the work and may involve physical limitations like not putting on the roof until the walls are built. These are referred to as 'mandatory' or 'hard logic' dependencies that often apply in a construction project. In a business project, most of the dependencies are discretionary, where 'soft logic' or 'preferred logic' are applied. For example, it might be unwise to start advertising until a new product is ready to be shipped to customers. So, while in theory tasks have clear dependencies, in practice dependencies may be fuzzy.
- In a business project, there may be many dependencies for a particular activity, especially where it involves input from external parties. Often dependencies only become apparent when an activity is underway. Even if one knew them, the Gantt chart would become too cluttered, so it's best to show only the main dependencies. This syndrome of unanticipated dependencies can cause activities which are only a few hours of actual effort, to take a week or more.
- There are other reasons for duration being hard to pin down. For business projects, the duration may depend on the skill of the person doing the work. A weak player may take five times as long and even then there may be rework. One might also assume that putting more people onto an activity will shorten it. This would probably apply to building a wall where two people might get it done twice as quickly as one. But business projects are different: skill, experience, and commitment are more important than numbers, and sometimes adding people actually slows the activity down.

To sum up: scheduling most business projects is not an exact science, and the best the PM can do is to track a schedule that represents the current reality.

9.7.2 Tips

- Allow for times when work will slow down considerably. Holiday season and public holiday long weekends are examples. Some types of activity like training should generally not be scheduled at such times.
- Negotiate leave plans with your team, and build them into your schedule. It may even be important to know when key business stakeholders will be away.
- Schedule for normal time. When the sponsor asks for a challenging deadline, it is tempting to plan overtime from the start. Resist such temptation as it is likely to result in an unrealistic schedule.
- Put milestones (zero duration events) into your schedules. Focusing on a milestone that is a few weeks away is more motivational than looking at the end of the project that is 6 months out. The team needs to feel the urgency of meeting a near-term deadline.

9.8 Setting a Baseline, Resourcing, and Scheduling Tools

9.8.1 Comparing Current Schedule with the Baseline Schedule

While I would like to say that business projects always run to schedule, often they don't. Therefore, the schedule is constantly changing with activities moved to reflect the current situation. But this makes it difficult to see where the activities were when the schedule was agreed upon and by how much certain activities have slipped. One way to do this is by setting a baseline which most scheduling tools permit – illustrated in Figure 9.8.

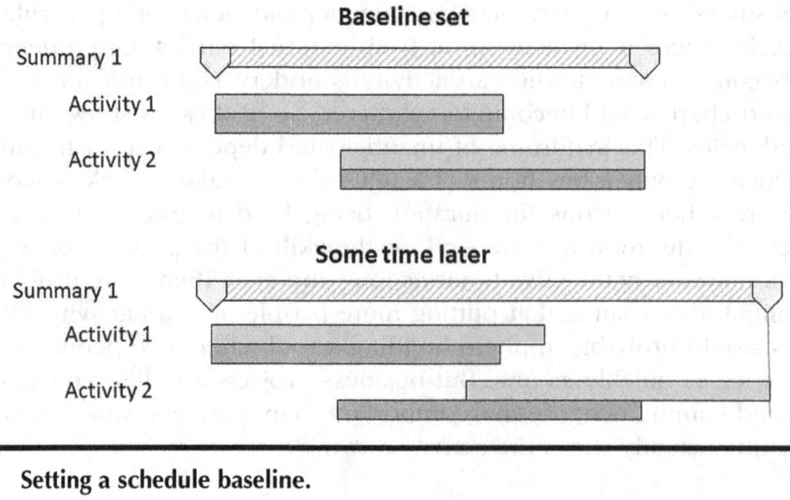

Figure 9.8 Setting a schedule baseline.

When the first agreed schedule is ready, the baseline facility allows one to place gray bars below each task (baseline set). Then some time later, as the project progresses, it may have been necessary to move certain activities. But the baseline remains, making it easy to see the deviation from the initial schedule. The figure shows that Activity 1 took a bit longer than planned, and that Activity 2 was moved out. So, one can visually see the amount of the shift. However, this only works well if the activities do not change. For a business project, activities are being added, deleted, and rescheduled all the time. For a new or changed activity, if they are baselined, they look up to date. Hence, I do not use baselines. What works for me is to save every new schedule with a date like 'Schedule Project X 220602'. Then, if necessary, I can go back to any earlier schedule and compare it with the current one.

9.8.2 Adding Resources to the Schedule and Resource Leveling

Up to now, our Gantt chart schedules assumed that we had unlimited skilled people (resources) – an unconstrained schedule. In practice, this seldom happens, and as someone once said "a schedule is not a schedule until resources have been committed". Resources are invariably limited, and often there will be parallel activities that need the same skilled person. Sometimes the person can work on both concurrently, in which case, both will stretch out and take longer. Alternatively, the one activity can be done first with the other being deferred until the first one is complete, leading to a resource-constrained schedule. Clearly, priority is given to critical-path activities. The bottom line is that a constrained schedule is likely to take longer. It could take twice as long, but increases of 30% to 40% are typical. It all depends on the resources available and the priority of the project. For a really time-critical project, it may be necessary to bring in skills from outside the organization, sometimes at considerable cost.

The process of adding resources to an unconstrained schedule and then changing activities so that resources are not overloaded is referred to as 'resource leveling'. Referring back to Figure 9.5, finishing at the end of week 10 might be feasible if we had a team to design and build the shed and in parallel, another team to build and paint the wall. If there were only one team that could handle any activity then the four activities might be strung out sequentially taking 17 weeks (2 + 5 + 6 + 4) – certainly longer than 10 weeks.

Most schedulers can automate resource leveling. But resource leveling tools need to make the assumption that resources of a particular type are interchangeable, for example, that any business analyst can do certain work. This may be true of bricklayers, but it is seldom true of professional staff. Also, some tools do not split or stretch activities. So, automated resource leveling can work for construction-type projects, but for business projects I always do it manually and negotiate with the people what they can reasonably take on, bearing in mind which person has the specific skill and experience required.

9.8.3 Use of Scheduling Tools

A scheduler can certainly save your time and take the drudgery out of maintaining a schedule when things are changing. Most schedulers have lots of sophisticated features and it may be tempting to use them. I urge you not to. Rather stick to the basics and produce the minimum output to track the project and communicate progress. For example, most schedulers offer cost control. I personally don't use it because there has never been time for me to learn how it works. Also, for a business project, trying to control costs at the level of activities is simply unnecessary work – high-level spreadsheets are usually all that is required. The same applies to enterprise-level scheduling tools. Yes, one must follow the organization's standards, but avoid letting standards divert you from the project's purpose.

Case 12 gives further practice at Gantt chart scheduling. Part 1 is done manually, while Part 2 uses the same data and explains how things are done using a scheduler, like adding resources, removing resource constraints, and showing progress. If you have a scheduling tool but are not experienced at using it, Part 2 will give useful guidance on the essential techniques.

9.9 Ways of Meeting Tight Deadlines

It often happens that the reasonable end-date proposed is not acceptable to management. Sometimes too, what started out as an achievable deadline no longer looks feasible later due to delays and problems along the way. In such situations, we need to find ways of reducing the remaining duration, albeit at a cost and sometimes also greater risk. There are three basic approaches to meeting a challenging deadline and often a combination is needed. I shall discuss them in turn.

9.9.1 De-scoping

This is the first avenue that I would look at. De-scoping is the term given to *not* doing work that was originally part of the agreed scope (the scope baseline). Certain activities are essential, but as the pressure mounts to complete a project, it usually emerges that some of the scope is of a 'nice-to-have' nature or work that is important but not urgent. It's best to de-scope it. The PM needs sponsor (or steering committee) approval for de-scoping, but sponsors almost always see such recommendations as proactive and are supportive of keeping the focus on only what is essential and time-critical. So, toward the end of a project, it is worth assessing the remaining work and only doing what is necessary.

> ***On one strategic initiative that had run for nearly three years and had been stopped more than once for political reasons, it became apparent that if a key milestone was not met timeously, the project might never be completed. The only way was to defer any activities that were not absolutely essential for that milestone. It worked and the milestone was achieved. Management were unconcerned that it took over a year to button up those deferred activities that still needed to be done.***

At the end of the project, in the closeout report, important de-scoped activities should be noted to avoid them being overlooked.

9.9.2 Fast Tracking

'Fast tracking' is the term given to overlapping activities that would normally be done in sequence. This might be done in a schedule using 'lead' dependencies. Examples might be: starting to plaster interior walls before the roof is on, or starting to build a prototype 2 weeks before the design is scheduled to be approved. Pulling work forward has risks. In the above examples, suppose that there is heavy rain before the plaster is dry or suppose that the design needs major overhaul after work has started on the prototype. Also, one needs to have sufficient resources.

When applying a lot of resources and doing many activity sequences in parallel, the risk increases. Suppose that project A has *one* critical path with a 70% chance of being completed without serious delays. Now consider project B which has *three* parallel paths, one critical and the other two close to the critical path with only a few days of float. If each of the three paths has the same 70% chance of no serious delay, and all are needed for project completion, then the overall probability of timely completion drops to around 35% (100×0.7^3). So, project B can be said to have greater 'schedule sensitivity'.

9.9.3 Crashing

'Crashing' is the term given to applying more resources to critical or near-critical activities. The aim is always to meet a deadline or to complete the project in an acceptable time. Crashing can be done in a number of ways. Bringing in more people is one; working overtime or shifts is another. Both have their benefits, but come with costs and some risks.

> ***Many years ago, towards the end of a large project, most of the team were working every weekend and it certainly helped to meet the objective. However, it was not good for team cohesion and morale. The contract staff were delighted to be paid at the higher overtime rate, the employee technical staff got a small allowance for overtime, while the business people got no extra pay and resented the impact on their weekends.***

One also needs to be careful about how much overtime people can handle (even if they are highly motivated). Overwork can make people irritable and unwilling to help other members of the team. They can even display 'dysfunctional behavior' like being downright rude to colleagues. Productivity can also suffer. Tired people make more mistakes.

> ***While in my 20s, I worked two consecutive ninety-hour weeks doing technical work. The results were hardly satisfactory. After a good rest, I could not believe that I could make so many errors. From then on, I seldom worked more than a 70 hour week.***

So when managing project teams, my general rule is that very hard workers can put in constant 50-hour weeks. They might be able to work 60-hour weeks for a few months, and 70-hour weeks for up to a month. But people should not work more than one 80-hour week. Beyond that, burnout beckons and team morale is likely to suffer.

Another potential pitfall is piling in resources near the end of a project. When a critical project is running late, management's first thought is to offer more resources. This only works if such resources are highly skilled and already knowledgeable about the project. Adding inexperienced people is more likely to delay things due to the learning curve. It is far more useful for management to give support in resolving issues and removing obstacles or by increasing the project's priority.

Here, I suggest that you do Case 13 on crashing, to consolidate your understanding.

9.10 Some Critical Chain Concepts

There was much excitement about critical chain scheduling some years ago, but nowadays it is not spoken about much. Nevertheless, let me mention two of its many concepts that I find particularly useful. You can decide whether to apply them to your own schedules.

- When estimating their activities, team members often add 'fat' in case there are problems. Once the longer duration is allocated, people start late or stretch the work to take the full amount of time and sometimes still overrun when it might have been done more quickly. Critical chain suggests that you allocate the minimum time to do the task, but allow a contingency project 'buffer' at the end to allow for problems along the way. Thus the PM starts with an ambitious schedule and manages the slippage so that it uses as little of the project buffer as possible.
- Normal scheduling starts non-critical activities as soon as possible even if the activity has a lot of float. Critical chain suggests starting them almost as late as possible, but allowing an activity buffer at the end of the task so that if it overruns, it is unlikely to affect the critical path. The benefits are that costs are incurred later and that there is more knowledge when the activity is started, reducing the likelihood of rework.

So, although I don't use critical chain scheduling, I mentally use some of its concepts.

9.11 Summary

Scheduling is essential for every project, whether it be using a Gantt chart, an activity list, or any other form. Initially, it helps you to plan the project. Thereafter, it helps you to track progress. Use the schedule to help understand the impact of issues or changes and expect the activities to change regularly. However, the schedule should not consume too much of your time – probably not more than 10%. Rather spend your time communicating with stakeholders which includes the team, and also resolving issues – all of which require having the schedule status at the back of your mind.

Chapter 10

Managing Project Quality

10.1 Introduction and Objectives

When we think of quality, things like a new Tesla automobile or the latest smartphone spring to mind. What we shall learn is that on projects, quality means something a little different. So the objectives are to:

- Understand the key concepts and terminology related to project quality.
- Know why more effort spent to achieve quality usually saves money.
- Distinguish between the quality of the outcomes produced and the quality of how we run the project.
- Be able to draw up a quality plan which includes listing the quality aspects of each deliverable, and then determining how to meet them.
- Understand the processes involved in quality.
- Learn about some useful mindsets related to quality.

A huge amount has been written about quality and yet it's not well understood. Years ago a junior PM asked me "what needs to go into my quality plan". My response: "Not sure, I'll have to think about that". So, it's not easy, but by the end of the chapter, you should have a good idea.

10.2 The Theory and Practice of Quality

First, let's understand that quality applies to almost everything: business, manufactured goods, food, IT systems, and of course, to projects. But what do we mean by quality? How would we describe it? Here are some answers:

- Quality is conformance to requirements which are often stated in specifications, generally referred to as 'specs'.
- Quality is meeting expectations. These could be the expectations of a customer or client, people that should benefit from the project, and even people that will not benefit.

DOI: 10.1201/9781003321101-12

- Quality is also about being 'fit for purpose'. For example, if I gave you a shiny new spade, but as soon as you tried to dig with it, it bent, then despite its good looks, it would not be fit for purpose, and hence not of adequate quality.

But there are also misconceptions. Quality is *not* about:

- Producing 'cool' and 'nice-to-have' things that were not specified, or having 'all the bells and whistles';
- Providing everything that your customer or the user asks for. That is where scope change control comes in – as will be explained in Chapter 15.

But, quality *does* include anything that is really important to the stakeholders, even if it is not in the specifications. The specs are seldom comprehensive; certain things are assumed and the PM needs to find out what they are. Setting reasonable expectations is part of the process. It's not easy, because stakeholders often have conflicting views as to the requirements, so there may be some negotiation.

10.2.1 What Is Needed to Produce Quality Outcomes?

Figure 10.1 gives an overview of how quality outcomes can be produced. I use the term 'outcomes' because they go further than the deliverables themselves. For example, often good communication around the deliverables enhances the overall outcomes. The PM needs to understand the quality requirements and then know what to do to meet them.

The three ovals are the quality processes recognized by PMI (the Project Management Institute) (PMI, 2017): First, plan how quality will be managed, which includes understanding the quality requirements. Second, manage quality during

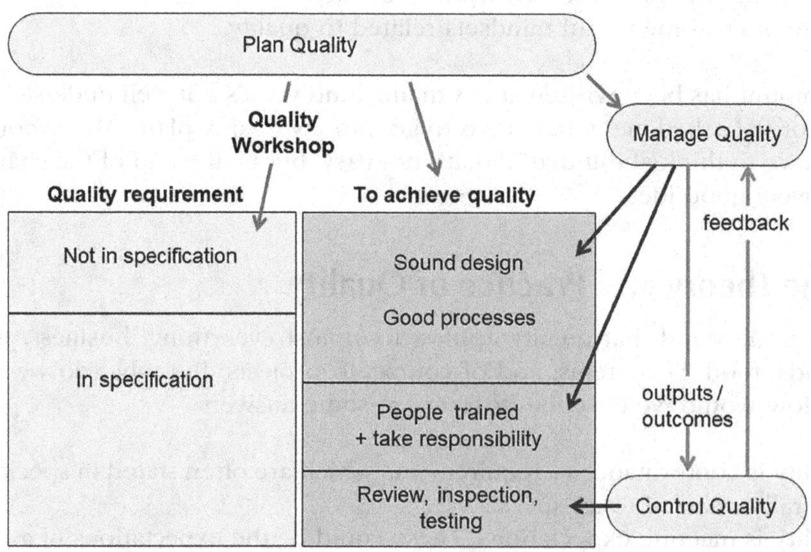

Figure 10.1 Project quality concepts.

project execution. Third, control quality by making sure that the deliverables meet the quality requirements, and feeding back to the 'manage quality' activities. OGC (2009) gives similar processes which are used in the PRINCE2 methodology. Because 'Plan quality' includes understanding the quality requirements, it should be given attention early in planning. Refer to the left-hand rectangles in Figure 10.1 and let us suppose that you have a specification – something in writing describing the deliverables. It could be broad, very detailed, or anything in-between. But, even if it is detailed, does it have everything? Probably not. And, it's up to the PM to find out what is not in the spec that is important. This is best done by involving your team and engaging with the project's stakeholders. It could be through one-on-one discussions or through a workshop, always documented lest important requirements be forgotten. The question to be asked is: "when this project is finished, what things will make you say that the outcomes were of satisfactory quality?" In other words, "what are you expecting?" What comes out of the discussion should reinforce or complement the spec and might have little effect on the scope. However, if something unexpected is required that amounts to significant extra scope, it should result in negotiations – the sooner the better. You would not want to wait until the end of the project to find that the users are unhappy – which could indicate a failed project.

Having understood what is needed, the darker rectangles to the right in the figure, indicate what to do to achieve satisfactory quality. First, make sure that any design is sound, and have it checked. The design could relate to a physical product, but it could equally relate to something less tangible, like an event. Also, have good execution processes. If these are right, it is likely that the output will be of good quality. Second, make sure that the team is trained on the processes and takes responsibility. For the people that do the work, taking responsibility includes checking what they produce. Here, it should be noted that, if the design is faulty or if the processes are inadequate, it will be near impossible for the team to produce quality output. Finally, there need to be some reviews done on the output. This may involve inspection; it may also involve testing which is a large part of producing an IT deliverable. But, most of the quality comes from the people doing the work, rather than from tests or inspections.

10.2.2 Quality Principles – the Total Cost of Quality

Let us now consider some of the principles behind managing quality, particularly those relating to what it costs. We talk about the *total* cost of quality and it has two components (PMI, 2017):

- The cost of *conformance* – making sure that quality will prevail, things like:
  - The cost of holding quality workshops.
  - The cost of building a prototype or doing a proof-of-concept.
  - The cost of training team members and others.
  - The cost of reviews, checking, inspection, and testing.
- The cost of *non-conformance* – the cost of things going wrong as a result of inadequate quality. Here are a few examples:
  - The cost of rework or additional work to fix product problems.
  - For a supplier, the cost of payments being held back.

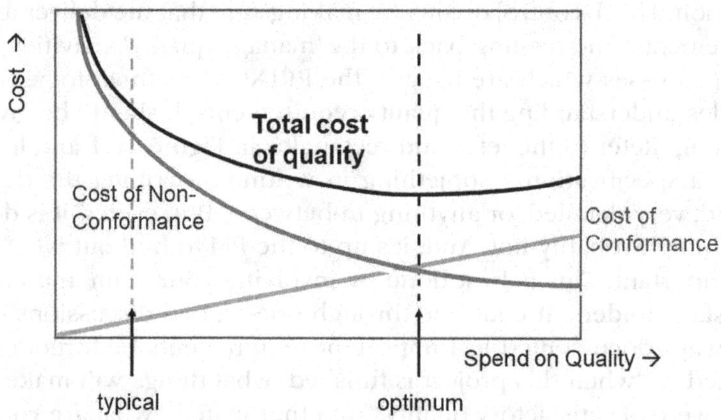

Figure 10.2 Spend on quality is seldom wasted.

- The impact on the organization's reputation and the cost of dealing with complaints.
- After the project, the cost of problems and higher maintenance.

Both achieving conformance and dealing with non-conformance cost time and money. Thus, the *total* cost of quality = cost of conformance + cost of non-conformance. If we spend very little on quality then the resulting mess will be expensive. If we spend too much on quality, then it just costs too much, but this is very rare. We need a happy medium. This is shown graphically in Figure 10.2.

Cost is on the vertical axis. Spend on quality is on the horizontal axis (with a different scale). The pale gray cost of conformance line is straight: the more we spend on quality, the more it costs. The darker gray curve, the cost of non-conformance, starts very high to the left (where nothing is spent on quality), drops rapidly as some money is spent, but reduces more slowly to the right where a lot is spent on quality. The black, total cost of quality curve, is the sum of the two. It reaches an optimum point (the minimum of the curve). That is where we should be operating, and fortunately, there is quite a wide range that is close to the optimum. But, sadly, because of the pressures that PMs work under, the tendency is to rush into things and take shortcuts – hence the 'typical' arrow, which has a higher total cost. The triple constraint triangle, explained in Chapter 6, suggests that if one wants more scope or quality, expect to pay more and take longer. That may be true for scope, but for quality, Philip Crosby expressed a different view. He said "quality is free". Spend more on it, and you will save money – almost always true if one is operating near the 'typical' mark.

Having covered the theory, it is worth mentioning that the costs mentioned above can be difficult to estimate and measure. They can also be difficult to predict. Nevertheless, there are quality metrics that are used, some during, but many after, the project. For example:

- Customer complaint statistics (Contact Center).

  When I was running projects in a financial services organization, I remember the business lead saying "we can't take that risk, if it goes wrong our help desk will be swamped with queries".

- Processing time (for example, the time from the customer request until the system is updated).
- Processing errors or reconciliation items to resolve.
- Customer servicing costs related to defects.
- For IT systems development, the number of errors needing to be fixed during user acceptance testing.
- Reliability: MTBF – mean time between failures.
- Maintainability: MTTR – mean time to repair.
- Availability: the percentage uptime of a system or a piece of equipment.

Overall, the principle is clear: Pay attention to quality and be prepared to spend time and money on it.

10.3 Project Quality

As mentioned, project quality has two different aspects: (i) the quality of the outcomes which are based on the deliverables and (ii) the quality of how the project is managed. Both matter and are related because if the project is well managed the outcomes are likely to be of satisfactory quality.

10.3.1 Quality Deliverables and Outcomes

First, we must ask "what is meant by quality outcomes?" Because of the variety of business projects, the list could be endless. No doubt the stakeholders will determine what is required for a particular project, but here are a few examples:

- Essential dates are met, so that opportunities are not lost.
- Stakeholders are adequately trained and know what to expect.
- Disruption during and after the project is minimized.
- Documentation supports a smooth handover.
- Involved business users are willing and able to do what is expected of them (see Chapter 23 on organizational change management).

For business projects producing a product or process:

- There is good customer communication with quality promotional material.
- Advertising is synchronized with product launch.
- Products are easy to use, leading to customer acceptance.
- Processes are not resource-intensive and are easy to audit.
- Process cycle times are short, leading to prompt results.

For IT systems development:

- The system is user-friendly and easy to learn; online response times are quick.
- The system is well tested with minimal downtime or processing errors.
- The programs are modular and inexpensive to maintain or enhance.

10.3.2 More About the Quality Processes

To achieve quality outcomes, it helps to follow the processes shown in Figure 10.1. But, rather than being isolated processes, they are woven into everything that is done on the project:

- Plan quality management. This includes checking what specifications exist, holding necessary discussions or workshops, and deciding how quality requirements will be met. Buy-in from the team on all such matters is essential. All this should be documented and could collectively be referred to as the 'quality plan'. It should also have the answers to questions like:
  - Who will be responsible for which quality aspects?
    On one large project, I was the commissioning manager. My only role was to confirm that everything worked properly and that handovers to the customer went smoothly.
  - Are there organizational standards that we must adhere to?
  - Are any QA (quality assurance) reviews mandatory?
    In a bank where I consulted, an IT architecture review was mandatory before development of any new IT system could begin.
  - What checklists should be used?
- Manage quality during execution. This involves planning the execution activities so that quality will be achieved. Some activities, like review and testing of deliverables, might be there specifically to ensure quality. You may need to make changes to the quality plan in collaboration with the team.
- Control quality would be done in parallel with execution. It might include the design of measurements and tests, maintaining records of quality activities, and involving other departments like Internal Audit or Compliance.

10.3.3 Project Management Quality

While the abovementioned quality processes are important for running a quality project, all the other essentials, covered in these core chapters, are also needed, like a capable team who know their responsibilities, effective communication, sound documentation that is accessible, risks responded to, and issues being dealt with. To achieve all this, use a simple methodology that is appropriate for the type and size of the project, and follow it rigorously. Welcome project health checks and project reviews; they are explained in Chapter 25 and help you to run a sound project.

10.4 Some Interesting Quality Standards and Philosophies

The following are included, not because you will necessarily use them, but to build your perspective and encourage a sound attitude. Some are contentious – expert views differ.

- ISO9000: You have probably heard of ISO9000. It is a set of international standards relating to quality. Organizations subscribe and can be 'ISO9000 certified'. It may seem like a lot of 'red tape', but in my simple view, what it aims to do is to have a suitable set of processes in place that are maintained, communicated, and practiced. It should not be a documentation nightmare, especially because most processes and documents are probably readily available via your intranet. But ISO9000 is not a guarantee of project success, nor is its purpose universally understood.

  In the late 1990s I called on a customer project sponsor to explain why we were running two weeks behind schedule. The sponsor reacted "but how can you be late? I thought you were following ISO9000?" My response was "yes we are, and its processes require me to keep customers fully informed".

  For many types of projects, nothing guarantees success, and the best we can do is to manage it properly and keep communicating.

- The 80-20 rule – the Pareto principle: It posits that 80% of problems come from 20% of the causes. It applies to certain types of projects, and even more to operations. So, the learning is, that to address quality problems, seek the root causes of the most common problems, and give top priority to solving them.
- DTRTRTFT: I hope that it is spelled correctly, and I cannot pronounce it. It stands for 'do the right thing right the first time'. It's a sound philosophy which suggests that taking time to do things properly is far more economical than fixing botch-ups.
- Zero defect: This is something to be striven toward. The concept arose because contracts for components used to specify an acceptance level of 95%, with only 5% being defective. The result was that the buyers got what they asked for – 5% defective. The Six Sigma concept became famous for aiming for fewer than four defects per million. It has since become a set of quality principles and practices, mainly used to improve processes.
- "The customer is the next person in the process": This is a mindset and in a project context, it means that we must treat others on the project as our customers and give priority to assisting them. The more the team members display this attitude, the better the quality is likely to be.
- Quality must be built into the design and process. We have already mentioned that if the design is poor, then no amount of effort will produce quality. Indeed research shows that 85% of quality comes from the design and the process. If we over-inspect then the people doing the work adopt a don't care attitude – "it's someone else's job is to find and fix my mistakes". So quality is designed in and *not* inspected in. But, I still suggest that you check things and validate the quality of deliverables.
- TQM (total quality management), when adopted, is practiced organization-wide. It's something that is instilled in everyone from top to bottom. For projects it means just what we've been talking about: dig out all the requirements and have the whole team work together to meet them.

- Continuous improvement: Once again, this is an attitude that applies to projects and processes. It proposes that what is competitive, or 'state of the art' now, will not be tomorrow. Therefore, we must continually strive to do things better. Indeed, this is a tenet of many methodologies, including TQM and Six Sigma.

10.5 Concluding Thoughts on Quality

Here is a question that is often debated: "who is ultimately responsible for quality? Is it the sponsor or maybe a QA department?" The broad consensus is that the PM is responsible. Many of the tasks can be delegated and stakeholders can be consulted, but the responsibility rests with the PM. Hence, besides following the processes suggested, the PM should be on the lookout for warning flags and then act on them. To return to our Tesla or latest smartphone: it is easy to take their quality for granted, but it is hardly possible that those products could have been produced without many projects where quality was well managed.

Now, to get practice at recognizing quality requirements, I suggest you do Case 14 where a factory move for EduToy7 is being planned and where there are many different stakeholder interests at play.

References

OGC. (2009). *Managing Successful Projects with PRINCE2*, 5th edition. In A. Murray (Ed.). Norwich: TSO (The Stationery Office) on behalf of Office of Government Commerce.

PMI. (2017). *PMBOK - Guide to the Project Management Body of Knowledge*, 6th edition: Pennsylvania, USA: Project Management Institute.

Chapter 11

Managing Project Risk

11.1 Introduction and Objectives

One might think that risks are a fact of life, and that not much can be done about them. The reality is almost the opposite. If risks are recognized in time, a great deal can be done to prevent them, or at least to mitigate them. And here, mitigation means reducing the probability of a risk happening and/or reducing the impact of the risk event if it does happen. Consider a simple example: You are on your way to a wedding and have a flat tire – a risk that can happen to anyone. If your spare tire is already pumped up, it can mitigate the risk by minimizing the delay caused by the flat tire. So the main objectives of this chapter are to:

- Know what project risks are, and how to identify them.
- Be able to describe project risks concisely.
- Prioritize risks by considering the probability of a risk event happening and its impact if it does happen.
- Use appropriate strategies to respond to risks.
- Learn how to manage risks throughout the lifetime of the project.

11.2 What Are Risks and When Do We Get Involved with Them?

A risk is an uncertain event or condition, that, if it happens, has a negative (or positive) effect on the project or on the organization. Indeed, there can be uncertainties that may be positive. An example would be where the outcome of the project is so successful that demand for the service produced far exceeds expectations. If the possibility is anticipated, then the organization may be better able to take advantage of it. But here, our main focus will be on the negative effects – things that can go wrong.

Another concept: a risk, by definition, is uncertain. If the negative situation were certain, it would be managed as an issue. Thus, an issue is a risk that has happened. Because dealing with issues is so important, issues are covered in Chapter 14. But, for most risks, there is much that can be done to prevent or mitigate them, and the question "how much effort is worthwhile?" will be discussed presently.

DOI: 10.1201/9781003321101-13

When do we get involved with risks? Right from when the project is first proposed and certainly before the project starts. Risks are a key input to the justification for the project, which is often documented as a business case. Here one might consider the sum of known risks and decide that the potential downside is so great that the project should not proceed. But even if we do proceed, expectations should be tempered with the likely cost of risks that may happen. Known risks are carried forward to the PDD (project definition document), and hence into planning and tracking. For risks, tracking is usually done by maintaining a 'risk register' and taking response actions to limit the overall effect of risks on the project. As the project progresses, further risks will emerge and some risks may happen or may no longer be possible. In short, the PM can never lose sight of risks because some may relate to the outcomes and benefits of the project. So, risk management is done throughout the lifetime of the project.

11.3 How Do We Identify and Describe the Risks for Our Project?

11.3.1 Identifying the Risks

First, we need to know what the risks are. The more we are aware of, and the earlier, the better we shall be able to handle them. But even with the best risk identification processes, some risks will emerge later, and sometimes issues will crop up without the risk having been foreseen at all. There are several approaches to identifying risks, and generally one uses more than one of the following:

- Discussions, interviews, and brainstorming. These involve focused discussion about what could go wrong, during or after the project, with one or more groups. It is also common to hold a risk identification workshop.
- Consulting with experts. In this context, an expert might be anyone that has already done a similar project or is a designated 'risk manager' – and some organizations have them.
- Looking at the documentation and especially lessons learned from similar past projects.
- Reviewing assumptions. Assumptions should be stated in any business case or PDD. The risk would be that the reality turns out to be significantly different from the assumption – which happens quite often. Sadly, even more often, an assumption is made but not stated, so the risk is overlooked.
- Using an online risk assessment tool. There are many available. Generally, they ask questions, and based on your answers, the tool suggests likely risks. If a risk checklist exists within your organization, it might serve a similar purpose.

Ideally one would want to use most of the above approaches.

> *At a bank where I was involved 20 years ago, we brainstormed all the risks we could think of, and then also used an online tool. Inevitably each approach raised valid risks that the other had not come up with.*

11.3.2 Describing the Risks

When describing a risk concisely, a possible format has three elements:

Given <the current situation>,
<risk event description> may occur,
resulting in <description of consequences>.

The following example is somewhat vague, but it does illustrate the format:

> Lack of business support: Given the current pressures on business people to produce more profit, it is possible that the requested business support may be inadequate, resulting in requirements being missed, and the stated benefits not being realized.

11.4 How Should We Document and Analyze the Risks?

Having identified the risks, Table 11.1 gives a useful format for prioritizing and tracking them. It is called the 'risk register' and could be kept as an MS Word or Excel document.

'Ref' is a reference number to allow reviewers to refer to the same risk during discussion. The risk description might use the format mentioned above. Often I put in a date, to say when the risk was identified. I also put in a date when there are additions or changes to a risk. The P, I, and X columns (used for prioritization), and the response action columns, are explained below. The scale here is shown from 1 (low probability or impact) to 10 (high), but any scale could be used. I give the document itself a date in the format 'yymmdd' which effectively versions the risk register, with the latest one always sorting (on name) to the bottom.

When a risk has happened and will not happen again, it is commented on under risk description referencing any issues raised, and then cut and pasted below 'closed – risk happened'. Similarly, if it is deemed that the risk can no longer happen, then it is cut and pasted below 'closed – risk did not happen'. This allows a focus on

Table 11.1 Illustrative Format for Documenting and Tracking Project Risks

Ref	*Risk Description*	*P*	*I*	*X*	*Response Actions*
R1	09Jun21: <description> 18Aug21: <additional information> possibly after an earlier response action was taken.	3	2	6	o Action 1 o Action 2
	Closed – risk happened				
	Closed – risk did not happen				

P = probability (scale 1–10), I = impact (scale 1–10), X = priority (generally P x I)

the risks that can still happen. This need not be a large document – typically one to three pages.

> *On a complex three-year project that I managed, the risk register only got to seven pages. Risks were color-coded according to their priority (X), and a discussion with the sponsor on open risks could be done in about half an hour.*

Two basic approaches to analyzing risks follow, each with variations.

11.4.1 Qualitative Risk Analysis

The first approach has already been alluded to above and is referred to as 'qualitative' risk analysis (PMI, 2017). Risks are rated using the PM's judgment for probability and impact. Using a 1-to-10 scale for probability means that:

- 1 or 2 would be low probability
- 3 to 5 medium probability
- 6 to 8 quite likely
- 9 or 10 almost certain

Likewise for impact:

- 1 or 2 minor inconvenience
- 3 to 5 impact will certainly affect cost or schedule
- 6 to 8 severe impact that may cause termination of the project
- 9 or 10 the project will almost certainly be terminated

Priority (X) is estimated by multiplying P with I. It is not necessary to follow the multiplication slavishly, so for a P = 2 and I = 3 risk, I might rate X as priority 5 (rather than 6). After all, these figures are a matter of judgment and are used for guidance. For a medium-risk project, there might be one or two risks above priority10, but most would be below 10. A priority of 1 (P = 1 and I = 1) is hardly worth documenting. Priority (X) will be discussed further under response strategies.

Business projects need to be particularly sensitive to risks that can have an organizational impact that can go way beyond the cost of the project. An example would be: enhancements to a financial system that accidentally cause incorrect payments to be made.

I use this approach on almost all business projects. It is relatively easy to do and remarkably effective.

11.4.2 Quantitative Risk Analysis

Only once have I used this approach, and then it was on a $30 million (in today's terms) project. It starts with the same identification of risk (PMI, 2017). However, now we calculate the probabilistic cost of each risk or the EMV (expected monetary value). To do this, for each risk, a percentage probability is assigned, as well as an impact cost in dollars. So, the probabilistic cost or EMV = probability percentage x impact cost. So if, for example:

- There is a 20% probability of a supplier delivering components more than a week late, and the cost of the delay is estimated at $5 000, then the EMV = 0.2 × $5 000 or $1 000.

To get the probabilistic cost of all the risks, we sum all the EMVs of the individual risks. This is quantitative risk analysis in its simplest form. There are many further sophistications that can be considered. Here are two of them:

- There may be multiple outcomes for a risk. For example, if the risk happens, there is a 30% probability that it costs $50 000, 40% that it costs $80 000, etc.
- There are interdependent risks, where a risk event depends on more than one probability. For example, there is a 0.4 (40%) chance of the problem occurring and a 0.2 (20%) chance of the contingency plan failing. So the probability of *both* adverse events would be 0.4 × 0.2 = 0.08 or 8%.

Quantitative risk analysis is seldom done for business projects, where less is known up-front and where responding to the risks is more important than calculating the probabilistic cost.

11.4.3 How Much Should Be Set Aside for Risks?

Because risks cost both time and money, reserves can be set aside to allow for them:

- Contingency reserve is money or time allocated to the project, over and above the basic cost and schedule estimates. Usually, the PM has discretion and would report on its use.
- Management reserve is money or time held outside the project for unanticipated risks and is only granted by the sponsor or steering committee after reviewing the facts.

Estimation of contingency is quite common. Based on qualitative risk analysis, one might conclude that a certain project is low risk, and allocate an 8% contingency amount. Another project might be deemed to be medium risk and get a 15% contingency amount. There are no hard-and-fast rules here. Where quantitative risk analysis is done the total EMV might be allocated as a contingency reserve. But, each organization has its own criteria and guidelines and some organizations do not even think about contingency. Nevertheless, where either cost or time are important, it would be unwise to start without some agreement on contingency.

11.5 How Should the PM Respond to Known Risks?

There are four types of responses to negative risks. The PM can avoid them, transfer them, mitigate them, or accept them (PMI, 2017). Here is a brief explanation of each:

- Avoid. The PM changes the plan to avoid the risk altogether. Examples:
  - We use a supplier that we know rather than a new one.
  - We stay with familiar software rather than upgrading to high-function software that we have not used before.
- Transfer (or deflect). The PM moves the risk to another organization (always at a cost):
  - We insure equipment for theft or buy warranties in case of breakdown.
  - We insist on penalty clauses in a subcontract to compensate us for losses due to late delivery to our customer.
  - We contract a deliverable to a company that has expertise that we lack.

  However, often such transfer of risk still leaves us with some risk. For example, if the company that we hire to produce a deliverable does a poor job, we still have a problem.
- Mitigate. The PM takes actions: to reduce the probability of the risk happening and/or to reduce the impact of the event, if it does happen.
  - We hold expert reviews to reduce the costs and delays caused by design flaws.
  - We involve business people early to ensure that we don't miss any requirements.
  - We do a proof of concept so that problems can be circumvented early.
- Accept. The PM records the risk but decides not to take any specific action.

For a complex risk, it may be necessary to use the above strategies in combination. Except for the 'accept' risk type, some actions will be needed. Depending on their size and duration, they may become activities in the schedule or action items to be tracked in the project minutes – always with a person responsible. However, it may not be necessary to state in the risk register who is responsible for the risk as a whole, unless the risk is specific to part of the project – like a subproject.

Once the response actions have been taken, the risk can be reassessed for probability and impact. It may now be possible to reduce either or both of the probability and impact, and to reduce the priority (X) accordingly.

Similar strategies apply to positive risks (possible opportunities). We may take actions to enhance their probability or consider sharing the opportunity with another organization.

11.6 Summary of Managing Risks Throughout the Project's Lifetime

Risk management starts while the project is still being conceived and proposed. Risks and their potential costs must be part of the business case, even if the justification is informal. In the extreme, risks may contribute to a decision not to proceed. During definition, stakeholders should be informed of the main risks; stated assumptions may be challenged or may highlight further risks. During planning, risks move from the PDD to a risk register. Response actions are documented and tracked until they are complete. Review of risks continues throughout execution. As the risk response actions are taken, the probability and/or impact may reduce, thus reducing the risk's priority. The highest priority risks are stated in every project report. As risks happen, or can no longer happen, they are moved to the 'closed' sections of the risk register. Even near the end when benefits are being realized, new risks can emerge. When the project is complete, risks would be discussed and documented as lessons learned. The risk register in its final state would be archived with the project documentation for future reference. So, risk management is done throughout the lifetime of the project.

This is a good time to get some practice at documenting risks in a risk register format. So I suggest that you do Case 15 which is about a project to film Cheetahs, and then compare what you have with the 'possible' answer given.

Reference

PMI. (2017). *PMBOK - Guide to the Project Management Body of Knowledge*, 6th edition: Pennsylvania, USA: Project Management Institute.

Chapter 12

Progress and Cost Tracking

12.1 Introduction and Objectives

The aim of this chapter is to give (i) a basic knowledge of cost management terminology and (ii) an understanding of how to track the work achieved via the schedule, at the same time as tracking costs. The main objectives are to:

- See how the 'triple constraint' relates to EVM (earned value management).
- Be able to use the terminology of project cost management.
- Avoid the commonest reporting error in cost management.
- Know where the three parameters used in EVM – planned value (PV), earned value (EV), and actual cost (AC) come from and how to estimate or measure them.
- Be able to monitor work achieved and hence track schedule and costs concurrently.
- Be able to report variances and indexes for a project, and explain what they mean.
- Estimate the percentage complete for a project and the likely cost at completion.
- Understand the difficulties of using 'classical' EVM for a business project.
- Learn to use the project progress tracker (PPTR) which overcomes EVM's difficulties.

12.2 Why Does a Business PM Need to Understand Earned Value Concepts?

The 'triple constraint' or 'iron triangle' discussed in Chapter 6 indicates that there are trade-offs to be made between scope, time, and cost. Scope and time are recorded in the schedule, where if an activity is shown as complete, the scope needs to have been done to an acceptable level of quality. In a business project, costs are seldom estimated and tracked for each activity (activities change too often). Rather, costs are

DOI: 10.1201/9781003321101-14

tracked at project level, and for a large business project, maybe at subproject level. Therefore, we need a way of concurrently tracking achievement against the schedule and against cost. The stakeholders are likely to be unhappy if the scope is complete on time, but with huge cost overruns, or, if the costs are acceptable but there is a huge schedule overrun. Indeed schedule (time) and cost need to be considered together. EVM (earned value management) is an approach that can achieve this (PMI, 2017). It is covered in almost all textbooks and professional certification examinations, so it's important that PMs understand EVM. However, while classical EVM may work well for a construction project, it has practical limitations for a business project. I use the term 'classical' to refer to EVM as it is covered in textbooks. Fortunately, the principles of EVM can be applied very effectively for business projects by simplifying the way that it is practiced. But first, an understanding of EVM is essential, and before doing so, let us go through some of the basics of cost management.

12.3 Some Cost Management Concepts and Terminology

Different organizations use terminology differently, but there are certain things that sponsors and other management want to know:

- What is the project status? What is the percentage complete?
- What has the project cost to date?
- Is the project on track? What are the variances?
- How much will it still cost to finish the project – ETC (estimate to completion)?
- What will the total cost be when finished – EAC (estimate at completion)?

12.3.1 Variances

Variances in project management usually apply to schedule or cost. They are calculated by comparing what has actually happened versus the plan or baseline. Variances can be positive or negative. The convention is that a positive variance is good, and a negative variance bad. So when considering costs, if we are under budget for specific work, we have a positive cost variance, but, if we have spent more money than planned and are over budget, then we have a negative cost variance. Likewise, when considering the schedule, if we are ahead of schedule we have a positive schedule variance, and if behind schedule, we have a negative schedule variance. So clearly, we need to be very specific about which variance we are talking about and what the measurement is – dollars, work days, or whatever is meaningful. In classical EVM, we shall see that all variances are in dollars. A small negative variance might not be serious, but a large negative variance would need to be explained. It might also need corrective action which, in most business projects, can realistically do little more than prevent identified problems from continuing.

12.3.2 Cost, Price, and Profit

When doing a project for an external party, cost and price are sometimes confused. The following explains the difference and gives some of the terminology often used.

> Suppose that a company contracts to do a market survey for a client. The contract price may be $10 000, but the estimate of the cost of doing the work may be $8 000 which includes a contingency amount for risk. The $2 000 difference is the gross profit that the company wants to make to cover overheads and have something for the shareholders.

In this situation, the *mark-up* on the cost of $8000 is $2000 or 25%, while the *margin* is 2000/10000 or only 20%. What determines the profit uplift? Many factors, but some of them are:

- Competitive pressures. If there is lots of competition, adding a large mark-up will not win the business; if this survey requires specialized skills and few others can do it, then a higher price might be accepted (margins are seldom disclosed).
- Availability of resources and projected workload. Where the employees are very busy, the company might seek a high mark-up, but when there is the threat of having people idle, then the company might accept a much lower mark-up just to keep their people busy and at least get *some* revenue.

Therefore, when managing a project, whether internal or for a client, there is usually some emphasis on managing the cost. While projected cost influences the quoted price, the price is a management decision.

12.3.3 More Terminology

- A **committed cost** is where goods or services have been ordered or contracted. Delivery has not yet happened, but a financial commitment exists. An example would be ordering specialized equipment which is in the process of being manufactured. It is too late to cancel the order without incurring some costs.
- A **sunk cost** is money that has already been spent. In a failing project, the comment might be made: "We have already spent $500 000, we can't stop now!" A more valid comment would be: "That $500 000 is a sunk cost, and should not affect our decision. We need to abort the project because the expected benefits are less than the remaining costs to complete the project".
- Costs may be described as **'fixed' or 'variable'**. A fixed cost might be the cost of buildings or equipment that will be incurred irrespective. Variable costs might be the cost of peoples' time working on a project or travel costs specific to the project. If the project stops, the variable costs also stop.
- Costs may be described as **'direct' or 'indirect'**. Direct costs would relate work done directly on the project. Indirect costs might relate to administrative work back at the office to support this project and others.
- **Depreciation** is a way of assigning a time value to an asset. Supposing that a specialized piece of equipment cost the company $100 000. It might be deemed to have a useful life of 5 years, and hence be depreciated at $20 000 per year. If your project then required the equipment for 6 months, it might be reasonable to charge depreciation for half a year, or $10 000, to your project. How depreciation is handled for tax purposes is another matter entirely and is up to the financial people.

12.4 Why Do We Need EVM and What Is It?

One of the reasons for using EVM is illustrated with a short example:

> Consider a project budgeted at $4 million.
> Suppose that it is planned that, at 30 June, $2 million should have been spent.
> Three days later, project accounts confirm that at 30 June, $1.8 million had been spent.

Is this project on track? What should the PM report to the sponsor? Many PMs would say "we are on track and in fact we are underspent on the budget". A report along these lines would go to the busy sponsor, who would make a mental note that the project was going well, and would think no more about it. However, the actual situation might not be so rosy. The facts might look like this:

- $2 million is half of the total budget of $4 million, and it was expected that 50% of the work would have been done.
- But, actually only 30% of the work has been done.
- Meanwhile, the project has spent 45% of the budget (100 × 1.8/4.0).

So, is the project on schedule? No, way behind.

30% of the work has been done against a plan of 50%.

And, what about the costs? Way overspent.

45% of the budget has been spent to do 30% of the work.

The sponsor would probably only find out when the deadline had been missed with the real costs heading for over $6 million. It is easy to make this mistake. Indeed I was guilty of something similar over 25 years ago.

> *It was a medium-size project, fraught with problems, with a budget of $4 million (in present day terms). We were 3 months from the scheduled end date and had spent $3.2 million. Everyone, including the sponsor, knew that we were in trouble with no possibility of meeting the end date. But, from a budget perspective, all looked fine, and I did not report the certain overrun. As it happened, the deadline was moved out progressively, and eventually, 18 months later we finished at a cost of $8.5 million. Although I was not blamed for the overrun, it certainly taught me a lesson. The cost issue should have been highlighted.*

Since then, I've observed this issue several times. If EVM principles had been applied, both cost and schedule issues would have been reported early enough to address them.

As you will learn with EVM, everything is planned and tracked in terms of money – dollars. So, if we plan a project activity to train 50 people, and if we estimate that it will cost $16 000 to do that training, then, when the training is complete, we can say that the project has *earned* an additional $16 000. If the PM assessed the training as 50% complete, then the EV (earned value) for the training activity would be only $8 000 at that point.

What follows outlines how EVM works.

12.5 Earned Value Fundamentals

12.5.1 Three Key EVM Parameters

When applying EVM, we only look at three parameters, and all three are in money amounts. They are shown in Figure 12.1.

The three values are always considered at a point in time – often the end of a month or a week.

- **EV (earned value)** is the most important, it comes into all calculations. It is a measure of what has been achieved at a point in time.
- **PV (planned value)** is what we planned to achieve at that point. Suppose that, by a specified date, say 30 April, we planned to achieve a value of $230 000, and we have already estimated the EV to be $250 000. Then, we have a positive schedule variance of $20 000 and are ahead of schedule.
- **AC (actual cost)** is what we have actually spent on achieving the EV. Some adjustments may be needed as payments to suppliers are not always synchronized with the performance of the work. So, suppose that on the date mentioned above, 30 April, the adjusted AC for the work is $260 000, then we have spent more than we planned, in achieving the EV of $250 000, and the cost variance is *minus* $10 000 indicating that we are slightly over-spent.

Figure 12.1 shows that comparing EV with PV indicates how we are performing from a schedule point of view, while comparing EV with AC indicates how things are going from a cost point of view. Very important to note that comparing AC with PV is meaningless! This is the mistake made in the earlier example, when saying that with PV of $2 million and AC of $1.8 million, the project is on track.

We now also understand what it means for a project to be 'on track'. It means that both the schedule and cost variances are zero or positive. A project might also be considered on track if one or both variances are slightly negative, but for reasons

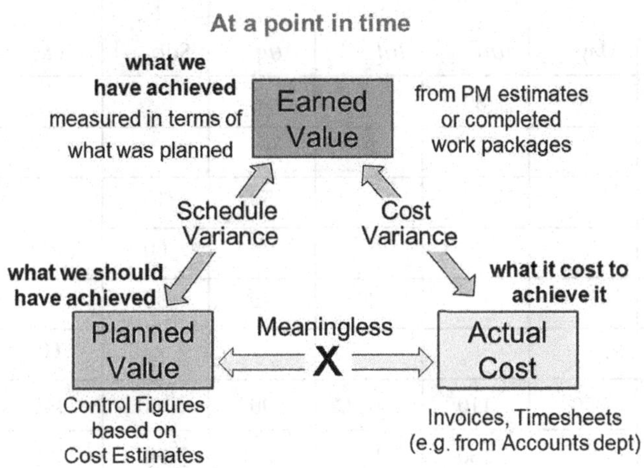

Figure 12.1 Triangle of parameters used in EVM.

that are understood and accepted by the sponsor. Another important point: It is entirely possible to have a negative schedule variance but a positive cost variance, or vice versa; in other words, the PM needs to know where things stand regarding *both* schedule and cost.

Thus far we have said very little about where the EV, PV, and AC data come from. They will be explained in the coming sections. PV comes first, as it is estimated during planning.

12.5.2 Producing a Time-Phased Budget for the Project to Get the PVs

If we wish to use EVM to track the schedule and costs for a project, we first need to plan what *should* happen – otherwise, we have nothing to measure against. So we need a time-phased budget that results in PVs (planned values). Table 12.1 illustrates how this might be done for a small project. The planned activities have been grouped into higher-level WBS packages A to F. The costs for each such package have been estimated, and a schedule has been produced with the project ending in November.

The timeframe of the project is indicated by the columns. Here we have shown it in months, but it could equally be done in weeks. (Weeks would give a finer level of control but would be more work). The packages are given in the rows. Once again you, the PM, can work at any level of detail. However, for a business project, one would not want too much detail for the budget – the detail can be managed via the schedule and task lists. Next, the estimated costs would be slotted in. Suppose that package A is estimated at $130 000 and should start in May, then based on the detail, you might estimate that $50 000 would be spent in May and $80 000 in June when activities in the package end. The same approach is taken for packages B through F. The numbers show when things are planned to happen. The actual Gantt chart for tracking the work would have more detail. The cost items are totaled horizontally

Table 12.1 Cost Planning Spreadsheet (Figures Are in Thousands of Dollars)

Activity Cost Items	*May*	*Jun*	*Jul*	*Aug*	*Sep*	*Oct*	*Nov*	*Total*
Package A	50	80						130
Package B		30	70					100
Package C				50	10			60
Package D					60	80	20	160
Package E			20	40	30			90
Package F						60	10	70
Total per month	50	110	90	90	100	140	30	610
Cumulative total	50	160	250	340	440	580	610	

to the right-hand column, and summing these totals downward gives the total cost of 610 which means $610 000. The costs in each month are totaled downward. For example, September has 10+60+30 = 100. The cumulative totals can then be calculated:

- May is 50 – same as the first month's total.
- June is 50 (from May) + 110 = 160.
- July is 160 (from June) + 90 = 250
- August is 250 (from July) + 90 = 340 and so on.

Not surprisingly, the cumulative total at end of November is 610 which should be the same as the total in the right-hand column. This serves as a check and balance because if they are not the same, then there is an error somewhere. The project's budget is therefore $610 000.

Typically, this exercise would be done on an Excel spreadsheet. The cumulative figures would become the PVs (or control figures) at the end of each month. For example, if the work is being completed as per the schedule, then the PM would expect to have spent about $340 000 at the end of August, so $340 000 is the PV for end-August. Note that everything here is an estimate: the times, the costs, and even the activities. So precision might be misleading, and an estimate of $57 803 might be shown as $58 000. We definitely do not want cents!

Here, I suggest that you do Case 16 which asks you to use a similar technique to estimate the PVs for a project that involves communications for a government department.

12.5.3 Tracking the Project as It Progresses

While we can estimate the PVs during planning, the EVs and ACs can only be determined when the project is underway. Let us illustrate how the figures are used with a very simple example, illustrated in Figure 12.2.

The project has just three high-level packages A, B, and C. The estimates of the PVs for each package and for the overall project are shown in Table 12.2.

The package budgets are given in the 2nd column which amount to 110 ($ thousands), the total project budget. Let us now consider a particular date of 19 April (not necessarily a month-end) when tracking will be done. Supposing that, on 19 April, the PM's cost planning spreadsheet indicates that A should be finished, B should

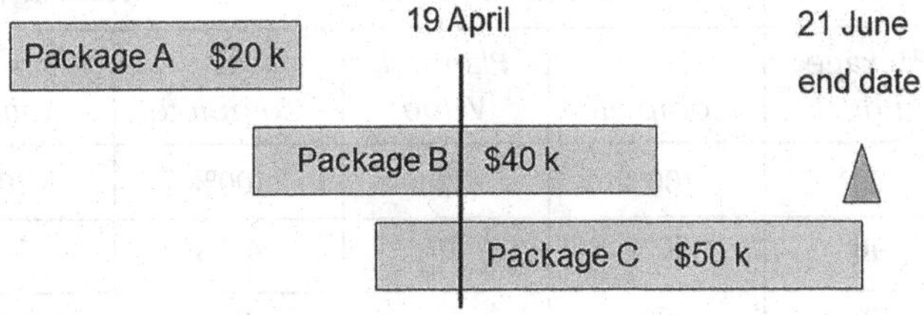

Figure 12.2 Simple project to illustrate EVM ('k' means thousands).

Table 12.2 Estimate PV from the Initial Plan (Figures in Thousands of Dollars)

From Project Plan		*Plan at 19 April*		*Actual at 19 April*		
Package	*Package Budget*	*% Complete*	*Planned Value*	*% Complete*	*Earned Value*	*Actual Cost*
A	20	100%	20			
B	40	50%	20			
C	50	20%	10			
Total	110		50			

be 50% complete, and C should be 20% complete. These figures are reflected in the Planned Value (PV) column:

- A, which should be complete has a PV of 20 (same as the package budget).
- B should be 50% complete, so its PV is 50% of 40 = 20.
- C should be 20% complete, so its PV is 20% of 50 = 10.

Adding them up gives a PV for the entire project at 50 on 19 April.

This reflects the plan. Let us see in Table 12.3 what has actually happened at 19 April.

The PM's estimates indicate that A is indeed complete, but that B stands at 45% complete and C at 28% complete. Hence the PM can calculate the Earned Value (EV) of each.

- A, being complete, has an EV of 20.
- B has an EV of 45% of 40 =18 (slightly behind the 20 planned)
- C has an EV of 28% of 50 = 14 (well ahead of the 10 planned).

Adding them up gives the EV for the entire project at 52 on 19 April. So, because the EV of 52 is higher than the PV of 50, we conclude that overall the project is slightly ahead of schedule. But what about the cost aspect? A few days later based

Table 12.3 EV from Estimated Percentage Complete (Figures in Thousands of Dollars)

From Project Plan		*Plan at 19 April*		*Actual at 19 April*		
Package	*Package Budget*	*% Complete*	*Planned Value*	*% Complete*	*Earned Value*	*Actual Cost*
A	20	100%	20	100%	20	
B	40	50%	20	45%	18	
C	50	20%	10	28%	14	
Total	110		50		52	

Table 12.4 Bring in AC and Compare to EV (Figures in Thousands of Dollars)

From Project Plan		*Plan at 19 April*		*Actual at 19 April*		
Package	*Package Budget*	*% Complete*	*Planned Value*	*% Complete*	*Earned Value*	*Actual Cost*
A	20	100%	20	100%	20	25
B	40	50%	20	45%	18	18
C	50	20%	10	28%	14	13
Total	110		50		52	56

on time-sheet and other information the PM gets the Actual Cost (AC) data, shown in Table 12.4.

From the AC column on the right the PM notes the following:

- A has cost more than planned and has a variance of minus 5 (20 – 25)
- B's cost is exactly where it should be: The AC is equal to the estimated EV.
- C's cost is slightly lower (better) than expected with a variance of plus 1 (14 – 13).

Adding them up gives the AC for the entire project at 56 on 19 April. So because it is higher than the EV of 52 we conclude that the project is somewhat overspent.

12.5.4 EVM Formulae

Schedule performance can be expressed using EV and PV:

$$\text{As a variance: SV (schedule variance)} = \text{EV} - \text{PV}$$

$$\text{As an index: SPI (schedule performance index)} = \text{EV/PV}$$

Likewise, cost performance can be expressed using EV and AC:

$$\text{As a variance: CV (cost variance)} = \text{EV} - \text{AC}$$

$$\text{As an index: CPI (cost performance index)} = \text{EV/AC}$$

These formulae need to be remembered and note that they all require the EV. In other words, if we have not estimated the work achieved, we cannot report meaningfully on the project. Also, variances and indexes can be calculated either at package or at project level.

For small and medium business projects, I generally track at project level and prefer the indexes. When considering the example given in Table 12.4, the indexes are as follows:

$$\text{SPI} = \text{EV/PV} = 52/50 = 1.04$$

and

$$CPI = EV/AC = 52/56 = 0.93$$

Two decimal points are sufficient because we are working with estimates, and do not want to imply accuracy that is not there. Indexes above 1 are favorable (like positive variances), while indexes below 1 are unfavorable (like negative variances). So in the example, an SPI of 1.04 says that we are slightly ahead of schedule, while a CPI of 0.93 indicates that we are somewhat overspent. Generally, indexes above 0.9 are not cause for great concern, but may need to be looked into.

Once the project has been running for a while, the CPI can help to forecast the EAC (estimate at completion) cost. It is done on the assumption that the CPI will remain unchanged through to the end of the project. The formula is:

$$EAC = \text{total budget}/CPI$$

For the above example given in Table 12.2, the budget is 110. Therefore, we can estimate the EAC = 110/0.93 = 118 (or $118 000). If later in the project, the CPI were to deteriorate, then the EAC would need to be recalculated. There are two methods of estimating the percentage complete.

- Method 1 is based on EV and total budget.
  Percent complete = EV/total budget
  Example: total budget = $100 000 and EV = $40 000 then,
  Percent complete = 40/100 = 40% complete
- Method 2 is based on AC and ETC (estimate to complete)
  First calculate EAC (estimate at completion) = AC + ETC
  Percent complete = AC/EAC
  Example: AC = $45 000 and ETC = $80 000, then EAC = 45k + 80k = $125 000, and
  Percent complete = 45k/125k = 36% complete – where 'k' indicates thousands.

Here is a simple example to illustrate the use of the above formulae. Consider a project which is scheduled to finish in July at a budgeted cost of $8.0 million. On 12 March, the PM has the following figures: PV = $4, 7 million, EV = $3.8 million, and AC is $3.7 million. Calculate the schedule and cost variances as well as the schedule and cost performance indexes. Based on earned value, estimate the percentage completion at 12 March. Also, estimate the likely EAC of the project. Comment on what the numbers mean. Answers:

SV = EV–PV = 3.8–4.7 = –$0.9 million; SPI = 3.8/4.7 = 0.81
CV = EV–AC = 3.8–3.7 = + $0.1 million; CPI = 3.8/3.7 = 1.03
Based on EV, the % completion = EV/budget at completion = 3.8/8.0 = 47.5%.
Based on CPI the EAC = budget/CPI = 8.0/1.03 = $7.8 million.
The numbers indicate that we are well behind schedule, but slightly underspent for the amount of work done.

12.6 Where Does the EVM Data Come From?

We have already seen that PVs (planned values) come from a time-phased budget, as shown in Table 12.1, done during planning. What about the AC (actual cost) and EV (earned value)?

12.6.1 Actual Cost

AC is usually more straightforward. Costs are tracked by the PM or a project administrator based on timesheets for people and from payments to suppliers. Sometimes costs are recorded outside of the project and notified to the PM regularly, in which case checking is essential. Mistakes are often made and the project could be charged for people that have not worked on the project, or for an invoice payment that belongs to another project. Already at estimating time, the PM needs to know which costs will be charged to the project. For example, will certain business stakeholders charge their hours? Whatever the case, the PM may need a spreadsheet to track costs. A further complication is that cost recording may be out of step with the work done or materials used. Most things are billed long after the goods or services that result in EV, are provided. But, sometimes suppliers demand some payment in advance. Both situations would result in adjustments to the AC figures, as the PM needs a realistic cost for the work actually achieved.

12.6.2 Earned Value

EV is difficult to estimate. For a business project, it would be based on the PM's percentage completion estimates for work packages or activities. Considerable discipline and judgment are needed by the PM as people often report very optimistically. It is common for a team member to report something as 90% complete, when asking questions would show that it is 60% complete at best. Construction-type projects sometimes use an algorithm like crediting half the EV when an activity is started, and the other half when it is completed, but I have never seen this used for a business project.

As mentioned earlier, all these estimates can be done at project level, or any level below. For most business projects, it is difficult to track costs below project level, because much of the cost is for peoples' time, which is spread across the multiple activities that they are involved in. Splitting the time by activity would be time-consuming.

12.7 Understanding EVM and the 'S' Curve

Although EVM formulae are relatively simple, the meaning of the numbers takes a while to understand. The best way is through practice. So by going through Cases 17 through 20 you will be better equipped to apply EVM in a variety of situations. It is suggested that you do the exercises, then look at the answers, and then days later repeat them, maybe even several times, until it becomes quick and easy.

One more vitally important consideration. EVM does not monitor the project's critical path. If a PM were to allow work on large, non-critical activities, EV could be credited. The project might look good from an EVM perspective, but the project could still be delayed if the critical path were neglected. So the PM needs to be aware of both EVM and the critical path.

EVM parameters can be tracked graphically as shown in Figure 12.3, with costs on the vertical scale and time going from left to right.

The starting point is the dark gray curve, the PV, which is already estimated during planning. The curve starts rising slowly because most of the resources are not planned to be on board yet. As execution gets underway, many resources will be involved and the costs rise more rapidly. Then toward the end, when people are planned to start moving on, the curve flattens again – giving a shape that somewhat resembles an 'S' shape. Where an S curve is produced for a real project, it might not be as smooth as the one in the figure. As the actual project moves ahead the EV and AC can be plotted at specific points in time. In Figure 12.3, at the 'now' point, shown by the thick arrow, we go up vertically and plot the EV and AC, giving rise to the black EV curve and the pale gray AC curve. In the case illustrated, the project is behind schedule and seriously overspent. Now one can visually see the schedule variance and cost variance (both measured in money terms and related directly to the EV). If we look at the EV point (at the 'now' point) and move left, it is seen that the PV curve expected that value to have been achieved earlier. The horizontal distance gives some indication of the schedule delay.

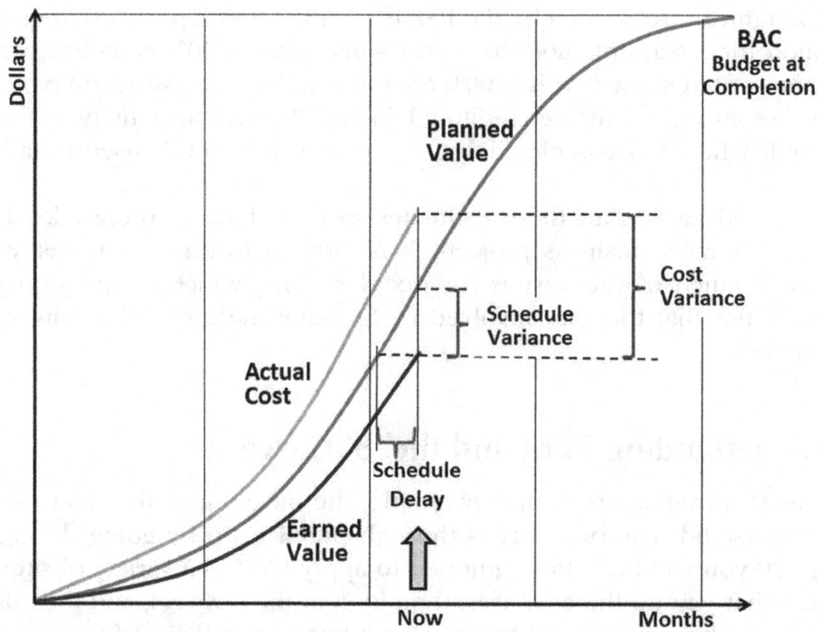

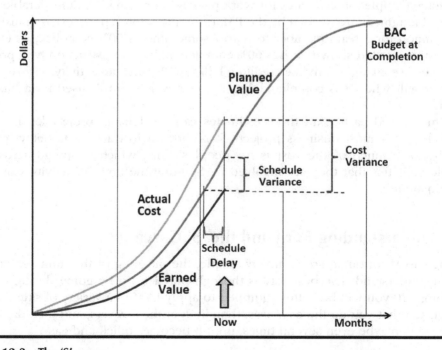

Figure 12.3 The 'S' curve.

12.8 Why Classical EVM Is Seldom Used for Business Projects – and a Solution

There are two aspects to EVM. The theory is totally valid. The practice, as described in textbooks (classical EVM), only works for certain types of projects, and certainly not for a typical business project. The reasons are given below and are followed by a description of PPTR (project progress tracker), a solution that honors EVM theory, but is easy to apply to a fast-moving business project (Einhorn, 2016). So what are the practical difficulties?

- Estimation of PVs requires us to understand the activities up-front. For most business projects a 'rolling wave' approach is taken, where later phases will only be detailed closer to execution.
- EVM is encouraged at activity or package level, requiring PV, EV, and AC to be estimated and tracked at a relatively low level. This may work for a large construction project where quantity surveyors estimate each package and where there are cost specialists to track the work. On most business projects the PM does not have time for such detail.
- Once the PVs have been estimated, it requires considerable effort to adjust for changes, and on a most business projects changes to activities happen frequently. It is also difficult to adjust if estimates are later found to be wrong.
- EVM uses money as the measurement. Activities must be assigned a PV in dollars (which becomes its EV when complete), and then its AC (actual cost) must be measured in dollars. This is problematic, even working with higher-level packages. One reason is that people are often working on many activities concurrently and, when recording, they may not remember to which packages to allocate their time.
- With EVM one cannot weight packages. A small, critical, high-risk activity gets low value (PV and EV) while a large, straightforward activity, possibly with high-cost procured items, gets high value. This can distort the status and take focus away from what is really important. So, dollars may not be the best measure for a business project.

While EVM may work satisfactorily for construction projects, the above difficulties are borne out by my observation that classical EVM is never used for business projects. It is simply too much effort; stakeholders and issues rightly take priority. However, the EVM concepts are fundamental, and without them, it is difficult for the PM to know the status of the project, let alone report on it. The result is that misreporting is common.

Fortunately, there are probably many solutions to these difficulties. The answer lies in a form of the Pareto principle, where 80% of the benefit is achieved with 20% of the effort. One such solution, called PPTR, is even better. I believe that it achieves *more* than 100% of the result with less than 10% of the effort, because classical EVM, due to its level of detail, is error-prone. Although PPTR is a simple technique, it requires some judgment, but the output is meaningful and representative of reality. PPTR works very differently from the textbook approach, yet it still uses the EVM concepts, so having studied EVM is not a waste of time.

Regarding cost: while tracking cost is important for most projects, there are some situations where it is not needed. Where most of the cost relates to a stable team of employees, and the PM has limited scope to bring in outside resources, the real cost is proportional to duration. The longer the project, the more it will cost. Here management will know that if deadlines are met, costs are unlikely to be of concern. Measuring progress toward the deliverables becomes the focus, and this is one of PPTR's strengths – measuring progress.

12.9 PPTR – Project Progress Tracker

The aim of PPTR is to give the PM, sponsor, and steering committee regular and reliable information on project status. It arose, over 20 years ago, when I was struggling to apply EVM on business projects. Since then, I've used it on every business project that I've managed, from very small ones to quite large ones. I have not found it, or anything similar in a textbook. PPTR works on HL (high-level) packages selected by the PM. For a typical small to medium business project, there might be about 20 HL packages representing hundreds of activities. The activities may change frequently, but the HL packages change much less. What follows is drawn from a paper that I presented at a conference in 2016.

12.9.1 The Starting Spreadsheet

The PPTR technique is done using a spreadsheet. It is illustrated below using an IT-business project, which goes through the typical phases from requirements gathering to go-live and early support. An existing computer application package will be extended to meet new business requirements, hence the project title is 'System Enhancement'. All dollar figures below are given in thousands of dollars. Thus $740 means $740 000 or $0.74 million. Figure 12.4 shows the starting spreadsheet reflecting a project start at around 10 May. The project end is indicated by the date at which the target percentage complete is 100, in this case, 18 October. The additional

10-May-22	PPTR - Project Progress Tracker																
Budget in $ thousands	740																
System Enhancement - Progress Chart			1, 2, 3		31-May		28-Jun		26-Jul		23-Aug		20-Sep		18-Oct		15-Nov
Package Description	Points	% Scope	Risk	%	Pt Earn	%	Pt Earn	%	Pt Earn	%	Pt Earn	%	Pt Earn	%	Pt Earn	%	Pt Earn
Planning, Managing, Tracking	11	8.9	1	0	0	0	0	0	0	0	0	0	0	0	0	0	0
Requirements definition	25	20.2	3	0	0	0	0	0	0	0	0	0	0	0	0	0	0
Systems design	16	12.9	2	0	0	0	0	0	0	0	0	0	0	0	0	0	0
Customize package application	22	17.7	1	0	0	0	0	0	0	0	0	0	0	0	0	0	0
Develop interfaces	15	12.1	1	0	0	0	0	0	0	0	0	0	0	0	0	0	0
System and User Test	25	20.2	1	0	0	0	0	0	0	0	0	0	0	0	0	0	0
Go live and support	10	8.1	2	0	0	0	0	0	0	0	0	0	0	0	0	0	0
Spare				0	0	0	0	0	0	0	0	0	0	0	0	0	0
Total	124	100			0		0		0		0		0		0		0
Progress (estimated % complete)				Perc =	0.0	Perc =	0.0	Perc =	0.0	Perc =	0.0	Perc =	0.0	Perc =	0.0	Perc =	0.0
Targets (planned % complete)					10		25		50		75		90		100		100

Figure 12.4 The PPTR starting spreadsheet with no progress shown.

column (15 November) is added in case of an overrun, but it could easily have been added later.

The spreadsheet is flexible and can be tailored to suit any project environment. The total project budget is given at the top as $740 (thousands). It would be updated every time a scope change is approved. The HL (high-level) packages are given in the left-hand column. Here seven HL packages are shown. There would be far more activities at the lowest level, which would reflect in the schedule, but not in PPTR.

- The first HL package 'planning, managing, tracking', is the work involved in managing the project. It is a 'level of effort' package, which recognizes that there is ongoing work involved in managing the project – estimated at under 10% of the total project cost.
- Each HL package is assigned a number of points at the discretion of the project manager. The absolute number is not important, but the numbers should reflect the size, and difficulty of the package in relation to the others. Here 'systems design' is weighted at 16 points indicating that it is expected to be less effort than 'customizing package application' which is weighted at 22 points. The project manager might solicit input from the team to get representative numbers, and can change them at any time should an initial estimate be regarded as too high or low. The total is 124 points, which means that a notional PV for the 'system and user test' HL package, would be $740 × 25/124 = $149 (thousands). This notional PV might differ from what we plan to spend on the HL package, but it does not matter because we shall track cost at project level, and shall not estimate package PVs.
- The '% scope' column is optional. It indicates the percentage of the project for each HL package. So, for 'system design' it would be 100 × 16/124 = 12.9%.
- The risk column is also optional, but indicates where focus is needed. In the illustration, 'requirements definition' is given a high risk because the project manager knows that there are many stakeholders and that reaching consensus may be challenging. Because of this concern, the 25 points allocated is possibly on the high side – but the project manager prefers to be conservative.
- Moving to the right, there are two columns per tracking date. Here the dates are 4 weeks apart, but the project manager can use any tracking interval. The first column is the estimated percentage complete. The second column (points earned) is the multiplication of points and percentage. If requirements definition were estimated at 20% complete, then 25 points × 0.2 = 5 points would be deemed to have been earned.
- Instead of using PVs, targets are entered at the bottom, by 'planned % complete' for each tracking date. They apply to the entire project. The 25% for 28 June means that the PV is $740 × 0,25 = $185 (thousands of notional dollars). This differs from classical EVM where each PV would be calculated based on the schedule and the estimated dollar cost of each package. It may be observed that the targets given reflect the typical 'S curve' which applies to most projects. While the 100% target would coincide with the project end date, the target percentages are based on the project manager's judgment. For example, if there were to be a holiday period during the project, the targets would rise more slowly during that period.

Actual costs do not reflect on the spreadsheet. They could be produced by a corporate cost tracking system, or by the project manager based on hours and rates. For the PPTR method, actual costs would be recorded at project level, rather than at package level, which significantly reduces the amount of administrative effort. However, they must still be synchronized with the work done.

For a very large business project, one might break it down into major subprojects and apply PPTR separately to each subproject. Summing up would give progress for the entire project.

12.9.2 Monitoring Progress

Figure 12.5 gives the status on 31 May.

- There has been solid progress with 'requirements definition' which is now (conservatively) estimated at 50% complete, resulting in 12,5 points earned. To this are added the points for the project management work (deemed to be about 10% complete).
- The total points are 13.6 – giving percentage completion as 100 × 13,6/124 = 11%. This compares favorably with the planned 10%.
- To get a visual picture of where there is progress since the last tracking date, percentages that have increased are shaded (or colored green).

31-May-22	PPTR - Project Progress Tracker						
Budget in $ thousands	740						
System Enhancement - Progress Chart			1, 2, 3		31-May		28-Jun
Package Description	Points	% Scope	Risk	%	Pt Earn	%	Pt Earn
Planning, Managing, Tracking	11	8.9	1	10	1.1	0	0
Requirements definition	25	20.2	3	50	12.5	0	0
Systems design	16	12.9	2	0	0	0	0
Customize package application	22	17.7	1	0	0	0	0
Develop interfaces	15	12.1	1	0	0	0	0
System and User Test	25	20.2	1	0	0	0	0
Go live and support	10	8.1	2	0	0	0	0
Spare				0	0	0	0
Total	124	100			13.6		0
Progress (estimated % complete)				Perc =	11.0	Perc =	0.0
Targets (planned % complete)					10		25

Figure 12.5 PPTR update at 31 May.

15-Jul-22	PPTR - Project Progress Tracker								
Budget in $ thousands	740								15-Jul
System Enhancement - Progress Chart			1, 2, 3		31-May		28-Jun		26-Jul
Package Description	Points	% Scope	Risk	%	Pt Earn	%	Pt Earn	%	Pt Earn
Planning, Managing, Tracking	11	9.2	1	10	1.1	20	2.2	40	4.4
Requirements definition	20	16.8	3	50	10	90	18	100	20
Systems design	16	13.4	2	0	0	40	6.4	100	16
Customize package application	22	18.5	1	0	0	0	0	40	8.8
Develop interfaces	15	12.6	1	0	0	0	0	0	0
System and User Test	25	21.0	1	0	0	0	0	0	0
Go live and support	10	8.4	2	0	0	0	0	0	0
Spare				0	0	0	0	0	0
Total	119	100			11.1		26.6		49.2
Progress (estimated % complete)				Perc =	9.3	Perc =	22.4	Perc =	41.3
Targets (planned % complete)					10		25		50
	reduce points for requirements definition								

Figure 12.6 PPTR update at 15 July, before the next tracking date of 26 July.

Figure 12.6 gives the status on 15 July, just over 6 weeks later.

- The 'requirements definition' is complete and approved. The project manager is relieved that the anticipated problems did not materialize and reduces the points from 25 to 20 to give a more realistic reflection of the effort expended. Reducing the points also reduces the points earned (to 20) and the total points for the project (to 119). It also affects the '% scope' column, but, the spreadsheet recalculates it automatically.
- The project manager is satisfied that the 41.3% completion (100% × 49.2/119) is now conservative. Although the 41.3% is well below the 26 July target of 50%, this is not too serious because 26 July is still more than a week away.

Figure 12.7 gives the status at 26 July.

- The estimate has improved to 44.5% complete (100% × 52.9/119), but this is still below the target of 50%, and might serve as an early warning.

Figure 12.8 gives the status at 23 August.

- The two completed HL packages are no longer shaded as they reached 100% at the previous tracking date. The 'planning, managing, tracking' HL package has been increased to 70% to reflect the approximate progress. 'Interface development' is well advanced, and testing is underway.

26-Jul-22			PPTR - Project Progress Tracker						
Budget in $ thousands	740								
System Enhancement - Progress Chart			1, 2, 3		31-May		28-Jun		26-Jul
Package Description	Points	% Scope	Risk	%	Pt Earn	%	Pt Earn	%	Pt Earn
Planning, Managing, Tracking	11	9.2	1	10	1.1	20	2.2	40	4.4
Requirements definition	20	16.8	3	50	10	90	18	100	20
Systems design	16	13.4	2	0	0	40	6.4	100	16
Customize package application	22	18.5	1	0	0	0	0	50	11
Develop interfaces	15	12.6	1	0	0	0	0	10	1.5
System and User Test	25	21.0	1	0	0	0	0	0	0
Go live and support	10	8.4	2	0	0	0	0	0	0
Spare				0	0	0	0	0	0
Total	119	100			11.1		26.6		52.9
Progress (estimated % complete)				Perc =	9.3	Perc =	22.4	Perc =	44.5
Targets (planned % complete)					10		25		50

Figure 12.7 PPTR update at 26 July.

23-Aug-22			PPTR - Project Progress Tracker								
Budget in $ thousands	740										
System Enhancement - Progress Chart			1, 2, 3		31-May		28-Jun		26-Jul		23-Aug
Package Description	Points	% Scope	Risk	%	Pt Earn	%	Pt Earn	%	Pt Earn	%	Pt Earn
Planning, Managing, Tracking	11	9.2	1	10	1.1	20	2.2	40	4.4	70	7.7
Requirements definition	20	16.8	3	50	10	90	18	100	20	100	20
Systems design	16	13.4	2	0	0	40	6.4	100	16	100	16
Customize package application	22	18.5	1	0	0	0	0	50	11	100	22
Develop interfaces	15	12.6	1	0	0	0	0	10	1.5	80	12
System and User Test	25	21.0	1	0	0	0	0	0	0	20	5
Go live and support	10	8.4	2	0	0	0	0	0	0	0	0
Spare				0	0	0	0	0	0	0	0
Total	119	100			11.1		26.6		52.9		82.7
Progress (estimated % complete)				Perc =	9.3	Perc =	22.4	Perc =	44.5	Perc =	69.5
Targets (planned % complete)					10		25		50		75

budget x target % complete	PV	555
budget x estimated % complete	EV	514
from invoices etc.	AC	580
	SPI	0.927
	CPI	0.887

Figure 12.8 PPTR update at 23 August with earned value parameters.

EVM information can be produced at any tracking date. The block at the bottom of the figure shows the method applied to 23 August. While the AC is in real dollars, the PV and EV are in notional dollars.

- Three figures are needed for a report at project level:

  PV = the budget of $740 × target % complete of 75% = $555.
  EV = $740 × estimated % complete of 69,5 % = $514.
  AC of $580 is obtained from cost records.

- The SPI (Schedule Performance Index) of about 0.93 (EV/PV) indicates that the project is somewhat behind schedule.
- The CPI (Cost Performance Index) of 0,89 (EV/AC) indicates that the EV achieved has cost $66 (thousand) more than planned.
- The project manager might in the next report warn that the project cost at completion is expected to rise to $740/0,887 = $834 – assuming that the CPI stays around 0,887.

Figure 12.9 gives the status on 03 September.

- Testing problems have emerged, and the project manager decides that the 20% previously reported for 'system and user test' was too optimistic, and reduces it to 15% – shaded dark (or colored pink) for negative progress. Although the 'develop interfaces' HL package is complete, most of the gain is negated by the reduction in the percentage for testing.
- A user request for training is approved as a change. An additional $40 (thousands) is approved, taking the project budget to $780. The end date moved out by 4 weeks, so the target completion for 18 October is reduced from 100% to 95%. The project manager assigns 8 points to the user training task, taking the total points to 127.

03-Sep-22	PPTR - Project Progress Tracker														
Budget in $ thousands	780										03-Sep				
System Enhancement - Progress Chart			1, 2, 3		31-May		28-Jun		26-Jul		23-Aug		20-Sep		18-Oct		15-Nov
Package Description	Points	% Scope	Risk	%	Pt Earn	%	Pt Earn	%	Pt Earn	%	Pt Earn	%	Pt Earn	%	Pt Earn	%	Pt Earn
Planning, Managing, Tracking	11	8.7	1	10	1.1	20	2.2	40	4.4	70	7.7	75	8.25	0	0	0	0
Requirements definition	20	15.7	3	50	10	90	18	100	20	100	20	100	20	0	0	0	0
Systems design	16	12.6	2	0	0	40	6.4	100	16	100	16	100	16	0	0	0	0
Customize package application	22	17.3	1	0	0	0	0	50	11	100	22	100	22	0	0	0	0
Develop interfaces	15	11.8	1	0	0	0	0	10	1.5	80	12	100	15	0	0	0	0
System and User Test	25	19.7	1	0	0	0	0	0	0	20	5	15	3.75	0	0	0	0
User training	8	6.3	1									0	0	0	0	0	0
Go live and support	10	7.9	2	0	0	0	0	0	0	0	0	0	0	0	0	0	0
Spare				0	0	0	0	0	0	0	0	0	0	0	0	0	0
Total	127	100			11.1		26.6		52.9		82.7		85		0		0
Progress (estimated % complete)				Perc=	8.7	Perc =	20.9	Perc=	41.7	Perc=	65.1	Perc =	66.9	Perc=	0.0	Perc=	0.0
Targets (planned % complete)					10		25		50		75		86		95		100

Figure 12.9 PPTR update at 03 September, before the next tracking date of 20 September.

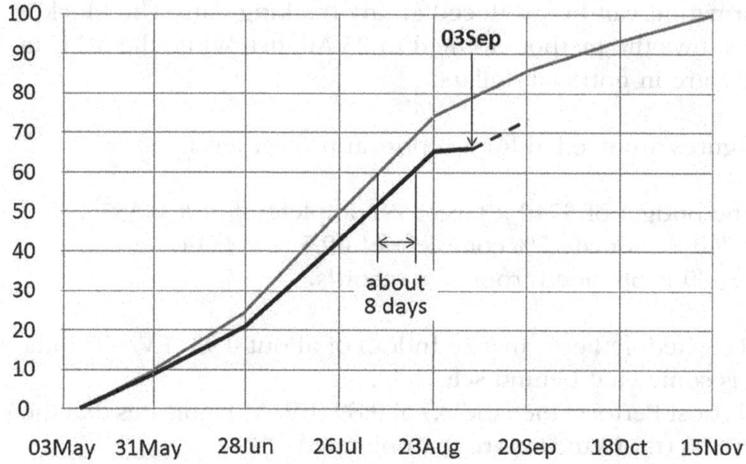

Figure 12.10 Chart drawn from PPTR showing actual versus plan as percentages.

12.9.3 Looking at Progress Graphically

Figure 12.10 shows the 03 September figures graphically, and this can be done automatically from the PPTR spreadsheet.

Some interpretation is needed. Up to the previous tracking date of 23 August, there is a small but steady negative schedule deviation from the plan. This suggests that, in the absence of additional information, there is no clear cause; it is even possible that the initial schedule was too optimistic. From the chart, it can be seen that around 23 August, the project was roughly 8 working days behind schedule. The figure at 03 September breaks the trend for two reasons. First, there were testing problems which impact both schedule and cost performance. Second, there are still more than 2 weeks to the tracking date. So, at 20 September, the graph can be expected to look better (shown by the dashed line), but nevertheless about 4 weeks behind schedule. Close monitoring is needed, and the changed situation should be reported.

12.9.4 Further Thoughts on PPTR

Supposing that, when using PPTR, a critical and challenging deadline, close to the end of the project, is looming. Here, the current points-earned can be subtracted from the total points for each HL package to give the points outstanding for incomplete HL packages. The remaining work should then be examined and decisions taken as to what work might be 'de-scoped' entirely, or at least postponed until after the critical deadline, with sponsor concurrence.

It might occur to you that PPTR points are similar to Agile 'user story points'. Yes, there are similarities, but also differences. For example, PPTR points are given to diverse HL packages that may require disciplines that differ from one another, and where all must be completed (unless de-scoping is approved). Story points relate to planned or completed functionality using similar skills. Their purpose is to determine what the team can reasonably take on in a given time, based on their historical story points delivery rate.

The above PPTR description indicates how, on an ongoing basis, figures are arrived at. It also shows how the PM might react to the output, and what information would be reported to the sponsor and other stakeholders.

12.9.5 Benefits of Using PPTR

In my experience, there are many benefits to using PPTR. Here they are:

- Creation of the PPTR spreadsheet is quick. The main information items needed are the HL packages, and an estimate of their weighting points. Detailed estimating is not essential, as points can be revised at any time.
- Tracking of the project is quick. All that is needed is information on the progress of currently active HL packages. A typical update might take a few minutes, and can be done at any time – not just at tracking dates.
- There is considerable flexibility. Points can be revised at any time, and HL packages can be added or removed. While sound planning is encouraged, for most business projects regular changes are inherent. PPTR is suitable for these, and also for projects where 'rolling wave' planning is used.
- 'What-if' analysis is easy. For example, the project manager might move a particular HL package to 100% to see what effect it would have on overall completion.
- While cost tracking requires the AC at each tracking date, the estimate is at project level. This is considerably easier than gathering costs at package or activity level, as encouraged when using classical EVM.
- HL packages involving large capital expenditure do not skew the picture because the cost is not the measure. For example, an HL package, estimated at $100 000 to commission a $5 million piece of equipment, would be assigned points that relate to the effort, complexity, and risk. The $5 million capital cost would be managed separately.

12.9.6 Things to Be Aware of When Using PPTR

- As a PM, you need sound judgment and a high-level understanding of all aspects of the project. Results might be misleading if PPTR is used by someone lacking experience.
- The method relies on integrity. It would be easy for a PM to deliberately mislead, by assigning too many points for HL packages already completed, or for crediting more progress than has actually been achieved.
- PPTR gives the status at project level. It does not drill down to package detail as might be done using classical EVM. To analyze deviations and take appropriate action, you would talk to people involved and gather necessary detail. This should not be difficult if you are holding regular tracking meetings and managing risks and issues.
- With PPTR, as with classical EVM, it is still necessary to monitor the critical path of the schedule. Progress on non-critical activities enhances percentage completion, but neglecting critical activities is likely to result in missed deadlines.

12.9.7 Suggestions and Tips When Using PPTR

- The value of PPTR is enhanced by involving the project team and other stakeholders. Besides producing sound tracking information, healthy discussion on the HL packages and their points allocation is likely to build team spirit and surface issues early.
- Be conservative, and err on the side of reporting less progress, especially for risky HL packages. Likewise, HL package points should be revised as soon as it is clear that they are over or under-stated.
- It might be useful to keep notes of reasons for changes to point weightings. These could be useful if stakeholders are uncomfortable with your use of discretion and you need to justify your progress estimates.
- It is sometimes helpful to look at past statuses. Therefore, I suggest that you save a dated version after each revision. Each spreadsheet is only about 20 Kbytes, so the volume will not be excessive. If a name like 'Project X PPTR 220920' were used, where the digits represent the date, then the versions, sorted by name, would appear in date sequence, with the most recent at the bottom.

12.10 Closing Thoughts

EVM has two parts, namely schedule tracking and cost tracking, which can be used independently (Brandon, 1998). Depending on the priorities, cost may be more important than schedule or vice versa. Sometimes both are important, Because PPTR gives input on EV, it can effectively be used for either cost or schedule tracking, or for both.

The term 'corrective action' is often glibly mentioned in project management literature, implying that, where you are behind schedule or overspent, action can be taken to still complete the project within the original time and budget. In my experience, this is seldom possible. Usually, the best one can do is to prevent things from getting further out of line. But, what is of benefit is to advise the sponsor of the current and projected variances and what is being done about them. This sets expectations and allows timely decision making.

References

Brandon, D. M. (1998). Implementing Earned Value Easily and Effectively. *Project Management Journal*, June 1998.

Einhorn, F. (2016). Earned Value does not work for most projects - but this does ! Paper presented at the PMSA Conference 2016, Johannesburg.

PMI. (2017). *PMBOK - Guide to the Project Management Body of Knowledge*, 6th edition: Pennsylvania, USA: Project Management Institute.

Chapter 13

Project Teams and Organization

People remain the most important aspect of a project and having an effective team is something to be striven toward. The characteristics of a team are outlined, together with its potential benefits to its members and to the organization. The process of building a team is discussed as well as potential inhibitors. The possible use of a team charter is given. The Tuckman model gives insight by presenting the five stages that a team might go through during the course of a project. Awareness is created of common team member behaviors – mostly desirable, but some that may need to be curbed. The characteristics of a high-performance team are summarized.

An overview of four common project organization structures (functional, matrix, projectized, and Agile) is presented indicating their merits and limitations, and hence the types of project to which they are suited. Next, the project manager's activities are outlined – to acquire the right people, assign responsibilities, and create a climate that will motivate them to perform. The project manager's sources of power are explored while contrasting the 'managing style' with the 'facilitating style'.

13.1 Introduction and Objectives

Despite all the technology and techniques associated with project management, people still remain the most important aspect. If the people are not committed and motivated, the most promising project will struggle. We have already covered stakeholders in Chapter 5. Here, we expand on the team that will do the work and the management structures around them. For many reasons, it may not be possible to build an ideal 'high performance' team. Rather it is something to strive toward and this chapter gives some guidance. The objectives are to:

- Know what makes a group of people a team, and how teams can benefit both individuals and the organization.

DOI: 10.1201/9781003321101-15

- Understand how teams develop, and the role that the PM needs to play.
- Create awareness of positive and negative team member behaviors.
- Know the ways that projects are done in organizations and their pros and cons.
- Know the PM's people responsibilities, and how motivation develops.
- Consider the PM's sources of power and what works best for business projects.

13.2 What Is Meant by 'a team' in the Project Context?

At one large Australian organization where I consulted, in the foyer of the head office, was the notice 'TEAM stands for Together Everyone Achieves More'. They took teamwork seriously and indeed it paid off. So, what is a team? Katzenbach & Smith (1993) provide a useful definition. A team is:

- A small number of people;
- With complementary skills;
- Who are committed to: a common purpose, with common performance goals, and a common approach;
- For which they hold themselves mutually accountable.

And conversely, a team is not any group of people brought together because they have similar skills or for administrative convenience. Let us consider the criteria for a team further.

How many is a small number of people? At the low end, anything more than one. Two people can collaborate and produce better answers than either one of them individually. At the high end, opinions vary. Between 5 and 7 is considered ideal, but above 10 one often finds that more than one team develops – which need not be a bad thing either. In practice, the number of people on a project will depend on the scope and often team members are part time. So, for business projects, it is quite possible for multiple teams to form, and a person may be a member of different teams concurrently (including teams outside the project).

What is meant by complementary skills? For an easy task, it is possible to find a single person that can do it alone. For a complex project, it is unlikely that one person has all the knowledge and skills. So to succeed, we need a team that, between the people, has all the skills needed, and by implication, they need to communicate with each other. So, where the group can work together, each contributing their own skills, to create something greater than any of them could have done individually, the skills build on each other and are complementary. This will happen most easily if a team is co-located. But with videoconferencing technology, it is quite possible for members to be in different locations or to do some of the work from home.

Having a common purpose sounds obvious, but each person in the group is likely to have their own agenda. So for them to become a team, the group needs to understand how they will each benefit from attaining the project's objectives. Much of their motivation comes from their contribution toward achieving something significant.

Finally, mutually accountable is an attitude which says "we are responsible, and we either succeed together, or fail together". Teams may, but do not always form naturally. Some things are beyond the PM's control because often the PM cannot choose the team. But, for any given situation it will become apparent, that the PM has much influence over whether effective teams form, or do not.

13.3 How Can Effective Teams Benefit Organizations and Individuals?

When people work cooperatively, it usually benefits everyone. This is especially so when people are brought together and can form a team. Where this happens, the organization benefits through increased creativity, productivity, and quality – quality because team members do not want to let the team down by producing substandard work. Provided that a variety of disciplines are represented there is likely to be better problem solving because of the broader input to the solution, often leading to better decisions. The individuals benefit because responsibility is shared and there are always people to discuss problems with, which for most members makes the work less stressful. There can be a greater feeling of self-worth because team members' contributions are appreciated by their peers. This is augmented where team members can learn from each other and broaden their own capabilities. Working in teams, there is often a sense of accomplishment because of the importance of what is produced with rewards and recognition being shared among the team. So overall, effective teams lead to higher morale which is in the interests of the individuals, the project, and ultimately the organization.

13.4 How Does the PM Build a Team?

13.4.1 About Team Building

First: what is team building? Team building is the process of transforming a group of individuals who may have different backgrounds, interests, and skills, into an integrated and effective working unit. Key to the process is creating awareness among the team that they are greater collectively than individually, and that better decisions are made through collaboration. Having fun together may be desirable, but does not necessarily build a team.

> *One of the most difficult situations that I experienced was, on a two year project, where two factions emerged with some animosity between them that sometimes hindered progress. A leader in the more difficult faction suggested to me that we go away for a day of 'team building'. This we did, and on that day there was considerable cohesiveness across the entire group. Unfortunately, as soon as we were back in the workplace the animosity continued.*

My lesson from the above experience is that the best teams are built on the job and that a fun day should be a reward for success rather than a way of fixing team problems. So, when building a team there is much for the PM to do, including some administrative tasks:

- Plan the skills and roles that will be needed. Negotiate for missing skills.
- Clearly define and communicate roles and responsibilities.
- Brief the team members and get their commitment, possibly by discussing the value of the project to the organization. An explanation from the sponsor or other respected business person can add credibility to the project's importance.
- Engage regularly with team members, one-on-one, to understand their backgrounds and personal needs, including what they hope to gain from the project. Hence, play a facilitating role in resolving any conflicts that arise.
- Establish a productive working environment, which may include office space, the right equipment, and procedures to follow.
- On an ongoing basis facilitate planning sessions, team meetings, and even celebrations, while subtly drawing attention to the contribution that each person makes.

But, doing these things is seldom easy, and there may be obstacles, the following being just a few examples:

- A high proportion of the team may be part-time and have other allegiances.
- Team members may have different values and incompatible styles of working.
- People may not communicate well, leading to confusion over roles and priorities.
- Upper management may not always be supportive and reasonable; changes to goals and priorities coming from them can be demotivating.
- Shortage of skills and support may cause frustration.

So even if the PM is doing an excellent job of building the team, there are usually challenges. PMs should not blame themselves for such problems, but need to continually work at making the best of the situation. Developing one or more experienced people as sounding boards often helps, and here a good sponsor can be a valuable advisor.

13.4.2 The Team Charter

One approach, to building the team is to, early-on, have the team produce a 'team charter' (PMI, 2017). The team are given an hour to debate their values in the context of the project and come up with the team charter – a list of around eight norms that they will expect each other to adhere to. Although some initial input may be needed, it is best if the PM is not a participant, lest the team charter be perceived as coming from management. Here are a few examples: We will:

- Put the sponsor's interests above our personal agendas;
- Share our knowledge and help others to be successful;
- Understand the other person's position before putting our needs across;
- Try to maintain a sense of humor, however tough the situation.

There are many such possible statements and while the output is important, much of the value is in the discussion that takes place. This is a true team-building activity!

13.4.3 The Tuckman Model for Team Development

The Tuckman model, developed in 1965, gives valuable insights into the challenges of building a team. Tuckman defines five stages that a team goes through during the project: Forming, Storming, Norming, Performing, and Adjourning (West Chester University, 2021). I shall describe them briefly:

- Forming. The project is new and there is often some confusion as to what must be done. The team members know little about each other. So, they may be polite, guarded, and somewhat impersonal. Some may 'test boundaries' by asserting themselves. This is where the PM needs to show leadership by communicating the common purpose, agreeing roles, and establishing a code of conduct. This stage seldom lasts long.
- Storming. Planning is underway and possibly some project execution has started. In a business project, the PM does not issue instructions on everything, but expects the team to display some initiative. This often leads to conflict among the team over control: Who decides what? Which way is best? Who should inform whom? Team members may seek status and power and attempt to create operating rules, sometimes leading to hostility and even open conflict. The PM needs to clarify roles and who should take the lead in which areas, as well as establish clear communications within the team so that everyone is informed. If this is well managed with a mature team, the Storming stage may hardly be noticeable; with difficult and disruptive individuals (often with good skills) some conflict may persist for far longer.
- Norming. The team now understand each other better and hostility reduces. There is more sharing of information. Trust and cooperation start to build, and norms develop. The team starts to develop an identity. The PM's role is now to ensure that the team's energy is directed toward achieving the project goals, and encouraging appropriate leadership from team members.
- Performing. The team now know and respect each other. Trust is established and the atmosphere is warm and informal. The team are conscious of their high productivity toward meeting project objectives. Members willingly cooperate and help each other. The PM's role is to support the team by facilitating communication, removing obstacles, and maintaining a productive environment.
- Adjourning. Every project comes to an end. The team feel positive about what they have achieved together. But they may have regrets that the working relationship will end or concerns about what comes next for them. People may even joke to deny their feelings. The PM now needs to give increased support to individuals which may involve discussion on what happens after the project.

Of course, on most business projects, the stages don't happen exactly as described. Often the team members will have worked together before and will continue their association after the project. Moreover, the stages may be even less pronounced where many members are part-time. Nevertheless, the Tuckman model helps the PM to understand what is going on and to use judgment as to whether and how to intervene.

13.4.4 The Benefits of Short-Term Objectives

Connie Gersick made a further observation in the late 1980s, that achievement is relatively slow until halfway toward the project deadline. At that midpoint, productivity ramps up possibly because people now realize that time is limited; productivity then continues at a higher level through to the end of the project. This is understandable because with a distant deadline, the mood is "there is still plenty of time". The PM can avoid this by ensuring that there are regular milestones for the team to strive toward that are visible to senior stakeholders. The Agile approach does this particularly well, with 'sprints' toward an objective that is typically only a few weeks away.

13.5 What Team Member Behaviors Should One Be Aware of?

In the 1980s, Meredith Belbin did extensive analysis on team roles and closely related to those roles are behaviors (Isaac & Carson, 2012). Although there are many ways of classifying team member behaviors, here I shall expand on just three behavior types. It is useful for the PM to be aware of them and what could lie behind the behaviors. So they may be classified into task-oriented, relations-oriented, and self-oriented behaviors. Task-oriented behaviors emphasize what the team needs to do to get the job done, and facilitate or coordinate making decisions. Relations-oriented behaviors emphasize the personal and relationship needs of the team, dealing with sentiments, viewpoints, and working together. Self-oriented behaviors are aimed at satisfying an individual's needs which could relate to identity, influence, power, and control. Let us look at these three behaviors in more detail by labeling the kinds of people that exhibit the behaviors, and accepting that a particular person may display several of the behaviors at different times

13.5.1 Task-Oriented Behaviors

- Initiators offer new ideas and suggest methods or strategies for moving ahead.
- Information givers offer relevant facts or thoughts pertinent to a current situation.
- Information seekers ask questions and clarify suggestions.
- Evaluators assess how the team is working together and question what other members are doing or suggesting.
- Coordinators coordinate team members' ideas, suggestions, and activities.
- Summarizers draw and state conclusions from team discussions.

13.5.2 Relations-Oriented Behaviors

- Communicators promote dialog between team members with participation by all.
- Encouragers give members the opportunity to contribute by welcoming their ideas; they accept and respond to the perspectives of others.

- Harmonizers reduce tension and resolve conflict by emphasizing areas of agreement and reconciling differences of opinion.
- Observers sense the mood and reflect it back for discussion; they share their own feelings about how things are going.
- Compromisers seek harmony by moving from their initial positions or by admitting mistakes.
- Standard setters seek mutually acceptable ways of interacting or doing things.

13.5.3 Self-Oriented Behaviors

- Blockers reject the views of the team and attempt to get their own way.
- Topic jumpers continually change the subject.
- Recognition seekers attempt to monopolize the discussion to gain attention.
- Dominators try to take over the discussion by interrupting the contribution of others.
- Dissenters resist decisions made by management and point out problems.
- Avoiders maintain an emotional distance from others, avoiding interaction or new ideas.

Some of the above behaviors are generally more desirable than others, and much depends on the circumstances. But what is important, is for the PM to recognize the behavior and assess the motivation behind it. Generally, the PM will not intervene, but occasionally, it may be necessary to encourage or discourage a behavior, or even to reign it in.

13.6 The High-Performance Team

Any project is more likely to be successful if the team works together effectively; this applies whether the team are dedicated full-time or have other responsibilities as well. Some indicators of a high-performance team are:

- A sense of purpose
- Trust and mutual respect
- Open communication
- Shared leadership
- Building on differences (backgrounds, cultures, skills)
- Effective working procedures
- Flexibility and adaptability
- Continuous learning

Some of these characteristics take time to develop and may not happen naturally. So especially for projects longer than 6 months, it may be worthwhile for the PM to put effort into fostering teamwork while still paying attention to the more technical aspects.

13.7 How Do Projects Fit into the Organization?

Let us now look at how projects are organized and led. There are many ways in which projects are managed in an organization, but four approaches are common. They are illustrated in Figure 13.1 and discussed in turn.

13.7.1 Functional Structure

Consider an organization that is broken into functions like Marketing and Production. Each function will have its own objectives and will have initiatives to meet them. Such projects, done almost entirely within the function or department, are considered to use a 'functional' organization. Almost all the team members would be drawn from that function and most would be part-time. A manager within the function would be asked to lead the project, probably on a part-time basis. This usually works well because specialists are available and most players have worked together before. But, there is one big limitation. It only caters to requirements contained in that function. An increasing number of business requirements cut across functional boundaries.

13.7.2 Matrix Structures

The matrix structure caters well to cross-functional requirements. As shown in Figure 13.1, Projects X, Y, and Z can draw resources from any of the functions. There are variations within the matrix environment. A 'weak matrix' structure would probably be for a small project, led by a coordinator with little formal authority, and having mainly part-time staff allocated from the functions. At the other end of the scale, a 'strong matrix' structure would be managed by a more experienced PM. It would have many full-time team members either from existing functions or brought in from outside the organization, thus allowing larger projects to be tackled. A balanced matrix structure falls somewhere in between. But, all matrix structures have advantages and disadvantages. Advantages are: (i) flexibility as to the types of project that can be undertaken, (ii) effective use of skilled people who may be allocated to

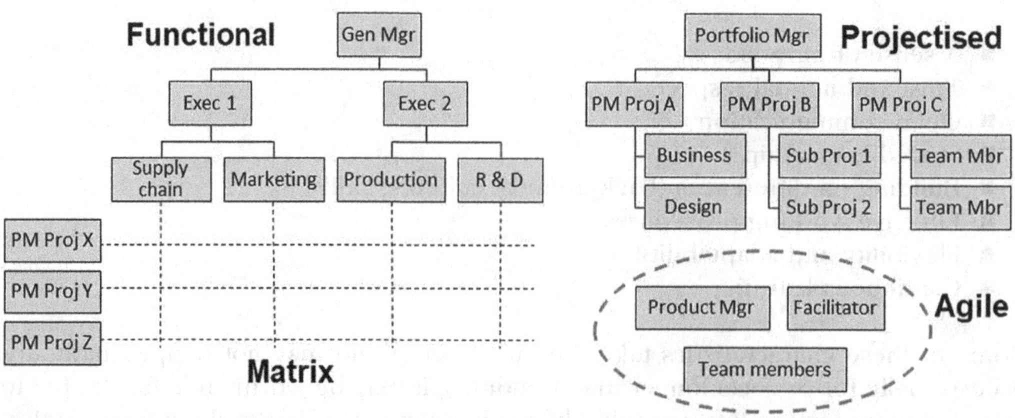

Figure 13.1 Organization structures for business projects.

several projects on an 'as required' basis, (iii) the learning that occurs when people from different disciplines work together. Disadvantages are: (i) Most project members report to a functional manager and also to the PM – known as the 'two boss syndrome'; sometimes it is difficult to please both, (ii) The PM needs to constantly negotiate for staff from the functions and then ensure that the work is getting the priority it deserves. The latter is difficult if the organization has taken on too many concurrent projects. Nevertheless, in the business world, often a matrix structure is the only one that is affordable and can meet the requirements. Some solutions to the difficulties are offered in Chapter 29 on dealing with business project realities.

13.7.3 Projectized Structure

This usually applies to part of an organization where the main mission is to deliver projects, often for external customers. The PM would have considerable autonomy and almost all resources would be dedicated. This structure is common for construction companies, but is also used where a powerful, multidisciplinary team is needed for the largest and most important business projects. There is less ongoing negotiation for skills, but sometimes scarce resources are not optimally used. For example, it can happen that one project is short of a skill, and another project has a person with the required skill, who is allocated to an activity that does not use the skill. A further problem is that when the project ends, people may not always be moved efficiently to the next project. Some organizations address this problem by having the skilled staff in a resource pool with a career manager to handle career paths and placement on projects.

13.7.4 Agile Structure

The Agile structure has some similarities to the projectized structure inasmuch as the team of technical people are dedicated and remain relatively stable. They are headed by a product owner and a facilitator rather than by a PM. The team would usually stay together when a project is completed and move on to another project. The product owner, essentially a business person, might change if a new business need were to be addressed. Agile is discussed further in Chapter 30.

13.8 How Should People Be Brought on Board, Motivated and Managed?

In business projects, most of the resources we deal with are people. First, the PM needs to acquire them, then enable them to be productive and at the same time satisfy their needs. This section will cover some of the main aspects at a high level.

13.8.1 Bringing People on Board (Resourcing) and Allocating Responsibilities

First one needs to understand what skills are needed for the project. This would be done concurrently with developing the project scope because the scope indicates the skills. For a large project, it might be desirable to tabulate the people requirements, and even draw up job descriptions which might include: title, main responsibilities, and then requirements in terms of skills, education, and experience (some essential, others desirable). The skills would be a combination of business, technical, and leadership. The latter is especially important on a larger project where subprojects need such leadership.

Finding the right people is one of the PM's most important responsibilities, and the approach may depend on the organization. Usually, the PM would first try to source the people internally by negotiating with HR and functional managers. Only if the right people cannot be found would the PM seek them outside, often through companies that offer contract staff.

When the resourcing process is well underway, and the scope well developed, the PM might draw up a RAM (responsibility assignment matrix), which would tabulate the alignment between the people and the scope. A RACI chart, shown in Table 13.1, is a commonly used format, RACI standing for Responsible, Accountable, Consulted, and Informed.

There are no hard-and-fast rules as to how a RACI chart should be used. It is there to help you as the PM, and often the thinking that goes into it is as useful as the chart itself. For a small project, it would be at project level, and for a larger one, it might be at subproject level. The meanings are:

- A (accountable): The person is held accountable for the work and would field queries related to the work.
- R (responsible): The person who actually does the work, and there could be more than one for any scope item.
- C (consulted/contributes): Here I prefer the word 'contributes' because it allows for a broader involvement than just giving advice. The person might even assist with the work itself (Costello, 2012).
- I (informed): The person should be kept abreast of decisions being taken and how the work is progressing.

Table 13.1 Illustrative RACI Chart, Linking People to Scope

	Person 1	*Person 2*	*Person 3*	*Person 4*	*Person 5*	*Person 6*	*Person 7*
Scope item 1	A		R	R		C	I
Scope item 2	A		I		C	R	I
Scope item 3		A			R		
Scope item 4		A	I			R	C
Scope item 5	A	R		C			C

The chart helps the PM to avoid overloading people and can show areas where conflicts might arise. It should be shared with the team so that everyone has a common view and can debate ambiguous areas.

13.8.2 People Management Activities and Motivation

Although I have occasionally had line management responsibility for people on my projects, more often my relationship with them is through a 'dotted line'. I manage their project responsibilities and give input to their manager who will do formal appraisals. Nevertheless, it is best for the PM to take on many of the ongoing management activities while people are on the project. These would involve:

- Understanding the person's career aspirations and trying to align their project work and skills development toward achieving them.
- Agreeing objectives, measurable where possible, which would be reviewed as required. At least quarterly there should be a discussion with feedback. Even experienced people want to know how they are doing and talk about how they can improve.
- Having regular one-on-one discussions which could be weekly, monthly, or as required, often depending on the person's maturity. Adopting a listening stance is best, where the person can tell what is on their mind. Some coaching might be helpful for inexperienced staff. Occasionally it might be appropriate to give counsel on personal problems, but only if they have a bearing on the person's ability to perform on the project.
- Possibly assigning a mentor for a team member who would benefit from regular interaction with someone more knowledgeable.
- Resolving conflict, which could be within the team or with outside parties – usually done through facilitated discussion.

The above would probably not apply to peripheral members of the team, who work less than 20% of their time on the project.

Motivation is a challenging area. Often one hears people say "you have to motivate your staff". But how? What does a PM actually *do* to motivate them? Probably not very much because people motivate themselves. But, the PM can do a great deal to create an environment where people will be self-motivated. Here it helps to understand a few concepts. In 1943, Maslow proposed that human motivation was based on a hierarchy of needs shown in Figure 13.2. It remains relevant today.

Each level gives a group of needs that a person will be motivated to satisfy – starting at the bottom. Only if a particular level is largely satisfied, will a person be motivated to move to the next level. The levels are further described as follows:

1. Physical needs include food, water, a comfortable temperature, air to breathe, sleep.
2. Security needs include personal and family safety, health, and employment.
3. A sense of belonging and social needs include intimate relationships, family, and friends.

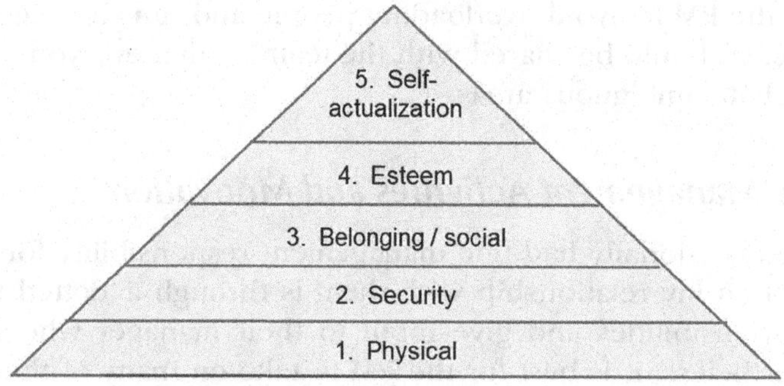

Figure 13.2 Maslow's hierarchy of human needs.

4. Esteem includes a feeling of self-worth, the respect of others, and having confidence.
5. Self-actualization includes striving to achieve, creativity, problem solving, and morality.

How does this help you as a PM? What you are looking for will mainly be in levels 4 and 5. You are looking for the drive to achieve and the self-confidence to be creative. What Maslow shows is that unless your team member's lower needs are met, you are unlikely to get the motivation that you need toward achieving the goals of the project. So things like a comfortable and productive working environment, reasonable job security, and being respected by the team all need to be in place for the team member to be motivated at level 5.

Maslow's hierarchy supports the next concept. Things that benefit your team members can be classified as hygiene factors or motivators. Hygiene factors are things that people expect. These factors may cause people to resign if they are *not* present, but will not motivate them toward achievement. Motivators are, by definition, things that stimulate superior performance. To get a better grasp, do Case 21 which gives a list of beneficial things, and invites you to explain why they are either hygiene factors or motivators. When you have compared your thoughts with the answers you will have a grasp of what drives project team members.

13.8.3 Some Approaches to Conflict

However mature the project team and however competent the PM, some conflict is inevitable. Sometimes the underlying cause can be rational, like different views on priorities or how an activity should be done. Other times it may be emotional, for example, where someone feels that their ideas are being ignored. Whatever the case, conflict is a natural result of change, and change is what projects are about.

Conflict is neither good nor bad, and can have positive or negative results for people and the organization. Much depends on how it is handled, and every conflict situation needs to be managed. There are several recognized approaches for the PM, and which is used depends on the situation which may be complex and involve emotions. The approaches are:

- Withdrawal. The PM decides not to get involved and let the people sort out their differences. This may be effective when the individuals involved are mature and where the conflict does not directly affect the work. It is unlikely to work for a serious conflict.
- Smoothing. This approach is best used in conjunction with other approaches. It involves playing down the differences. For example "does it really matter which way this gets done?"
- Forcing. This involves understanding the situation and then taking a decision. It should be used with caution and tact because at least one of the parties may feel that they have 'lost', and 'win-lose' resolutions are not good for morale. But in certain situations, it may be the only way, for example, where there is urgency or where you strongly agree with one party.
- Compromising. This would involve seeking a solution that both parties can live with, but where each gives up something. Compromising is not necessarily a sign of weakness or inability to decide. Sometimes a compromise is the best way forward.
- Problem solving. This involves seeking a solution that all parties will be happy with. It needs some brainstorming where alternative approaches are put forward and then sifted through. It could lead to a 'win-win' situation, or one may need to fall back to a compromise or a decision.

In situations where you, as a PM, decide to get involved, you would play the role of facilitator and listener – sometimes seeking clarification on a point. It is important that both parties have the opportunity to explain their positions. Hopefully, a resolution can be agreed, but if not, and if time permits, asking for time to think about it would be acceptable.

13.9 Leadership Style and the Use of Power

Power is the PM's ability to influence team members and others to do things that will accomplish the project's goals (Burke & Barron, 2007). There are several ways that power can be exercised, but without power, a PM will be ineffective. Here, we consider seven sources of power which are almost always used in combination. In the context of a leader, they are:

- Formal power. Decision-making power has been delegated to the leader from higher management. People must obey or risk sanction from above.
- Reward power. The leader can reward people with money or anything else that would please them, like being given the most interesting work or approval for time off.

- Coercive power. The leader can punish people by withholding things from them, by verbal reprimand, or through a negative report on their performance In the extreme, it can be removing a person from the team.
- Resource power. The leader can decide where money will be spent or on what activities people will work.
- Expert power. The leader has the knowledge, skills, and experience that the team needs, to be successful.
- Referent power. The leader is respected and liked. People want to work for the leader.
- Persuasive power. The leader is effective at promoting a point of view. In addition, the leader may be well connected and have a broad influence in the organization.

Figure 13.3 shows the degree to which these sources of power are used in two different styles, which I have labeled the 'managing' style and the 'facilitating' style (Einhorn, 2004).

Both styles make some use of all the sources of power, and notice that both styles rely more on reward power than on coercive (punishment) power. The differences lie in the emphasis. The managing leader uses formal, resource, and reward power, while the facilitating leader prefers to use persuasive, referent, and expert power. Neither style is right nor wrong. Nor does it mean that the leader with the managing style does not have the expertise, or that the facilitating leader lacks formal authority. It's more that certain styles are effective for certain types of project. For a

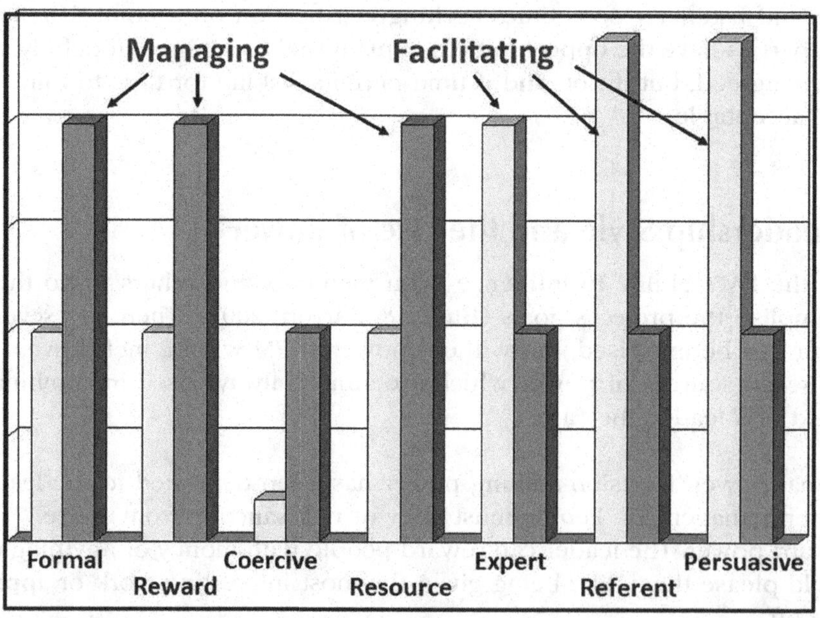

Figure 13.3 Use of power for two different PM styles.

construction project, a more managing style would be typical, whereas for a business project, a more facilitating style might be appropriate – the PM may prefer to discuss and agree with specialists on what needs to be done rather than tell them.

13.10 In Conclusion

Business projects succeed by the PM enabling the team to work together effectively. As one team member once said to me "we make the project happen, but you are the glue that holds it together". This would be a good time to tackle Case 22 where some serious team conflicts have arisen. Can you help Clement, the PM, to find the best way forward?

References

Burke, R., & Barron, S. (2007). *Project Management Leadership: Building Creative Teams*: Burke Publishing.

Costello, T. (2012). RACI—Getting projects 'Unstuck'. *IT Professional*, 14(2), 63–64.

Einhorn, F. (2004). The PM, Boss or Facilitator? Paper presented at the PM South Africa Conference.

Isaac, M., Carson, K. (2012). A Guide to Belbin Team Roles: How to increase personal and team effectiveness. *3Circle Partners*.

Katzenbach, J.R., Smith, D.K. (1993). *The Wisdom of Teams – Creating the High-Performance Organization*. USA: McKinsey & Company.

PMI. (2021). *PMBOK – Guide to the Project Management Body of Knowledge*, 7th edition: Pennsylvania, USA: Project Management Institute.

West Chester University (2021). *Tuckman's Stages of Group Development*. https://www.wcupa.edu/coral/tuckmanStagesGroupDelvelopment.aspx

Chapter 14

Managing Project Issues

14.1 Introduction and Objectives

Issues management is about problem solving, but in a structured way. I consider it important because, when managing business projects, I spend far more time on issues than on updating the schedule. However well a project has been planned there will always be problems; if they are not properly handled, they will have an impact on the project and could even derail it entirely. Unresolved issues also have a negative effect on the morale of all stakeholders. So, the objectives of this chapter are to:

- Understand why managing issues is vital to the success of the project.
- Recognize project issues and know how to document them.
- Be able to resolve project issues by facilitating the efforts of multiple stakeholders.
- Appreciate the benefits of effective issues management.

14.2 Project Issues and How to Deal with Them

Here, we shall discuss what an issue is, how to raise (or record) it, who should be involved, what documentation is needed, and how to resolve and close the issue.

14.2.1 What Is a Project Issue?

A project issue is a problem that threatens the success of the project. If it is not a threat then it's not a project issue. For example, a leaking tap in the bathroom may be a problem, but it would not be a project issue. We must also distinguish between a risk and an issue because the two are often confused. A risk is something that *might* happen, and yes we can take certain actions to make it less likely to happen or to reduce the impact. But an issue is something that *has* happened or that we have now become aware of. We have to take action to deal with it. Dealing with the issue may be within the PM's control, but sometimes, it is outside the PM's control. In such situations, the PM needs to work out who has to be involved to get it resolved and that may include business stakeholders or even the sponsor. Issues should be assigned a

DOI: 10.1201/9781003321101-16

priority. Some are critically urgent and must be resolved immediately, while others could wait for weeks or even a month or two.

14.2.2 Raising the Issue

Raising the issue means recognizing that it exists and describing it in the documentation. Some issues are obvious while others take experience to spot. So, where do issues come from? They could come from anyone and you almost want to encourage people, if they have concerns, to express them because some concerns may be real issues that need to be addressed. Often issues arise from meetings where somebody says that something is not possible or will be very late. However, many of the issues will actually be identified by you, the PM, because you have had experience and will anticipate things that are likely to cause difficulties. For example, seldom does a stakeholder raise political or interpersonal problems, but you might recognize them as issues.

Now, when an issue arises, the natural reaction of a PM is anything from frustration to despair. But, what should happen is for the PM to think: "this is an opportunity for me to make a real contribution to the project because I'm good at getting issues resolved". So I suggest that you seize the issue joyfully. There is no need to fear issues. In fact, maybe the issue to fear is the one that goes unrecognized and hits the project at the worst possible time.

So what do you actually do? The first thing is to document the issue as soon as possible, which includes talking to people and understanding the issue better. There are two records that need to be completed: The first is the issues log, a table where there is a one-line item per issue with basic reference information. The second is an issue record which describes important aspects of the issue. Usually, the record would be one page, but it could be more. Presently, we shall consider both in more detail. It pays to document the issue immediately because if this is not done, when one gets back to it, one might have forgotten some salient points. Worse still, the issue might be forgotten until it impacts the project!

14.2.3 The Issues Log

The entire issues log is seldom more than a page because each issue is just one line, and only larger projects have more than about 40 issues. For me the log is a Word document; others might use a different tool like a spreadsheet. The log takes the form of a table as illustrated in Figure 14.1.

Issues Log: Project Omega updated 12 Sep 22

No.	Prty	Resp	Open	Close	Description
Open					
E012	B	Joe	23Aug22		Users disagree with....
E013	C	Tracy	12Sep22		No support for design of ....
Closed					
E001	A	Thandi	07Apr22	22Apr22	Cannot meet spec on ...

Figure 14.1 The issues log.

Column 1 on the left, is the issue number. I use an 'E' prefix because 'I' can look like a number and because issues are sometimes referred to as 'exceptions'. Column 2 is the priority, A, B, or C which mainly reflects the impact of the issue. 'A' means that we must deal with the issue immediately and it needs to be resolved in the next few days. 'B' means that it must be resolved in the next week or two, and 'C' means that it could wait for a month or even more. Column 3 is the person responsible for getting the issue resolved – often the PM for a smaller project. Column 4 is the date that the issue was opened. Column 5 is the date that it was closed, so it starts out blank and is given a date when it is moved down to 'closed'. Column 6, on the right, is a title or brief description – just enough that you will recognize it.

The top section of the table is for 'open' issues, and it is here that new issues are entered. The bottom section is for 'closed' issues, and as soon as an issue is resolved, it is cut-and-pasted to the closed section. It is worth emphasizing that closed issues are never lost, but are kept on record as they may need to be referred to later. We may need to report on the issue and we may even need to re-open it if it crops up again. But generally the focus is on the open issues and hopefully there are not too many as most should have been closed.

14.2.4 The Issue Record

The issue record is illustrated in Figure 14.2.

It is usually a Word document, and note that it is relatively free format without lots of little boxes to be filled in or ticked. But there are a few items needed at the top to identify the issue. The title, the author, and the date are always essential while the issue number (E012) links the record to the log entry. Other items, some from the log, are at the discretion of the author.

There are headings to guide what should be recorded. The description is important, and might typically be half a page. When you or anybody else rereads the record, it should give a good appreciation of what the issue is about. If the issue is

Author: Thabo Issue Record 23 Aug 22

E012

Title: Users disagree with test method Priority: B

Target close date: 16Sep22 Actual:

Opened by: Belinda Responsible: Thabo

Description

1. The users want testing all day, whereas we need setup time.

Alternatives

- o Give them their own test-facility

Actions

Resolution

Closing Comments

Figure 14.2 The issue record.

caused by a known risk occurring, then also reference the risk. Sometimes an issue is triggered by somebody sending an email explaining the problem, in which case you might just copy that email into the issue record – whatever is easiest. Next, the alternatives. There may be several ways of dealing with the issue, and while you are describing the issue, you might think of some of them yourself. But later, when you discuss it with other people, further alternatives are likely to be proposed. There may be some actions to be taken immediately, but often actions arise during discussions. The resolution will only be known and entered later. The same applies to the closing comments which require the activities decided upon to be complete and the issue considered to be resolved. The closing comments thus summarize why we believe that we can close this issue. Sometimes when an issue gets closed, I cut and paste the closing comments to just below the title, so that if I reopen the issue, I can see at a glance why it was closed. Issues vary enormously in complexity and the amount of documentation needed. Some might never get to be more than half a page; others could be much longer.

> *The longest issue I ever had was over 20 pages. It took six weeks to resolve, including a lot of emotion because it involved the basis for payment of our business partners on a major project.*

Both the issues log and the issues records should be kept where they are accessible to stakeholders, so that they do not need to be circulated. This would preferably be in an issues folder for the project, sorted by issue number. There are some exceptions. Issues that are of a sensitive or confidential nature, like the one mentioned above, would not be shared. Problems that are specific to a discipline would be managed by the appropriate specialist, for example, design issues and decisions might be handled by the senior designer and would only become project issues if they were really serious. The same applies to testing or commissioning problems.

14.2.5 Resolving Issues

Having done the initial documentation of an issue, the next step is to decide who needs to be involved. This might already have been done if the issue was discussed in a project tracking meeting. The PM might also want to allocate a person to take responsibility for the issue, but on a small project, it would probably be the PM. If the issue is large and complex, it could almost be handled like a mini project in its own right. Having decided on the people, it's best to set up a meeting to discuss the issue, and the meeting might be like an informal workshop. Once the problem is fully understood by those involved, then it's worth coming up with alternative ways of solving it. Each potential solution should be documented with pros, cons, and other comments because it often happens, after the issue is resolved, that somebody says: "but why didn't you do it this way? it would have been much better" Then if you've got your alternatives, you might respond "yes we looked at your suggestion, and this is why we did not do it that way". Depending on the issue there are many forms that the solution might take. Sometimes what is needed is a decision, and usually important decisions must involve the sponsor. The solution might also involve changes to deliverables and how such changes should be controlled is covered in Chapter 15 which comes next.

When the best alternative has been selected, and it won't necessarily happen in the first meeting, then it's time to agree on what actions need to be taken and who will take them. If there's a lot of work then it might become an activity, or several activities, on the project schedule. If the solution involves a scope change, then refer to the number of the change request when it has been raised. But, whatever the case, it's up to the PM to ensure that the actions are tracked. Then, once it's clear that the issue is resolved and that project work can progress normally, the issue should be closed with comments in the issue record. It should be stated which alternative was selected, what the outcome was, and any related things like further risks arising from the resolution. Finally, the issue can be given a close date and moved to the closed section in the issues log.

14.3 Benefits of Practicing Issues Management

What are the benefits of using a method similar to the one described above, rather than just handling them 'on the fly' without any documentation? Indeed, there are many benefits. It allows the PM to prioritize issues. There may be several issues open concurrently and, by giving them an A, B, or C rating, the PM can decide which ones need attention first. The method is actually quite simple and ensures that no issue is overlooked. The thought process has to be gone through anyway and writing down the facts and considerations, helps the thought process without being a lot of extra work – even for complex situations. Managing issues in a structured manner keeps a project manager's mind active and brings definition to problems. It becomes easy to identify which issues need to be shown in regular project reports or discussed in reviews. The approach allows alternatives to be considered and even presented to stakeholders like the sponsor. It has happened that I've presented a number of alternatives to a sponsor, and recommended one of them, only to have the sponsor say "well actually I prefer that alternative, can we discuss it?". This is still a good outcome, and everyone knows that the situation has been properly thought through.

Issues often result in decisions being taken, and the issue record is a very good way of documenting such decisions and why they were taken. For some projects where many business decisions are taken along the way, I list those decisions on a 'decisions log' and circulate it to business stakeholders on a regular basis. At least, none of them will feel that decisions were taken without them knowing about it, and it gives stakeholders the opportunity to appeal a decision. Indeed, there have been occasions where previously made decisions were overturned, and a new one agreed.

Back to the benefits. If one is working with a client or customer, they are likely to be comfortable knowing that the PM is documenting and tracking issues. They will have confidence that nothing important will be overlooked. Finally, this approach to managing issues allows the PM to keep their 'finger on the pulse' of the project. The team are involved by identifying and resolving issues, but the PM remains in control.

14.4 Concluding Thoughts on Issues

You might wonder at what times most of the issues occur on a project. The following experience gave me the answer:

> *Early on, when I started using this issues management approach, we were at the end of planning a major project. Opinions on how to approach it were divided and we had dealt with a lot of issues. My thought was "now that planning is done, there shouldn't be too many more issues". How wrong I was. Issues kept happening all along the way, sometimes more sometimes less. Even in the final weeks of the project new issues needed to be dealt with.*

Another experience on a large and critical project where I was a subproject manager, indicated a way of handling an overload of issues:

> *The project was in 'red' status and new issues were coming up faster than earlier ones were getting resolved. We met every morning at 07:30 with a member of the customer's and our senior management present. Besides reviewing progress, we went through the list of open issues and got feedback from the responsible persons on the actions that were planned to address them. Amazingly, the issues melted away when they got the attention that they deserved. The meetings were only held for about a month and ultimately the project was a success.*

So, issues occur on all projects, and the more complex the project, the more issues there are likely to be. There are many ways of dealing with issues, but I have found the one described above to be effective without being time-consuming. Ultimately there is a choice. Either one manages issues thoroughly, or one needs to be very good at managing crises.

This is a good time to do Case 23 and get practice by documenting an issue that arises during the conversion of an IT system used for wealth management.

Chapter 15

Project Change Control

15.1 Introduction and Objectives

When project planning is complete, scope (deliverables), schedule (milestones), and cost (budget) baselines are agreed with the sponsor and other key stakeholders. Project change control, or simply 'change control', relates to the process of changing one or more of the agreed baselines or plans. Most changes start with a scope change – a stakeholder requires a change to a project deliverable. The stakeholder could be from the business, but could also be a project team member. Such changes need to be controlled because uncontrolled scope changes, referred to as 'scope creep', can cause projects to fail. The objectives are to:

- Distinguish between change control and other concepts using the word 'change'.
- Understand what constitutes a change, how changes arise, and the impact of not controlling them.
- Know the process to control scope and other changes, and its role in governance.

15.2 The Terminology Can Be Confusing

The word 'change' is used in different ways, so let's get some clarification:

- 'Project change control' relates to any change to a project's scope, schedule, or cost baseline – the agreed plan. The most common changes apply to scope – a planned deliverable of the project. *Control* means understanding the implications of the change and getting the appropriate approval, usually from the sponsor. Most scope changes also have schedule and cost implications. So, where a scope change request is approved, there is usually approval to adjust the schedule and cost baselines as well.
- 'Organizational change management', abbreviated to OCM, may sound a bit similar, but means something different. OCM is about working with the people who are affected by a project, and preparing them for the changes that the

DOI: 10.1201/9781003321101-17

project will bring. OCM is covered in Chapter 23 and may be an important part of the scope of some projects.
- 'Operational change control' refers to the organization's ongoing operations. For example, changes to an IT system can have a serious impact if they go wrong. Therefore, business management needs to control such changes by ensuring that sufficient preparation has been done. It does have a bearing on projects because often proposed operational changes are an outcome of projects.

Here, we shall only cover the first one – project change control.

15.3 What Is a Change?

Although changes can apply to scope, schedule, or cost, scope changes are usually the most difficult to deal with and have schedule and/or cost implications as well. A scope change can also be hard to recognize, which is part of the challenge. Generally, a scope change is:

- Any change to an approved scope deliverable. Normally a deliverable has some form of specification (or 'spec') associated with it, in which case a change to the spec would constitute a change, even if the change means *less* work. Often the required quality is mentioned in the spec, so any change to the quality would be a change to the spec, and hence to the deliverable.
- An additional required deliverable or the removal of a deliverable. Both would be changes even if the project team says that there is no extra time or cost. Removal of a deliverable is referred to as 'de-scoping' – often done when something is found not to be needed.

If any change, whether to the approved scope, schedule, or cost, is needed, then a change request should be raised and submitted for approval. But, some things that may *look* like changes are *not* changes, for example:

- A change in the details of *how* we shall do something is entirely up to the person doing the work and sometimes also the PM.
- Delays to the schedule, or cost overruns, are variances but not changes. They certainly need to be reported, but the time or cost baseline has not changed.

If there are justified reasons for changing a milestone date, or even the project end date, then a change request should be raised, because that changes the plan or approved baseline. Similar considerations apply if there are justified reasons for seeking approval for a budget increase.

15.3.1 Scope Creep: the Challenge of Small Scope Changes

Generally, small changes are far more difficult for the PM to handle than large changes, for a number of reasons:

- Stakeholders might see you as being petty for wanting to control small changes.
- Sometimes you don't even know that changes are taking place, and you find out when there is a query or when an activity has already slipped. That is why they are referred to as 'scope creep'. Each change on its own has a tiny impact, but collectively the impact can be huge.

Here is how small changes happen:

- A feature is assumed, for example, "we assumed that we could have Italian tiles rather than locally manufactured ones".
- Another party, often the customer or a user, is not carrying out their responsibilities, so, to make up for it, there is more work for your team.
- A stakeholder makes a request and a member of your team member says "we can do it at no extra cost".
- There may be a perfectionist in the team who wants to do extra work to produce an admirable output. This can be especially difficult because it is a matter of judgment as to whether an existing deliverable is good enough or whether it really needs to be improved.

Big changes suffer less from these problems; it's clear that they need approval. So what are the remedies? First, define the scope as tightly as possible. But, however thoroughly you do it, some things will always be subject to debate. Second, document every change however small. Even if you, as PM, have the authority to approve a small change, put it on record. Third, where the spec does need to change, get it approved, or at least formally notify stakeholders. Fourth, be selective, and maintain a 'futures list' (sometimes called a 'parking lot') for things that should only be considered post-project.

> *On one large IT project in a bank, we were falling behind schedule, but the main business stakeholder who had lots of good ideas, regularly asked for enhancements, citing some as urgent. My approach was to suggest that such enhancements be done as soon as the project was complete. When we finally did complete it, there were over a hundred items on the list. In the end we probably only did about five of them.*

15.3.2 The Impact of a Change That 'Requires No Extra Effort'

To illustrate the potential problems caused by an 'insignificant' change, here is a situation that might occur on a cabling project for a customer organization.

> On a routine site visit, one of your technicians mentions that Mr. Goven, a junior manager on the customer's facilities staff, asked him to modify the cabling to change the location of some of the network points. Your technician proudly says that he did it immediately, and that Mr. Goven is delighted.

What would be your thoughts as PM? What might be some of the consequences? These would be my thoughts: This is a change to the specification and no change control process has been followed. Even if I had a process in place, I would blame myself for not having communicated it well enough. Also, Mr. Goven did not have the authority to approve a change so the customer might ask me to fix it at our own cost. Even if the change were accepted, the drawings would now need to be updated. Moreover, this sets a precedent: Next time the customer wants a change, it will be expected at no cost. It could also be perceived as unprofessional, a lack of control. This highlights some of the problems that can result from even a minor change, and given the potential consequences, it is best to avoid such situations by having a well-documented process and communicating it to both the team and other stakeholders. Let us now see what sort of process we might need.

15.4 The Change Control Process

Suppose that your project and its scope, schedule, and cost have been approved. What process do you follow when changes arise later? As mentioned, changes can arise in many ways. There may be requests from stakeholders, or, the only way to complete the project might involve a scope change. There are many possible processes, but the simple process that I suggest involves two documents, probably both softcopy in MS Word: a change log, and a change record. This has similarities with the issues management process, but the processes are different. The contents of a change record are different from an issue record and even the log requires different columns.

15.4.1 The Change Request Log

The change log involves just one line per change, so, for an entire project, it is seldom more than one page. It is illustrated in Figure 15.1.

It would have a change number like C03, the person that proposed the change, the date that the change request was received, and a suitable title. The initial status would be 'raised' with no date completed. After a decision has been taken, usually by

Change request log:			**Project Omega**	**updated 07 Jun 22**	
No.	**Prop.**	**Date-O**	**Change title**	**Status**	**Date-C**
Open					
C03	Joe	07Jun22	Facility to audit compliance	Raised	
Closed					
C01	Thandi	18Nov21	New business rule for late premiums	Accept	02Dec21
C02	Tracy	02Mar22	Add $200k budget due to underestimate	Reject	04Mar22

Figure 15.1 The Change Request Log.

the sponsor or steering committee, the status would change to one of the following: accept (or approved), declined, deferred, or even 'no change'. The 'no change' status means that, after investigation, it is found that the 'change' is in fact, part of the original scope and not a change at all. Clearly, the log could be arranged differently and columns might be added. For example, when doing a customer project, one might want to record whether the change had been billed and paid.

15.4.2 The Change Request Record

Next we need a change record. Usually it would be just a single page but for large or complex changes it could be longer. The headings and a possible format are illustrated in Figure 15.2.

The change request record would link to the log via the change number shown bolded on the top right hand. The description should give enough information, and background, that the sponsor, or other stakeholders reading it, would fully understand the situation. Then, with the estimates of additional time and cost, they would know enough to take an informed decision. It is useful to state the impact of *not* making the change, and sometimes the impact is accepting more risk. Where the change relates to a risk or issue, then provide the risk or issue numbers so that they may be referred to. Finally, when there is a decision, its details get entered. Nowadays, because documents are seldom printed and signed, it would be wise to refer to how the decision was received. It could be via an email, or, the minutes of a meeting, and for either, the reference would be useful in case of a later query.

15.4.3 The Execution of Changes

Minor approved changes may be mainly for the record, but for larger ones, a fair amount of work can arise. Your schedules need to be updated and possibly activities reassigned in discussion with team members. Specifications may need an updated version, and there would probably be new schedule and cost baselines. These, and the fact that the change was approved, would be discussed in the next tracking meeting and reflect in the next project report. This should help you to ensure that the necessary communication has taken place. Thereafter, the new scope is tracked as part of the project.

Proposer: Thandi   Change Request   18 Nov 21
C01

Title: **New business rule for late premiums**

Description *(background, details)*

Impact if change not made

Schedule impact

Budget impact

Decision by: Status: approved   Status date: 02Dec21

Figure 15.2 The Change Request Record.

15.5 Further Matters Relating to Governance

Change control is part of governance, so it is important to define the responsibilities carefully, and they might not be the same for all projects.

Typical responsibilities would be:

- The PM would keep the records and manage the process.
- Schedule and cost estimates would come from the project team.
- Decisions, like approvals, would be given by the sponsor or a steering committee. They might even come from a 'change control board' (if it has been set up).

Levels of governance can differ depending on many things. For example, the sponsor may give the PM the authority to approve changes if the impact is below certain levels – say, less than a day of duration and a cost of less than $2 000. But, for sound governance, such changes should always be recorded, covered in the next project report, and mentioned at the next sponsor or steering committee meeting. A large change might need a two-stage process. The PM might need approval for the effort just to define the scope and estimate the change. After all, this kind of work may take more than a week and divert some of the team's most experienced people. Then, where the PM or the sponsor considers that the cumulative changes are of significance, the business case should be reviewed to make quite sure that the project remains justified.

15.6 In Conclusion

To handle changes effectively, it helps to define the deliverables and hence the scope as thoroughly as possible. This avoids lengthy debate and a large volume of changes later. You, as PM, need a process which is explained to the team, and they should consult you before doing anything that they think might be out of scope. Even if you have good cooperation from the stakeholders, you will still need to be vigilant and ask questions if you suspect scope creep. Document everything that looks like a change, even if it's just the 'one liner' in the change log that you will not pursue further. Finally, keep updating the milestone dates and budget so that they reflect the cumulative approved changes. These should be stated in reports lest stakeholders believe that the original targets still apply.

Chapter 16

Project Monitoring, Control, and Communication

16.1 Introduction and Objectives

This chapter gives an overview of certain monitoring, controlling, and communication tasks that the PM does throughout the project. The objectives are to:

- Understand how monitoring, control, and communication are related.
- Know which regular meetings to hold and why additional focused ones are needed.
- Be able to run meetings efficiently and to minute them economically.
- Motivate constant dialogue and follow-up between meetings.
- Mention some of the requirements for a productive project workplace.
- Present the communications challenge and ways of meeting it.
- Introduce the one-page report with its RAG (red, amber, green) status.

Here we do not specifically cover Agile projects. Although they have similar needs for tracking and communication they use different approaches, some of which are mentioned but are further described in Chapter 30. Nevertheless, there are many 'hybrid' projects which use both traditional and Agile methods. If you are involved in these, then select from this chapter what will work for you. I also accept that PM styles differ and what follows is what I practice. As a PM, you might prefer to do things differently, in which case I suggest you look for the common threads that apply irrespective of any particular method.

DOI: 10.1201/9781003321101-18

16.2 What Needs to Be Monitored and How Does the PM Control a Project?

First, what do the terms 'monitor' and 'control' mean in the project context? By monitoring, the PM observes many aspects of the project while gathering data and noting new risks, issues, and change requests. In controlling, the PM uses the information gathered during monitoring, compares it with what was planned, and makes necessary adjustments in collaboration with the team. So, monitoring feeds into controlling. Here, the term 'tracking' is used to cover both monitoring and controlling. Communication covers any interaction between people whether it be informal or in meetings, verbal or written. Communication invariably involves the passing of information.

Tracking is done in tracking meetings (or progress meetings) mainly to find out how things are going. Some actions might also be initiated in the meeting. But tracking also happens outside formal meetings and all aspects are covered in this chapter. Monitoring and control depend on communication to gather information and also to keep stakeholders informed or to advise them what actions they need to take. To this end, communication is covered here with an emphasis on regular project reporting. Many related disciplines that are detailed in other chapters are referred to, such as schedule, cost, risk, and issues management, as well as change control.

There are many ways that the PM does monitoring and controlling and sometimes it is hard to separate them because they go together. Some approaches are more formal like having meetings, others are very informal like chatting over coffee. But even meetings can feel informal, provided that there is reasonable discipline to avoid wasting time or leaving important matters unattended. But first, what should be monitored? I would suggest all aspects of the project, with the main ones being:

- Team workload and morale.
- The schedule, noting which activities are on track and which are behind or have problems. The same applies to action items from meeting minutes.
- Costs of people's time and other procured items.
- Risks – the ones on the risk register and any new ones.
- Issues – from the issues log and new problems.
- Change requests – usually relating to scope.

All of them might be covered in meetings or informally – we need both.

16.3 What Meetings Do We Need, and What Should They Cover?

We need many meetings, but we don't need too many people in them.

> *I remember one meeting in a financial institution that lasted for well over an hour. There were more than 20 people present, and only about three of them did any talking. The rest looked bored and on the verge of falling asleep.*

This is not the way to do things. Yes, we must keep people informed, but there are other ways of communicating. Given the high cost of people, this was also a very expensive meeting. So, the PM needs to: use judgment and try to, *only* have people in the meeting, who can contribute, or who need to agree to the outcome. Three or four people may be all that is needed to resolve an issue or to debate how to approach an activity. But usually, a few more- formal meetings are needed such as:

- The tracking meeting run by the PM.
- The steering committee meeting (also called the sponsor meeting or project board meeting) run by the project sponsor.

There are no rules for how frequent, or of what duration, these should be, as everything depends on the nature of the project. But I shall make some suggestions for typical business projects of between 4 and 12 months duration.

16.3.1 Team Meetings

Team, tracking, or progress meetings mean much the same thing. Such meetings might be held weekly, preferably at the same time, like Thursdays at 10:00. They would include all members of the team, and possibly a few other stakeholders. Anywhere between 5 and 12 people would be a typical number. Ideally, meetings would be in a conference room with people seated around a table so that they can see each other. But it is quite feasible to include people online or even to have a fully online meeting. My preferred format for the meeting is to go through the schedule, go through the agenda, and then end the meeting. This approach was developed when I spent 6 years working in a highly successful organization where the norm was to allow only half an hour for progress meetings. And this is the approach that I shall describe, including the method for taking minutes, whose action items form the agenda for the next meeting. In other cultures, PMs may wish to run meetings differently. Also, where people have had to commute to get to the meeting, one might take longer and cover more ground. But, whatever the length, I try to start on time, lest people get into the habit of arriving late – a problem if there is limited time. In meetings, I hand out two bits of paper.

- The schedule (less than a page) which only has activities that are currently in progress or about to start in the next month.
- The minutes from the previous meeting, possibly with some information-only items removed so as to focus on the action items.

We start with the schedule, and even if I already know the status, we go through each activity. For current ones the questions are: "will you finish by the scheduled end date?". If the answer is no, then "what problems have you encountered, do you need assistance, and when can you finish?" This is a mild 'carrot and stick' approach. The incentive for being on time is that I thank them for it, and the censure for being late is that questions get asked. For activities due to start soon we might discuss whether the dates are still reasonable.

Next, the minutes. There are only two types of items on the minutes, action items and information items. The information items which are there for the record, can be skipped unless someone has a query on them. The action items are covered in a similar way to the schedule: if the due date has passed, has it been done?

Where problems are raised, they may be discussed briefly, but then they get minuted as action items with a date, having agreed what the problem is, its urgency, and who needs to be involved to solve it. A meeting can easily be derailed because there is debate about a single item and sometimes the people that can help solve it are not even in the meeting. But, of course, there are exceptions, I can remember once allowing discussion to proceed on an issue which was *so* important that it had to be resolved for the project to continue. After all, it was possible for me to gather necessary information after the meeting by talking to people.

The above approach can work, with modification, in a variety of situations. For larger projects, the PM would meet with subproject managers who would hold their own team meetings. On one project, there was so much to change on the business front, that separate meetings were held with the more technical project team and with the business people. For Agile projects, the 'daily standup' meeting would serve a similar purpose. A 'Kanban board' would have both the main activities and any action items.

16.3.2 Sponsor or Steering Committee Meetings

The format for the steering committee might differ somewhat. Meetings would be less often, possibly once a month, and maybe once every 2 months.

> As an aside, avoid terms like bi-weekly or bi-monthly as they are ambiguous. For example, bi-weekly can mean twice a week or it can mean once every two weeks. Rather say "we meet every two weeks" or "we meet fortnightly".

The steering meeting would probably be chaired by the sponsor, sometimes referred to as the executive. There are two other roles that need to be present: at least one senior business person whose staff will benefit from the project, and at least one senior person who ensures that resources, like skilled people, are available (OGC, 2009). On a smaller project, the same executive might play more than one of the roles. For example, the sponsor might also supply the staff.

As a PM, you are a vital attendee and might play a facilitating role by preparing the agenda and doing the minutes. You would report back on the status and should be able to answer any questions, or, if unsure, agree to find the information and possibly append it to the minutes. For a small project, there may be no steering committee at all; you might just meet with the sponsor.

16.3.3 Decision Making

Controlling by its nature implies taking decisions. Most decisions, like who should help out on a task that is behind schedule, would be taken by the PM. But major decisions, like significant scope changes, need the sponsor's approval. Where to draw the line is a matter of judgment, usually following guidelines agreed with the sponsor. For the important decisions, there is seldom time to wait for the next steering committee meeting. So, the PM needs access to the sponsor while respecting the fact that the sponsor is busy. Often an emailed recommendation, backed up with a phone call, will get the required decision. The sponsor can choose whether to consult other stakeholders. However, it is paramount that all important decisions be communicated to key stakeholders, possibly by stating the decision in the next project report or by updating and circulating a 'decisions log' a tool that was mentioned in Chapter 14 on managing project issues. So, if the sponsor takes the big decisions, what is the PMs responsibility? The PM's responsibility is to *get* the decisions taken and to get them taken soon enough that impact to the project is minimized. This may take persistence, but it has to be done.

16.4 Meeting Minutes

16.4.1 Questions About Minutes

First, why are minutes needed? Many reasons. They record action items that need to be tracked lest they be forgotten. Minutes record what was agreed in the meeting, and form a vital record for the project. They may need to be referred to weeks later to understand or explain a situation.

Next, who should do the minutes? Opinions vary, but my preference is to do them myself. I understand the project well and can prioritize what should be recorded. Also by doing the minutes, I reflect on situations and sometimes have useful ideas that did not come up in the meeting. Doing the minutes also gives me some control over what will be covered in the next meeting. Delegating minutes to someone that does not understand the project may not be a good idea. Such a person may attempt to record everything that was said without extracting the meaning. However, on one large project, I had such a capable project administrator, that she took the minutes.

When should one do the minutes? Preferably immediately after the meeting while everything is still fresh in the memory. If one is listening carefully in the meeting, it is impossible to make notes of everything. Sometimes one or two scribbled words as a mind-jogger is all that there is time for. My experience is that if I wait even a few hours, the minutes take longer because I struggle to remember the details. So, I try to block out half an hour after the meeting to take care of the minutes. Another thing: If the minutes go out promptly, then there is time for people to check for action items for which they are responsible. Sending out minutes hours before the next meeting or not sending them out at all might be interpreted as slackness. Of course, there are exceptions. Sometimes more urgent things delay the minutes. But, while the above works for me, it may not suit every PM.

16.4.2 How Can Good Meeting Minutes Be Done in Just One or Two Pages?

What follows applies to regular meetings. Often, one receives many pages of minutes with headings like 'matters arising' and 'general'. I wonder how many people ever

Table 16.1 Possible Format for Project Team Meeting Minutes

Organization	Project Name	17 Jun 2021
	Tracking meeting 17 Jun 21 minutes	Author

Attendees: (P = present)

Name	P						

Ref	*Description*	*Date*	*Type*	*Responsible*
1.0	Project status			
1.14	Status as at today. The project is running a week behind schedule. The main focus is on getting the business specifications finalized. Costs are below what was planned for the work done.	2021-06-17	Information	
1.15	Send summary schedule to PM of project X	2021-06-17 2021-06-18	Action Due	PM name
2.0	Business			
2.8a	Business requirements workshop. It was agreed to hold the session on 23 June in the boardroom, lasting 2 hours. Tina will join online from Durban and Daniel from Cape Town.	2021-06-17	Information	
2.8b	Set up business requirements workshop	2021-06-17	Action	Person A
3.0	Interaction with related projects			
6.0	Project administration			

look at them or refer back to them. So here is an approach that I adopted from a colleague and have used for over 20 years. It has never resulted in more than one or two pages, and can be done in half an hour. The format of the minutes, which use MS Word, is shown in Table 16.1 and a brief description follows. The exact format does not matter, but the concepts do matter.

The 'attendees' block would have the names of all those that usually attend, and a 'P' is inserted for those that did attend. It is easy to add additional people.

Here the main section is divided into sub-headings shown in gray. Sub-headings, are optional and would be decided up-front. They can help to structure the content into areas of interest. The columns are used as follows:

- Ref: Each item is given a unique running number.
- Description: This briefly summarizes an information item, or states an action.
- Date, which links to the type column. For an action, it is the date that the action was initiated or is due or completed. For an information item, it is the date that it was discussed.
- Type initially indicates whether the item is an Action or Information item. For convenience, the column is also used for the status of an action item, which could be 'due' or 'complete'. It could also be 'revised' where a revised date is set, or 'cancelled' if the action is no longer needed.
- Responsible is only used for action items, and even if several people will be involved, it is best to have only one person responsible.

After the meeting, the previous minutes are opened and re-saved with the current date. Then, before new items are added, old items are cut and pasted into a 'minutes log' in Ref number sequence. Thus, the minutes log, which has exactly the same column structure, holds the combined minutes from past meetings. Old items would be all information items (which only need to appear once) and any action item that is complete or cancelled. So before adding items from the latest meeting, only the outstanding action items remain. And, with the new information added, the new minutes remain short. The minutes log builds up over time and might get to over 20 pages inside of a year. It is easy to search the minutes log for a keyword, which can be very useful if there is a query as to what was agreed.

While the approach just described is suitable for regular team or steering committee meetings, it is unnecessary for the many one-off meetings. These could be to discuss any number of things like cooperation with another project or how to deal with an issue. These should also be minuted, and besides heading, date, and author, all that might be needed is a numbered list of points made, of which some might be actions with a person responsible.

16.5 What Should Be Done Between Meetings?

16.5.1 Informal Interaction

Most tracking happens between regular meetings. Thus, when the PM is in a meeting there should be few surprises. Informal discussions and short meetings to discuss a particular matter are of immense value. Part of this is referred to as MBWA (management by walking about) and it would include talking to stakeholders outside the project. Where people are not in the same building, MBWA would be virtual, like having an online chat or a telephone call. Some of the many purposes are to gather information, and many people are far more willing to share their thoughts and feelings informally than in a meeting. So, it helps to pick up concerns, issues and risks, and also to know how activities are progressing long before the next tracking meeting. People also appreciate you showing an interest in what they are thinking and doing. But, here some judgment is needed. Some people like more interaction and others less. The PM walks a tightrope between neglect on the one hand, and 'breathing down a person's neck' on the other. The latter could even be interpreted as a lack of trust. Also, the nature of the work that some people do, like IT development requires intense concentration, and any interruption could cause the 'train of thought' to be lost. For such people, it may be better to approach them when they are not hunched over a laptop screen. While talking to people, risks that are picked up need to go to the risk register and response actions planned; issues that arise need to be logged and resolved.

The PM needs to be on the constant lookout for warning signs, like someone being unsure how to tackle an activity or doing out-of-scope work. The latter is sometimes called 'scope creep'. As was explained in Chapter 15, scope creep happens where small bits of work are done that do not form part of the scope. In specialized activities, it can be difficult to distinguish between doing the job properly and 'gilding the lily' which means doing unnecessary work to enhance something that already meets the requirements.

16.5.2 Follow-Up and a Productive Environment

There are often dependencies on other projects or stakeholders outside of the project team. Even if something has been committed in writing, it is wise for the PM to follow-up before the time. For example, if Marketing has committed to have a specialist available on a particular date, then the PM needs to confirm a few days or a week before the time, that the person is still needed and will be available. Then, if there is a problem, there is time to sort it out before the due date.

Maintaining a productive environment takes time and effort. Especially in an open-plan office, the PM needs to encourage a balance between healthy sociability and extended chats that consume time and distract others. Nevertheless, chats that help skills transfer to take place would be encouraged. The PM should arrange for the right equipment or software to be available for the team. Even getting a broken printer fixed might fall to the PM. Many things can be delegated, but on a small project, there is often nobody suitable to delegate to because one wants the skilled people to be focused on project tasks. So, sometimes the PM takes the attitude "if it is to be, it must be me" – accepting that simply doing something is the quickest way.

I suggest that you now do Case 24 which is about a PM named Delia. It describes a day in her busy life and then asks a number of related questions which would round out your understanding gained from this and previous chapters.

16.6 Communications – Practical Guidelines

Communication goes hand in hand with monitoring and control. While monitoring the project and making adjustments, the PM needs to communicate with a variety of stakeholders. According to some, PMs spend over 80% of their time communicating.

But the statement raises questions like: What should be communicated? In how much detail? How often? Formally or informally? Who should talk to whom?

16.6.1 The Communications Challenge

Let's start by considering a real situation:

> *Many years ago, working as a subproject manager on a very large project for a utility, our leadership group realized that there were hitches. Some customer executives heard similar things from several of our team, while others remained uninformed. We decided to try to align our team with the customer staff to streamline communication. On a whiteboard, we listed the names and drew lines linking people that needed to talk to each other. The whiteboard soon looked like a bowl of spaghetti!*

It turns out that the problem is inherent. The theory of the number of potential communication links between stakeholders is illustrated in Figure 16.1.

When two people are involved, there is one link. When five people are involved, there are ten links. And generally the number of links = (n × (n – 1))/2. Thus, if there are 20 stakeholders involved, there are 190 potential communications links. So, while one-to-one communication can be desirable, clearly it can also get out of hand. Nor is it a solution to channel all communication through the PM. Yes, there would be fewer links, but given the amount of information that must flow, the PM would become an overloaded bottleneck.

16.6.2 A Structured Approach to Communications

The communications challenge cannot be ignored, and the way to deal with it is to take a more structured approach. Drawing up a communications plan is such an approach and it would recognize: (i) who the stakeholders are, (ii) what should be communicated and how often, (iii) what communications mechanisms should be used, and (iv) from whom the communication should come. When produced, the plan might be done in tabular format.

What will become clear is that certain information needs to be available to everyone. Early on all stakeholders need to agree or be informed of the PDD (project definition document). As the project progresses, updated schedules, project minutes, and project reports may meet many communications needs. For example, schedules

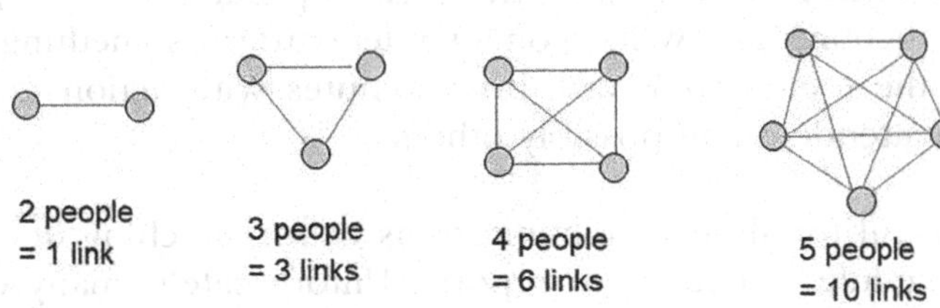

Figure 16.1 Links between stakeholders in project communication.

and minutes let people know what is expected of them, and by when. The project report is explained more fully below. How to communicate is a big subject, with lots of 'dos and don'ts' so here we shall touch on just a few aspects.

16.6.3 Interpersonal Communication

This applies as much on projects as it does in everyday life. Most people are good at talking, but listening does not always come naturally. Yet, listening is a valuable skill because it builds rapport and mutual respect. So PMs and others involved with projects can enhance their listening skills by developing the following habits:

- Have a comfortable body position which encourages the person to talk.
- Maintain eye contact.
- Give the speaker time.
- At intervals, summarize what you have understood, and allow the speaker to confirm or clarify (known as active listening).
- Acknowledge (but do not judge) the speaker's feelings.
- Ask questions, but only after getting the speaker's full message.

For effective communication to happen, the impact of certain barriers should be minimized, for example:

- Being rushed or having too little time – consider an alternative time.
- Noise and distractions – try to find a quiet place.
- Use of excessive jargon and terminology that may not be understood.
- Preconceived ideas or cultural differences.

Many of the above considerations would also apply to a phone call (with or without video).

16.6.4 Other Means of Communication

We have already discussed regular structured meetings and meetings between people. Here are a few other ways to communicate, with thoughts on each.

- Workshops or meetings to discuss a specific topic.
  It must be clear what topic will be discussed and the desired outcome. For example, "we need to agree how we will solve problem X". It is best to limit the number of attendees and to state the workshop duration. One person should facilitate the meeting, and writing on a whiteboard (or something similar) helps to maintain the focus. Afterward, brief minutes with action items should be circulated to attendees and possibly others.
- Emails
  These are useful for short communications or for attaching documents which might be schedules, minutes, or reports. Unfortunately, many emails will go unread, and some people will not even open them. But, at least people cannot claim to have been left in the dark.

- A shared repository for documentation
  This has been discussed, under documentation, in Chapter 3. The use of PPM (project portfolio management) software is also explained in Chapter 31 on digital tools. Nowadays, it is important that there is a web interface enabling people to access the repository from anywhere.
- Intranet or digital workplaces.
  These can be useful for keeping a wider audience in the organization informed. Dashboards, which just give basic facts and an updated status about one or multiple projects lend themselves to such communication.

16.7 Project Status Reports. How Long Should They Be?

There are many approaches to project reporting for stakeholders. Here is one approach which encourages regular reports, but limits each report to a single page, and preferably a bit less. Why one page? Well, most executives are busy, and will read no more than one page, especially where they are involved with many small- and medium-sized projects. Where an organization can agree on a standard format, so much the better because then executives will know where to look to find information. Conversely, getting many reports with different layouts can be confusing.

Information would be mainly in bullet form, but not so short that the meaning is lost. But the limited space does imply prioritization, and only the most serious risks or urgent issues would be reported. The frequency would depend on the project. Weekly is a good starting point, but some types of projects might report fortnightly or even monthly. PMs should present the picture as they see it. Bad news should never be withheld. For example, delays should be reported promptly even if a plan to contain the situation is mentioned. Figures should be representative and rounded rather than precise. For example, $1.36 million rather than $1 358 752.

16.7.1 A Possible Format and Content

Table 16.2 shows an illustrative one-page report. The exact format is not critical, provided that it is used fairly consistently.

Here are comments on some of the areas

- 'RAG' stands for Red, Amber, Green, and tells at a glance the overall status of the project, with a brief reason. Meanings are:
  - Green: There may be some minor problems, but they are under control.
  - Amber: Serious problems exist, but are being managed and are under control, or schedule or budget indexes are below a certain tolerance limit, like below 0.9.
  - Red. There are serious problems which require senior management intervention, or schedule or budget indexes are below tolerance limits. Red can also be used to signal the likelihood of missing a critical deadline if support is not given.

Usually the RAG is a judgment call by the PM, but on one project the sponsor wanted to agree a change in RAG status so as to be ready for queries. But generally, before

Table 16.2 An Illustrative One-Page Project Report

ABC Company	**Project Theta-B** Project Report	17 June 2021 Your Name

RAG	green	Reason: Close to schedule and no major problems

Highlights and lowlights for the past week

- o Discussions on supply chain restructure are completed and recommendation is under review.
- o
- o

Focus items for the next few weeks

- o Supplier information gathering continues, and the aim is to produce a supply chain map by 01 July.
- o
- o

Main issues

Issue description	Actions
Supplier X has been uncooperative regarding renegotiation of annual agreement	Involve head of dept. Y who have a strong relationship with Supplier X
Description of second issue	

Main risks

Risk description	Planned response action
We may have difficulty finding an alternative supplier for component Z	Investigate an alternative manufacturing approach that does not need component Z
Description of the second risk	

Performance information (values at 31 May 21)

Percent complete: 42%. Planned end date: 15 Oct 21 Projected end date: 05 Nov 21

Planned value: $850 000 Earned value: $810 000 Actual cost: $825 000
SPI = 0.95, CPI = 0.98.
Project is running 8 working days behind schedule. Costs are satisfactory.

going into red status, I would discuss the situation with the sponsor – executives don't like surprises.

- Highlights and lowlights require general comment on the situation: things achieved or where there was good progress, and disappointments or unsatisfactory areas.

- Focus items would generally look at the next 2 weeks, and would mention activities of current importance and those about to start.
- Main issues and risks should only mention the ones of greatest concern, or which relate to the RAG status.
- Performance information should relate to what stakeholders will understand, or what is relevant to the project. In one organization this section was omitted entirely, but we used four RAG codes at the top for schedule, cost, resources, and overall, and we also stated the estimated percentage complete.

My experience is that executives find this format more user-friendly than a Gantt chart, and I found doing regular reports a good discipline. Sometimes it seemed that the status was much the same as the previous week. This forced me to answer the question "why was there not more progress?".

To round-out reporting, I suggest you do Case 25, which presents four situations and gives you practice in choosing the appropriate RAG code.

16.7.2 How Should Executives Respond After Getting Reports?

By executives, we mean the sponsor, members of the steering committee, portfolio management, or any other senior stakeholder. There is more about the role of the sponsor in Chapter 17 on governance, but here we just consider the response to the regular report. Some of you may be executives that receive project reports.

First, you need to glance through the report, or at least at the RAG code. If the code is green, then detail may not be important. But, if the code is amber or red, then you need to check the reason, and understand enough to know whether or how to respond. Importantly, the RAG is not a reflection on the PM or team's competence or commitment. Thus, red does not mean poor performance, just as green does not mean good performance. Often there are circumstances beyond the PM's control. So, if the RAG changes for the worse, you would seek more information.

Reporting will be most effective if a PM-culture of honesty and sound judgment is fostered. Undue criticism of PMs who report honestly is likely to result in them hiding bad news and hoping that problems will magically 'come right' or go unnoticed. Under such circumstances the bad situation seldom improves; usually it gets worse and may even turn into a disaster. So, even if the PM has slipped up, it is more helpful to understand the background and then support or counsel, than it is to blame the PM. So, thank the PM for 'telling it like it is', or for raising issues in good time, and assist the PM in finding the best way forward.

Back to the PM. Yes, there will be executives that demand results without considering the circumstances, and this will always be challenging to handle. Fortunately, most executives have learned that, without being 'soft', a more constructive approach works best.

16.8 Summary

We have covered many of the day-to-day tracking activities that a PM might do while managing one or more projects. We have also discussed communication which supports those ongoing activities. We have paid particular attention to reports which not only give you a historical record of each project but may be the only information that reaches some of your stakeholders.

Reference

OGC. (2009). *Managing Successful Projects with PRINCE2*, 5th edition. In A. Murray (Ed.). Norwich: TSO (The Stationery Office) on behalf of Office of Government Commerce.

Chapter 17

Governance of a Project

17.1 Introduction and Objectives

Already in Chapter 4, we learned of the importance of governance at the levels of a single project and a portfolio of projects. We also learned that the business project lifetime overarches the project life cycle, starting before it, and ending sometimes long after it. While the PM is committed to the project during the life cycle, the project sponsor, sometimes supported by a steering committee, is accountable throughout the lifetime. The importance of the sponsor's role is touched on in Chapters 2 and 4, here we go into more depth. On larger projects, the sponsor is supported by a steering committee, or 'project board' as the PRINCE2 methodology refers to it (OGC, 2009). Here we shall shorten it to the 'Steercom'. So, where the sponsor is mentioned, the Steercom might also be involved.

While Chapter 19 expands governance to the portfolio, this chapter covers the governance of a single project, and the objectives are to:

- Restate what governance is, and how it can be seen as the organization wrapped around the project.
- Learn the qualities required of a project sponsor, which also apply to many members of the Steercom.
- Know what the sponsor needs to do as the project unfolds and also what the sponsor would expect of the PM.
- Understand the critical roles on the Steercom (which would all be played by the sponsor if there is no Steercom).
- Show how suppliers might be involved in the project and governance structure.
- Know how the 'gate review' approach can support project governance.

17.2 Governance Clarified

I know of no universally accepted definition of project governance. But, regarding governance as a 'set of principles and processes to improve the management of projects in the organization' rings true (PMI, 2017). So here we shall consider the

DOI: 10.1201/9781003321101-19

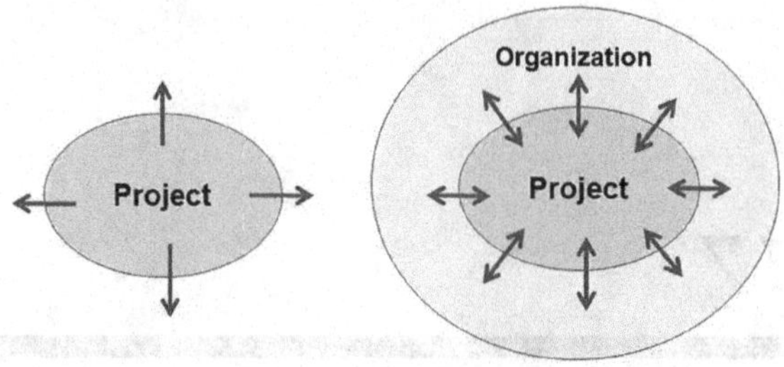

Figure 17.1 Project governance – the organization wrapped around the project.

principles and processes that apply to one project, which I see as 'the organization wrapped around the project' – illustrated in Figure 17.1.

On the left, we see a project that is being done in isolation. When there are problems, there is nowhere for the PM to go for help and the project might easily lose direction. There are many factors beyond the PM's control, and PMs might question their own ability when the real problem is a lack of governance. Contrast that with the project on the right where governance interacts with the project to ensure satisfactory results. There are many links with the organization, one being to the sponsor. Now there is lots of support, and even the most competent PMs need support at times. In fact, a good PM will understand the support structures and use them appropriately. Should there be any loss of direction, it will quickly be picked up and rectified.

At this point, it is suggested that you do Case 26, XP Insurance, which illustrates how easily a project can become isolated.

17.3 Qualities of the Sponsor and Steercom Members

Because the sponsor plays such an important accountability role, let's consider what qualities sponsors require. They need a level of seniority and formal authority to take decisions. They must have credibility within the organization as a whole and with the PM and project team. Sponsors need judgment regarding their involvement with the project: On the one hand, PMs need to be empowered to manage; on the other hand, sponsors must maintain an awareness of what is actually happening and pick up any warning flags. The latter is likely to happen where sponsors really care about project outcomes. Equally important is being available, particularly where a decision is needed or when an important document needs to be reviewed promptly. Members of the Steercom need similar qualities. Possibly they will not be as committed as the sponsor, but they must have the project's interests at heart.

17.4 Sponsor Activities Throughout the Project's Lifetime

There are many governances and other activities done by the sponsor throughout the project's lifetime. Steercom members may do some of them and assist with others. Figure 17.2 presents the high-level activities pictorially.

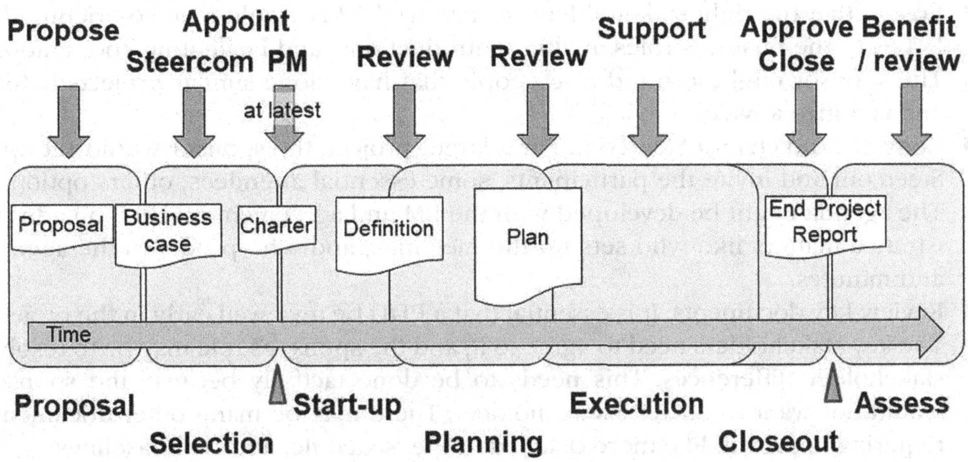

Figure 17.2 Sponsor activities during the project lifetime.

As a reminder, the project life cycle runs between the triangles, from start-up to closeout. The project's lifetime starts earlier and ends later. It runs from when the project is first thought of until after the benefits have been realized and the outcome assessed against what was envisaged in the business case. The assessment may only be final many months after closeout. The figure can be referred to as we progress through the sponsor's role, but in practice, the sponsor's involvement is situational and does not follow a neat sequence. So here is the list, and it's a long one:

- Initiate the project proposal: The proposal might be done by the sponsor or be delegated. Occasionally, where the need is understood but the approach is not clear, a feasibility study might be requested. A decision would be taken as to the approach on which to base the business case.
- Authorize development of a business case: Whether a few lines or several pages, a business case is needed for all projects – it formalizes the justification for the project. The sponsor would appoint a person or team, and ensure that time and money are allocated.
- Review the business case and decide: Based on the justification, the sponsor would decide whether or not to proceed, or, whether to submit the project to a corporate selection process. Where formal project selection is mandatory, the sponsor would motivate the reasons for going ahead, to the selection committee.
- Confirm that funding and resources will be available: The assignment of money and people may be part of project selection, but if not, the sponsor would need to provide them for the project.
- Appoint the PM and issue the charter: The PM may already be 'on board', but otherwise the sponsor needs to find and appoint one. Ideally, the charter would be a one- or two-page document outlining the project and authorizing the PM to get started. More often it would be a discussion, hopefully documented for the record. Sometimes, the resources for the project team would be 'in principle', leaving the PM to actually find the team members – but with the sponsor's backing.

- Ensure that the right stakeholders are involved: This would involve briefing the PM as to the business roles, making introductions, and facilitating cooperation. The sponsor might also indicate people that have done similar projects before and can give advice.
- Convene and chair a Steercom: For a larger project, the sponsor would set up a Steercom and invite the participants, some essential attendees, others optional. The agenda might be developed with the PM and agreement reached on administrative matters like who sets up the meetings, and who produces the agenda and minutes.
- Review key documents: It is essential that a PDD be reviewed early in the project. The key stakeholders need to agree to it, and the sponsor's role may be to resolve stakeholder differences. This needs to be done tactfully because the sponsor would not want to alienate stakeholders. There may be many other documents requiring approval, like more detailed scope, schedule, and cost baselines.
- Take decisions: At any time, decisions may be needed. Sometimes the sponsor would take them immediately and sometimes Steercom members or other stakeholders would be consulted first.
- Monitor the project and the environment: The sponsor would monitor the project by reading regular reports – especially if the project is in amber or red status. The sponsor would also be aware of things happening inside or outside the organization that have a bearing on the project's justification.

  I remember a situation where the announcement of a competitive offering caused us to change the focus of several projects to meet the threat – with a six week deadline for being business-ready. It was the executives that highlighted the need.

- Do reviews and take decisions: Project reviews, with the business case as input, might be initiated by the PM or a project office. But, the sponsor's input is essential, and ultimately the decision whether to proceed, change, or even stop the project, belongs to the sponsor.
- Handle exceptions: Issues and risks that can be dealt with at project level, merely need to be noted. But, where an issue is beyond the PM's control, or where a risk requires outside intervention, then the sponsor needs to be involved, with a briefing from the PM.
- Approve changes: Any changes to the baseline scope, schedule, or cost plans need sponsor approval. Often all that is needed is approval for a one-page document outlining the change. Major changes may take more, and include the involvement of other stakeholders.
- Approve project closure: Close to the end of the project, the sponsor would engage with the PM and agree to things that still need to be done. This might include closer involvement of business people for handovers and checking that benefits will be achieved. If there is a tight deadline then certain 'de-scoping' may be called for – agreeing activities that are not needed, or, that can be deferred until after the project is complete. Finally, an end-project report would be reviewed and discussed with the PM.
- Monitor benefits realization: Seldom does the sponsor's involvement stop at closeout. Business benefits still need to be achieved. Now a business person

might take over responsibility from the PM, but the sponsor remains accountable. At this time, the sponsor might also give feedback on the PM's performance, or even on the performance of other team members.

- Assess outcomes: This might be done, over a period after closeout. The actual outcomes and benefits would be compared with what was planned in the business case (or in some other way). Action may need to be taken where difficulties or new opportunities arise. The sponsor, as the most interested party, would ensure that such action is taken.
- Support the PM and team: This is needed throughout the project and is a major contributor to success. The sponsor may occasionally act as a sounding board for the PM, and might interact informally with team members. It should be agreed up front that the PM can contact the sponsor at short notice, should the situation need a quick decision. Even if being available and present takes little time, a powerful message is sent: "this project is important to me". Similarly, the occasional 'thank you' note never goes amiss.

All of these activities by the sponsor belong to governance. Often members of a Steercom assist with them and the activities may only take a few hours per month. Yet, I have never seen them formalized in an organization's processes. It is assumed that sponsors know what to do. Therefore, it is important for the PM to understand the sponsor's role. Sometimes the sponsor is not familiar with the role, in which case the PM would need to tactfully coach the sponsor as to what is expected and explain what support is needed. Whatever your current management responsibilities you may now or in future, play the sponsor role.

Because the sponsor gets involved in many aspects of the project in limited time, a great deal is expected from the PM – besides the day-to-day running of the project.

17.5 What Might the Sponsor Expect from the PM?

Just as the PM needs governance structures to guide the project, so the sponsor needs and would expect a great deal from the PM. Here are some of the items:

- The PM should produce a thorough plan, starting with a PDD (project definition document) that is easy for stakeholders to understand. Plans that need review must be provided in good time, and not 'at the last moment', expecting urgent review. The plans should not be padded with unjustified time and costs, but motivating some contingency based on risk, is acceptable.
- There should be no 'surprises'. Ongoing reporting must be honest, and neither overly optimistic nor pessimistic. Deviations from the plan should be made clear. Where serious problems arise, the sponsor should be made aware without delay. For situations beyond the PM's control, the sponsor should be given alternatives, with recommendations as to how they might be handled.
- While the PM cannot take certain decisions, the PM must be proactive in *getting* them taken. On a project involving many stakeholders, this might be facilitated via a 'decision rights matrix' whereby the sponsor indicates up front who is expected to take decisions in defined areas. Having identified who needs to

take the decision, the PM would provide background information, make recommendations, and explain why a decision is needed in a given timeframe.
- The PM might orchestrate regular sponsor or Steercom meetings and also suggest periodic reviews of the business case, especially where changed circumstances bring the justification for the project into question.
- Stakeholder relationships must be well managed. This includes dealing with the inevitable conflicts that arise in a project team, and also maintaining a productive relationship with customers and suppliers. Listening skills are a valuable quality in this regard.
- Even when things are running smoothly, the PM should communicate regularly with key stakeholders, who should be comfortable that they are well informed. This might include arranging interaction between the business and the team, or even inviting the sponsor to brief the team on the project's importance.

While some misunderstandings and crises may arise, if the PM demonstrates integrity, they will be overcome without relationship damage.

Because the sponsor-PM relationship is so important, I suggest that you do Case 27 which gives eight situations that a sponsor might encounter, several directly involving the PM. It invites you to suggest how the sponsor might handle each of them.

17.6 Governance Structures and the Steercom

Here we shall consider the key roles on the Steercom and then see how it might work in a project where a major supplier is involved.

17.6.1 Key Steercom Roles

I support PRINCE2's suggestion that there are three main roles on the Steercom, namely (OGC, 2009):

- The sponsor (sometimes also called the project owner or the executive),
- The 'senior business person' representing the people that will ultimately benefit from the project,
- The 'senior resource supplier', the person who controls the people that will do the work.

On a small project, all three roles could be played by one person, for example, where the sponsor also plays the business role and provides most of the project team. This might happen in a departmental project where the department manager would probably play all the roles. On a larger project, where several business departments are involved, the Steercom might have more than one senior business person. There might also be more than one senior supplier where project staff come from more than one department or where suppliers provide people. Where suppliers are involved, an excellent relationship between the sponsor and supplier at the executive level often gets issues resolved quickly without having to wait for a meeting.

The PM, who can provide up-to-date project information, is also part of the Steercom with a dotted reporting line to the sponsor. There may also be other Steercom members like representatives from Finance, Legal, Procurement, or any other involved function.

17.6.2 An Illustrative Governance Structure with Supplier Involvement

Figure 4.1 (Chapter 4) shows the governance structure for a project run *within* an organization. Now we shall consider a situation, shown in Figure 17.3, where a major supplier is involved. Clearly, the figure is illustrative because there can be multiple suppliers and each situation will need its own structure – the possibilities are endless.

The Steercom is shown in the upper half of the figure and indicates the variety of members. Here a supplier executive is a member, and also plays a role as a 'resource supplier'. Typically, a Steercom would meet monthly to be updated on project progress and to discuss project matters.

The project team is shown in the lower half of the figure. In this situation, the project team has both internal and supplier staff. The PM would usually come from the same organization as the sponsor, but might also come from outside. Sometimes there is a supplier PM (dark gray) working closely with the organization's PM (pale gray). This might happen where the supplier brings special skills and takes on certain responsibilities.

QA (quality assurance) where it exists is necessarily independent and usually plays an advisory role. A 'change authority', sometimes called a 'change control board', might be set up with powers delegated by the Steercom. But more often, the sponsor, assisted by the Steercom, decide on proposed changes.

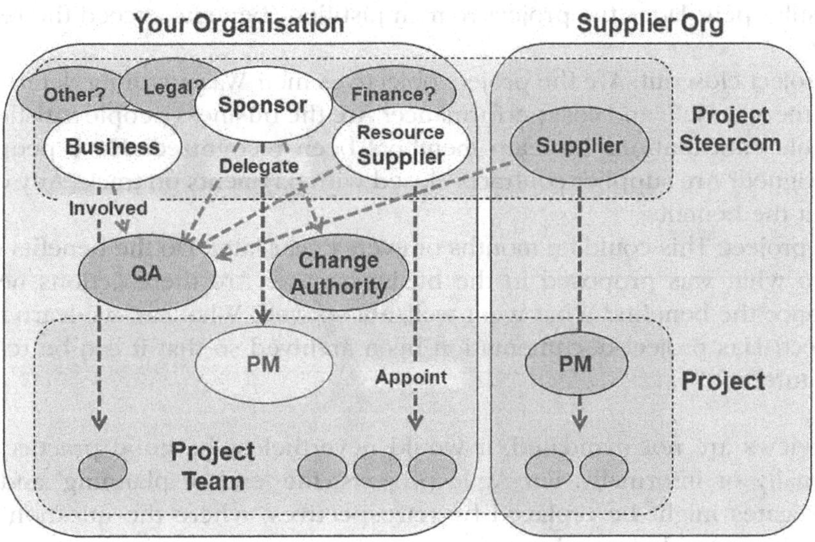

Figure 17.3 Governance structure involving a supplier.

17.7 Governance Through 'gate' Reviews

It has already been mentioned that periodic project reviews are needed. Some organizations have a standard that reviews be held at specific times during the project's lifetime. These are known as 'phase gate' or 'stage gate' or simply 'gate' reviews (Larson & Gray, 2018). The sponsor and PM would always attend and might be joined by other stakeholders like portfolio management or PMO staff. The purpose is always to determine whether the project should proceed, make changes, be placed on hold, or be terminated. As soon as it is developed, the business case becomes a key input and may be changed following the review. Each organization handles governance differently, but here are some points at which any gate reviews would typically be held, with questions that might be asked:

- Proposal: What problem are we solving or what is the opportunity? Is this strategic, operational, or to comply with legislation?
- Business case developed or project selection: Who is the sponsor? What are the benefits, who is responsible for them, and how shall we measure them? How long will the project take and what will it cost? What are the risks? Can we estimate the rate of return on our investment? Do we have the skilled resources, or must we find them? Can the project wait?
- End of planning: Is the plan complete or is there missing information? What assumptions are we making? Are the resources available? What are the greatest risks and what actions will be taken to respond to them? Has contingency been allowed for? Are key stakeholders in agreement (with the PDD or equivalent)? Is the business case still sound?
- During execution: Depending on the project's duration, this review may be held more than once. Are deliverables, schedules, and costs on track? What changes have been raised, approved? What are the main risks remaining? Which issues are still open? Does the project remain justified (benefits exceed the remaining costs)?
- At project closeout: Are the project objectives met? Was anything deferred? How was the schedule and cost performance? Are the business people satisfied? Have notable contributions by team members been recognized? Have people been reassigned? Are supplier contracts closed with payments on track? Any concerns about the benefits?
- Post project: This could be months or even a year later. Do the benefits measure up to what was proposed in the business case? Are there actions needed to enhance the benefits? What went well/not so well? What can we learn from the project? Has project documentation been archived so that it can be referenced in future?

If gate reviews are not mandated, it would nevertheless be good practice to hold them formally or informally. For Agile projects, the 'end of planning' and 'during execution' gates might be replaced by retrospectives, where the question "are we getting value?" should always be raised.

17.8 In Conclusion

What has been covered assumes a level of structure and formality. In environments where there is little structure, governance is still needed and sponsorship is still vital – some executives must want the benefits. But, whatever the situation, the PM and project team should never be 'going it alone'.

References

Larson, E. & Gray, C. (2018). *Project Management: The Managerial Process. International Edition*. 7th edition. New York: McGraw-Hill Education.

OGC. (2009). *Managing Successful Projects with PRINCE2*, 5th edition. In A. Murray (Ed.). Norwich: TSO (The Stationery Office) on behalf of Office of Government Commerce.

PMI. (2017). *PMBOK – Guide to the Project Management Body of Knowledge*, 6th edition. Pennsylvania, USA: Project Management Institute.

Chapter 18

Closing the Project

18.1 Introduction and Objectives

Closing the project, or 'project closeout', is what happens toward the end of the project. For many business projects, even if the project scope is complete, realizing the benefits may continue long after closeout. When the PM has moved on to something else, business people remain involved, and this is why evaluation of the project, by the business, may be deferred for several months – to give time for things to settle and for new processes to bed down. Nevertheless, there are many things that need to happen during closeout, and just *what* things, depends on the project. But for almost all projects, how they are done, leaves a lasting impression irrespective of how successful, or otherwise, the project might have been. So, the objectives of this chapter are to:

- Understand the various closeout scenarios – some well-handled, others not.
- Know the activities for closing a particular project and that they start well before the project's scope is delivered.
- Know how to perform the closeout activities.

Indeed there are many aspects to closeout, and although each situation is different, some of the activities are needed for every business project. First, let's look at the closeout scenarios.

18.2 Closeout Scenarios

As we shall see, not all projects are wonderfully successful, but all projects need to be properly closed. Let us consider what some of the scenarios might be (Larson & Gray, 2018).

DOI: 10.1201/9781003321101-20

18.2.1 Normal Closeout

This could occur even if the project is late or over budget. But the project objectives should have been met, with the scope substantially complete. I say 'substantially' because there may have been some de-scoping by agreement with the sponsor. De-scoping simply means: either not doing something that is found to be unnecessary, or, deferring something until after the project, as a follow-on activity or part of a new project.

18.2.2 Premature Closeout

There are many possible reasons for closing a project before it is complete. Perhaps there is no longer a business case – the cost or benefit assumptions, or the risk profile may have changed. Possibly a key element of the project has proved unworkable. Stopping such projects early is not necessarily a failure. It could indicate sound governance. It's also important to understand that premature termination does not imply poor performance on the part of the PM or the team. Conversely, poor performance is not a reason for terminating a *justified* project. But whatever the premature scenario, things should not just be dropped. Proper closeout is still needed. There are people to consider, partial deliverables to be salvaged, costs to be accounted for, and lessons to be learned.

18.2.3 Changed Priorities

There is also the scenario of changed priorities. Portfolio management, through project selection, may be constantly reviewing the justification for new projects and of projects that are underway. Changes in strategy and the business environment need to be taken into account because they affect business cases. This may result in changes in priority, and such shifts could be minor or major. The projects are competing for resources, particularly for money and skills. So, a critical new project, may cause projects that are already underway to be put on hold, or even terminated to free up the needed money and skilled people. Such actions are always challenging. The team members are usually committed, and should not be shown up in a poor light for something that was beyond their control. There may also be supplier contracts to negotiate to a close. But, as with successful projects, and for the same reasons, even projects going on-hold need proper closeout. It should cover the possibilities of the project being re-started later or never being re-started.

18.2.4 Badly Handled Scenarios

So far we have dealt with scenarios that are well-handled. Here is a scenario that is poorly handled. The 'runaway' or 'perpetual' project scenario sometimes happens. The project drags on in spite of delays and budget overruns. The business requirements may be unclear leading to uncontrolled change requests and scope creep. Leading indicators of failure are probably being ignored, such as lack of ownership, no sound business case, or vague scope – all typical symptoms of projects that lack a committed sponsor. Massive amounts of money and people can be wasted over long periods for little or no return.

Now, where does closure come into the picture? Well, it needs to be considered. The most important thing is for someone in authority to take stock and review the justification for the project. If it is justified, then it needs to be brought back onto a sound footing as a well-defined project, or as a properly managed program of projects. Either way, it would need a business case and a committed sponsor. This is certainly not easy because there are probably many demoralized people involved. Moreover, the benefits and even the projected cost estimates may be subject to emotion. But, if such a project, turns out *not* to be justified, then the quicker it is terminated the better. Proper closeout is needed because, once again, there are people, contracts and many other things to be dealt with, and some lessons to be learned.

18.2.5 Other Closeout Possibilities

Not all closeouts fall neatly into the above scenarios; indeed there are too many to enumerate. The following two scenarios are quite common and need the PM to decide how they should be handled. The first is where part of a project comes to an end before the entire project is finished. Possibly a major milestone has been reached and some team members or a supplier are no longer required on the project. The second is where the project is heading for completion, but there is a logical follow-on project. An example would be where a pilot implementation of new processes was done for one region, with rollout to other regions following on. It might be treated as a new but related project. Some work on the new project would probably even start in parallel. Another example would be where completion of a project within a program leads naturally to another project which may involve many of the team members. In such scenarios where closeout may not be as clear-cut, even more discipline on the part of the PM is needed to take the appropriate steps.

So we see that, whatever the scenario, proper closeout is needed. Let's now look at some of the closeout considerations.

18.3 Closeout Considerations

First, closeout is a process: a set of activities to bring the project to an orderly completion. Like any scope, the activities need to be defined and managed. Second, as mentioned already, similar activities are needed whatever the scenario. The activities cannot wait until the rest of the scope is finished; many of them must start much earlier. In fact, one might say that, closeout starts during the planning. Deliverables must be defined in such a way that it is clear when they can be accepted, and contracts must be drawn up so that it is clear what happens at the end of the project. Because these are activities, they will take people-effort and budget, so time and cost must be allowed for them.

To complicate matters, there are normal project activities that must happen in parallel even after handing over the main deliverables. For example, where business people are getting used to new processes, a support or 'hand-holding' period may be needed, with its own priorities like resolving problems that arise. Another thought: it really helps if the same stakeholders that were involved at start-up can be involved during closeout – especially for reviews.

Let's also accept that closeout is difficult, and requires even more discipline than planning or execution. The PM and team are often tired, so elements are easily overlooked and loose ends left hanging – often things that are quite easy to do. Moreover, the team members are usually not in the mood for 'dotting i's and crossing t's'. As far as they are concerned, their work is done. But, the professionalism that the PM shows during closeout is what may be remembered by the sponsor, the business stakeholders, or any customers involved.

18.4 The Closeout Activities – What Needs to Be Done?

Let's take a look at the steps, the closeout activities, bearing in mind that they happen in parallel with other critical tasks and can be iterative. So we cannot expect a neatly defined sequence.

18.4.1 Review the PDD or Contract and Deliver the Solution

Well before closeout, have a good look at the PDD for an internal project, the contract for a customer project, or any other relevant documents. Check that the specified deliverables are or will be ready, taking into account approved changes.

Next, deliver the solution. This can take many forms, but it might involve implementing a new or changed business process, doing handovers, training, or supporting business users. It could be presenting the results of a survey or study, or handing over any other documentation. In parallel, check the issues log and project minutes. Check that no issues are open that will affect deliverables, and that there are no important action items remaining on the minutes. Talk to stakeholders like suppliers and business users. Solicit their input because it may highlight things needing attention.

You might be required to give metrics to the PMO, like schedule data, costs, resource utilization, or whatever. I'm not entirely convinced as to their value because I have seldom seen project metrics used effectively. But, they may be important in your organization. Where metrics are required, they should have been noted during planning because it is difficult to generate data later, that should have been collected along the way.

18.4.2 Bring Supplier Activities to an Orderly Close

Liaise with your suppliers, especially those providing people or services. Check what is needed to close your contracts with them. Ensure that they have fully delivered, and then arrange payment which forms part of your project's financial closure. At this time, misunderstandings are common, so make sure your discussions are confirmed in writing. This helps to avoid unexpected and irritating issues surfacing post-project. It is also good practice to evaluate your suppliers (also known as 'vendor evaluation') and give them feedback. Your procurement or SCM (Supply Chain Management) function may welcome the information.

18.4.3 Perform Financial Closure

This may be a 'non-event' for small internal projects, but for larger projects, many organizations monitor budgets and need to know the final cost. Finalizing those costs can be quite a bit of work, especially where suppliers are involved. So, request final invoices or proforma (preliminary, estimated) invoices from suppliers, even if you will only authorize final payment when the work or delivery has been checked. Depending on the financial processes, you may even need to 'make provision' in the accounting system if the actual payment (to offset the provision) will only be made after the project account has been closed. Having approved the supplier payments, check that payment was actually made.

> *I learned the lesson from a situation where a supplier phoned me two months after I had authorized payment, asking where the money was. Only then did I find that Procurement had rejected the invoice due to a missing bit of (unimportant) data, without notifying me or the supplier.*

Where people are charging their time to the project, make sure any time capture is complete so that project costs can be finalized. If there is a project accounting system, and when all known costs have been received, arrange for the project account to be closed.

18.4.4 Take Care of the People

For part-time team members working in matrix mode, there is little problem; their department will quickly reassign them. But, for dedicated people, especially contract staff, plan their moves well before project closeout. It is less stressful for the people and good for your reputation as a PM that people want to work for. If they are good performers, there are usually other projects looking for staff. This has the additional benefit that they will be available to handle incidental queries post-project. Whether they are contract or permanent staff, have an arrangement that support can be obtained after they have moved, if needed.

Do appraisals where necessary, or give feedback, even if the formal appraisal will be done by another manager. A career discussion with some people may be worthwhile. Cultures differ regarding recognition. Letters of thanks take little time and are always appreciated. In some organizations, there is a formal award nomination process – sometimes for teams, sometimes for individuals. I am always wary of recognizing the best performers, visibly and with the team present, when everyone has been putting in extra effort to achieve the objective.

18.4.5 Tidy Up and Archive the Project Documentation

Where governance is well established, project documentation gets archived for future reference. But first, the documentation needs to be brought up to date. This includes many types of record, but any that relate to sign-off or acceptance of deliverables would be particularly important. A tidy-up of folders would help you, or anyone else, if the project data will be referred to in future – very useful for similar projects.

The documentation may already be in a PPM (project portfolio management) system in the cloud. On the other hand, it may only be on your laptop, hopefully well backed up. Sometimes there is no central repository, but increasingly PMOs provide such a facility, or at least say where documentation should be lodged. Always keep a copy for yourself; sometimes one needs to refer back to past projects.

18.4.6 Produce the Project Completion Report and Involve the Sponsor

Even if there is no standard that demands a project completion report or 'closeout report', it is sound practice to produce one. It allows you to reflect on how things went and sometimes brings forgotten items to your attention. Therefore, it's a good idea to start it early – even many weeks before closeout. The format may depend on whether the project is internal or for a customer or client. Where you are the supplier performing a project for a customer, both may be needed: a report for the customer sponsor, and another for your own management. Much of the content would be the same, but the objectives of the two organizations, while aligned, are not identical.

A good starting point is to go back to the PDD or contract. Note the goals and project objectives, and comment on each. In my experience, seldom are all of them fully met. Some of the goals may only be met long after the project is complete. Explain things that were not achieved; maybe they were de-scoped by agreement. Give a list of things that should be considered for a future project or phase. Some of them may be items from your 'parking lot' or change requests that were turned down by the sponsor; others may be tasks, removed from the project's scope, which business people agreed to complete later. Clarifying which things were not part of your final scope reduces misunderstandings.

You should summarize the main approved changes and their impact on schedule and cost, and also the main risks that happened or issues that arose which affected the project. These will give context for the cost and schedule performance summaries that need to be included. 'Lessons learned' can be part of the completion report or a separate document. State what happened and the lesson drawn from it, remembering that one can learn as much from things that went well, as from things that went badly. The lessons could come from your own records or from a workshop held with stakeholders which includes the team.

Reviewing the completion report is a good way to involve the sponsor and even other key stakeholders. The main thing is to ensure that the PM, the sponsor, and stakeholders are 'in synch' as to how things went and whether anything else is needed. Revisit the latest version of the business case and confirm the degree to which the envisaged benefits have been, or are likely to be, met. Just after completion, check that the sponsor agrees with the content of the completion report.

18.4.7 Additional Miscellaneous Activities

Further items depend a lot on the projects and organizations involved. Norms, and what is expected, differ widely. You can discuss internal publicity with the sponsor, but however successful the project, any external publicity usually needs to go through a Communications function. So, be very careful about engaging directly with the press. A social event for the team can be quite informal, but if it involves stakeholders outside the team, then best discuss what is appropriate with the sponsor.

Governance requirements vary widely. But, where the outcome of the project will only be fully understood in future, it may be appropriate to schedule a review or stakeholder survey some months after project closeout – a standard in some organizations. Finally, where you are working on a customer site, return any equipment and leave it tidy. That goes without saying.

18.5 Summary

There are many closeout scenarios, some orderly, others messy. But, they all need to be handled professionally. We have seen that there are lots of things to do for closeout, over and above getting the project finished. Very often they are neglected because there are so many pressures towards the end of a project. If such neglect causes stakeholders like suppliers or business end-users to be frustrated, you may not become aware of it. But, although seldom formalized, stakeholder frustrations may affect your reputation. So, if closeout activities are not already part of the schedule, then an hour spent thinking through what needs to happen and adding them to the schedule or your own to-do list, is time well spent.

This is the last of the core chapters that cover what is essential for most business projects. Therefore, there are two cases:

- Case 28 deals with the problems faced at the Rescon division of a multinational. It has both closeout and governance elements.
- Case 29 gives 16 situations that might happen on any business project and need to be dealt with by the PM. You are asked to say what approach you would take, which disciplines would be involved, and what documentation you would produce. By thinking them through, you will not only use all the understanding gained thus far, but you will also decide what approach to use in each situation.

The chapters in the next part of the book cover a broad variety of topics. Some, like the business case and project selection, are things that senior management like sponsors and portfolio managers need. Others like procurement are also important for the PM, but only in certain projects. Nevertheless, all the topics should build the perspective of anyone that is involved in business projects.

Reference

Larson, E. & Gray, C. (2018). *Project Management: The Managerial Process.* International Edition. 7th edition. New York: McGraw-Hill Education.

3 SPECIAL TOPICS RELATED TO BUSINESS PROJECT MANAGEMENT

The essential knowledge and techniques that the PM needs for all business projects, from small and simple ones to large and complex ones, were provided in Part 2

Part 3 covers a range of special topics, which are of interest to a broader range of stakeholders, but also to the PM. Several topics are relevant for a portfolio of projects. Other topics are needed for some projects, but not for others. Procurement is an example because it may apply greatly to the scope of certain business projects, while others may involve no procurement at all. Further topics broaden the PM's understanding, like knowing how a portfolio of projects might be managed, or learning the fundamentals of negotiation which everybody needs to master.

DOI: 10.1201/9781003321101-21

Chapter 19

Governance for a Portfolio of Projects

19.1 Introduction and Objectives

Chapter 4 on the project environment has already given an introduction to portfolio governance. This chapter takes it a step further and is mainly for senior management, portfolio managers, and PMO (project management office) managers and staff. Nevertheless, PMs need to understand how portfolio governance *should* function, and be able to assess how it works in their environment. Possibly some of the problems that PMs experience are because portfolio management is not done, or is not handled well. And, by the way, I regard portfolio management and portfolio governance as almost synonymous.

In Chapter 17, we covered governance applied to a single project. Here we discuss how an organization might govern many, or even all, of its projects. Certainly, there is some overlap, for example, the business case or project justification is needed for a single project and to select between many projects (OGC, 2009). So the objectives are to:

- Show how corporate strategies need projects to implement them.
- Understand the challenges of strategy implementation and how portfolio governance can address them.
- Get an overview of the portfolio governance processes.
- Classify projects, and know the difference between projects and programs.
- Know the role players in portfolio governance.
- Understand the ways that a PMO might support portfolio governance.
- Gain insights as to where 'project management maturity' might fit in.

DOI: 10.1201/9781003321101-22

19.2 How Projects Arise from Strategy

Projects arise for many reasons, but possibly the main one is to achieve the organization's strategies (Larson & Gray, 2018). Figure 19.1 shows an ideal progression of how it might happen, as a sequence of process steps (the rectangles). It also shows some of the role players. But first let us consider the steps going from left to right.

The top executives would hold periodic strategy sessions. After confirming the organization's mission, they might analyze its strengths and weaknesses and also look at the opportunities and threats that exist – known as a SWOT (Strengths, Weaknesses, Opportunities, Threats) analysis. This would lead to new goals being set. Some would be monetary, like revenue from new products of a specified number of dollars over the next 2 years; others would be non-monetary like becoming more sustainable by reducing the carbon footprint by a certain percentage over the next 5 years. Then they would agree on strategies to achieve the goals. So far so good, but, strategies do not just happen; work needs to be done to make them happen, and the best way, certainly for major initiatives, is through projects. This is where the problems often start.

Although the executives may have agreed with some of the important projects, there are usually many smaller projects that are also needed to address the strategies. Added to them there are the 'other projects' shown in the figure. They are operational projects like refurbishment of machinery in the plant, and projects to comply with legislation, known in some sectors as 'compliance' or 'regulatory' projects. Even these could be considered strategic if efficient and legally compliant operations were part of the strategy. Unfortunately, there are always more proposed projects than the organization can undertake. It simply does not have the resources, either financial or people, to take them all on at once. So selection and prioritization are needed. Once this is done projects can be initiated and executed, and when the output has been delivered, benefits can be reaped and strategies fulfilled – the last process step in Figure 19.1. If deliverables are produced at milestones during execution, then some benefits can be achieved before the end of the project (Enoch, 2019).

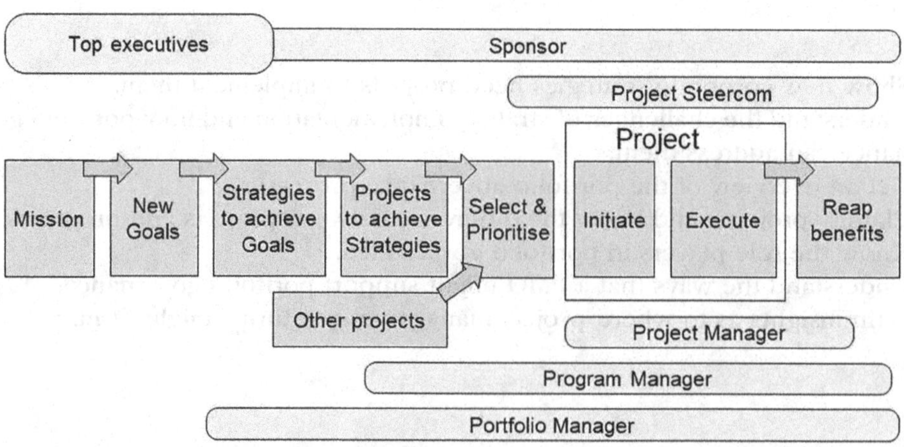

Figure 19.1 The portfolio management progression.

19.3 Managing a Portfolio of Projects

The scope of portfolio management is shown by the bar at the bottom of Figure 19.1. It starts by understanding the strategies and continues until the benefits of the required projects are realized and the strategies achieved (Marnewick, 2018). As mentioned in Chapter 4, a portfolio of projects is all the recognized projects in the organization or in a large and autonomous part of the organization. There may be hundreds of projects, and even the small ones can hold considerable risk or be critical dependencies for larger projects. So portfolio management is involved in optimizing the organization's projects by doing the right projects, and then 'doing them right'.

19.3.1 What Happens with No Portfolio Management

Let's now look at project portfolio management in more depth. First, let's consider what happens without portfolio management. Top management may have thought of some of the projects, and they may even have delegated them to the next level of management (Larson & Gray, 2018). However, a number of problems arise: (i) the projects need resources from multiple functional areas, and each area naturally gives priority to its own projects, (ii) the projects will have dependencies, which leads to further projects, (iii) organizational politics enters the arena, with influential managers linking their own projects to their career ambitions. The latter gives rise to 'pet projects' that may not be justified, but which nobody dares question. The result is some confusion and unproductive conflict, with too many projects being taken on. Many will be under-resourced leading to wasteful expenditure, and delays in strategy implementation. The task of the PM, working in a matrix environment, and drawing part-time skills from multiple departments, becomes more difficult, with much time being spent vying for the limited skills and explaining the delays.

19.3.2 The Scope of Portfolio Management

The solution lies in portfolio management, which can be broadly defined as 'the management of the organizations portfolio of change initiatives'. This means that portfolio management must coordinate the process and decisions to produce the most effective balance of organizational change and business-as-usual initiatives. So, the main activities are to:

- Understand the organization's strategies,
- Record proposed projects,
- Know what resources are available or could be sourced,
- Facilitate selection of the optimum set of projects, given the resource constraints,
- Monitor all projects in the portfolio, and
- Ensure that the planned benefits are realized.

19.3.3 Project Selection

This may sound easy, but some of the elements are not straightforward. For example, in selection of the optimum projects, the portfolio manager needs to understand the classes of project shown in Figure 19.2 – adapted from Matheson & Matheson (1998).

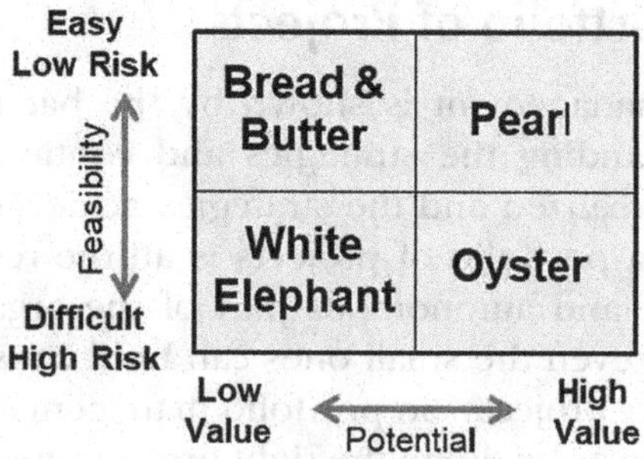

Figure 19.2 Classification for project selection.

It considers projects on two axes: (i) vertical: from difficult to do with high risk to easy to do with low risk, and (ii) horizontal: from low value to high potential value. Every portfolio manager would like to do 'pearls' – projects that are easy with high returns. Alas, there are limited such opportunities, and 'bread and butter' and 'oyster' projects also need to be done. The projects to be avoided are 'white elephants' which are both difficult and risky, but promise little return even if they do succeed. However, proposed projects do not come with these labels and the portfolio manager, with the help of business cases, needs to assess each project and ultimately make recommendations. In addition, even after briefing a selection committee, the executives may not agree with the recommendations or with each other. So the selection process is challenging. Nevertheless, it's far better than a 'free-for-all' where the most influential executives have their way irrespective of merit. Clearly, the portfolio manager plays a key role and is influential, but ultimately the decisions are usually taken by other executives.

19.3.4 Ongoing Project Review and Support

The portfolio role does not end at selection. Projects must be monitored and nurtured. Monitoring might be done through reviewing reports or dashboards and attending Steercom (steering committee) meetings and project reviews. Nurturing might be done through a PMO which will be discussed presently. Based on new projects that arise and the monitoring of existing projects, tough decisions may be needed. Corrective action may have to be taken where projects are in trouble. Projects may need to be put on hold to make way for higher priority initiatives. In the extreme, projects may need to be terminated. Although the decisions are not taken alone, portfolio management bears some responsibility and is measured on the overall success of the portfolio. Let us now turn to the other roles.

19.3.5 Other Roles in Portfolio Governance

Having discussed the roles of the executive group and the portfolio manager, let us refer back to Figure 19.1 and consider the roles of other players and their involvement spans:

- The sponsor: The role has already been discussed in Chapter 17. For large projects, the sponsor may be a top executive, and for small ones, a department head. Nevertheless, the sponsor is accountable from proposal through to benefits realization, so there would be ongoing collaboration with portfolio management.

- The Steercom, headed by the sponsor: Its members may already become involved during selection and prioritization. They remain involved throughout the project and many continue into benefits realization, especially if they represent the business.
- The program manager: The role was touched on in Chapter 2. A program, unlike a project, is open-ended but with a broad goal. It comprises multiple projects, some in sequence, some concurrently, and some overlapping. These, over time, collectively contribute toward the goal. The program manager would, within the program, play a similar role to that of the portfolio manager: agreeing on the program's strategy with the sponsor and motivating projects to make it happen. Then the program manager would engage with stakeholders, support the PMs, and ensure that the benefits are realized to support the goal. There are many possibilities: goals can be adjusted, and the program can be terminated. There are also many possible structures and the program manager might personally manage a project within the program.
- The PM: Generally the PM is appointed just prior to the project's start and would move on soon after closeout. But, it can happen that the PM is involved in justifying the project and sometimes the PM plays a role during benefits realization.

Not shown in Figure 19.1 is another structure, the PMO, which is covered below.

19.4 The PMO (Project Management Office)

The PMO is a structure that supports the governance both of individual projects and of the portfolio as a whole (Marnewick, 2018). A smaller organization might have no PMO at all, while a larger one might have more than one PMO. A PMO would work closely with, and support, portfolio management. The two may even be integrated.

19.4.1 Roles That the PMO Might Play

The roles of PMOs vary considerably, and entire books have been written on the subject. So the following is just an overview giving possible responsibilities:

- Engage with stakeholders: This is particularly important where the PMO is involved in the selection, prioritization, and management of projects. But, whatever the case, how the PMO and its staff are perceived by the business and technical functions has a great influence on its effectiveness. Ultimately it must be seen to be in touch with, and to meet the needs of stakeholders whether they be executives, project sponsors, project teams, or any people involved in projects.
- Maintain the projects register: This would be a central register of all projects, each of which would have its own status – anything from proposed to completed. Early on, projects would have very little information, later, there could be a considerable amount including the names of key peoples, descriptions,

financial numbers, and a link to the business case. The PMO might also maintain records of work requests that are too small to be managed as projects.

- Support project selection and prioritization: PMO staff might initiate meetings to select projects (decide in principle whether they are justified) and to prioritize them (decide which projects should start, and what priority they should have). Although executives would take the decisions, the PMO might provide information from the projects register.
- Deliver projects: Many of the organization's PMs might belong within the PMO, which would mean hiring and developing PMs as well as providing a career path for them. This could involve rotating people with the right ability, from other functions, through the PMO for some years. Project delivery also implies taking some responsibility for the outcomes.
- Maintain project standards: This would involve selecting or developing a methodology that is scalable for projects of different sizes. The standards would be communicated and PMs and others would need training in their use. Flexibility is needed as to what is mandatory and what serves as guidance.
- Provide and support specialized project-related software: Rather than every PM using different software, standardization is desirable. Besides reducing the workload of project staff, having standard software makes communication and the mobility of people between projects far easier.
- Maintain a repository of project information: There are many technologies that can make this possible including PPM (Project Portfolio Management) software which is generally cloud-based and becoming ever more affordable. However, even more important than the technology are the processes that go with it, and the PMO is well-positioned to provide them. The processes would indicate which documents are needed, at what times during the project's lifetime, and possibly also in what format. PMs would need to be trained on the processes, and some follow-up is usually needed where key documents are missing. The repository would be used, to varying degrees, during the project, and it would be a valuable source of input for future projects.
- Provide education: Education can consist of formal training or informal events like forums or workshops. Topics might include how to produce a business case or any other aspect of project management.
- Facilitate project reviews and health checks: By knowing the status of each active project, the PMO would be in a good position to remind PMs when reviews are due. PMO staff might facilitate reviews, whether they be minor ones, taking an hour, to major ones lasting several days. Where gate reviews are standard the PMO might be the custodians of documentation arising from them.
- Facilitate workshops: PMO staff might develop skills in facilitating workshops, and offer such services to the broader project community. Examples of workshops would be: project definition, risk assessment, quality planning, lessons learned, or benefits tracking.
- Communicate: This is broad and each organization will do it differently. Some examples: receiving project reports and creating summary dashboards; maintaining an intranet website with project status information; convening business 'town hall' meetings to communicate status, answer questions, and get feedback. The possibilities are endless.

- Track budgets and schedules: This would be in support of portfolio management with the overall aim of getting timely warning of budget or schedule overruns. Each project might maintain its own data and feed it to the PMO, or certain data, like people costs, might be gathered by the PMO as a service to projects.

19.4.2 Types of PMO

There are many flavors of PMO. Some are called 'Enterprise' PMOs or 'Strategic' PMOs with considerable influence at executive level. Others provide the essential services. Some PMOs are just one person, others many people. The larger the PMO, the more it can take on. But, whatever the situation, it is unaffordable for a PMO to attempt to do everything. So each PMO must select which responsibilities it takes on, and these responsibilities change over time to align with business priorities. Ultimately, the PMO will be judged by its contribution to the organization. Hence the emphasis on stakeholders, because it's only through stakeholders that value can be delivered.

19.5 Thoughts on Organizational Project Management Maturity

Project management maturity is not something that can be instructed by management because it has many cultural aspects. It is something for management and PMs to be aware of, and possibly even to strive toward. You might work in various organizations, and be able to observe how project management is practiced. It might influence what you expect from the organization and how you approach projects in it. So let me walk through the maturity levels and then we shall discuss them.

19.5.1 Maturity Levels

There are many approaches to assessing maturity with different names for the levels, and the practices in most organizations span more than one level. So this just gives an overview (Larson & Gray, 2018). You will probably observe that governance is increasingly prevalent as the maturity level rises:

- Level 1 Ad-hoc project management: There is no formal project selection, and no PM training, so each PM uses their own method, or possibly no method at all. Project management is just not part of the culture. The attitude might even be "why do we need project management?" Often projects are led by a person with no project management background, so results are unpredictable: some projects might go well, but others would suffer from avoidable pitfalls.
- Level 2. Formal project management: There are now some standards, and use of templates is encouraged, but there is little training for PMs. Any project prioritization would be informal, and when working in a matrix environment with project staff 'borrowed' from line managers, there might be some tension.
- Level 3. Project management is the norm: There are well-understood project management standards, but with the flexibility to cater to different types of project. Project selection and project management in general are formal. Things like

quality, change control, and cost management would be consistently practiced. A PMO might support and monitor project performance. Any project failures would be looked into.

- Level 4. Strategic coordination: No longer are projects looked at on their own. Portfolio management is done which considers projects and programs across the organization, keeping the organization's strategies in mind. A PMO might have a more strategic focus including planning resource usage across the portfolio. There would be a PPM application with a repository for keeping current and historical project data. Important projects would be reviewed periodically, possibly using a gate review approach.
- Level 5. Optimization of project governance and management: Managing project portfolios are part of the culture, and there is a constant striving for improvement. Because project management is so well established, there can be greater flexibility, with processes tailored for specific projects.

19.5.2 Benefits of Maturity Assessment and Some Caveats

Maturity is usually measured by consultants that specialize in it. Indeed, they can do much to give an initial reading and sound guidance. However, it can lead to organizations making a goal of reaching higher levels of maturity, where the *real* goal is to achieve business success. So, I have mixed feelings. There is a danger, that standards are put in place to tick maturity boxes, but that in practice, the standards are not appropriate and not adhered to. Maybe it is for this reason that some organizations do not even aim to reach level 5. Certainly it is worthwhile for an organization to know where improvements are needed. But maybe this can also be achieved by answering a basic list of questions. Such questions might be: how are we selecting projects? how are we managing resources across projects? how are we developing our PMs? how are we keeping our project documentation? how are we communicating with project stakeholders? how are we tracking costs? After answering the questions management can seek ways to improve using simple cost-effective means. So I question whether reaching a high maturity level should be a goal in its own right.

I spent a number of years in a highly successful company that did a few level 3 and 4 things, but mostly operated at level 1. Yet, things got done – it was all about culture and drive.

I also question the stated time required to move from one level to the next. Many texts give a benchmark time to move between levels, typically around 18 months. I agree that progress takes time, but becoming more mature does not happen automatically with time. Having progressed it takes constant effort even to maintain the higher level.

An organization that I had regular contact with, at one point practiced project management disciplines consistently. Then, over time it eroded to a situation where every PM seemed to do things differently. So, although the organization remained successful, from a maturity point of view, they appeared to have gone backward.

These are my thoughts, and no doubt others would see things differently.

Overall, my suggestion would be: by all means seek improvement, but rather decide what disciplines are really needed, and then focus on one or two at a time, always keeping things as simple as possible. One of the responsibilities of a PMO might be to facilitate such improvements. Having got the disciplines in place, put effort into maintaining them before moving on to the next objective.

19.6 Summary

In larger organizations, where there are many projects, it's not enough to manage each project properly. It's also important to select the optimum mix of projects, and to track them throughout their lifetimes. Inevitably priorities will change and gate reviews, or something similar, can help to manage not only individual projects, but the entire portfolio. Even with sound portfolio governance, it remains important for each project to be well managed, and to achieve its objectives. This is more likely to happen when the PMs understand the bigger portfolio picture and the role they play in project and portfolio governance.

References

Enoch, C. N. (2019). *Project Portfolio Management: A Model for Improved Decision Making*, 2nd edition, Hampton, New Jersey, USA: Business Expert Press.

Larson, E. & Gray, C. (2018). *Project Management: The Managerial Process. International Edition*. 7th edition. New York: McGraw-Hill Education.

Marnewick, C. (2018). *Realizing Strategy Through Projects the Executive's Guide*. Boca Raton, Florida, USA: CRC Press - Taylor & Francis Group.

Matheson, D. & Matheson, J. (1998). *The Smart Organization*. USA: Harvard Business School Press.

OGC. (2009). *Managing Successful Projects with PRINCE2*, 5th edition. In A. Murray (Ed.). Norwich: TSO (The Stationery Office) on behalf of Office of Government Commerce.

Chapter 20

The Business Case End-to-End

20.1 Introduction and Objectives

Research shows that governance supported by a business case is strongly linked to the success of a project and indeed, to the success of a portfolio of projects designed to achieve corporate objectives (Musawir et al., 2017). The business case is arguably the most important project document because it holds the justification for investing in the project. Project governance is about the oversight and decision making, undertaken outside of the project, that directly affects the project (PMI, 2016).

The business case is an essential input to governance without which governance is unlikely to be effective. Hence, the business case is extensively covered in PMI's governance handbook and in the PMBOK 7th edition (PMI, 2021). Furthermore, it is one of the seven key themes in the PRINCE2 methodology whose first fundamental principle is that the project's justification must be checked regularly (OGC, 2009). Understanding the business case is also valuable for the PM who can motivate the team by explaining the importance of what they are doing. Finally, when the going gets tough, the PM must be able to explain to any stakeholder why the project is needed and *must* succeed.

There is a popular misconception that the business case is only produced to get approval to do the project and thereafter has little relevance. For a business project, where things are changing constantly, not monitoring the business case could be dangerous (Einhorn, 2018):

- Management would be unaware if the project were to become unjustified due to changes to the projected benefits, costs, and risks. Such a project would probably not be stopped and would continue to consume resources wastefully.
- It might also tempt the proposers of a project to ignore risks and give unrealistic estimates of benefits and costs, just to gain approval – because they know that they will not be held to account later.

So, as we shall see, the business case should be updated and reviewed throughout the lifetime of the project – from when it is first approved until the benefits have

DOI: 10.1201/9781003321101-23

been substantially realized, which may happen long after the project is complete (OGC, 2009). Reviews might lead to the sponsor requesting major changes or even stopping a project, and early termination of an unjustified project is a success rather than a failure. Because the business case is so vital, our objective here is to answer the following questions:

- What goes into the business case?
- Who needs to be involved?
- What should the business case cost, and how detailed should it be?
- When and how is a business case used? What are the processes involved?
- What if I'm asked to start a project without a business case?
- What is a business case review and when should it be done?

Answers are provided in the sections that follow.

20.2 Contents of the Business Case

All projects need a business case, even mandatory ones that are done to comply with legislation; without a business case, additional benefits or synergies are easily overlooked. The business case would expand on any earlier proposal that had been put forward giving sufficient detail to support decision making. The contents might include:

- An overview or executive summary indicating the project type (strategic, operational, or mandatory).
- The business goals and project objectives.
- The preferred solution referencing any feasibility study that had been done.
- The broad scope based on the preferred solution, which is needed for estimating purposes.
- The estimated value of the planned benefits and any further possible benefits.

  The values should preferably be expressed in monetary terms with a time scale (for example: $0.7 million in year 1 after completion, $1.1 million in year 2, and so on). For non-monetary benefits, a way of measuring the result should be stated. For example, if 'improved corporate image' were a benefit, then it should be explained how will it be measured and what result is expected. In such a situation a 'before and after' survey might be needed.

- The business person(s) who will take responsibility for achieving each benefit. Realizing benefits could be a lot of work and without a responsible person, benefits are less likely to happen.
- The estimated timeframe. This should state when the project will be delivered and in what timeframe the benefits will be realized.
- The skills needed to do the project.

- The estimated cost of the project as well as any ongoing running costs which offset the benefits.
- The risks – all that are known, to answer the question "what could go wrong?" Such risks could apply during the project or after the project.
- Finally, the assumptions. These are important, because if the reality is different from what was assumed, then we need to reassess the justification.

There are many other items that could go into the business case such as alignment with corporate strategy, and some organizations even have templates for the business case. What we have covered above are the main ones.

20.3 People Involved in the Business Case

Let's consider who needs to be involved, and when:

- The project sponsor must own the business case from the initial proposal, until benefits have been sufficiently realized. The sponsor seldom has time to 'do the legwork', but must participate in periodic business case reviews and take decisions that arise from them.
- The business case developer (or a small team) needs to dig out, and document, relevant information. Seldom would the PM be involved during business case development because it is still uncertain whether the project will go ahead and the PM may not yet have been identified.
- The business stakeholders that want the benefits need to give their requirements. They should help to estimate the value of the benefits and every benefit needs to have a business person who will take responsibility for achieving it. During benefits realization, which may start even before the project is finished, business people should compare the actual benefits with what was envisaged in the business case.
- A variety of specialists may be brought in to outline the scope, estimate the skills required, and estimate the costs.
- An independent reviewer can add value by asking pertinent questions. This is especially important for critical projects or projects where stakeholders may have strong biases.
- If portfolio management is involved, then they would use the business case information to prioritize projects and to recommend which projects should proceed or be placed on hold.
- The PM would become involved as soon as the project is initiated. The business case would provide useful input to the PDD (project definition document), but at the same time, the PM must check that the business case is realistic and aligns with the PDD that gets accepted. During execution, the PM would monitor and report on progress and make sure that the business case is updated as the project unfolds. The PM should be involved in periodic business case reviews, and give early warning to the sponsor if anything changes that threatens the project's viability.

20.4 The Cost and Size of the Business Case

There are no hard-and-fast rules as to the cost to develop a business case and its length. Much depends on the size and importance of the project. Putting the business case together could take anything from a few hours to several months. The cost might be between 1% and 3% of the estimated cost of the project, depending on the risk – the greater the risk to the organization, the more effort is warranted. For a small project, the business case might be a page; for a large one, maybe ten pages. But where it starts getting too large, it's best to put detail into appendices and keep the essential elements concise and readable. It would be counterproductive to have a 50-page business case that nobody reads or understands.

20.5 The Processes Involving the Business Case

Figure 20.1 shows the main process groups – numbered 1 to 8. They are called 'groups' because each process group would contain smaller processes (Einhorn, 2018).

Here, I outline the ideal process flow. What happens in practice will vary considerably depending on the situation. However, where the business case is not done, or only done to 'tick a box', or done and discarded after approval, there is a much higher probability of failure. Because the main purpose of the business case is to support decision making, the typical decision points are shown with 'D' diamonds. Decisions might be: to go ahead, to make changes, or to terminate the project. I shall describe the process groups from left to right.

- Process group 1 covers preparation for the business case. Sufficient information is gathered to outline the project concept in a short proposal. Many proposals are rejected at this early stage. But where go-ahead is given, a person or team must be assigned the task of developing the business case.

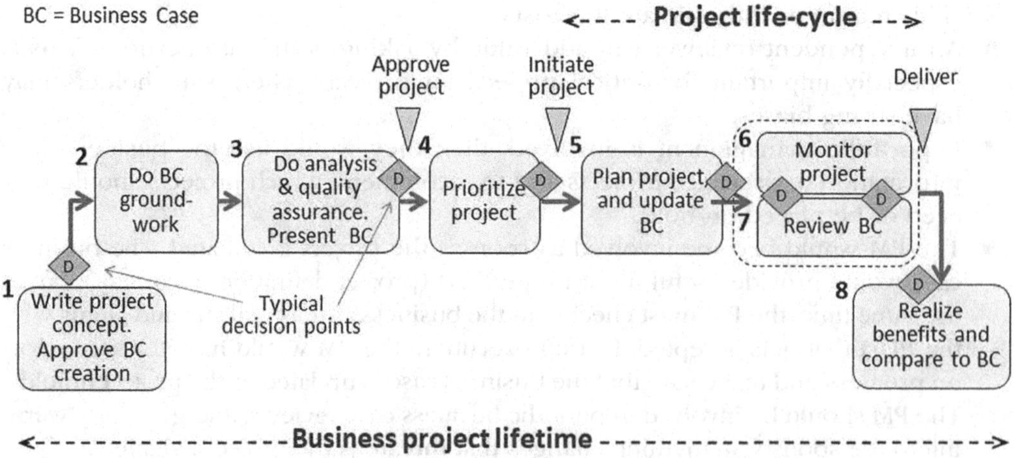

Figure 20.1 The business case throughout the project lifetime.

- Process group 2 covers the information-gathering groundwork. It includes identifying proposed benefits and determining the preferred approach, which in turn enables outlining of the scope, costs, and risks associated with it. Because it is difficult to get all the information, assumptions must be stated including where they came from. Assumptions lead to valuable discussion, and should be checked and updated later. The sponsor might intervene if there is insufficient cooperation from business stakeholders.
- Process group 3 involves selecting the most relevant information from what has been gathered, doing further analysis, and assembling it into a form that can be presented to decision makers. The draft presentation would be reviewed by key stakeholders and possibly also a person who thinks critically and is not directly affected by the project. The business case is then presented to senior management, and a decision in principle taken as to the way forward. What follows assumes a favorable decision.
- Process group 4 involves prioritizing the project against other approved projects, or even projects that are already underway. The scheduled start might be influenced by resource availability.
- Process group 5 starts when the PM initiates the project and the project life cycle starts. As mentioned above, the business case is an important input to planning, and especially to the PDD which should be done, early on, in collaboration with stakeholders. It is essential to update the business case to align with the project plan because: (i) much may have changed between the time that the business case was approved and project initiation and (ii) further information arises during planning. So at the end of planning, it must be confirmed that the business case remains sound.
- Process groups 6 and 7 are done in parallel during execution. Process group 6 covers routine monitoring and reporting on the project schedule and costs. It would highlight the main risks and issues, and any approved scope changes. Process group 7 involves periodic reviews of the business case in the light of the project's status or ad-hoc reviews to address concerns raised by stakeholders. Only two 'D' diamonds are shown, but there could be many depending on the project.
- Process group 8 starts near project closeout when the deliverables have been handed over. It is focused on the assessment of benefits realization which should lead to positive business outcomes. Benefits are compared with those in the business case and action needs to be taken by accountable stakeholders should there be a shortfall.

So, looking at the figure, we see that the lifetime of the business project extends for longer than the project life cycle. We also see that the business case must be updated and reviewed throughout – particularly after the project has started.

20.6 Starting a Project without a Business Case

What if you as PM, are asked to start a project with a briefing by the sponsor but without a business case? This is very common. I've only been given a business case for maybe one project in ten – not good but not a disaster. It just means that you will need to produce it. The PDD done early in planning, has most of the essential information. So most of the business case can be extracted from it. Indeed, the format of the business case could be similar to that of the PDD, but there are differences: The focus of the PDD is on how the project will be done, while the focus of the business case is on whether the project is justified. The PDD is frozen after it has been reviewed and superseded by the more detailed plan. On the other hand, the business case must continue to be updated and reviewed until all benefits have been realized to the sponsor's satisfaction.

From the sponsor's point of view, it may be better to ensure that the business case is solid at the *end* of planning, rather than to strive for a perfect business case before the project starts when there is bound to be missing information. However, for very high risk or critical projects, the business case needs as much detail as possible up-front.

The business case is also of value to the PM. It supports engagement with the sponsor if the project's justification becomes questionable. Thus it helps to avoid the problems of leading an unviable project where it is hard to keep resources and difficult to motivate the team who will sense that their effort is not well spent. Generally, an unjustified project is not good for the reputations of the team members or the PM.

20.7 The Business Case Review

After the project has been initiated, a business case review could be done on its own or as part of a broader review of the project. A normal review would be done sitting around a table. It might be facilitated by the sponsor and attended by the PM, a portfolio manager, and key stakeholders. The PM would summarize the projects status covering aspects like progress, costs, and stakeholder matters. The group would then walk through the latest version of the business case checking that the assumptions and expected benefits remain valid and that the project remains justified (the value of the benefits exceeds the remaining costs). If the project is going reasonably well, the review might take an hour or so. However, if serious problems have arisen it should lead to discussion and debate, possibly over several days, resulting in decisions on actions to be taken. Too often these tough discussions never happen and that is where expensive failures occur later.

After the project is complete, it is still relevant to review the business case even if some benefits came earlier. The sponsor, who owns the business case and remains accountable for business success, should compare the benefits actually achieved with those stated in the business case. Business people would continue to take the planned actions to realize the benefits, or else to note the reasons why they could not be achieved – useful learning for future projects.

20.8 Summary of How to Use the Business Case Effectively

The sponsor owns the business case and is accountable for business success. The PM who plays a key role during the project's life cycle must remain convinced that the project is justified. This enables the PM to maintain the team's morale by explaining how their efforts are making an important contribution to the organization.

The business case needs to be developed, and then maintained and reviewed throughout the project's lifetime – until the proposed benefits have been substantially realized. Discarding the business case after the decision has been taken to proceed with the project, is unwise. It leads to over-optimistic forecasts with risks being ignored. Lack of an updated business case also makes it difficult to take decisions when circumstances have changed. Except for the most critical projects, rather than try to create a perfect business case up front, it may be better to do a basic business case, with assumptions stated, and then to update and review the business case as more facts become known.

The business case is valuable in managing a portfolio of projects. It supports prioritization while taking resource availability into account. If projects that become unjustified are stopped promptly, resources can be diverted toward helping justified projects to be successful.

References

Einhorn, F. (2018). Effective use of the business case to enhance the success rate of business/information technology projects. (PhD), University of Johannesburg.

Musawir, A. U., Serra, C. E. M., Zwikael, O., & Ali, I. (2017). Project governance, benefit management, and project success: Towards a framework for supporting organizational strategy implementation. *International Journal of Project Management*, 35(8), 1658–1672.

OGC. (2009). *Managing Successful Projects with PRINCE2*, 5th edition. In A. Murray (Ed.). Norwich: TSO (The Stationery Office) on Behalf of Office of Government Commerce.

PMI. (2016). *Governance of Portfolios, Programs, and Projects: A Practice Guide* (pp. 1–122). Pennsylvania, USA: Project Management Institute.

PMI. (2021). *PMBOK - Guide to the Project Management Body of Knowledge*, 7th edition. Pennsylvania, USA: Project Management Institute.

Chapter 21

Project Selection: Financial and Non-Financial Criteria

21.1 Introduction and Objectives

Almost always, there are more projects proposed than the organization can tackle – given its limited people and money resources. The projects arise from strategy, from operations, and to comply with legislation (as shown in Chapter 19). Therefore, an important aspect of governance is to decide which projects to pursue. This is called 'project selection'. A key input to the project selection process is the business case which is covered in Chapter 20.

In this chapter, we shall assume that some homework has been done and we shall discuss ways of assessing projects, first looking at financial criteria and then looking at non-financial criteria. Both need to be taken into account for a balanced decision and several techniques are covered in textbooks such as Larson & Gray (2018) and Pinto (2013). Project selection needs to consider all projects, those proposed and those underway, because occasionally a viable project needs to be put on hold to provide resources for a critical new project. So, the objectives are to:

- Get an overview of a few financial techniques commonly used to evaluate projects, one quick and simple and others more thorough.
- Understand the problems that can arise if only financial calculations are used for project selection.
- Discuss other criteria that should enter the selection decision.
- Consider some structured approaches to project selection at portfolio level – where a portfolio of projects would support the entire organization or a major part of it.

Both financial and non-financial criteria should be covered in any project business case. Understanding sound project selection practice is essential for project sponsors, portfolio managers, and even for program managers and PMs. PMs seldom produce

DOI: 10.1201/9781003321101-24

the business case before the project starts, but in the many situations, where they are not given one at project initiation, they may need to produce a business case toward the end of planning. As explained in Chapter 20, PMs certainly need to be convinced that the business case is sound, and *that* may require a knowledge of the financial and other techniques.

21.2 Financial Techniques for Project Selection

For some projects, the business case only gives non-financial reasons for doing the project. However, many projects provide a financial justification and in some organizations it is a requirement. There are *many* techniques in use, but here we shall cover two common types which use the estimated dollar benefit and dollar cost to calculate:

- The payback period.
- The NPV (net present value) and the IRR (internal rate of return)

It should be noted that for almost all projects, the costs come earlier than the benefits, and this will be the case in the examples given.

Often the calculations are done by financial people, but once the PM inherits them with the business case, a sound grasp is needed. Both the sponsor and PM need to understand the underlying assumptions, and where the estimates have come from, in order to assess their validity. So, first we shall go through the techniques, and then we shall discuss some of the potential pitfalls. For both techniques, we shall use the simple hypothetical example given in Table 21.1 where we consider two projects A and B.

Both projects will take 1 year and cost $1 million, shown as –1 000 because all figures are in thousands of dollars and the minus sign indicates an outflow of money (for year 1). Both projects yield returns in years 2, 3, 4, and 5, with no further benefits after the 5th year. The signs are positive, implying a benefit or an effective inflow of money, and *showing* the plus sign reduces errors. The assumption is made that all costs incurred and benefits realized come at the *end* of each year. Both projects cost $1 million and return $1.6 million. The difference is in the timing. For project A, the biggest benefits come in year 2, while for project B they come in year 5. Let us now consider techniques for assessing projects A and B in financial terms.

Table 21.1 Example to Illustrate Financial Techniques (Figures in $ Thousands)

	Year 1	*Year 2*	*Year 3*	*Year 4*	*Year 5*
Project A $000	–1,000	+600	+400	+300	+300
Project B $000	–1,000	+300	+300	+400	+600
Project A cumulative	–1,000	–400	0	+300	+600
Project B cumulative	–1,000	–700	–400	0	+600

21.2.1 Simple Payback Period or 'Breakeven' Point

Here we calculate in simple terms how long it will take to recover our investment in the project. 'Simple' means that we consider a dollar after, say, 4 years to have the same value as a dollar now, or after 1 year. To do this we consider the cumulative values shown in Table 21.1.

- For project A, the breakeven point occurs at the end of year 3, where the returns of +600 and +400 equal the −1,000 (the initial outlay). We can say that at this point our investment of $1 million has been paid back.
- For project B, the breakeven point occurs at the end of year 4, so the payback period is 4 years from the start of the project.

Generally, executives are happiest with a short payback period, because of risks and future uncertainties. So, in this situation, executives would prefer project A. Note that we must be very clear as to whether we are stating the payback period from the start, or from the end, of the project. In this situation, it makes a whole year's difference.

21.2.2 Net Present Value and Internal Rate of Return

For the simple payback period, we assumed that a dollar in 3 years' time has the same value as a dollar now, and for quick paybacks, it may be a valid approximation. However, it is more rigorous to take the time factor into account. Supposing that I asked you whether you would prefer to have $100 now or $100 in a year's time. You would almost certainly prefer the money now, as you could invest it and get a return on your money and end up with more than $100 at the end of a year. Conversely, we can say that $100 in a year's time, is worth *less* than $100 now; maybe it would be worth only $90. And certainly, we would consider $100 in 5 years' time to be worth far less, maybe even less than $60.

When evaluating projects we are usually looking at a stream of estimated costs and a stream of estimated returns (benefits) going several years into the future. We need a way of evaluating them. We already know that we cannot compare money directly with money in the future, and much less can we, meaningfully, sum amounts at different times by adding them. So to make amounts comparable in order to sum them, we need to *discount* future amounts. This uses an approach called DCF (Discounted Cash Flow) or NPV (Net Present Value) which have a similar meaning. By all means Google DCF and NPV for more detail. To evaluate the dollar benefits of projects we may have a stream of costs during the project and a stream of benefits out into the future. To determine the 'net' benefit, we must make all amounts comparable by calculating their value *now*, or their *present* value, generally called their NPV or net present value. NPV says that to make $100 in the future comparable to $100 now, we must discount it, and the further into the future, the more we must discount it. By reducing all future costs and benefits to present terms, we can meaningfully add them up. Generally, if the NPV (the summed present values of costs and benefits) is positive the project is considered viable. Presently we shall show how this approach applies to the hypothetical example of Projects A and B.

Table 21.2 Discounting Factors

Discount %	*After 1 Year*	*After 2 Years*	*After 3 Years*	*After 4 Years*	*After 5 Years*
8	0.9259	0.8573	0.7938	0.7350	0.6806
10	0.9091	0.8264	0.7513	0.6830	0.6209
12	0.8929	0.7972	0.7118	0.6355	0.5674
14	0.8772	0.7695	0.6750	0.5921	0.5194
16	0.8621	0.7432	0.6407	0.5523	0.4761
18	0.8475	0.7182	0.6086	0.5158	0.4371
20	0.8333	0.6944	0.5787	0.4823	0.4019
22	0.8197	0.6719	0.5507	0.4514	0.3700
24	0.8065	0.6504	0.5245	0.4230	0.3411
26	0.7937	0.6299	0.4999	0.3968	0.3149
28	0.7813	0.6104	0.4768	0.3725	0.2910
30	0.7692	0.5917	0.4552	0.3501	0.2693

Each organization will choose its own discounting rate, which may vary over time depending on the economic situation. A discounting rate of between 15% and 20% might be typical. The formula for NPV is:

$$\text{NPV} = \$\text{ amount} \times \text{Discounting factor}$$

$$\text{Discounting factor} = 1/\left(1+\text{Rate}\right)^{\text{Y}}$$

- Rate is the discount percentage/100. So 18% would have Rate = 0.18
- Y is the number of years from the present time.

To get an understanding, it is easiest to use a table of discounting factors as shown in Table 21.2, which are all calculated using the above formula (or quickly produced using Excel).

Any amount of money now is *already* in the present and has a factor 1.0 *irrespective* of the discount percentage. Note that as the discounting percent rises, the discounting factors reduce more rapidly. Here are illustrative examples of how the table is used. Calculate the NPV of:

- $10 000 in 3 years' time at a discount rate of 12%.
  NPV = $10 000 × 0.7118 = $7 118 (intersection of 12% row and 3 years column)
- $200 000 in 5 years' time at a discount rate of 24%.
  NPV = $200 000 × 0.3411 = $68 220 (intersection of 24% row and 5 years column)

- $100 000 at the end of *each* of years 1, 2, and 3 at a discount rate of 10%.
  NPV = $100 000 × 0.9091 + $100 000 × 0.8264 + $100 000 × 0.7513) = $248 680
- $15 000 *now* at a discount rate of 16%.
  NPV = $15 000 × 1 = $15 000 (it is *already* a present value).

Supposing that you need to acquire a major piece of equipment. The supplier gives you the choice of paying $750 000 up-front, or of paying only $300 000 up-front, and a further $300 000 after 12 months and again after 24 months. Your finance people indicate that their effective borrowing rate is 12%.

Let us consider the delayed payment option using the 12% row in Table 21.2 The NPV of the three payments is:

$300 000 × (1 for the immediate payment + 0.8929 end year 1 + 0.7972 end year 2)

Which = $300 000 × (1 + 0.8929 + 0.7972) = $300 000 × 2.6901 = $807 030.

This is more than the $750 000, so, it is less expensive to pay everything up-front.

Having understood the NPV concept, let us consider Projects A and B and assume that the corporate discounting rate is 18%, given in Table 21.3. To remind you, we assumed that most of the cost of $1 million is at the *end* of year 1; if it were an up-front cost, it would be shown in year 0 with a 1.0 discounting factor irrespective of the rate.

Looking at the NPVs in the right-hand column shows that Project A, with an NPV of $112 800, looks more attractive than Project B, with an NPV of only $19 200. Now, supposing that the discounting rate were 20%, both NPVs would reduce, and, as we shall see Project B's NPV will actually go negative. This means that its IRR or 'internal rate of return' is above 18% but below 20%.

21.2.3 Discounted Payback Period or 'Breakeven' Point

This uses the same approach as in the simple payback period mentioned earlier. However, here we use the discounted amounts shown in Table 21.3. For Project A, we would start with –847.5 and progressively add the benefits of +430.9, then +243.5, etc. It would show that both Project A and B are estimated to break even during the 5th year, but A breaks even around 4 years and 1 month, whereas B breaks even later

Table 21.3 Calculation of Net Present Value at 18% (Figures in $ Thousands)

	Year 1	*Year 2*	*Year 3*	*Year 4*	*Year 5*	*NPV*
18% discount factor	0.8475	0.7182	0.6086	0.5158	0.4371	
Project A $000	–1 000	+600	+400	+300	+300	
Project A discounted	–847.5	+430.9	243.5	154.7	131.1	112.8
Project B $000	–1 000	+300	+300	+400	+600	
Project B discounted	–847.5	+215.5	+182.6	+206.3	+262.3	19.2

around 4 years and 11 months. Although this involves more calculation, it gives more realistic results than simple payback.

21.2.4 Estimating the IRR (Internal Rate of Return) of a Project

Another way of looking at projects is to consider their rate of return. A project that promises a 40% return is usually preferable to a project that only offers 20%. The most common measure is the IRR or internal rate of return. The IRR is defined as the discounting rate at which the NPV becomes zero. Given a future stream of costs and returns there are tools that will give an exact IRR, but to understand the concept Figure 21.1 may be more helpful.

Here the NPV for Project A and for Project B have been calculated at 18%, the corporate discounting percentage, and then at the higher rate of 24%. As expected, the NPVs for both projects are lower for the 24% rate. But we would like to know the discounting rate at which the NPV is zero. If the points were plotted for each percentage, they would show a gentle curve, but to get a close estimate, they can be joined with a straight line as shown in Figure 21.1. The IRR is the point at which the line crosses the zero NPV line. So, Project A's IRR is 25.8% (although it might look slightly less in the figure because a straight line was drawn). Project B's IRR is 19.0%, just above the corporate minimum of 18%, sometimes called the 'hurdle' rate. You will probably have noticed that if the project IRR is higher than the hurdle IRR (18% in our case) then the project meets the criteria.

The graphical technique shown below gives a sound understanding. If Excel is used, then it is possible to vary the rate until the NPV is zero, and hence get a fairly precise IRR. But always bear in mind that precision could mislead because we are dealing with estimates. So it's best to round the IRR percentage.

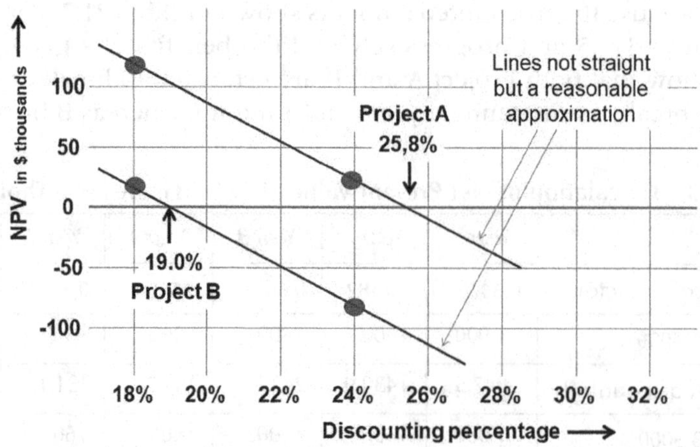

Figure 21.1 Plot to estimate the IRR (internal rate of return).

21.2.5 Why Is the Discounting Percentage (the Minimum IRR) So High?

You might be wondering who decides the corporate minimum percentage, and why it is so high. Surely a 12% return would be far better than what a bank would offer for money on interest? To answer the first question, the Finance function would usually recommend the required hurdle rate, and it might be approved by the executive committee. For the second question, let us consider an environment where inflation (often measured by CPI, the consumer price index) is around 3%, and, supposing that the organization can borrow money at 6%. Of course, the borrowing rate can vary widely depending on many factors like the economy and the borrower's creditworthiness. The organization might still require a minimum of 18% for projects. Some of the reasons are that projects have risks and the actual return might be far lower than what is projected. Even if the risks do not materialize, the organization will be taxed on the return, and something needs to be left over as profit.

21.2.6 The Sensitivity of Financial Figures to Incorrect Assumptions

It may be tempting for stakeholders to accept the NPV or IRR for a project when it is backed up by calculations. However, it is always wise to ask some questions, like, "who provided the estimates of costs and returns?" or "how did they arrive at the estimates?" Even if the answers are satisfactory, it may be worthwhile to do a simple sensitivity analysis. Such an analysis is based on 'what if' questions, for example, "what if the actual costs are greater than what was estimated?" and "what if the returns are less than expected?" Unfortunately, with business projects it is often difficult to produce reliable estimates. So, considering Project A which promises a return (IRR) of nearly 26%, doing a sensitivity analysis shows that (all else being as planned):

- If the project costs $1.2 million, the IRR drops to 14.7%.
- If it costs $1.5 million, the IRR drops to 3.0%.
- If all the returns are 20% lower than expected, the IRR drops to 12.4%.

Much will depend on the situation and the sponsor's level of confidence in the estimates. But, it is always worth understanding the implications of assumptions being invalid. So the takeaways are:

- Work out the numbers, but do not have too much faith in them and understand the assumptions on which they are based. Sometimes the estimates given are optimistically biased to get a favorable decision.
- Include a contingency amount for risks in the estimates. Doing so will reduce the impact of unpleasant 'surprises', and may result in expectations being exceeded.

21.2.7 Uncertainty and Precision

Often financial numbers are stated with a high degree of precision. An example would be if the IRR of Project A was stated as 25.811%. This would be misleading because it implies a level of certainty that is simply not there. With the methods mentioned, and in fact, most methods, we are working with estimates. These estimates may be reliable, for example, when we have had a firm quotation from a trusted supplier, but more often they are not reliable. We are often working with estimates with a range of plus or minus 20%, and sometimes even plus or minus 50%. Therefore, when stating your results, avoid precision and round the numbers appropriately. So, if the calculated payback period is 2.236 years, just put 2.2 years or 27 months. Likewise, if the value of total benefits is $1,537,406, just state $1.5 million. A rounded number is also easier for an executive to take in. By all means, state the confidence range to emphasize that the numbers are based on estimates (see Chapter 8).

21.3 Adapting Financial Estimates for Common Situations

Thus far we have considered some of the approaches to evaluating a project from a financial point of view. Here are two adaptations that may be necessary:

- For Projects A and B, we assumed that both the costs and benefits occur at the *end* of a particular year. What if they are spread out during the year? The easiest way to handle this is to split the amount to a portion at the beginning, and a portion at the end, of the year. For example, supposing that the costs for a project are estimated at $100 000, and that some of the cost occurs in the first 6 months. Based on judgment, you might split it into $30 000 at the start of the year, and $70 000 at the end of the year. If this were year 1, then the start of year 1 (end of year 0) would always have a discounting factor of 1. Given that we are working with estimates, this approach gives meaningful results.
- We have only considered costs and benefits to the end of year 5. What if there are benefits beyond year 5 that need to be taken into account? Many organizations only consider 5 years because the benefits after 5 years are uncertain and because the discounting factor becomes progressively smaller. However, for certain types of project, for example, when developing a mine, the benefits may stretch to 20 and 30 years, in which case a longer timeframe would be used.

So, in summary, for many projects, understanding the financial viability is very important. However, it must be re-emphasized that financial calculations are based on assumptions and estimates which may or may not, turn out to be valid. Therefore, the figures should be treated with caution, and revisited as the project unfolds. At this point, I suggest that you do part 1 of case number 30 which gives the estimated costs and the estimated value of the benefits for two projects that the company, Delectable Confections, is considering. You are asked to evaluate the projects from a financial point of view. However, there are always other factors to be considered, and we shall discuss them in the next sections.

21.4 Further Considerations for Project Selection

What we have learned thus far, is that many projects need a financial justification. We also know that the financials are based on estimates that may be sensitive to incorrect assumptions. Nevertheless, if the financials are unsatisfactory, it is unlikely that the project will go ahead. However, for many projects, there are important non-financial factors that may have an overriding influence on the decision. Indeed, there are projects where a financial justification is almost irrelevant, like a project to comply with legislation or a CSI (corporate social investment) project. For such projects, and possibly for all projects, non-financial factors need to be considered, and non-financial factors could even be included in the financial calculations if executives are prepared to place a monetary value on them. For example, an executive may tell you that the value of the improved corporate image, resulting from this project, will be worth at least half a million dollars, in which case we might use $500 000 as the value of a benefit in a financial calculation. But, in my experience, this is seldom done, and even very important factors remain 'intangible', in other words, they do not get a monetary value placed on them.

21.4.1 Dangers of Only Using Financials for Project Selection

Let's now think about some of the dangers of going for opportunities based purely on the financial numbers. Here are some of them:

- The project may not support the organization's strategy. This implies that it is important, when doing project selection, to understand the mission and strategies.
- The project might be a deviation from the organization's core business. We might lack the skills required to run a new undertaking which is the output of the project. It sometimes happens that organizations expand rapidly by buying up companies, while showing remarkable profit and share price increases, only to crash later when they are unable to manage the diversity of their businesses.
- Looking only at financials may favor projects that offer short-term gain. If we only consider 5 years for NPV calculations, we may miss projects whose greatest benefits come much later. Examples would be an innovative new product or a more flexible IT platform.
- Financials could tempt us to take on projects where the risk is not fully understood. Hopefully, some risk is already factored into the numbers, but often not sufficiently.
- The project may lack the support and commitment from both management and staff, which would play out negatively during execution or even post-project.

So, there are many reasons to look beyond the financial numbers.

21.5 Non-Financial Considerations When Selecting Projects

Having understood some of the dangers, let us consider questions that might be asked when weighing up a project:

- What are the risks that could affect the project's costs, benefits, or duration? Has any contingency been allowed for them in the estimates?
- Does this project depend on other projects?

- Does the project align with the organization's core business? and with its strategy?
- Does the project meet the stated corporate selection criteria? For example, the organization may want at least 25% of sales to come from products developed in the past 3 years.
- Do key executives support the project?
- Does the project fit in with the corporate culture?
- How does the output of the project affect awareness of our brands or our corporate image? An example of the latter might be a project with social investment aspects.
- Do we have the available resources (staff, skills, equipment, money) to do the project?
- Are aspects of the project mandatory, for example, to comply with legislation?
- Are there current threats or risks to the organization that the outcome of the project would mitigate?
- Will the project improve our competitiveness or create barriers to entry for competitors?
- Will the project improve our market share, or give us a more complete range of products or services?
- Will product quality, and hence customer satisfaction, be improved?
- How urgent is the project? Can it wait?
- What are the long-term benefits – beyond the normal 5-year window?
- Is the outcome sustainable? What are the associated ongoing costs?

There are probably many more. If a positive or negative value can be put on any factors, then they might be included in financial calculations, but many factors remain qualitative. So how should they be used when making a decision?

21.6 Score Sheets to Take Financial and Non-Financial Factors into Account

Score sheets are one possible answer. An illustrative example is given in Table 21.4 where a number of factors are scored out of 10 and averaged to give a score of 4.1, which would allow it to be compared with the scores of other projects.

However, valid concerns would be raised: Are all the factors equally important? Do the same factors apply to all projects? The first concern could be addressed by giving each factor a weight and arriving at a weighted score. Even then, the weights might need to vary depending on the project. Moreover, the second concern about factor relevance might be harder to address. There are techniques available that deal with these concerns, like Dr. Thomas Saaty's Analytical Hierarchy Process which is covered in Pinto (2013), but they are beyond the scope of this book.

A further difficulty with scoring is that sometimes the executives involved are not comfortable with the answer given. Their 'gut-feel' might prefer a project that does not have the highest score, or they might be uncomfortable with the project

Table 21.4 A Project Score Sheet

Factor	*Rating*
NPV and IRR satisfactory	7
Payback period acceptable	8
Supports corporate strategy	2
Consistent with the organization's core business	3
Risk level acceptable	3
Skills available internally	4
Positive effect on corporate image	3
Improve quality of products or services	0
Support from executives and workforce	3
Acceptable environmental impact	8
Average score	**4.1**

balance – for example, too many projects of a similar type undertaken (refer to Figure 19.2 – 'pearls', 'oysters', etc.).

What this shows is that a list of considerations is useful, and prevents factors from being overlooked. Even scoring could give rise to useful discussion, possibly resulting in scores being changed. But generally informed executive judgment often produces the best results. Informed means that both the financial and non-financial factors have been considered. So ultimately my belief is that people, and not scoring models, should take decisions, but that use of a checklist of considerations can ensure that the main factors are thought through. At this point, I suggest that you do part 2 of case number 30, where you will consider the non-financial aspects and then recommend to Delectable Confections how they should proceed.

21.7 Project Selection in the Real World and Some Conclusions

Having explained some of the techniques for evaluating project, it is worth noting that, in the real world, practices vary widely between industries and organizations. Here are examples:

- In many organizations, projects are not evaluated or prioritized – 'the boss decides'.
- Many executives use 'gut feel' rather than structured evaluation, sometimes effectively, sometimes not.
- Some organizations use rigorous methods that may be more appropriate for some projects than for others.

- A few might use sophistications like forecasting the economy and using variable discounting rates. They may also use probabilistic outcomes like there is a 70% probability of the benefit being $800 000 and a 30% probability of it being only $400 000.

So, do not be surprised if your organization, or a client organization, uses unfamiliar techniques. But, do get to understand their method and the rationale for using it.

Finally to summarize the main things: Use financial calculations where they are appropriate, but treat the output with some caution. Always consider the many other factors that may have a bearing, and especially think about the risks. These considerations apply not only to selecting projects but also to prioritizing the projects that have been selected. Finally, a point from Chapter 20 on the business case: understand that, for business projects, things change, and it is worth periodically re-evaluating the justification for projects.

References

Larson, E. & Gray, C. (2018). *Project Management: The Managerial Process: International Edition*. 7th edition. New York: McGraw-Hill Education.

Pinto, J. K. (2013). *Project Management, Achieving Competitive Advantage*, 3rd edition. Harlow, Essex, England: Pearson.

Chapter 22

Project Procurement, Outsourcing, and Partnership

22.1 Introduction and Objectives

Procurement is about buying things for the project, whether products or services. When buying a service, it is often referred to as outsourcing, and outsourcing can be just for a project, for a period of time, or indefinitely – until the outsource contract is terminated. Nowadays procurement is usually called 'supply chain' or SCM which stands for 'supply chain management' which includes looking beyond the immediate supplier, to their suppliers, and back down the chain. Some projects may involve little or no procurement; for other projects, the entire project may be about buying a complete solution, but even this means considerable work for the buyer.

Where procured goods and services make up a significant portion of the project, procurement may be done before the project starts, but, it may also be done as part of the project, in which case, many of the project activities would relate to procurement. The seller could even be another division within the same organization. As we shall see, much work goes into doing procurement thoroughly, and it would be unwise to rush certain aspects, so if procurement is needed, it should be planned from the start. Therefore, the objectives of this chapter are to:

- Be able to use accepted procurement terminology.
- Know how to fit the procurement processes into your project plans.
- Know the different types of contracts that result from procurement, understand their relative merits, and know which is most appropriate in a particular situation.
- Be aware of common procurement pitfalls – things that can go wrong from a buyer's or seller's point of view.
- Understand some of the pros and cons of outsourcing project scope.
- Learn best practices that help make outsourcing partnerships work.

DOI: 10.1201/9781003321101-25

22.2 The Project Procurement Environment

22.2.1 The Buyer and the Seller

The buyer is the person or organization that needs the goods or services. The seller provides them. But the seller is often referred to as the supplier, the vendor, or the contractor, and usually the terms are applied to the organization rather than to an individual. In a project situation where much of the work is outsourced, the PM could come from either the buyer or the seller organization, and sometimes from both. But, whatever the situation, a person from the buyer must remain involved. Much of my own experience has been as a PM from the seller organization working closely with a PM or sponsor from the buyer. The term 'performing organization' is sometimes used for the supplier that will do most of the project work.

22.2.2 Who Does the Procurement?

Procurement can apply to anything from acquiring a few laptops to billion-dollar contracts. Many of the procurement steps are similar. So, do we leave all the procurement work to the SCM (Supply Chain Management) function? Certainly not! The PM and team must remain involved because they understand best what is needed. But, the PM needs to involve SCM who can ensure that the right processes are followed, and without those processes, there are likely to be unexpected holdups later.

We've already mentioned that procured services or goods may be from within your own organization, in which case SCM may not need to be involved. The agreement could take the form of an MoU (Memorandum of Understanding) rather than a contract. But, many of the procurement activities still apply, probably with less formality.

22.2.3 Buyer and Seller Perspectives Differ

Even where buyer and seller organizations have worked in partnership for years, there will be differences in their perspectives and objectives. This is particularly true, where organizations have never worked together before. To set the scene, please do Case 31 where Upview Investments have engaged with M&P to discuss a contact center service. The purpose is to realize that, when two parties negotiate to enter an agreement, they have totally different needs and wants. These need to be aligned so that both parties can benefit.

22.3 The Procurement Processes

Procurement has planning, executing, and monitoring and controlling processes (PMI, 2017). Planning and executing take us to the point of awarding the business to a supplier; monitoring and controlling involve working with the supplier (or seller) to ensure that obligations are met and the benefits realized.

22.3.1 Planning Procurements – Specifying the Requirements

Planning has two main elements. First, we plan and specify what is needed. Second, we find eligible sellers and assemble documentation for them to respond to. So, starting with the requirements: what to procure, and when, could be considered during a feasibility study – if there is one. More often it is worked on after project start-up. There may be 'make or buy' decisions, in other words, "should we do this ourselves, or should we specify what we need, and get someone else to do it?" Consultants are sometimes used. They can play many roles, but ultimately they should bring valuable experience; after all, maybe your organization has never done a project like this before. Sometimes the buyer benefits from preliminary discussions with one or more potential suppliers, as in the Upview case. But one must be careful. The suppliers will often intentionally bias what you specify to favor their offering. Also, getting advice from prospective suppliers can create subtle obligations. For certain government organizations, such engagement might not be allowed, and even engaging a consultant may need to be a transparent procurement process. An alternative might be to issue an RFI (request for information) to several companies, but this takes time and lacks the interaction which can be so very useful.

The buyer must also weigh up whether to deal with a single seller (sometimes called a 'prime contractor') who will bring in, and take responsibility for, subcontractors, or to deal directly with multiple contractors. Managing multiple contractors saves money, but you, the buyer, assume the integration responsibility, and any technical or other incompatibilities between contractors become your problem. On the other hand, if you engage a prime contractor, they must deal with any integration problems.

Specification ends when you have a requirements document, with a statement of work (and exclusions), any specifications, and relevant dates. Getting this right is time-consuming but important because many problems and disputes later relate to poorly specified requirements. All this work involves project activities that must be planned and tracked.

Here are some terms that are commonly used. For something very specific, like buying nuts and bolts or a standard service, one would request a quotation, or 'quote'. Where the requirement is more complex with many possible ways of meeting the requirement, a proposal might be requested, with each responding company offering its own solution. Both quotations and proposals can be referred to as 'bids', and would come from several organizations. SCM should understand the processes needed to ensure that bidding is, and is perceived to be, fair and according to defined procedures. So, to do this, your organization would issue an RFQ (request for quote) or an RFP (request for proposal). Especially in a government environment, these might be referred to as 'tenders'. What follows are some guidelines that apply, mainly when requesting proposals.

- Provide a structure for the responses. There should be clear headings that will allow easy adjudication, because you may send different elements of the responses to different people for comment.

- The SOW (Statement of Work), and any specifications, must be clear, to minimize misunderstanding.
- Ensure that the terms and conditions are spelled out. Often it's good to include a draft contract, so that the bidder knows exactly what they will be asked to sign should they win the business. Once the award is made, the quicker the agreement is signed the better.

  I once managed a large project where there was urgency to get started using a letter of authority. But the contract negotiations dragged on for 18 months before being signed. This was a time-wasting nightmare and prior to the contract, the RFP and bid documents lacked the detail needed to avoid disputes.

- Allow for suggestions. Valuable ideas may be lost by *only* getting responses to narrow, restrictive questions. Thus, there should be a way for a knowledgeable supplier to suggest better ways of doing things.
- Ask sellers for references from their customers (and use them during the evaluation).
- From a procedural point of view, spell out the selection process. State how you will be evaluating the bid – some examples: (i) give any weightings of the responses that will be applied; (ii) indicate if there will be a second round for short-listed suppliers, and (iii) state whether you may decide to split the business between two or more suppliers.
- Specify the criteria for selecting sellers whose bids will be considered. Evaluating bids is time-consuming, so limit the suppliers to *only* those that are able to meet a variety of requirements like skills, experience, and financial stability.

22.3.2 Contract Types

Even if many contract clauses apply to any contract, there is a range of contract types that could apply for a particular bid. Each type has different risk implications for the buyer and seller. The contract type could be specified by the buyer or negotiated. Here are some basic ones.

- Firm fixed price (FFP) – mainly seller risk.
  When delivery is complete, as specified, the agreed price is fully paid. Whether it has cost the seller more, or less, is of no concern to the buyer. So the seller carries most of the risk. But the buyer also carries some risk. Fixed-price contracts are not change-friendly. If any buyer-initiated changes are required, they could be expensive; the seller may charge a full price for such changes, knowing that it's difficult for the buyer to go to another supplier. The buyer also needs to understand that sellers must allow for risk in their price. However, in a competitive environment, sellers often build in too little contingency for risk and tend to cut corners when under cost pressure. Therefore, the buyer needs to watch out for resulting quality problems. FFP is suitable for well-understood and fully specified deliverables. A standard education program would be an example.

- Cost plus percentage cost (CPPC) – mainly buyer risk.
  Here the buyer pays the seller for proven costs incurred, plus an agreed percentage of those costs. An estimate of the time and cost would usually be done up-front. But thereafter, it's easy to agree scope changes, because, even if estimating is needed, the basis for payment remains the same. Here, the buyer has control over what the money is spent on, but carries the risk of things costing more than planned. Nevertheless, the seller is usually cooperative because they want to meet the buyer's financial and other needs. A CPPC contract is most suitable where the buyer and seller enjoy a trust relationship, and where what must be produced is not yet fully defined. An example would be the development of a new product.
- Time and Materials (T&M) has similarities to CPPC – mainly buyer risk.
  The rates, at which people are charged, are defined, and the estimated number of hours stated, leading to an estimated cost. But, if more hours are needed the buyer pays more. The 'materials' often include things like travel costs. Once again trust is important, and the seller should warn, well in advance, if hours, and hence costs, are likely to exceed the estimates.
- Cost plus incentive fee (CPIF) – shared risk.
  Here, the seller has all their costs paid. Then, if the project ends up costing what was agreed, the seller gets an additional specified fee. For deviations, there is an agreed sharing percentage, say, 20%. So, if the seller cost is higher than the agreed amount, the fee is reduced by 20% of the overrun (but the fee can never be negative). If the cost is less, then 20% of the savings gets added to the fee. Here the deliverables would need to be reasonably well specified to arrive at an agreed cost, and the buyer would need to keep an eye on the quality delivered.Bear in mind that these are just some options, and even these could have variations, or could be used in combination to suit a particular project need. To understand the implications of these contract types better, I suggest that you do Case 32 before looking at the answers.

22.3.3 Conducting Procurements – Executing

Having completed, or being well advanced toward, documentation of the requirements, you need to find companies that can potentially meet all or a part of them. But, this would not be necessary where there is *already* an agreement, with an outside company, to provide the required goods and services. Assuming that you need to seek suppliers, there may be organizational standards to adhere to. Unless you are a very small organization, this is where SCM must become involved. They know the processes, they know the suppliers, and they know which agreements already exist. SCM might provide a list of sellers, to which you can add. You would then screen the sellers using the criteria developed earlier to limit the number of replies to be adjudicated. But, keep records of how you did the screening, in case of any appeal later. Sometimes, especially in government, it's mandatory to advertise a tender (RFQ or RFP). Think carefully about how much time to allow before the response deadline. Too little is unfair to the suppliers, and the responses may lack quality; too much time impacts your schedule. Then send the documents to the selected bidders.

You might hold an information session, also called a bidder conference. Having all bidders in a room at once will be perceived as fair, but bidders may not ask relevant questions for fear of disclosing ideas to competitors. Having sessions with one bidder at a time encourages openness, but could be viewed with suspicion. No easy answers here.

Finally, receive the responses. If you are the bidder, your response must be on time. If the buyer is from the private sector, you may get a second chance if you are late. But government regulations usually stipulate that late submissions are not even considered.

As the buyer, once the deadline is reached and you have the responses, you might send different sections of the response to different specialists for adjudication. Weighted scoring helps to identify which responses to consider further and which to eliminate. But the final selection may not necessarily take the highest score. You may be able to hold sessions with short-listed suppliers because inevitably there will be aspects of the responses that need clarification. There may even be final presentations to adjudicators before a decision is taken. Having selected the winning bid, it's only courteous to notify the other bidders and usually one would mention which company won the business.

22.3.4 Formalizing the Outcome with a Contract

Formal acceptance of a bid is usually binding, and that might be fine for a quote for nuts and bolts. However, where the bid is complex, acceptance should preferably be subject to a contract being signed. The contract should, at least, spell out: the statement of work, the deliverables and acceptance criteria, your responsibilities as the buying organization, and the payment schedule and terms.

At this point, it's worth re-emphasizing that what has been covered may involve many activities by many people, all of which should be part of the project plan.

22.3.5 Controlling Procured Services

Controlling procurements is like managing a project in its own right, with a few additions.

The buying company might periodically evaluate the seller and give feedback (sometimes called 'vendor evaluation').

> ***This worked very effectively for a bank rollout project where we had a contract to manage the rollout using three other suppliers. My co-PM did the vendor evaluations regularly and we got good cooperation and good results from the vendors. It took effort to evaluate fairly, but we believe that it was worth it.***

Even for fixed-price contracts, the seller may get progress payments, but it is worth holding back enough money that the seller has an incentive to complete the work. This also helps if, for any reason, the seller is unable to complete the work. At the end, there is a reconciliation to be done, especially if there were agreed changes.

For projects which include construction work, where there could be 'snags' after delivery, an amount is held back for a few months, called a retention – all agreed up-front. It is paid when any problems during the retention period have been dealt with.

A delivery audit might be needed. It's just a thorough check that what was specified has in fact been delivered and that the quality is satisfactory. Finally, at the end, there needs to be formal documentation and more detail is given in Chapter 18 on closing the project.

22.4 Miscellaneous Tips for Buyers and Sellers

This section gives some general thoughts and suggestions.

- Allow enough time. Clearly, a lot of work goes into procurement, and certain elements cannot be compressed – like giving sellers enough time to submit their bids. So, if the time for procurement is underestimated, or if it is left to the last minute, your project will be delayed.
- As PM, know what support is available to you. SCM, Legal department, and people that have experience are just some examples. So use the support, but realize that you know more about the project than they do, and be prepared to question advice given if you are not happy with it.
- As buyer, consider reducing the risk by using a phased approach, where each phase is treated as a separate contract. This applies especially if the initiative is very large, and it would be much like breaking a very large project into multiple smaller ones, done sequentially. An example might be where 'investigation and design', 'producing the solution', 'pilot rollout', and 'remaining rollout' could be separate contract phases. You could then terminate the contract at the end of any phase, and you have the option of engaging a different supplier for subsequent phases if the initial supplier does not meet expectations.
- Understanding the concept of 'back to back' contracts is important if you are the main contractor and employ subcontractors to meet your obligations to the buying organization (your customer). Your objective is to ensure that your agreements with the subcontractors mirror your agreement with the customer. If this is achieved, then your main roles are customer liaison and coordination of the subcontractors. But, it is not easy, and situations can easily arise where your obligations are not covered by subcontractor contracts, so that meeting the obligations costs you more.
- As a supplier, do not start work without a contract. You will often be pressured by the buying organization to start work because of the urgency. However, once your team has started work, it hugely reduces your power base in the contract negotiations. You know that you will not be paid anything until the contract is signed. So, if you have started work, then you will willingly sign almost anything, just to get paid. There is a way around this. If there is urgency, a letter of authorization from the buyer serves as a simple agreement specifying the hourly rates at which your team will work until the letter is replaced by a contract. At least you will be paid even if the contract is delayed or is never signed.

- As buyer, be wary of penalty clauses which reduce what you will pay to the seller if certain contract conditions, usually meeting deadlines, are not met. If you insist on penalties, then expect the price to be higher. The sellers will need to charge extra to cover their additional risk. A further problem may be that if your organization is in any way responsible for the delay, then expect the penalties to be challenged by the seller. So only use penalties if something is critical to you, and is worth paying extra for.
- If terminology is used, especially in contracts, that you are unfamiliar with, then learn the meaning. Many terms have legal implications and you need to know what those are.
- Be aware of risks. If you are the buyer, the seller could go insolvent. This risk is most severe when only one seller can do certain work. Watch for currency risks when you will pay for goods or services in a foreign currency. If you are importing major capital equipment then maybe discuss 'forward cover' with your bank, effectively allowing you to fix the exchange rate (at a small premium).

22.5 Project Outsourcing and Partnership

Outsourcing goes hand in hand with project procurement. In general, outsourcing involves contracting another organization to provide services that might have been provided in-house in the past (Larson & Gray, 2018). So, any project work done by another organization is effectively outsource. Most outsourcing starts with a procurement process, whether it be for specific work on a project, or to outsource certain organizational functions for a defined period.

As illustrated in the Upview case, the objectives of the buyer and seller (the outsource company) are different. However, over time, it is beneficial, to both parties, if their objectives become more aligned and mutual trust builds up. When this happens, the two organizations could be regarded as business partners, even if there is a formal contract between them. Where such partnerships work well, it is likely that the organizations will work together on further projects, thus reinforcing the partnership. Such partnerships are not just for services. Often, partnerships apply for goods, like complex components, that require advice and support, beyond just delivering a quality product. Nowadays it can even happen that organizations are both partners and competitors; they may compete in some areas and cooperate in others. So what are the drivers toward outsourcing and partnership?

22.5.1 Advantages and Caveats of Outsourcing

Over the past few decades outsourcing has grown enormously. One reason is that the complexity of products and the degree of specialization make it no longer economical for an organization to maintain the full range of capabilities internally. Another reason is that communication has become cheaper and more effective. Years ago, an offshore help desk would have been slow and cumbersome. Nowadays with high bandwidths, the internet, and the use of common software, geography is less of a barrier. An outsource partner can even be in another country. So, here are some of the benefits of outsourcing, and, in particular, project outsourcing:

- One can bring in specialized skills, equipment, software, or whatever, at a lower cost than trying to do everything internally. Moreover, other companies can do certain things better than one's own organization and may offer valuable ideas and insights.
- Outsourcing can save time. Another company may have skilled people readily available, whereas you would need to wait for such resources in your own organization, and even then, your project might not get high priority.
- Similarly, outsourcing can avoid having idle resources. You can bring skills in only when you need them.
- Working with a respected outsource partner can even add credibility to your offering.

However, there are some things to be aware of and also potential problems:

- There will always be a contractual overhead when working with another organization. But the more rigorous specifications can have advantages because in-company agreements are often a bit loose.
- There will be some loss of control because you cannot always dictate who should do the work, or how it should be done.
- There can be communication breakdowns and even conflict due to different languages, cultures, and agendas. The latter underlines the importance of having the interests of the outsource partner aligned and aiming for the same success scenario.
- Outsourcing can cause internal morale problems.

  A bank, in which I was managing a project, decided to outsource their entire IT test department, of over 100 people, to an offshore organization. The depression was palpable and it seriously affected our project because we relied on the test team, and knew many of the staff.

- It may be difficult to end the relationship if the outsource company is not meeting expectations. This can be very serious if the outsource is for a function that supports the entire organization. It is usually less serious where the outsource is limited to a project. Nevertheless, there would be an impact.

So, despite the potential disadvantages, being good at outsourcing can bring great competitive advantages. Whether the outsource is for a project or organization-wide project management is relevant, as the setup of an outsource arrangement, or any changes to it, will involve projects.

22.5.2 Some Illustrative Outsourcing Scenarios

Just to emphasize that there are an almost infinite number outsourcing scenarios, Figure 22.1 gives some illustrative examples.

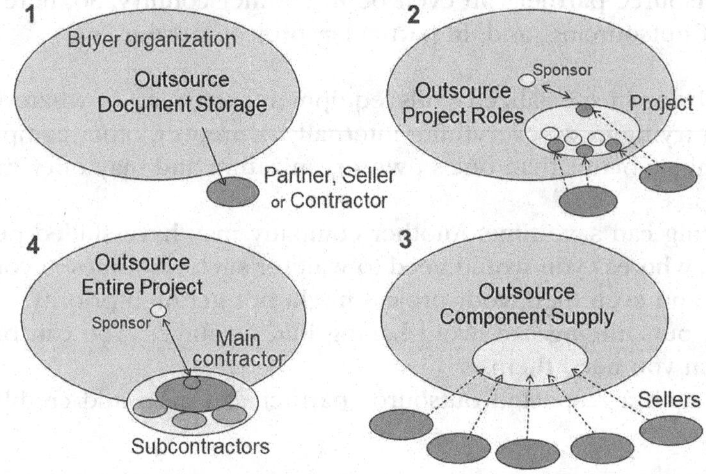

Figure 22.1 Illustrative outsource scenarios.

- Scenario 1 is where document storage for the entire organization is outsourced.
- Scenario 2 shows a project run within an organization, but where the PM and certain other roles are outsourced to two different suppliers. Such people might work as though they were employees of the buyer organization.
- Scenario 3 shows a production operation where the supply of many of the components is outsourced to multiple sellers, some of which might have a close working relationship with the buying organization.
- Scenario 4 shows an entire project that has been outsourced to a main contractor, who in turn employs subcontractors to do the bulk of the work. The link to a person in the buyer organization illustrates the importance of this collaboration, which could even involve a steering committee.

But even in scenarios 1 and 3 where ongoing operations are involved, there are always projects to set them up or when operations need to change.

22.5.3 Approaches to Moving Toward Partnership

Most organizations have many suppliers. For the important suppliers, it is desirable to move from a traditional relationship toward more of a partnership. This does not happen overnight; partnerships are forged over a period. On projects, where buyer and seller work as partners, there is less relationship overhead, people are more relaxed and productive, and overall the project is more likely to be successful. The left-hand column of Table 22.1 gives some characteristics of traditional seller relationships, and the right-hand column gives the partnering ones that organizations might strive toward.

A few elements need clarification. To facilitate open communication, seller staff often sign non-disclosure agreements, so that confidential information can more safely be shared with them. Executive relationships do not replace project relationships, but supplement them. Ideally, the project relationships between buyer and

Table 22.1 Partnering Versus Traditional Approaches

Traditional	*Partnering*
Suspicion	Trust
Guarded communication	Open communication
Project relationships	Executive relationships
Contracts – for use in a law court	Contracts – to reach understanding
Own agendas	Shared goals
Suppliers are not team members	Joint project teams
Push the risk to the other party	Risk is shared

seller are excellent. But, in the occasional situation where there is dispute or tension, it helps greatly if the buyer and seller executives are on good terms and can step in to facilitate a resolution.

> *More than once on my projects things have gone wrong, and well briefed executives have negotiated a fair solution. I've also experienced the reverse, where the project was going satisfactorily, but the outsource relationship was terminated because of customer changes at executive level leading to a breakdown in trust.*

With shared goals, the aim is to optimize the outcomes for both partners. Each partner still has their own agenda, but not at the expense of their partner, else trust will be lost. Finally, if risk can be shared, when the going gets tough, the mood of the team will be "we're in this together".

22.5.4 Sound Practices to Facilitate Partnership

What follows is mainly from the point of view of the buying organization. It applies particularly to a project involving several organizations, but many of the points apply to all projects.

- When people from other organizations join your team it is essential to brief them well as it is unlikely to have been done by their own management. If such people join at the start, then attending a definition workshop or an orientation session helps. But, if they join during the project, then discuss the importance of the project, the need for cooperation, and how the person can personally benefit.
- When communicating be aware of the cultures involved, and that people from the other company may have different assumptions. Due to language and culture, they may understand the meanings of an agreement or a deadline differently. It is safest to 'put things in writing' and then to discuss them to check that there is sound understanding, especially of the terminology used. For deadlines,

discuss why they are important and also what to do if there is difficulty meeting them. When defining the work to be done, there must be specifications or a clear description, indicating how work will be measured, and confirmation that the requirements are understood. Having team members co-located working in the same area helps communication but is not always possible.

- There needs to be a clear process to follow if disagreements arise. While it's best if team members, from whichever organization, resolve disagreements themselves. It should be clear at what point the problem must come to your attention, as PM. Such problem-solving situations are an opportunity to build the team by jointly finding the best solution rather than having a 'my way versus your way' conflict.
- Fair contracts are essential. Your supplier partner must feel that there is something in it for them. By all means, consider incentives, but use them with caution because there can be unintended consequences, such as when a supplier blames you for the fact that they could not achieve something.

Case 33 is about an outsource and the project to set it up that has gone badly wrong. Use what you have learned to answer the questions; then compare your answers with those given.

22.6 Summary

As PM in a buyer organization, where procurement is needed, you cannot fully delegate it to other people. Even the sponsor may not have time to avoid some of the pitfalls. So take it upon yourself to ensure that what is agreed in a contract is well understood, fair, and allows for risks. But involve the right people, and start in good time.

For both buyer and seller staff, try to build a partnership relationship, with shared interests, good communication, and trust.

References

Larson, E & Gray, C. (2018). *Project Management: The Managerial Process: International dition*. 7th edition. New York: McGraw-Hill Education.

PMI 2017. *PMBOK – Guide to the Project Management Body of Knowledge*, 6th edition. Pennsylvania, USA: Project Management Institute.

Chapter 23

OCM – Organizational Change Management

23.1 Introduction and Objectives

The outcome of many business projects is that people inside, and often outside, the organization, must change the way that they do things.

> *Back in the 1990s, I remember implementing a hospital system, at a hospital that had never before been computerized. Many of the staff had never in their lives used a computer. Customizing the software and loading the data for the hospital were not easy, but the process of enabling the staff to use the system effectively was far more challenging.*

That's what OCM (organizational change management) is about – all the things needed to enable people to adapt to a new way of working. Indeed, for many business projects, the project can only be successful if the people adapt to new ways and ultimately believe that the changes are an improvement. There are many facets to it, often involving people that specialize in OCM, or simply 'change management'. As we shall learn, people are complex, and the process to bring about change, is not straightforward. That is why PMs need to understand change management and build it into the project scope. Here, it should be noted that, although the word 'change' is common to both, OCM and project change control are different disciplines. OCM is about people change, while project change control is about scope, schedule, and budget changes.

For some projects, very little OCM is needed. For example, installing new network infrastructure may take considerable skill and money, but once it is commissioned, the job is largely done – network traffic will flow. But, for many business projects, the

DOI: 10.1201/9781003321101-26

job is only done when the people-change has happened. As with the hospital project, the OCM aspects form much of the project scope. Let us move on to the objectives, which are to:

- Understand the project contexts where OCM applies.
- Be able to assess the importance and scope of OCM for a particular project. The OCM component could be small or it could be massive.
- Learn the principles of OCM.
- Learn the Prosci organization's ADKAR model for approaching OCM. The letters stand for Awareness, Desire, Knowledge, Ability, and Reinforcement.
- Be able to apply some of the structures and techniques used in OCM.

23.2 OCM in Context

Let us consider the types of project where OCM applies. Organizational change could be a project in its own right, for example, a corporate restructure, or the introduction of employee time recording using a standard package. Organizational change could be the consequence of a project: if the project were to move a company to new premises, then there would be many people matters to resolve. You would be right if you suggested that the people and customer aspects should form part of the scope right from the start. Likewise, there are projects where it is known before the project, that organizational change is a large component. For example, a merge of two organizations clearly includes both systems and people aspects. Similar considerations apply to the replacement of outdated computer systems.

There are some fundamental things that PMs need to understand about change. First of all, change must happen, or else the company won't survive. Jack Welch, who headed up General Electric during successful times, is reputed to have said: "if the rate of change outside (the organization) exceeds the rate on the inside, the end is near". So, business projects are about change, but change won't happen unless the people support it. Unfortunately, change is not without challenges (Davies & Garrett, 2013). Most people fear and resist change. Also, some research has found that the people dimension is the most common cause of project failure – which I can believe. The bottom line is, that for many projects, the organizational change aspects need to be taken very seriously. Often the activities to manage people change, are overlooked when developing the business case, and even during project planning, leading to a major piece of scope not being allowed for.

23.3 The Principles of OCM

A project should be seen as having a change component if its outcome or execution affects peoples' jobs, status, way of life, livelihoods, or workplace culture. The following principles apply particularly for major changes involving people:

- From an executive point of view, strong sponsorship for the changes, and executive resolve, are essential. Supporting the new way needs *sustained* focus.

It's not enough to explain what will be done, with reasons, and then walk away – the change is likely to peter out. Executives need to understand the current situation and the desired situation after a reasonable timescale has been allowed for the change. Then they must remain involved throughout and communicate regularly.

- From the PM's point of view, usually the people change aspects are very different from putting business or technical infrastructure in place. So consider making the OCM aspects a major subproject. The main thing is that the right people are assigned, with clear responsibilities – communications, mentioned below, being key.
- For the affected people, change is unsettling and resistance is understandable (Davies & Garrett, 2013). Why? Well, it takes extra time and effort to learn new processes, and usually their normal jobs still have to be done. Moreover, the benefits of the changes may not be obvious. Power has shifted in many industries. So, no longer can management impose a change, with no questions permitted. The people want to understand the reasons for change, and they may not accept certain things, like greed (profit at any cost), or things that are bad for the environment. They expect to participate in the change and have management at least listen to any concerns that they may express. Also, in some countries, it is not easy to dismiss people for resisting change.
- The first-line managers play a key role because of their effect on the people. The managers' role is to communicate and enable the change. It has already been implied that merely telling people to change, is seldom effective. So a critical success factor is to help the managers to play their role well. They need to be a positive influence, and to support their staff through changes. Conversely, obstructive managers can derail the change process. Imagine if a manager told the staff: "The executives want this new thing. I think it's a load of rubbish, but you have to do it". Now, even if that is never spoken, people are quick to pick up on attitude, so having first-line managers committed, is vital.
- Communication and training. These are also essential. It is best to be open and honest and give as much information as possible. If anything, over-communicate. It may annoy some, but people will know that the change is important. By all means, send information by email, but on their own, emails will not get the message across. Workshops, and discussing the reasons for, and impact of, the change, are far more likely to be effective. Also, 'hands-on' learning where people practice new techniques or jointly solve problems, usually works better than listening to a presentation. And as we shall see, any form of learning will only work, if the need for the change has already been accepted.

While the above points may appear to be focused on people within the organization, most of them apply to customers and even communities that are involved. A role similar to that of the first-line manager might be played by financial advisors in the case of changes in how a wealth management company operates, or by community leaders where a government project is undertaken. There are many other examples, but it's important to get these influencers on your side.

23.4 The ADKAR Approach to Change

I once thought that Prosci was a person, but in fact it is an organization (www.prosci.com) founded by Jeff Hiatt in 1994. It did research, over several years, on about 700 companies and found the following: For successful change, there are five phases that must happen in a rough sequence, probably with overlaps. Each phase needs to be met, to an acceptable level, before moving on to the next one (Hiatt, 2006). Here they are:

- Awareness of the need (phase 1). This is not the awareness that there will be a change, but rather, awareness of the *reasons*. People must understand the potential negative consequences for the organization if the change does not happen.
- Desire (phase 2). People must not only realize that the change is good for the organization, but that it's better for them, versus the alternative of not changing. I accept that this is tricky in a situation where a few people will lose status, or even their jobs.
- Knowledge (phase 3). People need to know enough about the change to know their role in making the change happen.
- Ability (phase 4). Knowledge, on its own may not be enough. Suppose that you had read a book on how to play better football, but had never tried it out. You might have the knowledge, but not yet the ability. So gaining the ability includes developing the skills and behaviors needed to make the change happen. In the football example, it would mean practicing with others in the team.
- Reinforcement (phase 5). This may last for a year or more. Management needs to constantly talk about the new way, give feedback on the benefits, and deal with non-cooperation. It would be a bit like having a football coach, encourage your own development in the team, to help the team to play better.

When starting on an OCM initiative, the recommendation is to rate each ADKAR phase out of 5, where 1 would be 'does not exist' and 5 would be 'fully met'. Then, focus on the first in the sequence that is below 3 and get it to a 4 or 5, before moving on. Thus, if the majority already know why the organization needs a particular change, then maybe go easy on awareness communication and get on with the subsequent phases. However, the process should not be mechanistic: different groups may be in different places and the attitudes of some people may even move in a negative direction. So ongoing judgment is needed.

23.4.1 How the ADKAR Phases Relate to the Project Phases

Figure 23.1 shows how the ADKAR phases might relate to a typical project progression.

OCM needs to start early, and awareness might be created even while the business case for the project is being finalized. Then, while the concept and design of the project are being worked on, which could be process re-engineering, changes to IT systems, or even developing a new mine shaft, the OCM focus would shift to desire, and answer the question: "why will this be good for the people as well as for the organization?" Next, during execution and implementation, knowledge and ability

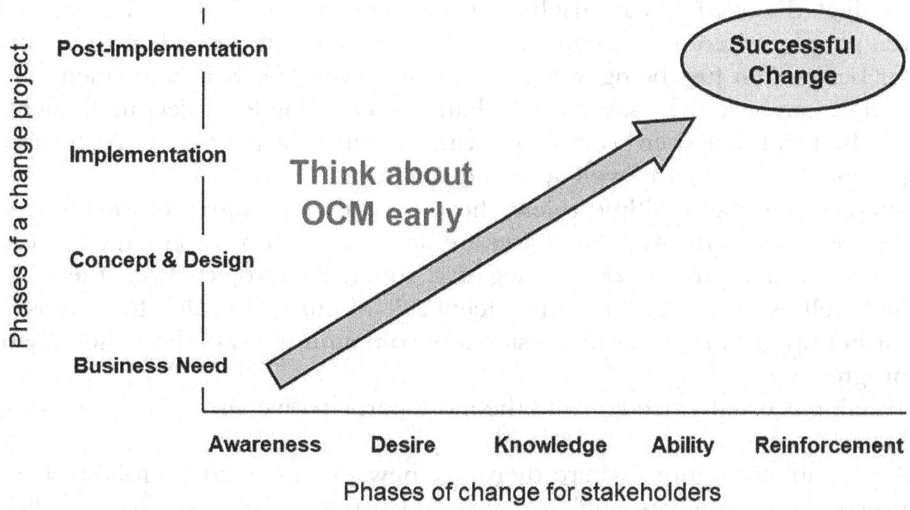

Figure 23.1 Linking ADKAR phases to the project phases.

must be created. And finally, after implementation, reinforcement from all levels of management is needed to bed down the new ways – resulting in successful change. Even if the need for OCM is only recognized late, the sooner it starts the better. This would mean discussions with the sponsor and possibly the steering committee because it involves asking for more time and money, and checking that the business case remains sound. Not easy, but better than a failed project later.

23.4.2 Putting ADKAR into Practice

Now that we know what must be done, how do we go about doing these phases: creating awareness and desire and then building knowledge and ability? Here are some approaches, which, for a small project, might be facilitated by members of the project team. For a larger project, the engagement might require a change analyst or even a change team.

> *Back in the early 1990s on a two year bank project, we had a change analyst join our team. She pointed out, and did, many things that I would not have thought of. But, it also goes to show that, while OCM has developed over the years, it's not new.*

Back to the approaches

- Managers need to brief their staff, and it has to be planned because it is unlikely to happen on its own. So the PM, or change person, would need to engage with the line managers, brief them, and offer support for sessions with their staff. Some resistance may be experienced, but that is still better than a revolt during implementation.

- Facilitated workshops are useful because they can be done with groups, of say ten people, where participants can ask questions and raise ideas or concerns – far better than just being 'told'. Even if not everyone is in agreement, at least people can have their say. Also, if challenges relating to project implementation can be identified, then workshops with the business people involved can often produce workable and well-accepted solutions.
- Surveys can play multiple roles. They can gather valuable information on the degree to which the ADKAR phases are progressing. It could emerge that respondents are unaware of, or are negative about, the project. Even the response level tells something. Structured feedback of survey results, to groups, gives further opportunities for discussion and communication on how the initiative is progressing.
- Training is usually needed, and the more participative and problem-solving, the better.
- After implementation, where there are new processes to be followed, 'super-user' support prevents staff from getting frustrated and going back to their old ways. A super-user is a person who, early-on, becomes an expert at a new process, and helps others to follow it.
- Finally, newsletters, on intranet or email, reinforce the notion that something is happening, even if they might have limited impact on their own.

23.5 Further Thoughts on OCM

The most important thing, for both PMs and sponsors, is not to overlook the OCM aspects of a project. As a PM, you are probably very involved in achieving the project's technical deliverables and may not have much time for the people-change aspects. Nevertheless, you need to be sufficiently aware of them to discuss how they should be handled, with the sponsor, especially if they can 'make or break' the project. Sometimes the sponsor may have ideas as to how best to handle the people change aspects. Then, on projects which affect large numbers of people, it may not be possible to engage personally with all of them. So, deciding how to reach the affected people would need discussion.

This might be a good time to think about your own organization, or the ones that you have worked with. Were there projects that involved OCM? How were they handled? Were all the 'affected people' considered? For example in a hospital project, it may not only be about the hospital staff; it may also affect the patients.

> *A delegate on an executive education program, told me about a project to implement an automated medicine dispensing machine. Not only did staff need to enter the right information into the system and load the right medicines, but patients needed to know how and when to use the machine to get their medication.*

This would be a good time to look at Case 34 which is about the changes caused by an early retirement program aimed at reducing staff numbers. Much of the learning is thinking about which groups of people are affected and how to engage with them.

References

Hiatt, J. M. (2006). *ADKAR: A Model for Change in Business, Government and Our Community: Prosci Learning Center Publications*, Loveland, Colorado, USA.

Davies, G., & Garrett, G. (2013). *Herding Professional Cats – Advice to Aspiring Leaders in the Professions*. Axminster: Triarchy Press.

Chapter 24

Contracts for Business Projects

24.1 Introduction and Objectives

Many aspects of project management involve other organizations, individuals, or even other parts of our own organization. A contract, is merely the formalization of an agreement between two parties. It should make it clear what each party will contribute and deliver and what compensation will be paid. Some believe that the main purpose is to go to court if the contract is breached, usually by obligations not being met. Another view is that, when a potential dispute arises, a starting point is to refer to the contact (or agreement as it is often called). Usually, the contract clarifies what was intended and a fair resolution is quickly reached. The preparation for a contract also involves quite a bit of valuable thinking. So, the objectives of this chapter are to:

- Consider the PM's involvement in contracts.
- Give a high-level understanding of contracts and their importance.
- Know the structure that is commonly used for contracts.
- Understand some of the terminology and important clauses that are likely to be included.
- Learn some of the things to watch out for, like liability, and to get legal support in good time.
- Know about ADR (alternative dispute resolution) as a way to resolve disputes without going to court.
- Enable the creation of contracts that are easy to understand and encourage sound project practices.

However, a few words of caution. I'm not a lawyer, and have used contracts to support a trusting relationship and thus to avoid litigation. I have never been in court over a project, and lack such experience. Also, the legal systems across geographies differ, and there is a range of attitudes toward contracts which vary by country and

DOI: 10.1201/9781003321101-27

industry. Nevertheless, it is hoped that all systems encourage fairness and sound understanding in business dealings.

24.2 Why Does the PM Need to Be Involved in Contracts?

Let us now consider why the PM needs to know something about contracts, and cannot simply leave it all to the lawyers. Here are some reasons:

- As PM, you generally need to be involved in any contract negotiations, because you will need to live with whatever gets contracted and will want to reduce the likelihood of disputes arising. This applies whether you are on the buying side, the selling side, or are going into a partner relationship.
- For a project of any size or risk, that involves contracts, it is wise to have legal people involved. Often your organization will make it mandatory because 'Legal' (as they are often referred to) can spot troublesome clauses. So, you need to be able to communicate with legal people, and this requires you to have a working knowledge of contracts and their terminology. Indeed, advice from Legal may be needed at any time during the project.
- But, Legal cannot handle contractual aspects alone. You have a better understanding of what must be delivered, and this applies particularly to the supplements of the contract where the details of a specific project are spelled out. Your input would be especially important if Legal has limited experience in the type of project at hand. Legal might be unaware of things that could go wrong, so you would collaborate with them on ways to mitigate such risks via the contract.
- Then, during the project, you need to understand the constraints mentioned in the contract. For example, you may need to introduce procedures to ensure confidentiality. You also need to understand things that introduce risk, like indemnity clauses which could be expensive should certain adverse events happen.

24.3 Some Important Facets of Contracts

Before going further here are some thoughts on legal aspects. First, the law is not an exact science. While some aspects of a contract are clear, many situations arise that are a matter of judgment, hence the need for judges. If everything were straightforward, a computer could adjudicate any dispute, but many aspects of projects are not clear-cut. Second, the term 'agreement' sounds friendlier than 'contract', but once an agreement is signed by both parties, it becomes a contract in the eyes of the law. Third, for projects, contracts are usually between two parties, but often there are many contracts related to a project because there may be many parties.

24.3.1 Do All Projects Need Contracts?

A few more questions arise: Do *all* projects need contracts? and what aspects of a project need a contract? Where a project involves other legal entities some form of contract is essential. It could be to formalize a buyer-seller relationship, or it could be used to bring contract staff on board, or to hire premises or equipment. But, where a project is entirely internal to an organization, with no additional suppliers, there would be no contracts. For other departments whose support is needed, sometimes a DoU or MoU (Document or Memorandum of Understanding) is drawn up, even if it lacks the legal status of a contract. However, while contracts can be time-consuming, they enforce a level of discipline because the project deliverables and other outcomes need to be thoroughly thought through. So, for internal projects, where there is no formal contract, the PDD (project definition document) might be considered as an agreement between the PM, the sponsor, and other key stakeholders. Even for projects where there is a contract, the contract does not replace the PDD. The PDD serves many other purposes, like ensuring that stakeholders have a common understanding because it is unlikely that all stakeholders will read the contract. Also, new facts often come to light, while preparing the PDD and during subsequent planning, resulting in contract modifications or variations (as they are sometimes called).

24.3.2 Requirements for a Contract

Certain things are required for something to be a contract: Both parties must have the intention to reach an agreement and know that they have entered into a contract. They must also concur on the material aspects of the contract which must be 'fair and reasonable'. Now you might ask: "surely these things would be perfectly clear?" Well, in a written contract, they probably would be. But they might not be if the contract were verbal, and a verbal agreement can be deemed a binding contract. The only problem is that, even with witnesses, it might be hard to enforce an oral (verbal) agreement. So, the moral of the story is: even if parties trust one another, it's best to have things in writing where there is less chance of misunderstanding.

There are more requirements: The contract must create obligations by both parties. If I put in writing that I will build you a house, it would not be a contract unless it specified what you would pay me for it. Also, the obligations must be possible to perform. Then, if there is an offer, and acceptance of the offer, it constitutes a contract when the acceptance is sent back to the offeror. This might be by post, but, depending on the offer, it might be by other means, like email.

24.3.3 Things That Would Negate a Contract

There are a few things that would prevent something from being a contract, and hence make it 'null and void'. Where the acceptance is subject to changes, and this can happen easily, it would be considered a counter-offer rather than an acceptance. Anything in the contract document that is illegal prevents it from being a contract. Then, there would not be a contract if either party does not have the capacity to enter into an agreement. Two situations are: a party not being authorized to sign and a party being under the legal age (18 in many jurisdictions). If there were duress involved, like blackmail or a 'gun-to-head' situation, the contract would be void. Undue influence might have similar consequence; if it were proved that a consultant to the party that signed, had been bribed, the contract would become invalid. Interestingly, a reasonable mistake could prevent something from being a contract until it is rectified. I am not sure what 'reasonable' would be, but possibly a typo which added an extra zero to a dollar amount? But, saying "I did not read that clause" would not be considered a reasonable mistake.

24.3.4 Is an Offer and Acceptance Good Enough?

In Chapter 22 on procurement, we discussed bids in response to an RFP (request for proposal). Supposing that an RFP was issued and responses were received. Then after evaluation, one seller is notified, in writing, that their bid had been accepted. Would we have a contract? Probably we would, because there was an offer and an acceptance. But, would the RFP and the response cater to most of what might happen? The answer is: probably not, which could result in some hard-to-resolve disputes. If anything on the project went to court, there could be unexpected laws coming into play. Therefore, unless the bid is for something very routine like purchasing nuts and bolts, it might be wise to make the acceptance subject to an agreement (contract) being signed between the parties.

24.4 The Structure and Content of a Contract

24.4.1 A Commonly Used Contract Structure

Let's look at the structure of a typical project contract which is illustrated in Figure 24.1.

One tries to have the clauses that are likely to apply to all kinds of work, and are unlikely to change, in one document – often called the main contract or body. This applies particularly if the buyer expects the seller (the other party) to participate in several future projects. Then, for each piece of work, there would be a supplement which is effectively an extension of the main contract (or agreement) and spells out the details specific to that piece of work including dates and payment amounts. Just one thing to note: where either the main contract, or more typically a supplement, refers to another document, like a specification, then that document becomes

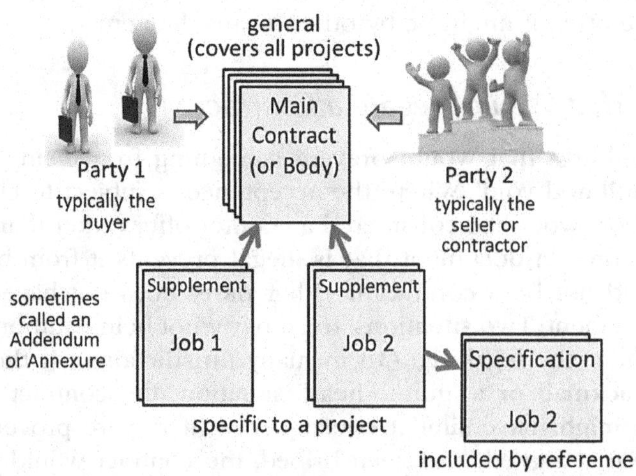

Figure 24.1 Typical business project contract structure.

incorporated (included) in the contract 'by reference'. So, one needs to be careful about what goes into a referenced specification. The main contract and supplements is quite a flexible arrangement, especially when there will be new work coming up periodically. No need to have lawyers go through the main agreement again – just work on what's in the supplement, which is usually shorter and more focused. A few more points:

- A contract supplement (sometimes also called an addendum or annexure) can override a clause in the body contract, but just for that supplement.
- The supplement should indicate the sequence of obligations: one party performs first, then the other party. There are usually overlaps, especially where both parties have responsibilities or where there are progress payments.
- Certain terms may survive the contract, like non-disclosure. It's worth mentioning that here, the word 'terms' means a contractual requirement, and the word 'survive' means that something applies after the termination (end) date of the contract. Yes, legal English can be confusing.

Having explained the two-part contract, a single contract that combines the clauses from the main contract and the supplement is the norm for something that is unlikely to be repeated, like an employment contract.

24.4.2 Clarification of Some Contract Terminology

There are many words in contracts that we do not use every day, and some that have specific meanings. There are also variations by industry, type of contract, and country. So, when in doubt, talk to Legal. Nevertheless, here is my understanding:

- Intellectual property refers to ownership or copyright of ideas, the content of documents, and sometimes computer programs, that are created as part of the contract.
- Confidentiality usually binds the contractor's staff not to disclose anything about the project to outside parties. This even applies after the contract ends. Often, each individual is required to sign a non-disclosure agreement.
- A liability clause might limit the liability of either party that might result from an error being made or something going wrong. Sometimes, liability only applies in the case of 'gross negligence', but this could be subject to judgment.
- Restraint of trade may prevent one party's staff from competing with the other party for a set time after the contract ends. This may also be subject to interpretation and is often difficult to enforce.
- A 'conflict of interest' clause may prevent a contractor's staff from working with the buyer's competitors for the duration of the contract.
- 'Domicilium' relates to where a party resides and can be reached.
- An 'assignment of rights and obligations' clause may prevent one party from getting an outside party to do their contracted work, without permission.
- A waiver clause may indicate that the buyer should not be seen to have accepted work that was not according to the contract, just because they say nothing. It may also spell out under what circumstances a contract obligation can be set

aside by the other party – like accepting that a contractor has painted the roof green instead of gray as stated in the supplement.

- A force majeure clause states what will happen if unforeseeable circumstances, which are beyond the control of a party, prevent them from meeting their contractual obligations.

'Terms and Conditions' or 'T's & C's' is a catch-all phrase for all the clauses that accompany a contract. Often you hear "terms and conditions apply", meaning you need to find out what they are.

This would be a good time to do part 1 of Case 35 which asks you to decide which clauses should be in the main contract and which in a supplement.

24.5 Tips Related to Contracts

Here are miscellaneous things for you to think about when entering into contracts. The list is by no means comprehensive because it is hard to think of everything – which is why we get Legal involved.

- Always keep a copy, even softcopy, of signed contracts. At the time that a dispute arises, you do not want to ask the other party "please can you send me a copy of the contract". It could weaken your negotiating position.
- As mentioned in Chapter 22 on procurement, where you are working with subcontractors, try to make the contracts 'back to back' so that the subcontractor will meet your obligation to your customer – sometimes easier said than done.
- Be careful of liability, for example, in an employment contract. Even if you are not being paid huge amounts, the consequences of an error can run into millions.

  One of the few times that I engaged with my own lawyer, was to discuss how to limit my liability if it were found that I had been negligent. My client accepted my need and amended the draft contract to limit my liability. Fortunately, no such situation arose.

- If you are the contractor (seller), make sure that the buying organization's responsibilities are spelled out. They go beyond paying. Their non-action can hold up the entire project, and you don't want to be blamed or lose money, for their tardiness.
- Be aware that the parties' lawyers often have different views and can become quite antagonistic. Contracts can go to and fro, consuming a lot of time, over minor details. Maybe, the quickest way is to arrange for the lawyers to meet online. This situation can also be eliminated by the next point.
- As buyer, it might be wise to include, in the RFP (request for proposal), the contract that you expect the seller to sign (as suggested in Chapter 22 on procurement). You can invite comments if a seller has concerns with any aspect of it. Then, when the seller is selected, get the contract signed promptly so that work can start.

- Get contracts reviewed by Legal with the aim of eliminating glaring risks. Also, watch out for the other side's lawyers putting in unfair clauses. If possible, get them changed. If there is a threatening clause, don't fall for "that's a standard clause, we would never use it". The person you are dealing with might not, but the lawyers might have other ideas.
- By all means, refer to important documents, but then treat those documents with the same care as you give to a contract.
- Watch out for conflicting statements within the contract and get them resolved. The more complex the contract, the greater the likelihood.
- As buyer, be aware that a contract does not always ensure that the outcome will be as expected. If the contractor defaults, remedies may depend on the situation. If you are dealing with a subsidiary company, the parent company may not step in to assist them.
- If you have the choice as to which contract wording will be used, then use your own, rather than the other party's, contract. You understand it better, and know that it is fair.

24.6 Handling of Differences Between the Parties

24.6.1 Some Causes of Differences

In this context, a 'difference' is a difference of view between the parties, on something perceived to be important. If it is not resolved amicably, it becomes a dispute. So, here are some possible causes of differences, and understanding them may help to avoid them:

- Interpretation of the scope. The parties may not see the details of the contracted scope the same way, especially if it was vaguely stated. For example, the seller may have misunderstood a requirement due to time pressure to bid. So, generally, try to get the scope as clear and complete as possible.
- Poor scope change control. This can lead to disputes if the buyer assumes that something will be done at no charge.
- The occurrence of an adverse event, where each sees it as the other party's problem. Adverse events happen on most projects and the contract may not have been clear as to who carries which risks.
- Poor quality deliverables. The cause could be a lack of skills, leading to disputes over rework.
- Personality clashes, where pride is at stake, and neither person is willing to negotiate. This is aggravated when the general relationship between the parties is poor.

Fortunately, there are factors that can prevent differences from becoming disputes. It helps greatly if the parties maintain a trusting, cooperative, relationship, especially at executive level, where working together, takes precedence over personal positions. Having a sound understanding of the contract also contributes to resolving differences quickly. Thorough, well-managed, documentation, with a record of facts like names and dates, is another aspect. Generally, the party with the better documentation is in the stronger negotiating position should differences turn to disputes.

24.6.2 Dispute Resolution

Supposing that a difference cannot easily be resolved and a dispute emerges. Litigation (going to court) should be seen as a last resort, and would only happen if one party adopts a 'win at all costs' attitude. Often the winner of a court case does not end up better off, partly because any relationship with the other party is probably severely damaged. Fortunately, there are ways of avoiding going to court, known as ADR which stands for Alternative Dispute Resolution. It may even be specified in the contract that neither party may litigate without taking certain ADR steps first. So what is ADR? It can take many forms and each form can have variations. A few of the common forms are:

- Negotiation. This would be more formal than merely discussing the situation.
- Mediation. This is similar to negotiation, but with an experienced, independent, mediator whose purpose is to facilitate a fair agreement between the parties. The mediator may even propose a resolution.

  I had an experience over 20 years ago, when my sub-contractor incorrectly specified some computer equipment, which cost us money. After several weeks of not agreeing as to how it should be resolved financially, one meeting with a knowledgeable third party, that we both trusted, led to a compromise.

- Arbitration. An arbitrator (sometimes more than one) would be appointed, and would, after a thorough discussion of the facts, give a ruling. Adjudication, practiced in some countries, is used for a quick ruling on a specific situation, like, determining what dollar compensation would be appropriate.

Usually, the parties would start with negotiation, then consider mediation, and only resort to arbitration if the earlier approaches have not worked. ADR has a number of differences from litigation (going to court):

- The proceedings are confidential to the parties, whereas court proceedings are on public record.
- In court, the judge does not ask questions, but listens to the evidence led. It is up to the lawyers to ask the right questions. In arbitration, the arbitrator may ask questions.
- In ADR, the mediator or arbitrator will probably have some experience with the type of situation. With litigation, there is no such guarantee; the judge may have little understanding of the salient features of a case.

Before engaging in any form of ADR, a number of things need to be considered:

- Is there benefit in first getting an expert opinion on the merits of the case?
- Will each party engage voluntarily, or only because ADR processes are specified in the contract?

- Will the mediator or arbitrator be agreed between the parties or be appointed by an outside body?
- Is any agreement reached, binding on the parties?
- Is the decision of an arbitrator final, or can it be appealed in court?
- Will the lawyers from both parties participate?
- Will ADR be quicker or cheaper than litigation? Arbitration is usually quicker than litigation but not necessarily cheaper because both lawyers and arbitrators charge.

After any dispute is settled by ADR, ensure that the resolution is well documented to prevent it, or something similar, 'blowing up' again.

Practices vary between countries, so, should a serious dispute situation arise, you, as PM or sponsor, would need to find out, possibly with Legal assistance, how to proceed. ADR works best where the amounts at stake are not vast, and where both parties want a fair resolution – conditions that usually apply when the parties are working together on a project. However, despite the benefits of ADR, the best way of minimizing differences in the first place, remains a well-thought-through contract.

24.7 Standard Contracts to Support Sound Practice

There are many free contract templates available on the web. There are also organizations with many years of experience that offer a range of contracts and can advise on their use. The range is needed because there might be significant differences between, for example, a services contract (often used in business) and a construction contract. Whatever you use, it is wise to have the contract checked by a lawyer, especially if it is for something large or high risk. Contracts relating to projects should have certain desirable features. These are things for the drafters of contracts to strive toward, and some standard contracts do them well:

- The contract should be based on sound project management practices, and include things like how scope changes will be controlled and how issues will be managed.
- The scope should be thoroughly defined. Because the scope is specific to a project, a standard contract could only give pointers as to what should be covered like timeframe, quality criteria, volumes, geographic data, etc.
- Terminology, like the people roles, is defined and used throughout, to avoid confusion.
- Plain, understandable language is used with short sentences and simple words. The opposite might be a contract that only a trained lawyer could make sense of.
- The present tense should be used where possible.
- There should be minimal, and preferably no, cross-referencing, so that the reader does not need to scroll up and down to find things.
- Requirements should be stated to be as specific as possible. This means avoiding adjectives or adverbs that are subject to interpretation. For example, 'designs must be reviewed promptly' is not specific enough. Rather put 'designs must be reviewed with feedback given in three business days'.

- The contract should encourage collaboration between the parties and doing things in a professional manner.

All of the above points support the contract being used to achieve a common understanding and to foster professional, cooperative, relationships.

24.8 Summary

We have covered why you, as PM or sponsor, need to know about contracts. We have discussed various aspects of a contract like its structure and some of the clauses. We have learned about things to watch out for, and then, some ways to resolve differences. Nevertheless, the greatest value that a contract adds is to achieve understanding between the parties and to support a trusting and productive relationship.

Of particular importance is to state the scope in a clear manner that covers all important aspects in adequate detail. So, this would be a good time to get some practice, by doing part 2 of Case 35, which involves drafting the supplement for a major training project.

Chapter 25

Project Review

25.1 Introduction and Objectives

We hear many terms used like: project review, project audit, and project health-check. They have much in common in that they all 'take a step back' and provide feedback on the project, with recommendations. The words have different nuances which we shall discuss, but here I `shall use the term 'review' to cover all of them. Some PMs find reviews threatening, but my experience has been positive and I shall mention a situation where a review probably rescued my project. The word 'review' can apply to lots of things, but here we are talking about a review of an entire project or an important aspect of it. So, the objectives are to:

- Know the different types of project reviews.
- Appreciate the benefits of periodic reviews, to you, your project, and to the organization in terms of project governance.
- Learn three important steps for conducting a major review.
- Get some guidelines for reviews to be meaningful and effective.

25.2 Types of Review

The term audit comes from the financial world. Audits by external auditors are legislated; auditors are obliged to report on the processes and controls and to substantiate the organization's financials. A negative audit can affect peoples' careers, although fortunately this does not happen often and the relationship with auditors is usually good. Internal auditors play a similar role, but what they look at is more discretionary.

The project environment is different. The purpose of a project review (or a project audit) is to check that the project is viable and is being managed properly. I have never seen a review lead to negative consequences for the PM, but I suppose that it could happen.

DOI: 10.1201/9781003321101-28

25.2.1 Terminology

Let's introduce the various types of project reviews. Each organization does things differently, so what follows are my perceptions.

A project audit is usually thorough, and quite formal. It could last for several days, depending on the size of the project. The word 'audit' sounds threatening. It suggests that someone will come and ask for documentation, ask a lot of questions, then go away and write a nasty report which will be seen by senior management before you see it. Then, your boss will call you in and ask for explanations. No wonder many PMs are wary of audits. The reality is not nearly so bad. Most project auditors are actually quite nice, especially if you have been managing responsibly; often their suggestions are really helpful.

A project review could last for several days like a project audit, but probably with less formality and more interaction. It could also be far shorter, like a session lasting for an hour, or it could be anything in between.

The term 'project health-check' is not commonly used and the technique is not well known. When I was with IBM in the 1990s we had many PMs working on customer projects, and we regularly did what we called health-checks, as follows: The PM would sit down with a peer (a fellow PM who knew something about the project) and walk through a checklist. An example can be found in Appendix 3. The checklist's headings are the main project areas, and within each heading is a list of things to be checked. We jointly rated each item on a zero to three scale. Zero meant either that everything was in order or that the item was not relevant to the project. Three meant there were serious gaps needing urgent attention. Ratings of one and two were somewhere in between. Interestingly, when there was a problem area the PM rather than the peer, would almost always spot it first. We found project health-checks to be short (seldom more than an hour) and useful.

A 'lessons learned' review might be done at the end of a project or major part of a project, and would typically last for an hour or two. It would involve the project team and possibly business stakeholders. The purpose is to look backward and discuss what can be learned from the experience. In the Agile environment, the term 'retrospective' means something similar and is explained in Chapter 30. Retrospectives do not wait for the end of the project; they are held more frequently, almost always at the end of several weeks of intense work.

As mentioned, I shall use the term 'review' to cover all of these. Each should produce documentation, with an appropriate level of formality and made available to the agreed people.

25.2.2 Various Focus Areas and Various Reviewers

Figure 25.1 illustrates the main focus areas, and the players that might conduct project reviews. It only gives some of the possibilities. Note that: where there is a buyer organization that owns the project and a seller organization that does most of the work, a review might be initiated by either organization. They would usually involve the other because their objectives should be aligned. The buyer organization would

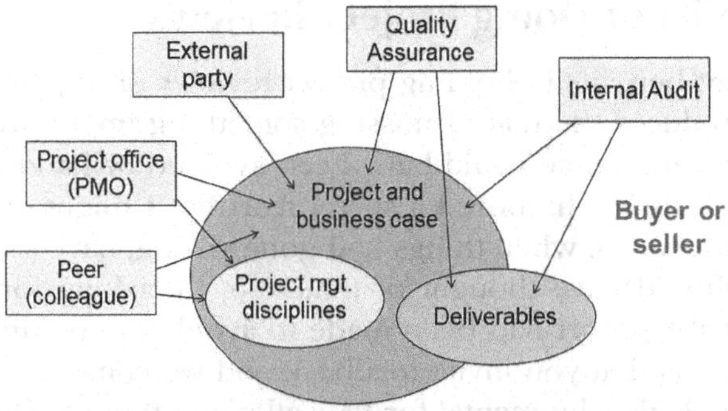

Figure 25.1 Illustrative project review scenarios.

focus on the business case and check that the benefits remain realistic and that the project will meet them. The seller organization would also want the business case to be sound, but might look more closely at whether they will be meeting their contractual obligations, while adhering to time and cost targets.

The ovals in the figure show the focus areas which may be:

- The project as a whole. This would include the justification for the project – the business case.
- The project management disciplines. It would check that due process is being followed, that required documents like a PDD (project definition document) are present, and that schedules, logs, minutes, and reports are up to date and available to stakeholders.
- The deliverables. The review might be to confirm that the quality will be adequate.

> *This was done on a project to move investments to a new platform. Internal audit, besides reviewing the processes being followed, ran extensive data extracts, mainly to gather proof that no investment value was unaccounted for.*

As shown by the boxes, there are several players that may be involved. Starting at the left and working clockwise: A peer would do the health-check mentioned above and the checklist considers not only project management disciplines but also the project as a whole. The PMO (project management office) may be involved in many aspects of review. A common role would be to schedule and conduct reviews of various sizes, on a prioritized basis. An external party would be brought in where impartiality is essential or where an outside perspective is needed. Quality assurance, if it exists in the organization, would be particularly interested in deliverables, but might also want to see how the overall project is progressing. Internal audit might want to look at any of the areas. All major reviews take time and cost money, so the organization needs to be clear from which budgets the funding will come.

25.3 The Benefits of Doing Project Reviews

There are significant benefits in holding project reviews of any kind.

First, a review reduces the risk of missing something important. There are many causes of project failure. Some could have been avoided or handled better, by picking them up early. I always harbored a secret fear that I might overlook something fundamental and afterward, when things had gone wrong, have someone say "Surely a competent PM should have thought of that?" So, by asking for a short review, I knew that a reasonable effort had been made to avoid overlooking things. In short, my recommendation is that you invite feedback and welcome it.

Second, a review is developmental for PMs allowing them to share their concerns and get 'sounding-board' kind of input.

> *Early in my career, playing the technical lead role for a large IT project, I was the de-facto PM because no PM had been formally appointed. The project got into trouble because I was trying to play too many roles and lacked project management experience. So, my organization brought in two experienced overseas managers who did a thorough audit. They made six main recommendations that helped to turn the project around. We finished late, but overall the outcome was successful. I was not blamed for the problems and learned a great deal from the review.*

This experience explains why, on the few occasions that my projects were reviewed, my position was: "I'll happily give you all the information that you need, but I want to see your report as soon as it's finished so that I can fix anything that needs attention". Reviews can also broaden the experience of the reviewers; they might find new approaches that they had not thought of.

Two final benefits: If the organization has project management standards, reviews help to encourage them and support project governance (PMI, 2016). Even more important, a review should send a message to the whole team: "we would not be reviewing your project if we did not see it as important".

Sadly, in my experience, many important business projects are never reviewed and yet management lament that failure rates are too high. There are many possible reasons why reviews are not done. Possibly reviews are simply not thought of? Possibly there is a hidden fear as to what the review might reveal? PMs will seldom request a review because they are under pressure and have other things to think about. So, maybe it is up to the organization to make appropriate reviews a standard that is driven by a portfolio manager or a PMO.

25.4 The Timing of the Reviews

Recognizing that reviews take time and can be disruptive, a question that is sometimes debated is: "should a major review be done *during* the project or only *at the end* of the project?" If it is done during the project, the main purpose would be to improve the probability of a successful outcome, in other words: "what needs to be done while there is still time?" If it is after completion, then the aim would be to learn for future projects. It might also give input to appraisals or metrics maintained in a PMO.

Generally, I believe that there is a better return on the effort spent, if the review, whether small or large, is done *during* the project while the outcome can still be influenced. For a long project, there should be more than one review and regular project health-checks which are quick and effective. At the end, we get feedback in any case, via a lessons learned review, an end-project report, and maybe a bit later from stakeholder evaluations.

25.5 Steps When Conducting a Major Project Review

What follows explains how you might conduct a major review, lasting perhaps a week (Larson & Gray, 2018). But, whether the review is shorter or longer, many of the same approaches apply. It assumes, irrespective of who initiated the review, that the sponsor wants the review. Without the sponsor's 'buy-in', the review is unlikely to be effective.

25.5.1 Initiating the Review

To get started, it is always a good idea to have an executive like the sponsor send a note to the PM asking that the team be made available for the review. It might state that it is a routine review done as part of governance on our most important projects (so that the PM does not feel targeted). If the review arose due to serious concerns, then the approach might be different. Also, agree who will get the review report and how it will be used. Next, identify the review team. Unless it's a very critical project, a large team is unaffordable, but it really does help to have at least one other person to share ideas with. It helps particularly if, as the review progresses, you suspect that problems like interpersonal conflict are being covered up. The timing is important. Check what dates would be suitable for the sponsor, the project team, and especially for the PM.

25.5.2 Preparing for the Review

It helps to meet with the PM the week before the review to get more background, reiterate the purpose, and listen for any concerns that the PM may have. At this meeting, you might ask for documents (softcopy) like a business case, PDD, project reports, and more, so that you can look through them and 'hit the ground running' the following week. Discuss the team members and agree who should be interviewed, when, and where. If remote, the interview might need to be by video conference. Also, identify key stakeholders that are outside of the team. Their input is vital to ensure a balanced picture. Next, draw up a timetable allowing time for making notes, further discussion, checking of facts, as well as structuring and writing the report. Drawing up a list of questions is essential; the project health-check template (Appendix 3) would be valuable input and there is more on the web. Going through some of the project's documentation will raise further questions. Such planning prevents a situation where you are busy preparing the report, only to find that important areas were not discussed. Finally, decide to which interviewee the questions will be put and if you have co-reviewers, agree on who will interview whom. Key questions may need to be discussed with more than one interviewee because perspectives may differ. For example, if a major supplier is involved, then the relationship with that supplier might be covered in several interviews.

25.5.3 Conducting the Review

The first phase involves the review team gathering information via interviews and then analyzing it. At the end of each interview, keep the door open by getting contact details and asking permission to phone if anything needs further clarification. Also, allow a bit of time after each interview to reflect on what was said and make additional notes. If you have co-reviewers, allow time to meet and share your findings.

25.5.4 Producing the Report

As review lead, you would be responsible for producing the report. Consider looking at one or two previous review reports just to get a feel for the format and style, but do not assume that they are perfect. Try to use standard headings, and here are some suggestions:

- Brief project description, with key numbers that indicate the extent of the project.
- Findings and analysis. This may be the most difficult and important part of the report. You might indicate the source of the findings, but if not, at least know the source and how you arrived at any finding.
- Recommendations. These are the main things that should be done to improve the project as a whole or to address any problems encountered. Lessons learned would only apply if specific things need emphasis or if they will affect later parts of the project or similar future projects.

The report itself should be concise and readable. Keep details in appendices and refer to them from the body of the report. But most important, get the report in on time – by the agreed deadline. A brilliantly written review report in 2 weeks' time is simply too late. Not only will things have changed, but everyone will have lost interest.

25.5.5 Some General Guidelines for Getting the Most Out Of Reviews

The lead reviewer must have access to the sponsor and even a short interview is essential.

> *Once, when doing a supplier-initiated project review, the sponsor (from the buyer organization) did not have time to see me. This suggested that the sponsor did not see the project as a priority, which was itself a key finding.*

Ensure that the interviewees are representative and can, between them, cover the full range of interests. When reporting, stick to project issues and only comment on individuals or groups as they affect the project. Even relevant statements about people may be impossible to verify, so just indicate that an event was told to you or that something is a perception. Lastly, be aware of likely reactions to the report. Even negative feedback can be stated sensitively, so as not to pose an undue threat to members of the team or to other project stakeholders.

However well a review was done, it will only be of value if it results in: (i) a better understanding of the project and (ii) any actions that flow from that understanding. It would be an exceptional project if the review concluded that everything was in order and that nothing needed to change. For such follow-up, the persons that initiated and authorized the review including the sponsor are responsible. They should ensure that recommendations are weighed up and where necessary actioned. These could mean changes to the project's plan or changes involving stakeholders that are not part of the team. To achieve this, discussions involving the PM, the sponsor, and possibly others are needed. Thereafter, the outcomes should be monitored as the agreed actions are taken.

25.6 Closing Thoughts on Project Review

Up to now, we have mainly considered the governance and the reviewers' points of view. So what can the PM do to be relaxed about reviews and get the most out of them? Here are a few ideas.

- Periodically, go through the project health-check, even on your own. Acting on it will give you confidence that nothing obvious has been overlooked.
- Brief the Internal Audit function on your project. Should they wish to become involved, check whether they will charge time to the project and discuss it with the sponsor.
- Do regular and honest reporting. That way there will be no surprises when any review findings are delivered.
- Log lessons learned as they happen, whether positive or negative. State what happened and then the lesson that can be drawn from it. A positive lesson is where you tried something out and it worked so well that others can also benefit.
- Take the initiative; request a review if you believe that it can help the project. Then manage any agreed actions after the review has been done.

In summary, reviews can be a good experience for the PM as well as for the reviewer. The PM's purpose should be to get an independent view of the project which enables improvements and to learn as much as possible.

References

Larson, E & Gray, C. (2018). *Project Management: The Managerial Process: International Edition*. 7th edition. New York: McGraw-Hill Education.

PMI. (2016). *Governance of Portfolios, Programs, and Projects: A Practice Guide*. Pennsylvania, USA: Project Management Institute.

Chapter 26

Ethical Conduct and Adherence to Legislation

26.1 Introduction and Objectives

It almost goes without saying that PMs, and others associated with projects, should be ethical and professional, and should adhere to legislation. However, there are many pressures on PMs, and what is expected of the PM may not be well understood. Similarly, the legislation that applies to a specific project may not be clear. So this chapter has the following objectives which are to:

- Understand what ethics means, and how it links to morals and integrity.
- Know why ethical behavior is important and why we should not always do what seems expedient at the time.
- Know how to apply the four cornerstones of the PMI Code – Responsibility, Respect, Fairness, and Honesty (RRFH will help you to remember them).
- Offer guidance on how sponsors and PMs can find out what legislation applies to a particular project.

As PM, you are urged to read PMI's 'Code of Ethics and Professional Conduct' which is freely downloadable from the web, and which all PMs are expected to adhere to (PMI, 2019). During the chapter, you will be referred to exercises that give practice on how to apply the code in a variety of situations.

26.2 Morals, Ethics, and Integrity

Before getting into ethics, let's describe morals. Morals are about assessing what is right or wrong even when there are confusing shades of grey in-between. Morals are also about distinguishing between good or bad human behavior, and the good or bad human traits that cause the behavior. Then, ethics is about applying moral principles

DOI: 10.1201/9781003321101-29

that govern a person's behavior or the conducting of an activity. Ethics are effectively rules of conduct. But, the term 'ethics' can be used negatively, for example, "I don't like that person's ethics". Generally, when someone is viewed as ethical, it means that they do what is right and behave in a responsible manner. A person who exhibits sound ethical principles is said to have integrity, and integrity sometimes takes courage when others are not meeting similar standards.

Now for a question that is often debated: "is ethics situational? In other words, does ethics depends on the situation at hand?" Some people see everything as simply right or wrong. Others might say that something is right under certain circumstances and wrong under other circumstances. For example, the decision to drop the first atomic bomb in 1945, involved heated debate. So ethics, per se, may not be situational, but how it is applied may be. There is not always a *perfect* ethical solution, so, perhaps some compromise is needed. My own belief is that ethics *is* situational, which actually makes it *more* difficult. If everything were clear-cut, right or wrong, then it's easy – just do what is right. But some situations are neither clear-cut nor simple. The best test for what is ethical is the well-known 'noticeboard test' or 'newspaper front-page test'. Supposing that what you did, or decided, was put on the noticeboard for all your colleagues to see (nowadays that might be a digital display), would you feel comfortable? Or if it were on the front-page of the local newspaper for your friends and family to see, would you feel comfortable?

26.3 The Importance of Ethical Behavior

Let us now consider why sound ethical behavior is valuable in an organization. There are many reasons; here are a few:

- Consistently good ethics builds trust, and trust is one of the most valuable things an organization can have. People trust each other. Customers trust the organization. Things happen faster and more efficiently – hence Covey and Merrill's book 'The Speed of Trust'.
- The organization's external image and reputation have much to do with the actions of its people and hence with ethics.
- Leadership needs ethics; leaders need integrity. People observe their leaders and do likewise. So if leaders don't display good ethics, the standards in the organization, from top to bottom, are likely to stray. The same applies to the PM and the project team.
- High ethical standards reduce the need for controls (but does not eliminate them) thus reducing the amount of red tape, frustration, and cost.

Ethical behavior is also important for PMs and for the project management profession:

- Ethical standards guide your behavior toward people and in project situations. They give you valuable support for taking wise decisions where the right path is not always obvious. Ethical standards help you to become a better practitioner.

- The reputation of the project management profession rubs off on all PMs. As a PM, you would want stakeholders to assume that you are a person of integrity. You would not want them to view you as potentially devious and self-serving.

26.4 The PMI Code of Ethics and Professional Conduct

There are many codes of ethics, and each organization may have its own code. But, they are all likely to support similar values. So here, we shall discuss the PMI's Code of Ethics and Professional Conduct (PMI, 2019). It is used worldwide in the project management community. The code deals with four basic values: Responsibility, Respect, Fairness, and Honesty. For each there is:

- A *mandatory* standard which is the minimum expected. It may limit one's behavior, but in a positive way. In the extreme, violations can result in loss of PMI certification.
- An additional *aspirational* standard. This is something that must be striven toward, but may be harder to measure.

To some, I have added comments that are not part of the code. However, just a caution here: PMI is based in the USA, so a dilemma may arise when working in a culture where the norms are different. But, at the end of the day, maybe the noticeboard test, mentioned earlier, will be your best guide. What follows is a summary, omitting definitions, where I try to give the most important dos and don'ts. The PMI text has the details.

26.4.1 Responsibility – Taking Ownership of Our Actions or Lack Thereof

Mandatory standards:

- We must get to know the laws, policies, and rules that relate to our work, and then report unethical or illegal conduct to management and affected stakeholders. This may be hard to do, but that's what is required.

Aspirational standards. We should:

- Meet commitments we have made.
- Own up to errors and fix them.
- Protect confidential information entrusted to us.
  (Could these first three be mandatory?)
- Act in best interests of society, safety, and the environment.
- Only take on work that is within your capabilities. This can be hard to judge, and sometimes we all need to take on challenging assignments. But, maybe we should warn stakeholders that we shall be learning on the job.

26.4.2 Respect – Showing Regard for Ourselves, Others, and Resources

In this context, resources include things entrusted to us like money, equipment, reputations, and the environment.

Mandatory standards. We must:

- Negotiate in good faith. As mentioned in Chapter 27, you will be working with the people that you negotiate with, so seek outcomes that are in the interests of both parties and do not hide anything.
- Never be abusive toward others. Respect their rights, for example, to spend time with their families.
- Not misuse our knowledge or position at the expense of others. Conversely, do not take advantage of other people's lack of experience or influence.

Aspirational standards. We should:

- Listen, and understand the other person's point of view. (Always sound practice).
- Talk directly to people with whom we disagree or have conflict. In other words, we should not go to someone's boss until we have spoken to the person. Also, we must not 'talk behind people's backs'.

26.4.3 Fairness – Make Impartial Decisions and Act Objectively

We must be aware of our own interests and not let them influence our decisions.

Mandatory standards. We must:

- Proactively disclose conflicts of interest. In other words, don't wait to be asked whether you have a conflict of interest – it will probably not come up (until later).
- Only take or influence decisions if others (to whom you have disclosed your conflict of interests) ask for your involvement.
- Show no favoritism or discrimination in hiring or rewarding.

Aspirational standards. We should:

- Be transparent and explain the real reasons for our decisions. (This should be the norm).
- Provide equal access to opportunities and information. This may be subject to judgment or constraints imposed by the organization.

26.4.4 Honesty – Speak and Act Truthfully

I like the cynical quip attributed to Mark Twain (author of 'The Adventures of Tom Sawyer'): "when in doubt, tell the truth". But there should be no doubt, we *must* tell the truth. Besides, it's so much easier.

Mandatory standards: We must:

- Not deceive or mislead others. There are many situations where it is tempting to sweep the truth under the carpet, like when there are problems on our project. But it's always best to give the bad news early. Also, we must not condone others giving misleading information.
- Not behave dishonestly for personal gain or anything that disadvantages others.

Aspirational standards. We should:

- Provide accurate and timely information. This is part of the PM's job, but occasionally it may be desirable to defer giving bad news for an hour or two, to give one time to find possible solutions.
- Seek to understand the truth, and create an environment where others can safely tell the truth. The latter part is common sense: if people do not feel safe, they will hide things from us.

26.4.5 *Summary of the Code and An Opportunity to Get Some Practice*

In summary, PMs and indeed all stakeholders should be professional and show integrity. Integrity helps you to build trust, which not only gets things done faster, but also makes the project environment less stressful for all the stakeholders. As PM, following the code will create the right image for you and for the project management profession that you represent. Now have a look at Case 37 which presents some examples of the kinds of dilemma that PMs are faced with. If you are working with a group, they make for useful debate, but I do not provide a 'model answer' because there may be multiple valid solutions.

26.5 Adherence to Legislation

Projects need to adhere to legislation, and here I use the term 'laws' to cover legislation, statutes, regulations, or whatever is applicable. Sometimes it may be difficult for the sponsor and PM to know which laws are important. This is complicated by the fact that each nation, and possibly even part of a nation, has its own laws, which change periodically. Certain laws may apply across several countries, such as in the EU (European Union) where some rules are mandatory across all EU countries. For some projects, laws may hardly be a consideration; in other situations, the main purpose of the project may be to adhere to new laws.

26.6 The Drivers of Legislation

What are some of the changes that have taken place over the years that are driving legislation? Here is a short list, and you can probably add to it:

- A greater value is placed on human health and life. One avoidable accident or death is seen as one too many. The result is more health and safety laws, and greater emphasis to adhering to what already exists.

- Managers are now more accountable. They are expected to prevent mishaps, rather than to merely respond to them.
- Mental health is increasingly recognized as an occupational hazard, and PMs are expected to avoid undue stress on team members and to watch for warning signs.
- Global warming and the fragile environment are on everyone's minds – a huge change from even 20 years ago.
- White-collar crimes like fraud and money laundering have increased, so there are more compliance requirements to inhibit them.
- With the ease of storage and transmission of large amounts of data, and the regular misuse of such data, there is increasing legislation to protect personal information.
- The degree of inequality has grown and, with it, a greater focus on treating people equitably.
- Many new materials and medications are being developed, with pressure to bring them to market, but whose effects may not be fully understood. This has led to additional laws that ensure that they are introduced responsibly.

Fortunately, there is collaboration between nations, and there are international bodies that facilitate and influence legislation. Thus, there is a reasonable alignment between nations. Part of the reason is that trade may only be permitted if nations adhere to compatible standards.

26.7 The PMs Responsibility Regarding Legislation

As was mentioned in Chapter 10 on project quality, the PM plays a key role in ensuring that quality objectives are met. The same applies to laws. Contracts and specifications might state the requirements for deliverables, but may not be specific as to *which* laws must be adhered to. So, while the PM will seldom know all the applicable laws, it's up to the PM to find out which ones apply. The best way is to talk to the right people, and who is 'right' will depend on the situation. Besides the sponsor, here are some examples:

- The Legal department should be able to indicate which laws need attention for a particular project. Even a small organization might have access to external advice.
- In many countries, it is mandatory to have at least one Health & Safety officer. Such a person should be able to give advice that is not limited to physical safety. For example, they would know of rules that limit the number of hours that people can work at a stretch.
- EA (Environmental Assessment) practitioners can advise on what approvals are needed for any projects that might have an environmental impact.
- In financial institutions, the main role of the Compliance function is to ensure that the myriad of financial rules is adhered to. Often a compliance person is a part-time team member.

The takeaway is that the PM should understand the legal requirements and build them into plans, communications, and quality checks. There may also be risks that relate to adherence to laws, but each such risk should be considered and a decision taken as to the response action (even if it is to do nothing). Some of this may be a matter of judgment, like:

- How much safety training should we give?
- If we miss the statutory deadline, how likely is the organization to incur a fine?
- What is the likelihood of customer data being stolen and abused?

So, there is a balance between doing too little and doing things that may be unnecessary.

Reference

PMI. (2019). *PMI Code of Ethics and Professional Conduct.* Pennsylvania, USA: Project Management Institute Inc.

Chapter 27

Project Negotiation

27.1 Introduction and Objectives

PMs are believed to spend over 80% of their time communicating, to which I could add that much of it is spent negotiating. So negotiation is a skill that's essential for PMs, but also valuable for everyone. Having read on the subject, and practiced negotiation during my career, I found the teaching of George Siedel, Fisher and Ury, and Herb Cohen (see references) valuable, and many of the explanations given here are influenced by their thinking. The concepts that we shall cover can make a big difference in any negotiating situation and most such interactions we do not even see as 'a negotiation'. Accordingly, the objectives of this chapter are to:

- Recognize the aspects of projects that we negotiate on.
- Know when *not* to negotiate.
- Recognize two fundamental negotiation scenarios, one of which is very applicable to project management.
- Explore the importance of relationships and trust, and hence seek common interests which usually result in a better outcome for both parties.
- Learn the importance of preparation even for minor negotiations.
  Preparation includes an assessment of your and the other party's 'power base'. It also considers BATNA (best alternative to negotiated agreement) which affects the power bases.
- Understand another new term: ZOPA (zone of possible agreement).
  This also forms part of preparation. It is about estimating the range of outcomes that is likely to be acceptable to both parties.
- Familiarize with ethical and legal standards which tie in with Chapter 26 on professional conduct.
- Learn the techniques of how to negotiate.
  Most of them are fair and open, resulting in a better outcome. There are also tools and traps: some are fair, but others are things that you need to watch out for in case other people use them.
- Draw some conclusions, like putting whatever is agreed, in writing.

DOI: 10.1201/9781003321101-30

27.1.1 Exclusions

Negotiation is a vast subject area. Therefore, we shall not cover things here that seldom arise on business projects or things that are covered in other chapters. For further reading, there is lots on the web. We shall not delve into how negotiation is affected by the legal systems in different countries. We shall not consider situations where more than two parties are involved (coalition bargaining). Nor shall we cover agency situations where you or the other party appoint an agent and give them certain negotiating powers. Even though it seldom happens on business projects, if you suspect that you are dealing with an agent, it is essential to get the principal to confirm preferably in writing what authority has been given to the agent. Anything about concluding negotiations via a contract, we cover in Chapter 22 on procurement and Chapter 24 on contracts. The latter also touches on ADR (alternative dispute resolution) which involves negotiation.

27.2 Principles of Negotiation

27.2.1 What Do PMs Negotiate About?

For a negotiation to take place, there must be common interests as well as some points of conflict. For example, if I want to buy a boat but the other party does not have a boat, there can be no negotiation. If they *do* have a boat and are willing to sell, we probably still have conflicts to resolve about the price and the terms. But, PMs don't usually negotiate about boats, so what do they negotiate about? Here ae some of the items:

- Resources for the project – usually people.
- Money: agreeing a reasonable budget for the project.
- Business requirements and quality. For example, a business person may ask for something that your analyst believes is a lot of work but is unnecessary, and you would prefer not to bother the sponsor for a decision.
- Priorities. For example, when you are debating with other PMs around which project has the greater need for limited equipment.
- Agreeing who will take on which activities.
- Asking people to put in extra effort or work overtime. The negotiation may be around what the project needs versus what people can reasonably manage.
- Supplier contracts and service level agreements.

The list is endless. So, if you are uncomfortable negotiating, then maybe you won't be happy as a PM. Fortunately, negotiation can be learned and there are lots of opportunities for practice. Also, it's a skill worth investing in because the fundamentals of negotiation change very little – unlike technology which changes constantly.

27.2.2 Situations in Which You Might Not Wish to Negotiate

Not every interaction is a negotiation. There may be times when you decide not to negotiate. Here are some such situations:

- The negotiation will take preparation, and is not worth the time and effort.
- Negotiation may be uncomfortable and is likely to affect relationships. For example, you may not want to negotiate prices when you entertain a client in your favorite restaurant – it would spoil the ambiance.
- There may be risks. For example, if you try to negotiate changes to an employment contract the offer could be withdrawn because the employer may not want someone who will be unhappy with their remuneration.

27.2.3 The Importance of Execution – Carrying Out What Was Agreed in the Negotiation

Negotiation could be classified into two scenarios: one, where you are unlikely to meet the other party again (like selling a used vehicle) and two, where you will need to cooperate with the other party after the negotiation. As a PM, you almost always need to continue a working relationship with the party you are negotiating with. Whatever you agree, execution is still needed and a person who believes that the resolution is fair is more likely to be committed and perform well – important for the success of your project. Fairness is sometimes a perception, so the negotiation *process* is important: nobody must be bullied or tricked. The ongoing trust relationship is critical. You want to be partners, not adversaries, so you need a fair arrangement. And, once you are working together, if subsequent negotiations break down and you cannot reach agreement, then usually both of you lose. Having, emphasized cooperation, some conflict is ok if it leads to better solutions.

> *I remember a talk by the project director for results-gathering and distribution at the 1996 Olympic games, a very complex project. He said that negotiating consensus among the involved stakeholders was his most important contribution.*

On a project, all of the above is particularly applicable where there is a buyer-seller (or supplier) relationship.

27.2.4 Further Negotiation Aspects

There are more things to consider when entering a negotiation:

First, are we resolving a dispute? Or are we doing a deal to the advantage of both parties? And where it's a dispute, can it be turned into a deal? Siedel (2014) gives an example:

> *A software company is in dispute with a customer who, against the contract, is building an adaptation of their software with intent to market it. Negotiations have broken down and they are about to litigate (win lose). Fortunately, someone saw the opportunity of creating a joint venture to market the adaptation – and an agreement was reached that was in the interests of both parties.*

Second, is the situation position-based or interest-based (Larson & Gray, 2018)? Examples of position-based situations are: "we want delivery tomorrow" versus "we can deliver next week" or "we want a 60% share" versus "we are offering 50%". This is like deciding how to share a pie of fixed size – there's just one variable, the amount of pie that each person gets. Interest-based is different. It involves exploring to find out what the other party *really* wants. Often it is possible to find a solution that meets all or most of each party's needs. It's like creating a bigger pie. Then the debate is easier because each party can get something that they will be happy with. Even something that looks position based like selling a vehicle can have interests such as timing, payment arrangements, and accessories – all of which can make the outcome better for both.

27.3 Preparation for Negotiation

Most day-to-day negotiations happen 'on-the-fly'; one is not planning to negotiate so one cannot prepare for it. However, where something important will be negotiated, like taking on a new assignment, it would be wise to do some preparation and there is usually enough time because preparation may not take long. Some of the elements of preparation follow.

27.3.1 Power Base and BATNA

You need to understand your own power base – things that give you an advantage and make it easier to get what you want. The needs or weaknesses of the other party are part of your power base. It is also important to understand the other party's power base. Here are some examples:

- If time is on your side and they are in a hurry, it strengthens your power base and weakens theirs.
- If you desperately need the business and they have other alternatives, it weakens your power base (so you probably would not disclose that you are desperate).
- If you have critical skills and they need your skills, it strengthens your power base.

It may be the *perceptions* of power base that ultimately influence the outcome rather than the *actual* power base. So a few considerations:

- Should you emphasize your strengths? You probably want the other party to know your strengths, but you might need to do it subtly so that they do not feel threatened. Should you divulge your weaknesses? Probably not, unless you are asked a direct question.
- Avoid doing things that reduce your power base or strengthen theirs. If you show enthusiasm for their offering, you are strengthening their power base. However, if you show understanding of the benefits of their offering, it may be seen as competence which could help your power base.
- Returning to the situation mentioned in Chapter 22 on procurement, where a contract still has to be finalized. What is the effect on power bases if the

customer has urgency and at their request, you as the seller start work before the contract is signed? Until you start, you have power (they are in a hurry and need you to start quickly). But, once you start work, the power shifts to them (you need the contract signed so that you can get paid). Such a shift can materially affect the final contract.

A key element of your power base is your BATNA (best alternative to negotiated agreement) (Fisher et al., 1991). Let us look at a few examples. If:

- You are buying a service or product, your BATNA is to have an alternative supplier.
- You are selling a service or product, your BATNA may be to withdraw and spend time on other prospective customers.
- You are trying to reach agreement on a scope change requested by a stakeholder, your BATNA may be to accept that the stakeholder will go to the sponsor rather than you proposing the change.
- A dispute arises with a supplier on a large project and you would like to resolve it directly. Your BATNA might be to escalate the dispute to the steering committee knowing that the supplier will not be comfortable doing so.

So how does BATNA affect your power base? A strong BATNA greatly strengthens your power base. For example, as a buyer, if lots of other suppliers can provide a similar service, you have a strong BATNA and power base. Similarly, a weak BATNA weakens your power base. For example, if you are bidding for a contract and are faced with the time-consuming task of finding other business if you do not win it, you might have a weak power base.

27.3.2 ZOPA (Zone of Possible Agreement)

ZOPA gives a view of the range that the possible outcome might have. The simplest form is where there is just a money amount at stake. Figure 27.1 gives an example where you wish to sell a car and one potential buyer has made contact.

You, as the seller might come up with three figures:

- Your 'reservation' amount of $12 000 is the lowest that you would accept.
- The likely amount of $15 000 is your estimate of fair value.
- Your 'stretch target' of $20 000 is the best that you could possibly hope for.

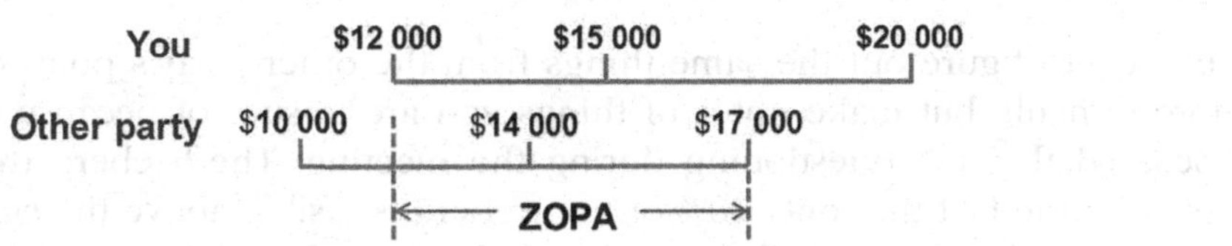

Figure 27.1 Estimating the ZOPA – zone of possible agreement.

Then think about it from the potential buyer's point of view. Their reservation amount might be $17 000 (they will not pay more). Their stretch target might be $10 000. From the figure, you can see that the final agreement is likely to be anywhere between $12 000 (your reservation amount) and $17 000 (theirs). Of course, you don't know the other party's figures; you can only estimate them.

In practice, there are likely to be other considerations (or interests) that will decide where the final agreement may be struck, but you will only learn those during the discussion. Because of the fairly large ZOPA in Figure 27.1, it should be possible to reach agreement, but where it will end up may also depend on your respective power bases and of course on negotiating ability. In a different situation, where you believe that there is no ZOPA (no overlap) then maybe it's not worth negotiating.

27.3.3 Culture and Style

A number of other factors can complicate negotiations: negotiating culture and style is a big subject and the following just gives some pointers. Be aware of the negotiating style of the other party, sometimes called their surface culture. For example, are they aggressive or conciliatory? Try to assess their deeper values, like how important is it to get the contract? versus how important is it to establish a trusting relationship? When dealing with other cultures, try to understand the other culture and know what might be offensive. But, be careful of stereotypes. For example, there may be a perception that people from a certain culture will not show their feelings. You may be wrong, so be prepared to modify your perceptions as the negotiation unfolds. Also, do not try to emulate their style by doing what is unnatural for you. Rather show respect and try to avoid those things that you believe might offend them.

27.3.4 Summary of Preparation for Negotiation

We have covered, some preparation items and it's a good idea to write down answers to the following questions:

- What is our overall goal, and why?
- What are our interests – the main things that we want from this negotiation?
- What is our power base and our BATNA in case agreement cannot be reached?
- What are the three ZOPA outcomes: our walk-away point, the likely outcome, and what we would really like to achieve? But bear in mind that the outcomes may be scenarios rather than numbers.

Next, try to figure out the same things from the other party's point of view. This is more difficult, but make notes of things you are unsure of because these could be discussed through questioning during the meeting. The 'iceberg theory' which is based on the fact that only 10% of the iceberg is visible above the surface, supports this. It suggests that, usually, only the obvious things get discussed. The implication is that, if the hidden needs of each party (the 90%) can be uncovered by questioning, there may be benefits to both parties which would 'enlarge the pie'.

This is a good time to tackle Case 38 where you, as PM of an important project, are preparing to negotiate with the head of the intranet department to get development work done as quickly and inexpensively as possible.

27.4 Conducting Negotiations

27.4.1 Ethical and Legal Matters

Here are some aspects that apply to both negotiating parties and should tie in with Chapter 26 on professional conduct. One needs to be both ethical and legal, and that includes not lying which would be fraudulent. Reasonable questions need to be answered, and the material facts that you give and that the other party will rely on, *must* be true. But there is an exception: If the other party asks questions about what you will accept, you can be evasive, after all the negotiation is not over yet. Also, you may not talk about alternative options like offers, if you do not have them – that would be deception.

Lying is difficult to detect until afterward, and maybe for that reason, the other party is unlikely to tell an outright lie. However, they may well omit telling you relevant information. What that means is that you need to ask questions about *all* the things that are important to you, like timing, guarantees, terms and conditions, or whatever. And, having the questions lined up is all part of your preparation.

A few more things. Negotiators have a fiduciary duty. For example, there must be no undisclosed conflicts of interest. Fortunately, such situations would seldom affect a PM, but an example might be if you had received a job offer from the party that you are negotiating with. And now for a big word: 'unconscionability'. It means that you must not take advantage of a situation where you have a lot more power than the other party. For example, if you work for a large company and are negotiating with a small supplier. Yes, you have a strong power base, but be careful how you use it. The result could be perceived as unfair and even the process could be seen as unfair. There could be reputational and legal consequences.

27.4.2 Before and During the Negotiation

There are no hard and fast rules because everything is situational. Nevertheless, the following suggestions apply to most negotiations.

Build relationships, particularly with people that you don't know or hardly know. Get to know the other party as a person. Build rapport. It applies particularly to other cultures. In Western culture, one might want to get down to business as quickly as possible. Other cultures may want to take it more slowly so as to get to know you first, and many countries have a variety of cultures. Therefore, negotiation is almost always better face to face with handshakes and lunch (except perhaps during a pandemic), rather than using a video-conferencing tool. But, where distance prevents 'across the table' contact, then video tools or even a phone call may be better than trying to negotiate by email.

> *I had the experience, while doing my PhD, of having to persuade busy executives to complete a 20 minute survey. If I could get them on the phone, at least 50% responded, versus less than 5% when sending emails.*

Past relationships and executive relationships also help.

> ***While at IBM, occasional situations arose with customers, that would have been difficult to negotiate formally. But, somehow, because there were long-standing relationships, especially at executive level, things got sorted out relatively quickly.***

Ask questions and seek clarification. We've already mentioned that the other party may not raise certain things but will not deceive when answering your questions. Actively listen to their answers and here, active listening includes summarizing what you have understood and getting their confirmation. The more you know the greater your power. In other words, your power base is not fixed; you can strengthen it during the negotiation.

Avoid having to give an immediate response to a proposition. Try to make time to think something through. For example, when dealing with a difficult stakeholder, it helps not to have too much authority. It buys you time if you can say "I'll need to discuss what you are asking for with the sponsor". Similarly, if the other party has a team, it can reduce the pressure if you are not alone. Once again, you can create time by asking your colleague "do you have any thoughts on this?"

During the negotiation, work on your relative power bases and BATNAs. As already mentioned, part of the preparation is to get a 'first take' on their BATNA. If you can find out more about it by asking questions you might weaken their BATNA by pointing out potential pitfalls with their alternative. Likewise, as part of the preparation, talk to others and find the best alternative options before the meeting, which usually strengthens your BATNA. If they ask you questions and you have a strong BATNA, then you can sensitively disclose it. On the other hand, if your BATNA is weak, then hope that they don't ask and if they do, try to gloss over it.

27.5 Negotiating Tools and Traps

Some negotiating tools are ethical and productive. There are also traps – things to watch out for if the other party uses them – but fascinating nonetheless.

Anchoring is very powerful and is often used. Here's an example: the other party is selling to you, and early on they say "look, for what you are wanting, we are talking in the region of at least $90 000". The chances are that the negotiation is then around $90 000, and maybe you feel good about beating them down to $85 000. But what if the reasonable value of what they are offering is around $60 000? So anchoring can be a trap and the best protection is to have done your homework. Even then, and assuming that you still want to do business with them, you will need to be tactful about how you call their bluff and allow them to save face when coming down to a reasonable figure. But of course, it will affect the trust. That is why you want to be aware of the trap and only use anchoring to propose a figure that you believe can be defended.

First offer strategy: Having agreed to what will be provided, there is lots of debate about whether you should be the first to propose a fair price. Many believe you should get the other party to go first. This may be valid but it gives them the opportunity to anchor. Also, what if they do propose first and come up with something that you believe is very favorable. Should you accept immediately? It is probably better to 'hum and hah' a bit and ask questions before accepting. If you accept too quickly, they may come away unhappy and feeling that they should have gotten more. It is tricky if neither party wants to propose first. You just have to keep talking, and ultimately you might put forward your stretch target scenario.

Overconfidence: Watch out for believing that you understand everything, and rushing into an agreement. Look at the risks. Check all the assumptions. Think about what things might prevent you from reaching agreement. For example, when renting premises ask: "can we move in next week?", "will defects be fixed at your cost?" But generally, just be a bit cautious.

Framing: This amounts to stating exactly the same thing in a way that makes an offer sound good. For example: "20% of your costs will be fully reimbursed" sounds better than "80% of the costs are for your own account". Yet, the meanings are identical.

Look beyond the information presented. The other party may present information that makes what they are offering look better. In adverts for houses, the pictures make the living area appear vast but when you get there, it's actually quite small. Even if what they show is not be relevant to your situation, it may still influence your decisions. Never let competitive pride divert you. If the other party tells what wonderful things another customer is doing with their product, do not try to be better but keep *your* needs in mind.

Look at the situation from the other party's point of view. What do they really want? This is not intuitive and requires questioning and listening. Yet, it can enable you to propose something that will be appealing to them. Conversely, if the other party proposes something that would be in *your* interests, guard against 'reactive devaluation'. In other words, do not reject something purely because it came from the other party. Rather listen, question, and evaluate their proposal on its merits.

Encourage reciprocity. Do something small that will be appreciated by the other party, like giving the link to an interesting article. They will feel an obligation to reciprocate in some way. It's a powerful human emotion. Even asking their advice on something will increase the relationship. But, always be wary if they offer you something.

The Contrast principle. If you can present some poor options and then one that is better, by contrast, it will look great. But of course, this could be used on you. So always evaluate what they are offering in isolation.

The power of silence: It's hard not to fill the gap after the other party has said something that you are not happy with. But sometimes your silence will get them to talk more and give you valuable information.

So, it is helpful to know the approaches (tools and traps) just mentioned. It can be difficult to recognize them when they happen. One experienced negotiator kept a list of them to glance at during breaks, just to assess whether they were being used. So use them, but appropriately and sparingly because the other party may see what you are trying to do, and trust remains vital.

27.6 Miscellaneous Additional Advice

The tips here are drawn from an interview with Herb Cohen who had a reputation as an outstanding negotiator, and who wrote extensively on the subject (Deacon, 1998).

- Start your interaction with the other party by discussing things that are of shared interest, even if they do not relate to the negotiation at all.
- Where you have had to travel for a major negotiation, never disclose your return date. The other party may keep delaying until you are forced to accept their terms, just so that you can catch your flight.
- If the other party says "no" to something, do not assume that it's final. If *you* have to say no, then do it as gently as possible maybe sounding regretful, like "we would really like to help, but . .".
- Concessions are things that you offer to the other party. Do not make concessions too early because it can limit the solution. Also, do not make concessions without something in return because the more effort the other party puts into getting you to concede something, the more they value it.
- If others are aggressive, don't fight back. Rather ask questions like "how did you come to that conclusion?" Also, if the other party requests something unreasonable, do not agree or disagree. Rather say something like "we'll have to think that through". It does not help to show the other party that they are wrong, but if something is bothering you, it needs to be discussed and resolved.
- As a PM, manage your stress when negotiating. You need to care about the outcome but not *too* much. Accept that there will be times when your BATNA is the way to go.

27.7 Final Thoughts on Negotiation

Here is an important point that has hardly been mentioned: Besides your preparation, make notes as you go along. Making notes triggers questions and may prevent you from overlooking something. Then, when agreement is reached, confirm it 'in writing'. If this is not done, the other party may conveniently forget about concessions that they made during the negotiation. Putting things in writing applies whether you are agreeing something internally or with another organization.

After negotiations related to projects, there should be no clear winner and loser because such outcomes are seldom sustainable. Nevertheless, you want to get the best outcome for your project or your organization. Nor should negotiations feel like combat against an opponent. Often they can be about working together to find a solution that will suit both parties. In projects, negotiation is not always about being the most brilliant or toughest negotiator. It is more about doing good homework, asking the right questions, and looking for a fair outcome that is in both your interests.

References

Deacon, T. (1998). *Negotiation: It takes Two to Tango – Interview with Herb Cohen. ProjectPro*, Vol. 8, p. 16, Monument Park, South Africa.

Fisher, R., Ury, W., & Patton, B. (1991). *Getting to Yes: Negotiating Agreement Without Giving In*, 2nd edition. New York: Penguin Books.

Larson, E. W., & Gray, C. F. (2018). *Project Management: The Managerial Process: International Edition*. 7th edition. New York: McGraw-Hill Education.

Siedel, G. (2014). *Negotiating for Success: Essential Strategies and Skills*. Edenton, NC, USA: Van Rye Publishing.

Chapter 28

Managing International Projects

28.1 Introduction and Objectives

It is impossible to give firm guidelines on how to manage projects that involve other countries. There are simply too many variable sets of conditions that apply in different parts of the world. Therefore, the objectives are to:

- Give examples of international projects.
- Become aware of the research and the planning needed for you to be involved in projects in one or more other countries.
- Recognize the possible cultural and environmental factors that may affect you and provide useful checklists of things to find out.
- Know what to expect and how you might prepare. Learn the meaning of the term 'culture shock' and how to manage its effects.

In this chapter, to avoid confusion, 'local' refers to your own country and 'foreign' to other countries.

28.2 Types of International Projects

There is no limit to the projects that could be considered international. Although they could be done on behalf of government, like setting up a trade initiative, most are done by private enterprise. Here are some examples, starting with the ones that are common, and moving to those that happen less often but have a greater impact on your life:

- You are working locally but your project has elements that involve other countries such as customers and suppliers. You communicate regularly with, and occasionally visit, your foreign associates.

DOI: 10.1201/9781003321101-31

- Your company is international and may require you to manage projects that affect business processes in several countries. Working for an airline or supermarket chain might have such elements.
- The project is done abroad by or for a local company. Such projects often relate to the supply chain. The company may want to market to people or organizations in another country, sometimes called 'downstream' supply chain. It could also involve 'upstream' supply chain like sourcing materials, components, or even skills from another country. Setting up such operations would certainly involve one or more projects.
- You might be working for a foreign firm in your own country. They might say "we have a new project in Brazil, and we'd like you to manage it". You might live at home but make lengthy visits and hold regular video calls, probably in a different time zone.
- Your company might say "We do a lot of business in Malaysia, and we'd like you to move across there, on a three year assignment, to manage projects for us".

Each of the above scenarios would involve some disruption to your life, and be different from only working at home or at the local office. Each scenario would need a greater or lesser grasp of the foreign countries involved.

28.3 Considerations for Working Locally But Having Links to Other Countries

Let us start with the simpler scenario where most of your time is spent in your local office, but where you regularly interact with overseas people and periodically visit them. Here there are some logistical challenges like managing across different time zones and allowing for each country having its own daylight saving schedule. The main challenge is to bridge the cultural gap and this is covered next, but some of the environmental factors covered thereafter almost certainly apply.

28.3.1 Cultural Factors

Here is a checklist for cultural factors that may affect the interaction whether it is done by video conference or by a visit to another country.

- Time taken building relationship (before talking business).
- Task versus relationship focus.
- Punctuality, meeting deadlines, and sense of urgency.
- Ways to say things: direct or indirect; give open criticism or allow face saving.
- Acceptance of women in managerial roles.
- Nepotism – the expectation that family or friends get preferential employment.
- Taboos – things that must never be done or mentioned.
- Degree of formality, such as for greetings and taking leave.

- Things that gain respect, for example, dress, position, status, experience, age.
- Religious norms – each country may host several religions.

The culture basics are likely to be found on the web by Googling the country, but deeper cultural factors are harder to find. The best way might be to talk to foreign persons, and so much better if they also know your project and their country's business environment. The alternative is finding out 'the hard way' from experience later. So, let's talk about cultural factors. As mentioned, even within a country, cultures can differ widely. The bullet points above merely indicate the kinds of things to consider.

In some, like the American or European cultures, it's ok to get down to business pretty quickly. Other cultures expect that people will share their backgrounds and talk about things of general interest. They will want to know *you* before talking business. To them, relationships may be more important than the project tasks at hand. You will find that the sense of urgency varies. Western nations value people with a sense of urgency. In other countries, emphasizing urgency may come across as aggressive, and other things take priority over meeting deadlines. The way that things are expressed differs. In some cultures, one can say directly but tactfully, if something is unsatisfactory. In other cultures, one needs to be careful about how criticism is delivered and allow the recipient to save face.

Punctuality for meetings, whether they are physical meetings or via video, may vary. So, don't be too surprised if people are late or don't even show up. Then there are some mindsets that may differ from your own. In Western cultures, women are seen as equals, and nepotism, which means preferring to give jobs to family or close friends, is frowned upon. Other cultures may have different norms. Likewise, gifts may be expected rather than perceived as potentially corrupt. There may be taboos, things that 'we just don't talk about'. It may take time, or an informed friend, to tell you what they are. We probably have some taboos in our own cultures. Be aware of the degree of formality, and this applies particularly when greeting or saying goodbye. Foreign people may have expectations. They want to deal with somebody in authority and this may be indicated by your dress or your demeanor. For example, in the USA, the CEO can wear jeans, but in other cultures, a suit and tie might be expected. When there are problems, people may bring religion in. So, for example, if there is a delay, it may be 'caused by God' when you know that the delay was avoidable – it can be difficult to question this kind of reasoning.

28.3.2 Hofstede's Cultural Dimensions

Further insights into cultural differences may be obtained from Hofstede's cultural dimensions, some of which are available from Hofstede Insights (2021). The dimensions in Table 28.1 are used and countries are rated on a 0 to 120 scale. The scores are not intended as good or bad but rather as a reflection of the prevailing culture, which affects business and projects.

Interestingly, even among developed nations, there can be marked differences. For example, France has a higher score than Denmark for 'tough versus tender'.

Table 28.1 Descriptions of the Hofstede Cultural Dimensions

Dimension	*High Score Meaning*	*Low Score Meaning*
Power distance	A hierarchy exists where people know their place. Decisions from above are seldom questioned.	All stakeholders have a say about the project.
Individualism versus collectivism	The focus is on individual needs and aspirations.	Group goals and achievements are emphasized.
Tough versus tender	A competitive, culture exists where males tend to dominate.	Caring and quality of life are valued. Women are equals.
Preference for certainty	Structure and rules, which bring certainty, are preferred.	Flexibility and change are norms. New approaches are encouraged.
Long versus short-term orientation	A long-term view of projects is taken.	Short-term benefits are essential. People-contracts can be short.
Expression versus restraint	Peoples' thoughts and desires are openly expressed.	Norms of restraint exist. People control their desires and impulses.

Another example is that for 'long versus short term' China, a developing nation, has a higher score than the USA.

28.4 Considerations for Operating in Another Country

Let us now consider projects which require you to relocate or at least spend extended periods in another country. The cultural considerations apply, but in addition, environmental factors play a significant role. If your assignment is to move to another country for a number of years, possibly to set up an entirely new operation, you will need a really good understanding of the environment. Taking a family with you adds to the things to investigate.

28.4.1 Environmental Factors

Here is a checklist of some of the environmental factors in another country:

- General education level. Wealth disparity.
- Skills availability. Employment costs, regulations, and labor unions.
- Political stability. Inter-government relations. Location of your embassy.
- Perception of your country by foreign people.
- Laws, different from your own, that will affect your projects.
- Ease of doing business, work visas, visitor visas, other permits required.
- The extent and nature of corruption.

- Economic factors: currency stability; availability of credit.
- Utility services: electricity, water, internet, post/courier.
- Business services: banking, legal, consultants.
- Transport: airport, roads, rail, other logistics.
- Language barriers.
- Accommodation, schools.
- Safety, security, crime.

For environmental factors, Googling the country usually gives a lot of information. Some of the items are worth expanding on. You will need to consider not only yourself and possibly your own family, but also the people that are living in the country. There are big advantages to having foreign people, who know the environment, as members of your project team, and to having the project seen as one of theirs. So you'll need to know about the general education levels, the availability of suitable skills, and what those skills will cost. Also, you may be marketing your products to people or organizations in the country.

It is important to know how people from your own country are perceived, and this could be influenced by the relationship between the governments. It could also be affected by the country's history, and a basic knowledge of the history is useful and makes a good impression. You'll need to know: something about the laws, especially those that differ from your own country, and whether any constraints apply to people from other countries; also, about factors affecting the ease of doing business, like visa requirements, and how long it takes to process applications for things. Dealing with endemic corruption is always challenging. A few companies might appoint an agent in the country, to get certain things done in whatever way works. Other companies will decide to avoid the country concerned or to simply suffer the delays of not paying 'sweeteners'.

The state of the economy might affect your project, so too will services like electricity, water, and access to the internet. Business services like banking and legal will certainly be needed by your project because you will probably move money in and out of the country. Language could be a barrier; if there is no common language like English, you would need a reliable interpreter. Even with a common language, it takes extra effort to ensure that foreign people understand you, and vice versa. Then there will be logistical considerations like transport: Is there an airport nearby and are flights regular? What are the roads like and how efficient is rail?

You will need accommodation, and schools if you have a family. Special security arrangements may be advisable. Before accepting a relocation, you will want to fully understand the cost of maintaining an acceptable standard of living – it's easier to negotiate about these things before you move. Even things like the weather and holidays may be considerations.

28.5 Culture Shock and Getting Help

So, given the cultural differences, and compounded by environmental factors, PMs and other managers should expect to take time to adjust to a foreign country that is very different from their own. This applies particularly if you are relocating to, or spending large amounts of time in, other countries. Your feelings might be that nothing is getting done and that all the things that are effective back home, just don't work here. This is sometimes called 'culture shock' (Larson & Gray, 2018). Family could be a further complication, for example, children not settling down in school or a bored spouse.

> *I had a situation where an excellent IT specialist from India, brought his wife across to South Africa. She was a dancer and very sociable. But she just could not find a circle of like-minded friends. The result was that she became sick and it all ended with the specialist going back to India and working on our project from there.*

So, how do you prepare for an international project? Get training if it's available, and certainly find out everything possible from the web. Think of social aspects as well as just project-related things. Try to find an intermediary; that is, a person from the country that you can trust and talk to. If your organization already has an office there, then the office manager or a member of staff could play the role. Otherwise, you may want to look for a consultant. But ultimately, when you arrive in the foreign country, it helps to watch how people conduct themselves and to do quite a bit of listening. Also, be careful of assumptions and stereotypes. Even within a foreign culture, people are not all the same.

28.6 In Conclusion

Some countries will be easier than others. For example, for a South African, the USA, Canada, Australia, and most European countries involve relatively minor adjustments. Even Namibia has many similarities, but going further North in Africa or to the East might require a greater adjustment. Wherever you go, you still need to apply the essential project management disciplines. The project needs a business case and definition. Engagement with the team and stakeholders remains key. Schedules may change regularly and costs may have complications caused by foreign currency and volatile exchange rates. So, while these disciplines still apply, you may need to apply them differently and with greater flexibility.

Whatever the country or countries, prepare as best you can. but expect upsets and some culture shock. Seek and welcome support to speed up your adjustment process.

References

Hofstede Insights. (2021). *Cross-cultural management*. Retrieved from https://www.hofstede-insights.com/

Larson, E & Gray, C. (2018). *Project Management: The Managerial Process: International Edition*. 7th edition. New York: McGraw-Hill Education.

Chapter 29

Dealing with Some Realities in Business Projects

29.1 Introduction and Objectives

In this chapter, we discuss three realities often faced by business projects, namely:

- The projects are usually relatively small.
- They often have a matrix structure with mainly part-time resources.
- They sometimes take place in an unstructured or even chaotic environment.

Each brings its own challenges, so, the objectives are to:

- Discuss the background of each reality in turn.
- Make some suggestions as to how to deal with them.

29.2 Smaller Projects

Let's start by asking: how big is a small project? a medium-sized one? I have found no clear or universal definition. It's difficult to define size in terms of dollars because the value of any currency depreciates over time. Also, for business projects, most of the cost derives from the hours that skilled people work on them. So my suggestion is as follows:

- A small project is between 5 and 50 person-months.
- A medium project is between 50 and 500 person-months.

These person-months relate to the PM and the team. They would not include the hours of stakeholders outside the project team, which in some instances could be considerable. Work that requires less than 5 person-months might be considered a

DOI: 10.1201/9781003321101-32

'work request', but even a work request needs some of the project management disciplines. Clearly, these criteria do not apply to, say, construction projects, where even 500 person-months might be considered small. So, in what follows, we shall discuss *business* projects.

29.2.1 Are Smaller Business Projects Easier and Less Important?

Let's start by asking some questions about small projects.

- Are small projects easier? Not really. Managing a $200 000 project to implement a new financial services product might be more difficult than a much larger project to build five kilometers of new road on a firm, well-drained, surface. I do not underestimate the complexity of road building, but financial products designed by actuaries, with many business rules, can become very complex.
- Does a small project make it lower risk? Not always. A badly conceived enhancement to the HR retirement package could do damage far exceeding the cost of the project. By comparison, the road described above might be relatively low risk.
- Does it matter much whether a small project is successful? It certainly might. Some matter a great deal. A small project might enable a key marketing strategy. It might address new legislation, which, if not adhered to, could result in huge fines. It might address a mine safety issue that could cost lives if not resolved.

So, small projects can be difficult, risky, and matter a great deal. Further, for every really large project, there are many thousands of small projects underway all the time. So, small- and medium-sized projects really do matter.

29.2.2 Managing Smaller Projects

There are some common problems with smaller projects. Some companies have rigid and demanding methodologies and standards. So, for project managers who often manage several projects concurrently, there is simply no time to follow rigid standards. Then, with unexpected things popping up regularly, many PMs give up and use no method at all.

> *Many years ago I spent a year managing an IT department of 45 people. Many were experienced technical and business people, but, even though the company was highly regarded, some projects slipped with little warning to management, causing frustration and affecting our credibility. So, I discussed with the team leads, a list of eight items, like having a table of tasks with estimated dates, that would help them to track and report on progress. The result was not what I had hoped for. Most were reluctant, and possibly not able, to follow relatively straightforward project management procedures, even though they were otherwise good at their jobs.*

These were almost all small projects carried out by an average of around five people. In retrospect, there are a few lessons: Adopting even simple project management processes was a change and hence uncomfortable – as we learned in Chapter 23 on organizational change management. Perhaps I asked for too much at once? However, it does emphasize that any project method should be as simple as possible if it is to be used. So, for smaller projects, the 80–20 rule applies: 80% of the benefit, with 20% of the method. On a mega-project, probably 80% of the benefit is not enough. The remaining 20% of the benefit could be worth many millions of dollars. So, we would need the rigor and have it carried out by experienced people.

As we noted in the introduction to Part 2 of this book, there is a minimum for any project. And, for very small projects, even the minimum list might be trimmed. For example, we may not need cost management, because we know what the three people working on the project are costing per month. But one thing is worthy of note: whatever is done, needs to be done consistently. For example, it is little help if scope changes are only *sometimes* logged; they need to be logged whenever they occur.

So, in conclusion: for smaller projects: (i) Management should encourage flexibility in the application of standards. (ii) PMs should motivate following the minimum methods that are essential, and doing them thoroughly. To repeat: do the essentials, and do them well.

29.3 The Matrix Environment

Figure 13.1 in Chapter 13 illustrates the matrix project structure where skilled people are shared between projects. Although the matrix structure brings many benefits, it does indicate that people with skills face conflicting demands on their time, and you as PM, need to contend for your share.

Let us briefly reiterate some of the main aspects. Matrix projects can be of any size and exist in small or large organizations. There are many functional disciplines involved and many of the people are specialized. They have their normal work to do, and sometimes this involves keeping part of the operation running smoothly. So, if there are operational problems, they must deal with those first, resulting in an uncertain impact on any project that they are involved with. Project sponsors are interested in their projects, but have little time to negotiate for resources.

29.3.1 Likely Problems with Matrix Projects

So, what problems might you as a PM, experience when working in this mode? Here are some possibilities:

- The organization starts too many projects. A new project comes along. Management does not know where the resources will come from but decides to start the project anyhow intending to 'borrow' resources as they are needed.

  Some years ago, I attended a TenStep interactive webinar with an international audience of around 300. We were asked about the number of projects running concurrently. 70% responded that their organizations took on too many projects. Almost nobody indicated that they took on too few projects.

- Several projects are all 'priority 1', making it difficult for specialists to know what to do next if they are working on two 'top priority' projects.
- People are affected. They may be involved in several projects – two (fine), three (maybe ok), but if there are many more, people will be constantly switching between projects, and taking time to refocus. They probably feel important because there is such demand for their skills, but actually, they may be relatively unproductive. There could also be morale problems should the people feel that management expects too much or keeps changing priorities. For the latter, this might lead to apathy: "nothing seems to get finished".
- The projects are affected. They are scheduled for the resources working an agreed amount of time, but when this doesn't materialize, the projects just slip. Project meetings are poorly attended and are unproductive because much of the meeting becomes excuse monitoring.

> *Once, on a (supposedly) medium-priority matrix project, no progress had been reported in two successive tracking meetings. I put the project on hold, without even consulting the sponsor who had many other projects to think about. The decision was never questioned.*

29.3.2 Some Solutions

Solutions to the above problems come mainly from management. They should aim to get the benefits of sharing skills while minimizing the negative effects. They need to consider both the interests of the organization and of the people; usually the two go together. If you are a PM, you can point out to management, the problems hampering your own projects, and tactfully suggest solutions. Here are some possibilities:

- Do fewer projects concurrently. Put some on hold so that people can focus on fewer projects at a time. The principle is illustrated in Figure 29.1. It compares two ways of handling the same four projects which all use similar resources. The

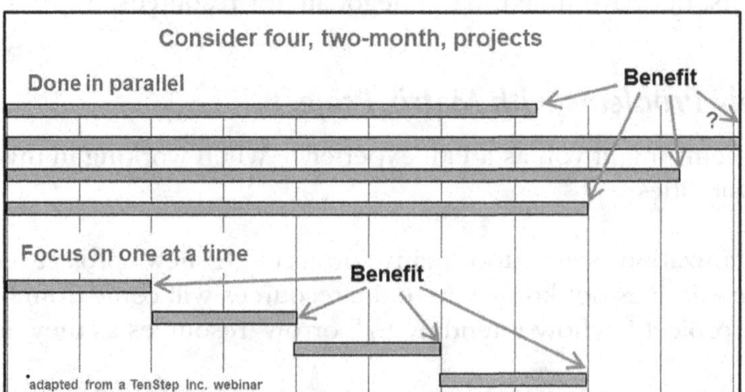

Figure 29.1 Earlier benefits by focusing on fewer projects.

minimum time for each project is around 2 months. In the 'parallel' scenario, with people spreading their time across the four projects, each project will probably stretch to around 8 months, with most of the benefits being reaped after 8 months. However, in the 'one at a time' scenario, the highest priority project is given focus and benefits are achieved after just 2 months. Thus, not only are the people more productive, but prioritized benefits come far earlier.

Clearly, with many resources, there can be several projects running concurrently, and the number of concurrent projects should be influenced by the resources available.

- Prioritize projects formally. An executive, or a management group, should decide on priorities and communicate them. There should be no joint priorities. Project priorities are from 1 to n, where n is the total number of projects running (whether matrix or not). The priorities should be adjusted regularly, say, once a month, or as required. Anyone should be allowed to query priorities via their own, or a designated, manager, and preferably in writing, stating reasons. Minimal time should be spent discussing priorities between meetings, but the queries should be debated at the next priority-setting session. Generally, people should work on their highest priority project until it is finished, or is held up, and then revert to their next highest. However, cooperation between PMs and judgment is needed. Some examples:
  - A person working on the priority 2 project might give 10 minutes assistance to someone working on the priority 5 project.
  - A PM might produce a draft PDD for a lower priority project, just to understand it better (and then put it on hold).
  - A critical path task on the priority 3 project might be done before a non-critical task on the priority 1 project.
  - Judgment might even be at deliverable level, where a lower priority project might have a deliverable that others depend on.
- Assign people to projects for a percentage of their time. This can only be done by the management team based on the current project priorities. For example, in the next period:

  > Mohamed should work 70% on project A (priority 2), 20% on project B (priority 4), and spend 10% on operational issues.

  These would be guidelines because there may be no operational issues. Moreover, things change, so meetings need to be every few weeks to revise the assignments. Then, both PMs and people would know what to expect, and PMs could monitor, to make sure that the time they are getting, is close to what was committed. PMs can adjust their plans as allocations change, and explain any impact on the schedule. This approach should also reduce the stress on the PM of continually having to contend for resources.
- Where the involvement of resources from functional departments has been agreed, it should be documented. This would be done by the PM and it includes

keeping functional managers informed of changes to plans. For example, "we shall only need Mary to start on 17 October; is that ok?" Also, confirm details close to the time, maybe even by email, like "just to confirm our agreement, Mary will do business testing for 2 weeks, starting on 17 October".

29.3.3 Summing Up Matrix Management

As indicated, many of the challenges of the matrix environment can best be alleviated by management, but PMs certainly play an important role. In summary, the number of matrix projects done concurrently needs to be limited to minimize churn, if necessary putting some on hold. Projects need to be assigned unique priorities, with all involved people being informed. Part-time staff should be assigned to projects for agreed percentages of their time. And finally, agreements on staff, with functional managers, should be well documented.

29.4 The Unstructured, or Even Chaotic, Environment

From the outside, many organizations look well-run and are widely respected, but when you are on the inside, things may be different. Some parts of the organization might be highly structured, or even too rigid, while other parts might be unstructured, even chaotic. Even within *part* of an organization, certain aspects may be structured while others are not. So in this section, we are dealing with 'chaotic' as it relates to the running of business projects. We probably cannot change the organization that we are in, so we have to make the best of the reality that we find. First, we shall discuss how to identify a chaotic project environment, and then we shall discuss how to manage within it.

29.4.1 Identifying a Chaotic Environment

What do we mean by chaotic or unstructured? There are a number of indicators to consider. In Chapter 19 on portfolio governance, we discussed project management maturity levels. A chaotic project environment would be at level 1, which means that you would not expect projects to be formally selected and prioritized. How a project is managed (or not managed) depends entirely on who is running it; possibly nobody is running it. Project management goes 'against the grain' of established norms and is not part of the culture. If someone is running a project, they would probably have a title other than 'PM'. Besides maturity, the organization might also be in some turmoil with lots of change happening, which often leads to lack of understanding as to who is responsible for what. But, it must be emphasized that change per se, is not a bad thing; we learned in Chapter 23 that if there is little change, an organization may not survive for long.

There are also some possible misconceptions: It might be reasonable to suppose that: (i) chaos only happens in small organizations, (ii) that larger organizations are constantly improving, and (iii) that chaotic organizations are generally unsuccessful. I have not found these to be true. Here, you might want to compare my observations with your own, because countries differ. In my experience, even the best organizations have a measure of chaos, sometimes for short periods of change and sometimes ongoing. It is also not true that organizations become progressively more structured and mature. Some go backward. Chaos is also not confined to small organizations, in fact, one of the most structured organizations that I've been exposed to is a small one. It certainly doesn't only happen in unsuccessful organizations. Some highly successful companies have a measure of chaos. In short, one cannot make assumptions as to what one will find in an organization.

29.4.2 How to Manage in a Chaotic Environment

Having recognized a chaotic project environment, how should one manage within it? Most of the things have been covered in previous chapters, and this is merely reinforcement.

- Be aware of what you cannot change. Accept the organization the way it is. Of course, if you are very highly regarded, or are given the job of making improvements, like being appointed as PMO manager, you might be able to introduce more structure.
- As PM (or whatever title you are given) make sure that you have a committed sponsor, who has reasonable power and influence. Likewise, if you *are* the sponsor, then you will need adequate power given the size and scope of the project. If this is not met, it may be wiser not to start the project.
- As PM, be committed to delivery because that is what you *can* influence. Expect some frustrations and adopt an agile mindset – in other words, be willing to change rapidly should the need arise. Even if problem-solving is part of your job, recognize what is genuinely beyond your control and don't blame yourself for everything that goes wrong.
- Apply the basic PM disciplines. This is key, and the following points relate to it. Whatever is going on around you, work in a structured way. Nobody can stop you.
- Maintain a repository for all documentation, not just project management stuff. Probably nobody else is doing this, and you can add value when people come looking for things. Just remember to keep good backup.
- Build relationships. In a chaotic environment, you will need help from many sources. It may even mean helping others in small ways or doing favors, but not so much that you lose focus.
- Identify the main stakeholders and get their agreement on the contents of your PDD – face to face if possible. It may only be three or four pages. but it should give an outline of the objectives and scope. Try to get approval for reasonable contingency for time and cost.
- Keep the most important stakeholders informed through short visits. Report regularly and honestly to all stakeholders, using the amber or red status codes where appropriate.
- Follow up on things, and negotiate personally with stakeholders. Then summarize the understanding in emails. Keep records of decisions taken and agreements made. Keep emails filed so that you can find them.

All of the above points apply to any project, but they are particularly important in a chaotic environment, especially the people-relationship aspects. They will help you to run a project successfully whatever is going on around you.

Sometimes, in a chaotic environment, there is some finger pointing, and you may be accused of things that were beyond your control. Having good records will enable you to give rational explanations where things deviated from the plan, and to produce a factual report when the project is delivered. In Chapter 3 while discussing documentation, I referred to the ability to defend your actions as CYA (cover your assets). As mentioned there, CYA should never be the main purpose of sound documentation – but it might be a useful byproduct in a difficult or aggressive environment.

29.5 Summary

There are many realities that can make business projects challenging, and here we have discussed only three of them. Much of this needs to be addressed by executives, and portfolio management can be part of the solution. PMs that understand the realities can still achieve results and might even have some influence toward improving matters. Nevertheless, whatever the situation, applying essential project management disciplines and fostering good cooperation with the sponsor and other stakeholders will make the difference.

Chapter 30

Agile Approaches

30.1 Introduction and Objectives

Understandably, there is much confusion about the term 'Agile' which only started to become prominent in the early 2000s. Agile can be used to describe a project approach which we shall elaborate on below. Agile can be used to qualify an organization's culture, which manifests as an attitude held by its people: "we shall adapt rapidly to changes". Agile can also refer to the structure of the organization itself. Here, we shall only cover the Agile project approach, but it does require all involved players to have an agile attitude. So the objectives are to:

- Explain the traditional 'Waterfall' approach to IT development projects.
- Show how an Iterative approach addressed some of Waterfall's difficulties.
- Present the Agile manifesto.
- Show how the Agile principles can be adapted for business projects.
- Explain how the Agile approach might be used in practice.
- Give an overview of 'hybrid' Agile, which is still being debated.

Referring to the Agile project approach, there is no single standard way of applying it. Each organization may use it differently or not at all. Similarly, there are many differing opinions held by people with Agile experience. Nevertheless, nobody questions the impact that Agile has had on the project world; indeed when the 6th edition of PMI's PMBOK guide came out, it was accompanied by the 'Agile Practice Guide', produced in conjunction with the Agile Alliance (PMI, 2017). Here, the aim is for you to understand Agile better and to be able to use some of its concepts.

30.2 The Traditional 'Waterfall' Approach

Agile does not *only* apply to IT development projects, but since it started there, I shall use a typical IT project to explain the concepts and the motivation to move to

DOI: 10.1201/9781003321101-33

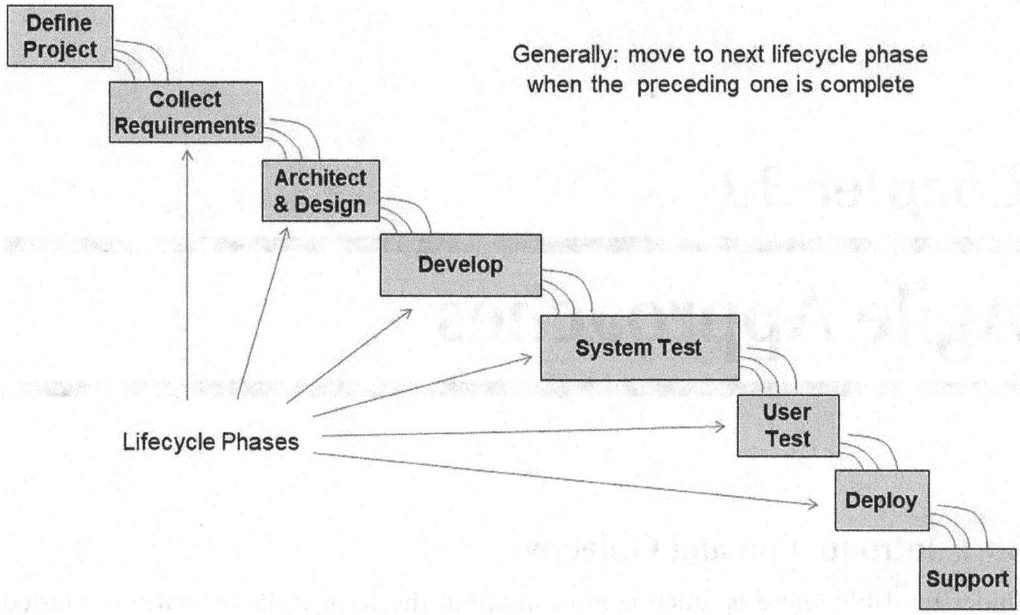

Figure 30.1 The Waterfall or traditional approach to IT development.

Agile (Mochal, 2013). Moreover, many business projects have IT elements and their aim is to support business stakeholders.

First some history. Prior to 1980, IT application development often lacked formal methods. Some IT projects were highly successful, but many failed. There was a need for more structure. So, in the 1980s, the 'Waterfall' approach, now also referred to as the 'traditional' approach, became accepted. Waterfall is illustrated in Figure 30.1. It is a logical progression of defining the project, collecting business requirements, doing design, developing the solution, testing the solution, having the business users test, deploying the solution to make it available, and, for an agreed period, providing support to business stakeholders.

Theoretically, it is very sound, but as will be shown, there are some practical problems. You can see the life cycle phases that the IT project team goes through; this does not even include any OCM (organizational change management) activities that need to happen for business people and customers to adopt the new functionality. Here, 'develop' would mean customizing a package and/or programming. System test may take many months and even UAT (user acceptance testing) may take several weeks. From the figure, you can see why it is called Waterfall. The Gantt chart looks like a waterfall. One only moves to the next life cycle phase when the earlier one is complete and approved (maybe with minor overlap). Waterfall has advantages:

- Lots of planning is done. There is usually a sound design, with most design problems solved early.

- Systems are thoroughly documented and approved by stakeholders before moving on.

  We jokingly said that things needed to be 'signed in blood' – meaning that once signed, the business had no right to change anything. Of course, that never worked very well.

- The method is structured and suited to well-understood requirements that are not going to change much. This hints at one of the disadvantages.

So let's list the disadvantages of the traditional Waterfall approach:

- Waterfall is rigid. It does not respond well to changed requirements. Even in the 1980s, requirements did change and today requirements change even more rapidly. In the private sector, the competitive landscape forces change and even in the government sector the voting public is becoming more demanding of change.
- Business users are often not good at articulating and specifying their requirements. IT people were often heard to lament that "the business folk don't know what they want". Even when they *do* know what they want, they are not always good at articulating their requirements. Even though business analysts are involved, misunderstandings can occur.
- With Waterfall, testing is started long after the design activities are complete. Often flaws due to misunderstood business requirements only surface during testing, forcing considerable rework.
- It is difficult for business users to see what they will get until well into testing, and sometimes they are not happy with the result.

30.3 The Iterative Approach

In the 1990s, some of the problems were addressed by using the Iterative approach which is illustrated in Figure 30.2. In the early phases, it is similar to Waterfall, but delivery is broken down into smaller more manageable chunks.

Besides the advantages of Waterfall, Iterative has some further advantages:

- Testing of the first iteration is done in parallel with development of the second, so the learning can be applied to later iterations.
- It is more able to respond to changing requirements.

Although the Iterative approach offers improvement for many projects, some of the difficulties remain: it still assumes that business users can specify their requirements, and it still requires most of the documentation before delivery starts.

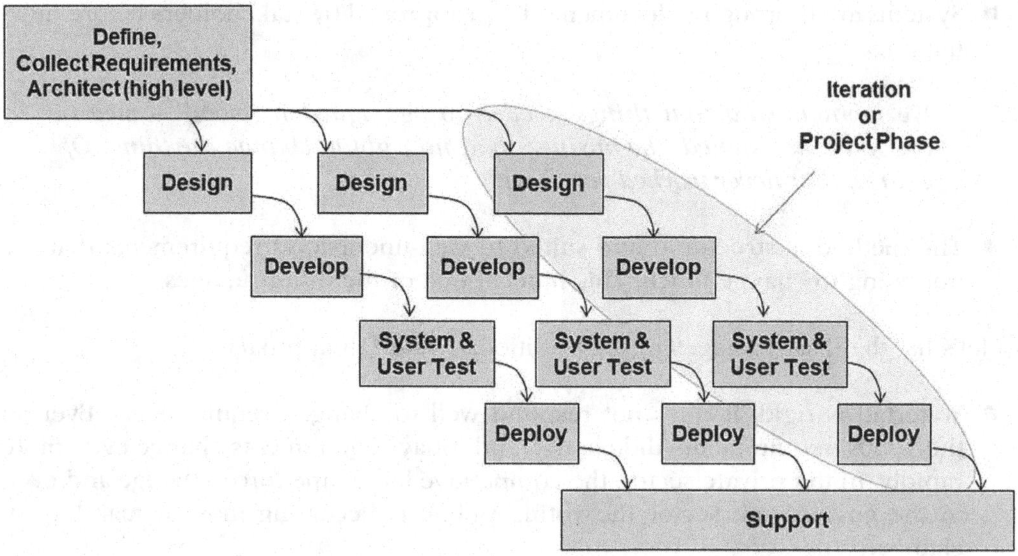

Figure 30.2 The Iterative approach to IT development.

30.4 The Agile Approach

Agile took off in the early 2000s. It was a bit like a return to the early days where the programmer interacted regularly with a business person and produced what they asked for. But Agile is more structured and can be used for larger teams and greater scope. It is also iterative, but the philosophy is very different. As mentioned, it's still evolving and there are many methodologies that use the Agile philosophy.

30.4.1 The Agile Manifesto and Agile Principles

It started in 2001 when a group of top specialists got together and created the Agile Manifesto which reads as follows:

We have come to value:

Individuals and interactions	over	Processes and tools
Working software	over	Comprehensive documentation
Customer collaboration	over	Contract negotiation
Responding to change	over	Following a plan

While there is value in the items on the right, we value the items on the left more.

So, even though plans, processes, and documentation are important, motivated individuals who collaborate and respond to change are more important. This led to the development of 12 Agile principles that are specific to IT development projects

(Agile Alliance, 2021). Many of them apply beyond IT projects, and here are some adaptations that apply to many types of business projects:

- The priority is to satisfy the customer.
- We welcome changing requirements.
- Regular deliverables that offer benefits to the customer are the measure of progress. (This may not be possible for all business projects, but sometimes deliverables at a milestone can produce early business benefits).
- Business people must work with the project team throughout the project.
- We need motivated people. Trust them and give them support to get things done.
- The best communication happens through conversation – ideally face to face, but online collaboration also works.
- Attention must be given to good design and technical excellence.
- Keep it simple and avoid unnecessary work.
- The project team should constantly evaluate how it is performing and make adjustments.

30.4.2 The Practical Modus-Operandi for an Agile Project

Now let us see how the Agile approach might be applied, using an IT development project as an example and drawing on a method that is referred to as 'Scrum'. The Agile team would typically consist of the product owner (a business person), between five and nine IT developers with complementary skills, and a facilitator often referred to as a 'scrum master' (I'm not sure that I like the word 'master' here). The facilitator plays many project management roles but tends more toward removing obstacles for the team and resolving issues, than telling the team what to do. This style is sometimes called 'servant leadership'.

The Agile project would be started with an initiation session, led by the business, which would in broad terms define what will be produced and the justification for doing it. Next, a planning session would be held to map out the releases and what will be delivered in each. Once again the planning is broad and the plan is subject to change. Each release would be achieved through a series of 'sprints', the duration of which is typically between 2 and 6 weeks. The sprint duration is determined in advance with very specific end dates. Generally, an Agile team will use the same sprint duration and get into a sustainable rhythm. Each sprint is illustrated in Figure 30.3.

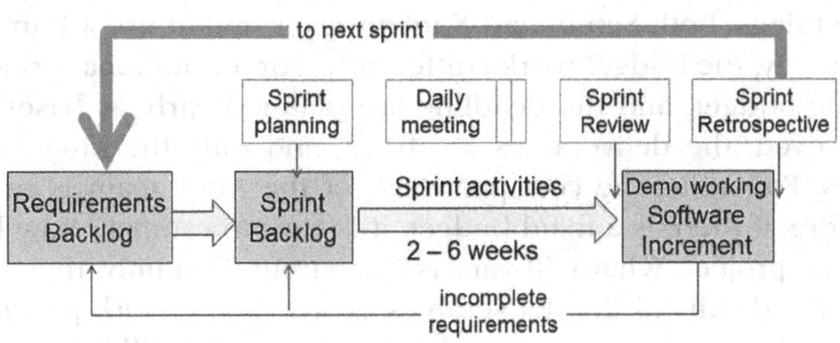

Figure 30.3 A typical Agile sprint for IT development.

The team starts each sprint with a backlog (effectively a to-do list) of remaining requirements. Sprint planning involves the product owner negotiating with the team as to what they can reasonably achieve in the set sprint period, say three weeks. The team then works collaboratively for this period, engaging with the product owner to produce the agreed deliverables. Daily there is a short meeting (maybe 15 minutes) the purpose of which is to discuss progress and plan the day ahead. The meetings are referred to as 'standup' meetings because there are no chairs. They are usually held around a whiteboard, often called a 'Scrum board' or a 'Kanban board' where tasks and progress are recorded. The purpose is for everyone to be able to see what is going on. Electronic Kanban boards are available to support teams especially where members are working remotely.

At the end of the sprint, the product owner facilitates the sprint review which looks at how the product has developed against what was planned. Consideration is given as to what might be included in the next sprint. In a similar timeframe, the working software is demonstrated to business people and feedback is noted. Last, there is a facilitated 'retrospective' where the team members discuss what went well and what did not. For the future, the team might agree on things that they will keep doing, start doing, or stop doing. Then on to the next sprint.

30.4.3 A Summary and More Aspects of Agile

Generally, each sprint develops working deliverables. The exception may be a 'sprint zero' which accepts that some initial design might be needed. The product owner is part of the team and must ensure that the output meets the business need. Therefore, the product owner remains in charge in terms of deciding on what needs to be done in each sprint. This is different from the traditional Waterfall approach where, once sign-off is given, the IT people are in charge. Ideally, the team members sit together in the same area and are largely self-managed, usually with the help of the facilitator. The team, rather than any single individual, takes ownership of deliverables and they agree to what they can reasonably achieve in the time. Individuals do whatever they are capable of and review each other's work. The requirements for each sprint might be specified up-front, but any further documentation is done along the way – only what is essential for later maintenance. There would seldom be a Gantt chart – more likely a task list on the Kanban board.

There are also different flavors of Agile: The Scrum approach described above works with sprints. With the 'Kanban' approach the team works continuously, but only taking on new work, prioritized by the product owner, when earlier work is complete. Just to confuse things, both Scrum and Kanban teams might use a Kanban board.

Very importantly, the budget works differently. For a traditional project, the scope deliverables, the budget, and the deadline are planned early as baselines. Unless a change is approved, the deliverables are fixed, and only the time and cost might show variances. For Agile, the cost per week of the Agile team is reasonably well known. Therefore, if there is a fixed budget, it is easy to estimate how long the team can spend on the project. What will vary is the output. Certainly, there will be broad objectives, but the details of the deliverables evolve as the work progresses. Even if an Agile project's budget is fully spent, the decision could still be taken to work for longer if there are clear benefits to doing so.

For larger projects, two or more Agile teams might work in parallel, in which case liaison between the teams is needed.

30.4.4 Benefits of the Agile Approach

Agile offers many advantages:

- The output is what the business needs and is usually of high quality. The few misunderstandings on requirements are speedily rectified.
- The team output is generally much greater than for a team working in traditional mode.
- Only necessary work is done. With traditional methods, the business people put some 'nice-to-have' items into the requirements because there is little opportunity to get something later that was not in the original specification. With Agile, backlog work is prioritized, so non-essential items tend not to get done – with significant savings.
- The approach can be used outside of IT. New product development of any kind might benefit from the flexibility and collaboration that Agile offers.

But Agile also has potential disadvantages:

- The main disadvantage lies with the assumptions. We assume that the team are mature, trustworthy, and can manage themselves. We assume that the business person is dedicated to the project, knowledgeable, and represents the real needs of the business. These assumptions are not always valid and may result in executives wanting more controls.
- The close cooperation required by Agile becomes more difficult when the team is geographically distributed.
- Agile is not suitable for all types of project. It may be unsuitable where a thorough and detailed design is needed before work starts. For example, I would not want to see a bridge being designed 'along the way' using Agile – it needs a firm design up-front.

30.5 Hybrid Agile

Agile has massive strengths for the appropriate type of project, but because of its potential limitations, 'pure' Agile is not common. More often an adapted form, called 'hybrid Agile' is used. There is still debate as to what the term means, but basically hybrid Agile is any deviation from a pure form of Agile as described above. Examples:

- A project where some elements are done using more traditional approaches while others are done using Agile approaches.

   We used a hybrid approach when making major changes to a wealth management system. The back-end work on the business rules relating to investments and the database structure used traditional methods;

they were tracked using a Gantt chart. The end-user web changes were done by an Agile team. It worked well.

- Management may be uncomfortable giving an Agile team free reign. They may impose some of the governance disciplines like a formal business case, a more traditional project manager, a budget, regular reporting in a prescribed format, and periodic reviews.
- It may not be possible for the whole Agile team to be full-time. This might apply particularly to the product owner who may be in demand to do other work in parallel.

Purists might say that these situations are not really Agile. They may be right, but in practice most projects referred to as Agile, are of the hybrid kind, to suit the organization and the business situation.

30.6 Some Conclusions on Agile

Agile has come a long way and is still evolving. As mentioned above, few organizations use Agile in its pure form. Hence, there are many flavors of hybrid Agile, some involving more formal project management disciplines. In fact, contrary to what some Agile proponents say, project management is still needed. Issues still come up and need to be handled. Executives still want to know what's going on. However, the person who takes care of these things in an Agile project may not be called a project manager.

Agile is not just for IT. The concepts can apply to anything where the requirements are changing and where the final deliverable is not fully specified initially. For example, for the refurbishment of equipment, activities may be prioritized as new things come to light. So, as with Agile, in many business projects, there is a broad objective but the scope detail cannot be pre-defined. It evolves and is prioritized along the way.

Even if you are not involved in Agile IT projects, many of the principles apply to all business projects. Things change and all involved stakeholders – the sponsor, the business, the PM, and the team – need to be able to rapidly reassess the situation. This could result in changed goals, changed scope, or changes in the approach to doing something. In such an environment, ongoing collaboration is needed. So the purpose of this chapter is for you to know the benefits of having an agile mindset and to see which of the Agile philosophies and approaches apply to the business projects that you are involved with.

References

Agile Alliance. 2021. *12 Principles Behind the Agile Manifesto* [Online]. Available: https://www.agilealliance.org/agile-essentials/

Mochal, T. 2013. *IT Development Lifecycles*. New Jersey, USA: TenStep webinar.

PMI 2017. *PMBOK – Guide to the Project Management Body of Knowledge*, 7th edition. Pennsylvania, USA: Project Management Institute.

Chapter 31

Digital Tools for Project Management

31.1 Introduction, Objectives, and Some Terminology

Nowadays it is imperative for organizations to adopt appropriate digital strategies. It can mean things like: selling online, use of artificial intelligence for assessing credit-worthiness, analyzing large volumes of data to understand consumer trends, or automating processes. Indeed, pursuing a digital strategy involves a series of projects. Here, however, we shall restrict our view to digital tools that directly support *business* project management. We shall also not discuss digital tools that are mainly used in a particular industry. For example: In the world of construction and engineering projects, there are tools to manage contractual commitments and cash flow. The tools may even apply to some business projects. In IT, some of the tools have IT development aspects like controlling the status of developed code, but also have project management aspects like recognizing dependencies between IT development activities. So, it certainly gets complex. There are many thousands of digital tools available commercially and they are evolving all the time. Therefore, in this module, where our aim is to put things into perspective, the objectives are to:

- Introduce some terminology.
- Review which digital tools are already in common use.
- Understand which aspects of project management may need digital tools to support them.
- Consider the kinds of tools needed to manage a portfolio of projects. These are sometimes referred to as PPM (project portfolio management) software.
- Get general guidance on how to use digital tools effectively for project management, and possibly even beyond project management.

DOI: 10.1201/9781003321101-34

31.2 Terminology

This just gives the meaning of a few of the terms used here.

- A software package usually runs on a smartphone, a laptop, a server, 'in the cloud', or on a combination of them. It meets one or more business needs.
- The term 'application' or 'app', used in the context of computers, is software that helps you to do something useful.
- Freeware is software that you use without paying for it, like most web browsers.
- Cloud software is licensed to a person or organization, and is accessed via the web. Besides your own device, no hardware is required, and payment is generally based on usage and/or time. Data captured, and accessed, also resides in the cloud, but is not available to outside parties. Gmail is an example of cloud software that is free.
- PPM (project portfolio management) software. Here the term is used for software that enables the management of many projects. It may also include features like a scheduler or templates, that can be used on individual projects.

31.3 Commonly Used Digital Tools

What exactly is digital? Put simply, it is the use of IT. So let's not get too excited about 'moving to digital', because in project management, as in most other things, we have been using digital tools for a very long time. Consider the following, and here I shall sometimes mention tools that you know, rather than the generic terms:

- Word processors have been around since the 1970s, followed soon after by spreadsheets. MS Word, Excel, PowerPoint, and even Access with its database capabilities, are regularly used to manage project data.
- Email has been widely used since the 1990s and electronic calendars, with their meeting scheduling ability, are in regular use.
- Videoconferencing for online meetings and collaboration, while already in use earlier, came to prominence with the Covid pandemic. Zoom, Google Meet, and MS Teams have many additional features like sharing a document or presentation.
- Web browsers which give access to vast amounts of information are now available to almost everyone. They provide the user interface to cloud-based applications and to many locally hosted ones. The corporate intranet is just one of many examples.
- There is a choice of devices for working digitally. Laptops have the advantage of a larger screen, while smartphones are more portable. Most project people use both, sometimes concurrently.
- Multi-user applications, which were in-house and server-based, are being replaced by cloud software. There are many ways of pricing cloud software, but a common way is by concurrent user. So, for 20 concurrent active users, one might pay a certain monthly charge, but for 100 concurrent users, one might need to pay more.

- Scheduling tools, like the MS Project scheduler, have been available since the 1990s. After entering the activities, durations, and dependencies, the schedule is commonly displayed as a Gantt or bar chart, but can also be shown in precedence or network format. Whiteboards (like Kanban) are used for Agile and other projects, with columns showing the status of development items, e.g. not started, in progress, or completed. These boards can also be electronic, allowing team members to collaborate from anywhere.
- Projects needs a central place, or repository, where project data is stored, updated, and accessed by many role players – from portfolio managers to project teams, and from project sponsors to business people. Project portfolio management (PPM) software goes a step further, and is increasingly used in larger organizations, typically supported from a PMO (project management office). Besides providing a repository for project data, PPM software offers tools to manage individual projects, and for the governance of a portfolio of projects. Let us now look at PPM capabilities in more depth.

31.4 Project Portfolio Management Software

A PPM application is needed in organizations that run many concurrent projects. It would almost certainly be cloud-based and accessed by a wide variety of role-players through a web interface. Here are some of its functions:

- As mentioned, it would have a repository to store information about projects that are in a variety of statuses. Projects might be proposed, approved, in progress, or complete. They might also have been placed on hold or outright rejected. Whatever the situation, all essential data is kept for the record. The repository would store documents related to each project, such as business cases, project definition documents, meeting minutes, status information, lessons learned – almost anything.
- Then project data can be extracted through a variety of enquiries and reports. Reports for multiple projects might be called 'dashboards'. When executives need to select and prioritize projects, the input would certainly be extracted from the PPM system.
- Resources, particularly skilled people and their allocation to projects, might be kept track of. The aim is to avoid starting projects without necessary resources, and to prevent people from being overloaded.
- The PPM tool might have its own scheduler, but more commonly it would support a variety of schedulers by storing: activities, dependencies, resources, progress, or whatever is needed, and making the data available to the scheduler of choice.
- Just as the PPM software might interface to a scheduler, it may need to integrate with other systems. A typical requirement would be the interface with an accounting system so that project cost tracking can be done for projects that require it.
- Other entities like risks, issues, and scope changes could also be documented, possibly using customized templates. All such entities would be linked to specific projects so that they could be reported on, at project level.

- The PPM system would be updated with approvals. These could be for a document, or to allow a project to take the next step. The system could be configured to issue warnings if certain documents or approvals were missing. But it could also be set up to prevent a project from proceeding if certain approvals following a gate review, were missing.
- Access control, sometimes called 'permissions', is essential. It would cover what a particular person may see and what they may change, both by function and by project.

Of course, this list is not comprehensive. But one thing is worth noting: PPM software is unlikely to give management a 'birds-eye' view of what is going on in multiple projects; communication between PMs and other stakeholders remains essential.

31.5 Choosing Appropriate Project Management Tools

This section is intended for management who take decisions as to which project software the organization needs. It also offers the PM a broader perspective on tools. The use of some digital tools is essential for sound project management and governance. No doubt you will ask yourself: "which tools should we use, and how should we use them?" Most PMs use what is required by their organizations, but some also advise management on which digital PM tools to acquire.

As guidance, it is probably more effective to use basic tools (like spreadsheets) well, than to use sophisticated tools poorly. What do we mean by poor use? Some examples:

- There are no standards or training, and the use of tools is variable or not at all.
- Some people spend hours trying out 'cool' features that deliver no value.

For certain basic tools like email and messaging (like WhatsApp), following standards may not be critical, but even here there are norms of good behavior like not 'copying the world' on an email, especially one that criticizes something.

Every organization has different needs and the needs vary from user to user. This is exacerbated by the sheer number of packages, with new or improved ones becoming available regularly. The sales pitches may not help much because they tend to mention the positives, and not the limitations. So one needs to be wary, ask lots of questions, and possibly try out a demonstration version. You always need to consider how a particular tool will work in *your* organization. So, acquiring project management software is much like acquiring any other kind of software – it takes effort. New software also comes at a cost. What is paid to the vendor is only part of the cost. There is also people-time to familiarize with the software, training, and most of all increased complexity, So, before accepting the expense of new software, one would need a clear idea of the requirements – the problems we are trying to solve. For an organization with few projects a manual approach using simple tools should suffice. Where there are many concurrent projects in a larger organization, using spreadsheets and trying to control many documents becomes cumbersome. Here, PPM software may add great value, but requires an investment.

But even if one acquires high-function software, it may be best to use the minimum subset that meets the need. So when introducing PPM software, start with the basic functions. Even this will need a culture shift from people who may find the procedures and increased discipline restrictive. They will also need to develop new skills. So when adopting new functions, it is best done as a project with technical, process, and OCM (organizational change management) aspects. Unless the people buy in, the new processes are unlikely to be effective. PPM software will also need housekeeping, cyber security, and ongoing user support. It is seldom affordable to have more than one or two people playing this role.

Be aware of the dependencies on internet access and the cloud. While today, cloud access is very reliable, internet access may be restricted when PMs travel. Also, be wary of software that you don't pay for. It's fine for things like WhatsApp which is widely used for communication, but for something like PPM software, the cost of the software is a fraction of the total cost. For such systems, support from the vendor or a consultant may be critical, and the availability of such support may be as important as the functionality of the package. For PPM software, there will also be compromises needed. Who will be allowed to use which functions and access or update which data? Maintaining these access permissions is part of the housekeeping mentioned.

And finally a caution: No tools, not even the best ones, replace people competencies like: (i) justifying and defining projects, (ii) dealing with stakeholders, and (iii) solving problems. But if the people have these essential skills and a disciplined attitude, tools can add great value. So, the effectiveness of advanced digital tools, even well know ones like schedulers, is proportional to the quality of the people. And the corollary is: Do not expect technology to solve people problems like a lack of competence, discipline, or commitment.

31.6 Summary

Digital tools to support project management are already used widely. They may be fairly manual, like the use of standard templates and storing documents in structured folders. Or they may be highly automated and centrally controlled. There is everything in-between. Digital capabilities have come a long way, even since the start of the millennium, and are improving all the time. But a balance is still needed between avoiding digital tools and drowning in their complexity through being too ambitious. Finally, as indicated, digital tools support competent PMs but do not replace them.

Chapter 32

Trends: The Future of Business Project Management

32.1 Introduction and Objectives

The world is changing rapidly, and project management is changing with it. This chapter considers what has changed over the past 50 years, and more importantly, it speculates on what is likely to change in future, particularly regarding *business* project management. So, the objectives are to:

- Walk through the history of project management over the past 50 years, including approaches and techniques, technology advancements, and the role of governance.
- Consider changes that are already happening and those predicted to happen soon.
- Reflect on the skills required by a competent PM and how these might change.
- Think about whether PMs will be needed in future.

There are few universal truths, and much ongoing debate, on many of the above topics. So, by all means, compare your perspective with what follows.

32.2 Changes Over the Past 50 Years

Some of the history is given in Figure 32.1 which shows progress over the years in the three key themes of project management (middle), technology (bottom), and governance (top). The themes go hand in hand and influence one another. The items in each theme do not have firm dates associated with them, so the positioning merely indicates the rough time frame in which they were used or started to be used.

DOI: 10.1201/9781003321101-35

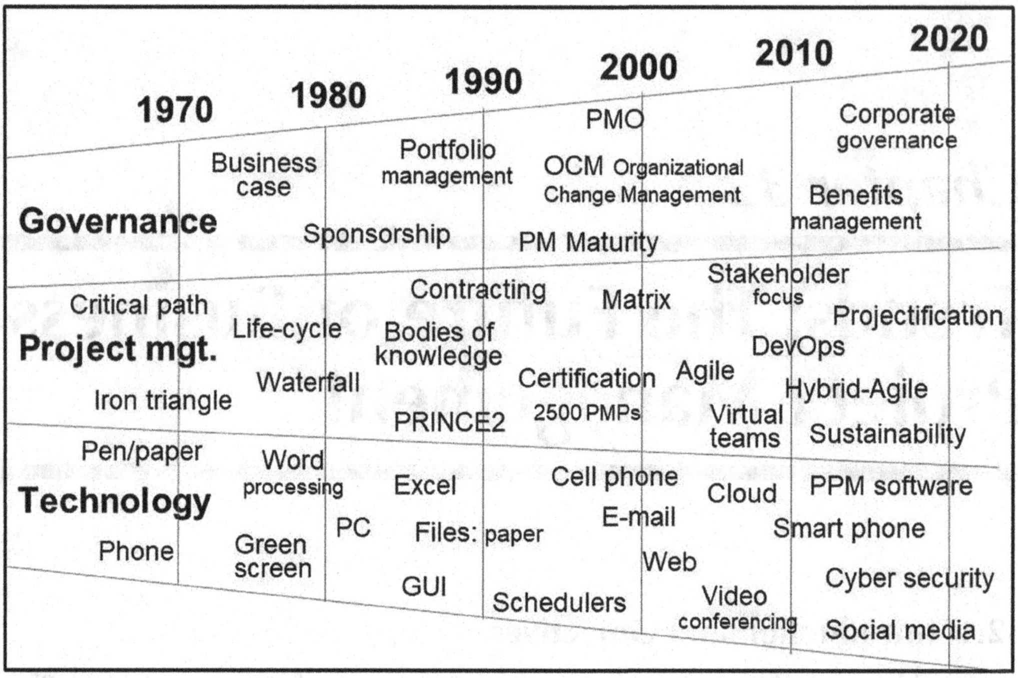

Figure 32.1 Three key themes over the past 50 years.

32.2.1 Changes in Project Management

Let's start in the middle with the project management aspects, working from the left:

- Critical path theory and earned value management gained traction in the 1960s starting mainly in the USA.
- It became accepted that there needed to be trade-offs between scope, time, and cost, known as the triple constraint or iron triangle.
- The project life cycle consisting of initiation, planning, execution, and closing became recognized.
- Early IT successes gave way to quite a few failures in the 1970s. To address this the traditional Waterfall approach of requirements specification, design, development, test, and go-live became widely accepted.
- PM methodologies became better documented and PRINCE2 was released in the late 1980s. In parallel 'Bodies of Knowledge' started being produced, the best known being the PMI's guide to the PMBOK which even in the mid-1990s, was not the glossy covered or electronic handbook that it is today (PMI, 2017).
- Contracting gathered momentum in the late '80s, and in the '90s many project resources were contracted in, rather than being permanent employees.
- PM certification was in its infancy. When I got my PMP in 1994, there were about 2500 PMPs worldwide. The figure is now over a million – four hundred-fold growth in less than 30 years.

- Prior to 2000, even business projects tended to have dedicated resources. Thereafter more and more resources were shared in matrix mode, as people became more specialized and the pressure grew to run more projects concurrently.
- Agile approaches were conceived around year 2000 and, since then, they were expanded into many sub-disciplines like Scrum and Kanban. However, the needs of organizations varied, with some requiring more controls. This led to many adopting a form of 'hybrid Agile'.
- With the rapid development of the internet, in terms of coverage and performance, virtual teams became more practical with project resources spread across buildings, cities, and even countries. This way of working received a major boost from the lockdowns resulting from the Covid pandemic. It is likely to remain prevalent, even though the benefits of project team members solving problems while sitting around a table are still recognized.
- Project failures did not go away, because the complexity of business projects grew just as rapidly as the capability to manage them. With the complexity came a wider variety of stakeholders that needed to be engaged with. Indeed in 2013 stakeholder management became a recognized project knowledge area.
- In 2007, 'DevOps' started to become formalized in the IT world. Previously development teams, which worked in project mode, were separate. Merging them with operations support resulted in regular new functionality and better support for business users.
- Around 2010, sustainable project management, with its 'people, planet, profits' slogan, was becoming talked about. This was driven in part by threats to the environment and to the growing number of stress-induced mental conditions on projects.
- Projectification is the term given to organizations bringing about more and more of their changes through defined projects. Although it had been growing for many years, the concept only became recognized more recently.

32.2.2 Changes in Technology

Moving to the bottom of Figure 32.1, the changes in technology, as applied to projects, was even more dramatic.

- In the early 1970s, projects were managed with pencil and paper, with the phone and maybe post ('snail-mail') as the means for distance communication. Neither were cheap, particularly distance phone calls.
- In the late 1970s, monochrome (green on black) screens started appearing on PMs' desks. They usually offered clunky word processors and access to limited mainframe facilities.
- Enter the PC around 1982, and everything changed. Spreadsheets (like Excel) and better word processors came on the scene. Some years later GUI (graphical user interface) made the screens more capable and user-friendly. But even in the mid-1990s, project files were still in binders kept on shelves or in cupboards.

- Prior to 1990, Gantt chart schedules were mainly done on paper or via Excel. Then schedulers emerged which could display data in Gantt or network format.
- Around 1995, we got the first mobile phones, and email started to become practical. Laptops started replacing desktop PCs, with the corresponding mobility benefits. Mobile phones first became smaller and then they got smart. Today, smartphones are used for almost everything that a laptop can offer.
- Around year 2000, with improved browsers, the web moved from being used mainly by nerds (technical specialists), to use by everyone, but dial-up was still painful. By 2010 that had all changed. The web was directly accessible, most organizations had intranets, and video conferencing became common.
- Cloud computing really blossomed after 2010. The uptake was rapid, and today most application software, including software used on projects, is cloud-based.
- PPM (project portfolio management) software, for handling project data of all kinds, came of age and became available on the cloud. While a PMO is often involved in supporting it and taking regular backups, projects can easily store documentation and access it from anywhere via the web. PPM software also facilitates getting consistency across an organization.
- There is a risk introduced by these advances. Cyber security has become a consideration. While it is normally handled by specialists, PMs increasingly need to participate in the security of business data which depends on both technology and on people.
- Social media, like LinkedIn, can help PMs to stay in touch with one another. It can also facilitate the finding of suitable team members.

The project management tools that we take for granted today were almost unthinkable 50 years ago. But, even then, projects did happen, and people landed on the moon without them. It should also be noted that, despite the rapid advances, some of the manual techniques like activity lists and diagrams scribbled on paper or a whiteboard can still add value.

32.2.3 Changes in Governance

Governance is shown in the upper part of Figure 32.1. There had been an increasing realization that projects can seldom exist in isolation. Business projects are the way that organizations implement change, and, as discussed in Chapters 17 and 19, they need governance and support from outside the project itself.

- Justifying projects through a business case grew gradually, and the need for sponsorship (or ownership) became more apparent during the 1980s.
- Portfolio management became accepted as the way to prioritize and manage projects across an organization. PMOs were set up to support the portfolio in a variety of ways.
- Consultants started to measure an organization's project management maturity.
- During the 1990s, it was increasingly realized that many business projects relied on people to accept change, or to change the way that they do things – even after project closeout. Accordingly, OCM (Chapter 23) became a recognized discipline that formed part of, or worked alongside, many business projects.

- Benefits management became a hot topic soon after year 2000, to ensure that envisaged benefits actually materialized after the project was complete.
- In many countries, corporate boards are expected to ensure that proper project governance is carried out. This arose because of the significant impact that project outcomes can have on organizations.

It is now understood that governance, starts before a business project is initiated, is done during the project, and continues after closeout. Therefore, over time, governance has become recognized as essential for the success of projects and portfolios of projects.

In summary, there have been massive changes over the past 50 years, and at no time did the pace slow down. So, given that change is likely to continue, let's consider what the next 20 years might bring.

32.3 Possibilities for the Next 20 Years

In most areas of project management, nobody can say for certain what will happen. What follows uses research done some years ago, and is adjusted for observations since then (Gemünden & Schoper, 2014). The management of business projects is unlikely to become easier, because of the rapid rate of change and greater uncertainty. Indeed, one view of plans is that they cannot be used to control the future, they merely make the PM aware of deviations from the plan that need attention. In what follows there are some generalizations, so expect there to be exceptions.

32.3.1 Megatrends

Let's first look at some mega-trends.

- Globalization: Although it took a knock during the Covid pandemic, with supply chain risks coming under increased scrutiny, globalization still remains a trend. So, there will be more international projects.
- Cyber-crime: This is causing considerable executive concern. Any project that relates to systems or the web will need to consider it as a risk, with response actions becoming scope items.
- Diversity and soft skills. Cultures in most countries are becoming more diverse and there are more women in leadership roles. Leadership styles are also changing. Soft skills are becoming more important and the tough, macho PM is suitable in fewer business project situations.

32.3.2 Projectification

With growing projectification, project management skills are becoming a core competency required by *every* manager. Even professionals who are involved in projects will be of greater value if they have a broad understanding of project management. Because of the variety of business projects undertaken, it is becoming more and more difficult to apply a single methodology for all situations. In the future, there must be diverse approaches to cater for different industries, sizes of project, and types of project. Even within an organization methods will need to be flexible with a few core elements and the rest tailored for the situation.

32.3.3 Complexity

The more capable we become and the better our tools, the more we take on and the more complex will be our projects. This is driven by competitive pressures, arising from the need for innovation and rapid product development. Projects are crossing more boundaries, involving multiple departments, multiple organizations, and multiple countries. This increases the variety of stakeholders. There is more information available ('big data' being just one example), and more automation (with artificial intelligence (AI) and the internet of things (IoT) being contributors). There will be more matrix projects, and because we already take on too many projects, we shall have to prioritize better. The level of complexity adds to the need for more flexible methodologies. The core disciplines will still apply but things like schedule and risk management must be tailored to the context. Earned value concepts need to be applied differently for projects that have uncertainty and use rolling wave planning. The PPTR (project progress tracker) approach, explained in Chapter 12, is one such response. An agile mindset will be needed, where PMs are willing and able to respond rapidly when something does not work or to changing requirements. This applies even if the project is not using an Agile or hybrid-Agile approach.

32.3.4 Further Technology Developments

The tools we use today may be considered archaic in 20 years' time. There will be bigger and better repositories, leading to a greater need to manage information overload. Project management will become more virtual, and be done from anywhere. Better online collaboration tools will make it easier for team members to be remote, but yet work as though they talking around a whiteboard. Simulation tools will become more available. Already 'digital twinning' is being used in the engineering and process industries by building an electronic model which simulates (acts just like) the real environment. For business projects, simulation may be used to test many scenarios, by varying parameters and observing the effect. The approach taken in business games can be extended to project management. In future, 'gamification' will be used more often to train PMs, making learning a game, sometimes even competitive.

32.3.5 Strategic Project Management and Benefits Realization

Hitherto, PMs have been seen mainly as implementers of strategy, and producers of defined deliverables. There is a trend toward involving PMs in strategy formulation. Already a number of SPOs (Strategic Project Offices) have been set up, which not only guide executives as to what is possible, but also get involved in the prioritization and execution of initiatives. Indeed, it has been predicted that PMs will be seen more often in corporate boardrooms. This has a number of implications. PMs will need to understand the organization's strategy, and how their projects contribute. They will need to look beyond the deliverables, to the benefits that will accrue to those deliverables. This means working closely with the business stakeholders that take responsibility for benefits realization. Executives are also affected because project and portfolio success influences their careers. The project sponsor, and product owner in the Agile world, will need to demonstrate that the benefits used to justify the project, are actually achieved. This may curb over-optimistic proposals because the business cases will be used for a reality-check when project outcomes are reviewed. But overall, sound governance and effective sponsorship will remain important for executives.

32.3.6 Chartered Status for PMs

Finally, project management is starting to have a chartered status. Employers and people contracting PMs expect an appropriate certification, and there are now many overlapping forms, like scrum master and program manager, to name just two of them. The value of project management will become better recognized and lead to new career paths. So, whereas project management will be a skill for all managers, there will still be a need for specialist PMs. Interestingly, whereas most professions like accounting, engineering, or medicine are entered through tertiary education after leaving school, this is not typical for project management. Many PMs start with another discipline, whether business or technical, and then move to project management when they show interest and have an aptitude for it. It is then that they realize the need for formal project management education and a certification. Having done that they are able to broaden into managing projects in a variety of domains.

32.4 Which Aspects of Project Management Have Hardly Changed?

People involved with projects need to be aware of the changing landscape. However, it is also important to recognize the competencies that have changed relatively little over time and will remain relevant in future. Think back to Figure 2.2 which shows the four legs of project management capability. Under generic skills, computer literacy needs constant updating, but the rest stay the same. Business knowledge needs to keep pace with change in any case. Leadership changes very little, except perhaps to give strategy more emphasis and to pay attention to the soft skills like facilitating and removing obstacles (sometimes called 'servant leadership'). The PM leg might change a bit more but the essential skills and techniques change very little. So what this indicates is that project management competence is worth developing, through experience on challenging projects, and will never become obsolete. The things that a PM does like engaging with stakeholders, defining the project and agreeing it with the sponsor, negotiating for resources, communicating the project's justification and status, managing risks and issues, will always be needed.

32.5 In Conclusion

Going through the history of project management and looking ahead shows that change is here to stay and may even be accelerating. The roles of the project sponsor and the PM will continue, but the PM may have any number of different titles like 'scrum master' or 'product owner'. The competencies of the PM will change very little. Communicating, negotiating, engaging with people, and solving problems remain relevant, and the PM will continue to be judged by the outcomes produced given the challenges faced. In short, project management skills will still be needed, and while they may be assisted by artificial intelligence and robots, they will not be replaced in the foreseeable future. Because of projectification, project management will grow as a profession, but many aspects of it will become essential skills for all managers and many other professionals.

References

Gemünden, H. G., & Schoper, Y.-G. (2014). *Future Trends in Project Management*. ResearchGate. Retrieved from https://www.researchgate.net/publication/303375998_Future_Trends_in_Project_Management/link/573f19a708ae9ace84133ad7/download

PMI. (2017). *PMBOK – Guide to the Project Management Body of Knowledge*, 6th edition: Pennsylvania, USA: Project Management Institute.

WRAP UP OF THE BOOK AND STUDY MATERIALS

4

Part 4 of the book has a variety of chapters:

- Chapter 33, the wrap up, covers the main requirements for project success in some depth. It gives thoughts on the true-false questions raised in Chapter 1 and summarizes the essential disciplines that apply to almost all business projects.
- Chapter 34 offers a study guide which indicates different ways in which the book might be used – everything from light reading to offering an advanced program.
- Chapter 35 gives quizzes, each relating to a specific chapter. Only the core elements and some of the special topics have quizzes. They are referred to from the study guide and their answers allow you to quickly check your understanding.
- Chapter 36 has 'cases', some of which are exercises and others are case studies. They are referred to from the chapters as well as from the study guide and allow you to further develop your learning.
- Chapter 37 provides answers for the cases. For the exercises, there should only be one correct answer; for the case studies where there could be many valid answers, 'possible answers' are given.

DOI: 10.1201/9781003321101-36

Chapter 33

Wrap-Up and How to Achieve Success

33.1 Introduction and Objectives

This is the final chapter, other than the study guide, learning materials, and appendices. So the objectives are to:

- Know that success can be viewed in different ways.
- Learn some basic causes of failure and how to avoid them.
- Revisit the 'true-false' statements posed in the introduction (Chapter 1).
- Wrap up by summarizing the essentials for managing a business project.

Before we relook at those questions and wrap up, let us consider what is meant by project success.

33.2 Project Success and Avoiding Failure

33.2.1 What Is Success?

One view of project success is 'on time, on cost, and on scope'. I find this a bit narrow. My view is that if the business stakeholders believe that the project's output is giving business value, and provided that the time and costs are not excessive, the project can be deemed a success. Various authors have had similar thoughts. I like Bannerman's analysis from a 2008 conference paper (Bannerman, 2008). He suggests five levels of success: (i) the project management processes used effectively, (ii) the production of agreed deliverables on time and within budget, (iii) the acceptance of the output by stakeholders, (iv) business success through use of the deliverables, and (v) strategic success which may only be known later when one looks back on the project and its outcomes. The verdict for each level might be different, but Bannerman suggests that the higher levels are the most important. Thus, if it has

DOI: 10.1201/9781003321101-37

delivered business and strategic value, it may not matter much if the project itself was not run perfectly. Bottom line: there are different ways of looking at success.

33.2.2 Avoiding Failure

One of the contributors to success is knowing the most common things that lead to failure and avoiding them. So here is a list of things to watch out for.

- Sponsorship is insufficient: This could happen in a number of ways; here are some: (i) the sponsor may not be senior enough or may lack influence, (ii) the sponsor may not care about the outcome, (iii) sponsors may not understand their responsibilities or not give enough attention to the project, and (iv) no sponsor may have been assigned. None of these are easy for a PM to handle. If the deficiency is apparent up front, then declining to take on the project may be an option. If the problem manifests itself along the way, then the first approach might be to talk to the sponsor and politely explain the support you need. If that gets a negative response or leads to no improvement, then you might be able to discuss it with another interested person, like your own manager or the portfolio manager if there is one. Keeping a factual log of the difficulties experienced along the way, will help. Case 27 (XP Insurance) deals with this kind of situation and suggests possible answers.
- No business case has been approved: Business cases do not need to be formal documents with an approval stamp on them. But, it really helps to have something in writing that outlines the justification for the project. This should be versioned and reviewed periodically because many things can change, including the assumptions. Where there is no business case, the benefits, costs, and risks section of a PDD (project definition document) cover similar ground – which should have been agreed with the sponsor.
- Goals are unclear, requirements are misunderstood, or scope definition is poor: Once again, producing a PDD and getting buy in from the sponsor and key stakeholders should avoid this. Other symptoms of the problem may be stakeholders that appear dissatisfied or team members not being sure of how to tackle certain activities. Where the problem is identified, then revisiting the PDD or holding a workshop to iron out differences may be worthwhile. Such issues cannot be ignored; they need to be attended to and resolved.
- The customer or business stakeholders are unprepared to play their roles: When dealing with a customer, their responsibilities should be clearly stated in the agreement (contract). Where there are breaches, then raise an issue, and think about how to get it into the open and dealt with. Talk to your own management before confronting the customer sponsor. When dealing with internal business stakeholders, the sponsor would be the person to discuss the impact with.
- Stakeholder expectations are not set and managed: This would only happen if there were no PDD or if some important stakeholders had not understood it. But even if the PDD has been studied, stakeholders may have misinterpreted something. So, engage with stakeholders periodically and discuss how they will benefit from the project. Then it will quickly become apparent if there is a misunderstanding which could, in turn, lead to scope change requests.

- A large number of scope changes or uncontrolled scope creep occurs: Three things should help to avoid this. First, understand the requirements and agree the deliverables while doing the PDD and more detailed scope planning. You may not know all the activities, but you should have some knowledge of the deliverables. Second, have a change control system in place – the simpler the better because then, when someone spots a change, it can be quickly discussed, documented, and a decision taken. Third, talk to the team about the importance of bringing any mooted changes to your attention. They can be your eyes and ears, and prevent scope creep from 'just happening'.
- The schedule is unrealistic: This can happen when there was over-optimistic estimating to get a business case approved, or when an executive wants something urgently and insists on an almost impossible deadline. Two main options: Decline to take on the project unless the deadline changes. But, more likely, you have little choice but to do it. So, write up what you believe to be a more reasonable date estimate, stating all the assumptions, and have a discussion with the sponsor. Often a compromise can be reached like reducing the scope or delivering part of the scope by the requested date. You might also be able to make delivery subject to conditions like having specific skilled people assigned. Always document the agreement, with assumptions, and send it to the sponsor, because memories are short and conditions are easily forgotten. At least you will have set expectations by communicating that the deadline is optimistic and will be able to defend yourself should you fall behind schedule.
- People skills are inadequate: First you need to know and be able to justify what you need. Next, communicate it clearly to both sponsors and stakeholders that provide skilled people (referred to as the 'senior resource suppliers' in PRINCE2) (OGC, 2009). The reality is that often you are assigned people and only have limited control over others that you acquire. Hiring contractors is not easy, and some work out better than others. As the project progresses, monitor performance and report on any skill shortages. If serious, treat them as issues to be resolved. At least, set expectations by reporting regularly on the situation.
- Roles and responsibilities are unclear: This is quite common, but a PM should be able to deal with it through discussion, documenting the responsibilities, and resolving conflicts.
- Risks are not managed: Things go wrong that could have been avoided. This also happens often, but should be dealt with by following normal risk processes. Stay alert to people expressing concerns. Their concerns may be risks in another guise. Get them onto your risk register, and in the few minutes that it takes to describe the risk, you will often think of response actions. At least you will not have been caught by surprise.
- Issues remain unresolved: Usually this only happens when issues are not being logged and dealt with. So, follow the issues management process. Usually, you and the team will be able to resolve them, but if not, you will be able to ask for support through the sponsor.
- A supplier is unable to deliver: This only leads to failure if the supplier was doing something critical. So, where you will rely on a supplier, go through the procurement process thoroughly. There are many checks to be done but doing them diligently greatly reduces the likelihood of a default. Then, treat supplier

failure as a risk and think about how to respond. Having an alternative supplier helps, but sometimes, once the solution is decided upon, changing suppliers is not easy. Monitoring the supplier's delivery is important. Far better to know of problems early than to find out, on the due date, that delivery has not happened.

- People who need to be involved are unprepared for the change: The OCM (organizational change management) aspects of a project are often overlooked. So, while putting the PDD together, think about which people or groups will be affected, or will need to work differently for the project to be a success. Then include OCM as project scope activities, which may affect your budget or schedule, and possibly even the justification for the project. Alternatively, ensure that OCM activities will be handled outside the project, but treat them as dependencies.
- Technology is new or immature: This mainly applies to technology and IT projects. There is constant competitive pressure to do new things that require the use of 'leading edge' software or other technology. The salespeople will tell you what the product *should* do, but often there are subtle problems that they may not even know about. So, some suggestions, based on my experience in the IT industry: Try to find other organizations (not direct competitors) who are already using the technology and learn from their experience. If you must be the first, then get special support agreements from the supplier. Be especially wary of a new solution from an unknown supplier, which effectively means two risks (the supplier and the solution) that compound each other. Other ways of mitigating risk are to do a 'proof of concept' before you make a full commitment; you will be able to assess the technology and familiarize your team. Alternatively, use the technology on a smaller non-critical project before taking on bigger ones.

Clearly, the list is situational and not comprehensive, but if we can eliminate the common causes, then our probability of success is that much greater. As indicated, many of the problems are addressed by following the core disciplines outlined at the beginning of Part 2 and explained more fully in its chapters. Some of the disciplines covered in Part 3 also apply.

I recommend that you do Case 39, TRSA records management, which sketches a project scenario that could happen in any organization. See whether you can spot the danger flags, and recommend how to turn this into a likely success.

33.3 Discussion on the True-False Statements from the Introduction

Now that you have done the reading and hopefully most of the cases, let us revisit those true-false statements from 'setting the scene' in Chapter 1. My comments are below each, and my conclusions at the end:

- With sound training in project management anyone can be a good PM.

  The PM 'capability stool' in Chapter 2 shows there are many attributes that make up a good PM. People with most of the other attributes will be better PMs if they develop project management knowledge. But, project management training cannot fully compensate for a lack of ability in other areas like communications and problem solving.

- If one follows a methodology, project management becomes straightforward.

  Following a methodology certainly helps considerably, but project management is seldom straightforward. Sure, there are simple projects, but given the varied stakeholders, the personalities in the team, and the complexities in the organization, most projects require problem solving which the PM usually facilitates and contributes to.
- The first thing a PM should do is schedule the project from start to finish.

  There are many things that must happen before a meaningful schedule can be developed. The requirements need to be gathered, the scope defined and the activity durations estimated based on the available resources. All of these are challenging and take time. Moreover, for the more agile projects, the activities only become known shortly before doing them.
- Risks are a fact of life, so there's no point in bothering about them.

  There is a huge amount one can do about risks. Some risks can be greatly reduced, for example, by convening discussions to avoid delays caused by stakeholder conflict. Most risks can be mitigated at an affordable cost, and a few can be accepted. Even those that are accepted serve as input to deciding whether the project remains justified.
- Project management software allows one to manage projects effortlessly and efficiently.

  At best, software can provide valuable tools and help a capable PM to get organized. Unfortunately, at the current state of the art, software is not good at managing people or resolving tough issues. So sadly, project management is never effortless and efficiency depends a great deal on the PM and the team.
- If we are behind schedule, it is easy to catch up by having people work overtime.

  Theoretically, this may be true, but having people work overtime is seldom easy. Also, in my experience, I have never caught up more than a few days through overtime. Usually, the best that I could achieve was to prevent the project falling even further behind schedule.
- If there are problems, the PM should keep them to herself so as not to upset management or threaten team morale.

  You might find this statement amusing, but I've seen it happen in practice. It is tempting to hide problems, and one might put off unpleasant discussions for a while. But, for the longer run, honesty remains the best policy. The truth will come out, and the sooner everyone knows, the sooner problems can be dealt with. You, as PM, will build trust if you 'tell it like it is'.
- Documentation is a waste of time because it does not contribute to getting the project done.

  Unless one can write something down (or capture it on a keyboard), one probably does not understand it. The corollary is that documenting things ensures that one understands them, or at least highlights what one needs to find out. In other words, it supports the writer's thought process. Having thorough and well-organized documents is of great value when decisions are needed. It also helps when communicating with stakeholders, whether by reporting, resolving issues, or motivating changes.

- The PM takes most of the key decisions on the project.

  Although the PM takes many decisions, like who should do which activity, the big decisions belong to the sponsor. For example, the sponsor or Steercom would decide whether a major change is justified or whether the project should be placed on hold. Whereas the PM and other stakeholders may influence or even guide the sponsor, the sponsor ultimately decides. But, the PM does have a very important responsibility: the PM needs to highlight decisions to be taken, and get them taken in good time to minimize the impact on the project.
- Once thorough planning has been done, very few issues arise.

  I wish this were true. Experience has shown that issues arise all along the way – some even in the final weeks of a project.
- Unless a project is on time and within budget, it is a failure.

  As discussed above, this is a limited view. It may apply in certain situations, like when you are managing a well-defined, fixed-price, contract. But for most business projects, the Bannerman criteria help to determine the degree of success.
- However challenging the project or tight the deadline, a good PM will get it done successfully.

  One experienced project manager said to me "if I can see that the project is not doable, I will decline to take it on and explain the reasons". PMs are not supermen or superwomen. A good PM will recognize targets that are unachievable and negotiate the best way forward with the sponsor.
- Project management is no longer necessary. With an Agile approach, the team always does what is most important to produce business value.

  First, without the facilitating role played by the PM (or scrum master or Agile coach) who works closely with the product owner (or business person), the team may not always do the 'right' activities. Second, there is still a need for people management, reporting, and many other things that team members are often reluctant to do.

So overall, I would rate all the statements as 'false', but no doubt, there are grains of truth in many of them.

33.4 The Essentials for Managing a Business Project

To end, it's worth re-stating the core, and essential, disciplines that were outlined in the overview of Part 2. From what I have observed, even these basic things are often not done. Certainly, there are situations that need more sophistication, but for most business projects the essentials, done consistently, are what is needed:

1. Ensure that you have a sponsor.
2. Talk to the stakeholders regularly.
3. Maintain a structured documentation repository.
4. Produce a PDD and have it reviewed.

5. Define the scope and the deliverables from the PDD in greater detail.
6. Develop and track a simple schedule, noting the milestone events.
7. Develop a cost budget and track the costs (where appropriate).
8. Hold regular, short, minuted, team meetings.
9. Document and manage project risks, issues, and changes.
10. Produce regular one-page reports – usually weekly or fortnightly.
11. Close with a report, and review it with the sponsor.

This list does not cover portfolio governance because, important though it may be, it is done outside of the project.

33.5 Conclusion

We have covered a broad range of topics that should be of interest to PMs and other stakeholders involved in business projects. While I have attempted to place the chapters in a logical order, in practice many things are happening concurrently, so knowing what to focus on next is never easy. Nevertheless, whether you are a PM, a project sponsor, or one of the other role players in the projects arena, I hope that you have found the book of value and that you can apply some of the approaches in your business or personal life.

References

Bannerman, P. (2008). Defining project success: A multilevel framework. Paper presented at the PMI Research Conference, Poland.

OGC. (2009). *Managing Successful Projects with PRINCE2*, 5th edition. In A. Murray (Ed.). Norwich: TSO (The Stationery Office) on behalf of Office of Government Commerce.

Chapter 34

Study Guide

34.1 Introduction

This chapter suggests a variety of approaches to learning from this book. Which approach, or which combination of approaches, will depend on your objectives. You might wish to:

- Enhance your general understanding of how to manage business projects.
- Give yourself an advanced program in managing business projects.
- Facilitate such a program for a group of people.

These requirements are covered in the sections that follow. They all refer to Table 34.1 which gives the chapters, any quiz (heading 'Q') or cases associated with the chapter, and discussion items. Table 34.2 is a guide to the cases that are referred to. While the chapters are in a reasonable learning sequence, in project management there is no perfect sequence as much happens concurrently. You can select your own sequence because as far as possible, the chapters can be studied in isolation and most do not rely on earlier chapters. However, where a concept is not clear, the glossary in Appendix 1 or the Index should assist.

To get value from this book, it is not necessary to adopt all the views expressed or the techniques covered. The book presents an approach; no doubt there are many others. Even if you choose a different approach, there is value in comparing your preference with the approach suggested. Please send any comments to me at fdeinhorn@gmail.com.

The questions and discussion items in the right-hand column of Table 34.1 may need clarification by looking at the chapter. They are just some suggestions because you will probably think of far more items that are worthy of debate.

DOI: 10.1201/9781003321101-38

Table 34.1 Study Guide

Topic	*Ch.*	*Q*	*Cases*	*Possible Questions and Discussion Items*
				PART 1 – OVERVIEW
Introduction	1			■ How do business and construction projects differ? ■ What thoughts do you have on the true-false statements? ■ Why should project management be kept as simple as possible?
Business projects and their management	2		Self-assess	■ What is a project? Does it need a sponsor? ■ What could happen if a project is not managed? ■ Can anyone be a good PM if they go on a PM course? ■ What skills does the PM need?
Methodology from unusual angles	3			■ Will a project management methodology ensure success? ■ What are the strengths and limitations of methodology? ■ Certification: is it worth it? ■ Is documentation needed? What value does it add? ■ What is a glossary? How might it be used? ■ Will PM software tools replace methods?
The business project environment	4		1	■ How do business projects arise? ■ How does the organization decide which projects to do? ■ Why do we need governance and a project structure? ■ How does the project 'lifetime' relate to the 'life cycle'? ■ Which documents are used to govern and manage the project during its lifetime (pre, during, post-project)? ■ What is a PDD? When and why is it produced?
				PART 2 – CORE ELEMENTS
Engaging with stakeholders	5	Y	2	■ What makes a person or group a stakeholder? Examples? ■ Give examples of how stakeholders can affect a project ■ On what dimensions can we classify stakeholders? ■ How should we engage with them? All the same way? ■ What information about stakeholders should be kept?

(*Continued*)

Table 34.1 (Continued)

Topic	*Ch.*	*Q*	*Cases*	*Possible Questions and Discussion Items*
Project definition	6	Y	3, 4	■ Why do we need project definition? ■ How do we get input to a definition document? ■ What is the 'triple constraint'? Why should we prioritize its elements? ■ What are the main headings in the PDD? Discuss the less obvious ones like 'exclusions' and CSFs. ■ Why do we need a business case if we have a PDD?
Scope definition	7	Y	5, 6	■ The scope is in the PDD; why do we need more detail? ■ How do requirements relate to scope? How do we gather them? ■ What is a WBS? How might it be created and presented? ■ How does the WBS relate to the project schedule? ■ What happens to the WBS when the schedule is approved?
Project estimating	8	Y	7, 8	■ What is an estimate? Why can it usually not be accurate? ■ Why do we need to estimate? ■ When and how does one estimate? ■ Explain the difference between a top-down and bottom-up estimate. Which is more reliable? ■ What are some of the estimating techniques? Explain them. ■ What is 'contingency' and how does it relate to estimating?
Project scheduling – time management	9	Y	9, 10, 11, 12, 13	■ What is a schedule and what forms can it take? ■ Why are milestones useful? How do they differ from activities? ■ Explain finish-start and start-start dependencies. What is meant by a lag and a lead? What is meant by float (or slack)? ■ What is the critical path? Why is it important and how do we recognize it? ■ For business projects, why might a Gantt chart be preferred? ■ What is meant by resource leveling? Is it easy to automate? ■ What can we do to meet tight deadlines?

(*Continued*)

Table 34.1 (Continued)

Topic	*Ch.*	*Q*	*Cases*	*Possible Questions and Discussion Items*
Managing project quality	10	Y	14	■ What is meant by project quality? Give some criteria. ■ If we have specifications, why do we need more input? ■ The 'cost of quality' has which two elements? Give examples. ■ What approaches are there to achieving quality outcomes? ■ What are ISO9000, the Pareto principle, other principles?
Managing project risk	11	Y	15	■ What is meant by project risks, and why consider them? ■ When and how does one identify risks? ■ How should the PM document, analyze, and track risks? ■ Summarize how qualitative and quantitative risk analysis differ. ■ What risk-response strategies can the PM use?
Progress and cost tracking	12	Y	16, 17, 18, 19, 20	■ What do terms like sunk cost, variable cost, etc. mean? ■ To assess project performance what do we track? ■ What is meant by EV (earned value), PV (planned value), and AC (actual cost)? Why is each important? ■ What is the danger of comparing PV to AC? (Figure 12.1). ■ Work through the example in Figure 12.2. ■ Explain schedule and cost variances. What does a positive or negative variance mean? ■ What is meant by SPI and CPI? Is greater than 1 good or bad? ■ Why is 'classical' EVM seldom used for business projects? What practical alternatives exist?
Project teams and organization	13	Y	21, 22	■ What do we mean by a team in the project context? ■ What does Tuckman tell us about how teams develop? ■ What can the PM do to build a team that works effectively? ■ Give examples of task-, relationship-, self-oriented behaviors. ■ What are the common project structures? What types of project are they suited to?

(*Continued*)

Table 34.1 (Continued)

Topic	*Ch.*	*Q*	*Cases*	*Possible Questions and Discussion Items*
				■ Give examples of hygiene factors and motivational factors. ■ What forms of power does the PM use to get good outcomes?
Managing project issues	14	Y	23	■ What is a project issue and how does it differ from a risk? ■ How do issues get recognized? What should the PM do? ■ Explain the documents that are used to manage issues. ■ How should issues be handled? Who needs to be involved? ■ What is a decisions log and how might it be used? ■ What are the benefits of managing issues consistently?
Project change control	15	Y	In text	■ Several disciplines use the word 'change'. How do they differ? ■ What does project change control cover? ■ What is (or is not) a scope change? ■ Which is harder to manage big changes or many small ones? ■ Explain the process for managing changes. ■ Discuss the example of a change that 'takes no extra effort'. ■ What is 'scope creep', and how should the PM manage it?
Project monitoring, control, and communication	16	Y	24, 25	■ What do the words 'monitor', 'control', 'track' mean? ■ How can team meetings be used to track progress? ■ How are project meetings recorded? How is it done in Agile? ■ What should the PM do between meetings? ■ What are the PM's responsibilities regarding decisions? ■ Why is communications challenging on a larger project? ■ What are some guidelines for effective listening? ■ Status reports: how often, how long, and what content? ■ Explain how a RAG code is used.

(*Continued*)

Table 34.1 (Continued)

Topic	*Ch.*	*Q*	*Cases*	*Possible Questions and Discussion Items*
Governance of a project	17	Y	26, 27	■ What is governance of a project? What are the benefits? ■ What is the project sponsor role? What qualities are needed? ■ How do sponsors contribute throughout the project lifetime? ■ What would the sponsor expect of the PM? ■ What is a steering committee? Who is on it? What is its role? ■ What pros/cons of having key suppliers on the Steercom? ■ Explain 'gate' reviews. Who does them and when?
Closing the project	18	Y	28, 29	■ What are the closeout scenarios? How does handling differ? ■ Why is closeout often neglected? ■ Explain some of the people activities around closeout. ■ What is financial closeout? How are suppliers involved? ■ What would the sponsor expect around closeout? ■ Explain the purpose and content of the closeout report. ■ Which other things should be considered at closeout?
				PART 3 – SPECIAL TOPICS
Governance for a portfolio of projects	19			■ Explain how projects arise from strategy and the likely problems. ■ What are the considerations for managing a portfolio of projects? ■ Who are the role-players in portfolio governance? ■ What is meant by a PMO? What services might it provide? How are its objectives decided? ■ What is 'project management maturity'? How should it be used?

(*Continued*)

Table 34.1 (Continued)

Topic	*Ch.*	*Q*	*Cases*	*Possible Questions and Discussion Items*
The business case end-to-end	20			■ What are the purposes of a business case? ■ Why is the preferred approach to the project, vital input for the business case? ■ Who is involved with the business case? What are its contents? ■ When should the business case be created? ■ If the business case is approved, what happens to it? ■ What if the PM must start a project without a business case? ■ How might it be used in reviews. What decisions follow?
Project selection – financial and non-financial criteria	21	Y	30	■ Explain how the organization might decide which projects to do. ■ What financial criteria might be input to a selection decision? ■ Why are future costs and benefits discounted? Explain NPV. ■ How does in internal rate of return (IRR) relate to the NPV? ■ Why might executives treat the proposed IRR with caution? ■ What non-financial aspects might be major considerations? ■ What is a project scoring model? How might it be used?
Project procurement, outsourcing, and partnership	22	Y	31, 32, 33	■ Give examples of projects with a procurement component. ■ What is a buyer, seller, supplier, vendor, contractor? ■ What is an RFP? What are its major activities for the buyer? ■ Explain a few contract types indicating who carries the risk. ■ Give tips for PMs who are either buyers or sellers. ■ What is meant by outsourcing? How might it give advantage? What are the risks? ■ Give tips that make for effective partnership.

(*Continued*)

Table 34.1 (Continued)

Topic	*Ch.*	*Q*	*Cases*	*Possible Questions and Discussion Items*
OCM – organizational change management	23	Y	34	■ Give some examples of changes that involve people – inside and outside the organization. ■ How do people respond to changes that affect them? ■ Should the people-change aspects be part of the project? ■ For change, what is the role of senior and first-line managers? ■ What do the ADKAR elements mean for a project? ■ What are some approaches used? How effective are they?
Project contracts	24	Y	35	■ What is the purpose of a contract? How should it be used? ■ Why should PMs understand contracts? How are Legal involved? ■ What is needed for a document to be a contract? What would prevent it being a contract? ■ Is a seller offer and a buyer acceptance enough? ■ Explain how a contract for projects might be structured. ■ What are common clauses and what are their implications? ■ Give tips that apply to either party regarding contracts. ■ What causes disputes? How might they be resolved? ■ What contract attributes support sound project practices?
Project review	25	Y	36	■ Explain the kinds of project reviews. What gets reviewed? ■ What are the benefits of reviewing projects? ■ When should reviews be held and who needs to be involved? ■ What are the steps for conducting a major review? ■ Give tips for reviewers and reviewees.

(*Continued*)

Table 34.1 (Continued)

Topic	*Ch.*	*Q*	*Cases*	*Possible Questions and Discussion Items*
Ethical conduct and adherence to legislation	26		37	■ What do morals, ethics, and integrity mean to you? ■ Why is ethical behavior important? Is it situational or absolute? ■ What are the four values in PMI's code? Give examples of each. ■ Mention factors that are driving legislation that affects projects. ■ Who might the PM turn to for advice on legislation? ■ Share some laws that affect projects in your industry.
Project negotiation	27	Y	38	■ What gets negotiated on projects, formally or informally? ■ How do position-based and interests-based negotiations differ? ■ In negotiation, what is important for ongoing cooperation with the other party? ■ Explain what is meant by 'power base', BATNA, and ZOPA when preparing for and engaging in negotiation. ■ What are some of the dos and don'ts in negotiation? ■ Explain some negotiating traps that one should watch out for. ■ What should be done after a negotiation?
Managing international projects	28			■ Give some examples of projects that involve other countries. ■ Explain some of the cultural factors to consider. ■ What are Hofstede's cultural dimensions? Can one generalize? ■ What environmental factors affect living in another country? ■ What is 'culture shock' and how might one prepare for it?
Dealing with some realities in business projects	29			■ Comment on smaller projects, say under $500 000, with respect to complexity, risk, importance, and project methodology. ■ Mention possible problems where many projects are done in matrix mode (shared resources). What solutions can be applied? ■ What are the indicators of a chaotic environment? How might the PM cope and achieve success?

(*Continued*)

Table 34.1 (Continued)

Topic	*Ch.*	*Q*	*Cases*	*Possible Questions and Discussion Items*
Agile approaches	30			■ Contrast the traditional (waterfall) approach with Agile. ■ What values did the Agile manifesto express around 2001? ■ Which Agile principles apply to most business projects? ■ For what types of project is Agile suitable? What are its benefits? ■ What is hybrid-Agile? Why might it be preferred to pure Agile?
Digital tools for project management	31			■ Which digital tools have PMs used for many years? ■ How has 'the cloud' made project tools more effective? ■ What is PPM (project portfolio management) software? What facilities does it offer to PMs and to the organization? ■ How are digital tools selected/managed in your organization? ■ What project needs will digital tools not solve?
Trends: the future of business project management	32			■ What changes have already taken place that affect projects, considering project management, governance, and technology? ■ Which mega-trends will affect PMs in future? ■ Explain projectification. Have you noticed it? ■ What changes are you observing or expect? ■ Will PMs (by whatever name) still be needed in 20 years' time?
				PART 4 – WRAP-UP
Wrap-up and how to achieve success	33		39	■ How would you evaluate project success? ■ What are the common causes of project failure? For each mention what can be done to avoid it. ■ Discuss each of the true-false statements from Chapter 1. Which might have more than one answer? ■ What are the essentials for successful business projects?

Table 34.2 Guide to Cases

Case	Subject	Description of Case Study or Exercise
1	Project charter	Endura holdings. Produce a meeting agenda with aim of preparing a project charter.
2	Stakeholder analysis	Waluma hospital. Do stakeholder analysis and produce a power-interest grid.
3	PDD	Triple constraint. Prioritize scope, cost, time for three situations.
4	PDD	Trandy Inc. Produce input for a PDD (project definition document) under given headings.
5	Scope	Classify the 27 statements given as to whether each gives: an objective, a requirement, a scope statement, or an exclusion.
6	WBS	Produce a WBS (work breakdown structure) for the NMA (National Medical Association) conference.
7	Estimate	SpeedWall. Produce a definitive estimate for building a wall. It gives practice at estimating, where facts and experience are available.
8	Estimate	Estimating for three different situations. Determine when estimates might be done and what techniques might be applied. For each situation, list considerations that need to be clarified before a valid estimate can be done.
9	Schedule	Market survey schedule. Produce a precedence (network) diagram and a Gantt chart. Calculate relevant parameters like float, and determine the critical path.
10	Schedule	Schedule to organize a conference. Produce a Gantt chart for a more complex situation involving both finish-start and start-start dependencies, and also lags and leads.
11	Schedule input	Activity precedence from conversation. Produce a table indicating which activities precede a given activity based on excerpts from conversations. I.e. work out the dependencies for the given activity.
12	Schedule	Hospital project schedule. First, produce a manual Gantt chart from the data given. Next guidance is given as to how to use a scheduler to create a similar schedule and then do updates like entering resources, leveling resources, adding an activity, and entering progress.
13	Compress schedule	Market survey schedule compression. This uses the same data as Case 9. The cost is given of crashing certain activities. Hence, produce the most economical way of saving 2 weeks to meet a tight client-imposed deadline.

(*Continued*)

Table 34.2 (Continued)

Case	Subject	Description of Case Study or Exercise
14	Quality	EduToy7 factory move. Determine what is needed for stakeholders to be satisfied with the quality of the move. If there is a scope of work or specification, it is unlikely to have all the things that the stakeholders really want. Either list likely stakeholder quality requirements or hold a syndicate quality workshop to produce the list.
15	Risk	Nature Films have an assignment to film Cheetahs in the wild. Complete a first-cut risk register indicating the risks, analyzing the risks, and determining response actions.
16	Cost/budget	Math11 budget. Produce a time-phased budget, arriving at control figures or planned values by month.
17	EVM – earned value mgt.	Painting a wall. The simple project is planned for 5 days. Produce earned value figures for each day from the data given. Comment on what the figures mean.
18	EVM	HR job description project. Answer 19 questions which include calculating earned value figures as the project moves through its 4-month duration.
19	EVM	Project Theta. Answer six questions based on the data provided.
20	EVM	Project Inter-World. The project is broken into phases. Answer 12 questions based on the data provided.
21	Motivation	Six attributes are given. Determine whether each is a motivator or a hygiene factor, giving reasons.
22	Teams	HVD (Heavy Vehicle Distributors). New business processes need to be rolled out. Early on, there is already conflict and the project is in some trouble. Make recommendations that will help the PM.
23	Issues	Wealth-Man conversion. A serious problem has arisen. Get practice at documenting the issue from the information provided.
24	Monitoring and Control	Delia is a PM. A typical day is described from morning until evening. Comment on the skills that she displays and on what she experiences as a PM.
25	Reporting	Determine the RAG (red, amber, green) status in four situations.
26	Governance	XP Insurance. The project to launch a new insurance product is in trouble. Comment on the governance situation, and make recommendations.

(*Continued*)

Table 34.2 (Continued)

Case	Subject	Description of Case Study or Exercise
27	Sponsor	Eight different situations involving the sponsor are described. Determine how the sponsor should handle each of them.
28	Governance, closeout	Rescon division. High-risk projects are the nature of the business. Recommend how they should apply governance, and terminate failing projects effectively.
29	All core areas	16 typical situations are outlined that happen on projects. State how the PM should handle each, and mention the documentation and communication needed.
30	Project selection	Delectable Confections must choose between two projects. Use both financial and non-financial criteria to recommend which should be pursued.
31	Procurement	Upview investments need to resolve their contact center problems. They arrange to meet with M&P who provide such services. For each party, list the main concerns that they might have and issues to raise in the initial discussion.
31	Contract types	Three different contract types are given, each with different actual cost scenarios. For each, calculate the profit or loss that would be made.
33	Outsourcing	M&P have completed the project to set up an outsource of the contact center for Upview investments. The outcome is unsatisfactory. Indicate how it might have been handled better, and recommend what should be done now.
34	OCM	Lorion are planning an early retirement program. Indicate who is affected and the issues arising. State the approach you would use to manage the change.
35	Contracts	BCT (Bowden Consulting & Training) will undertake a training project for a bank. Indicate into which part of the contract the various clauses should go. Draft a contract supplement for the training assignment outlined.
36	Project review	The Warestar retail project is underway. Plan a major review for the project – including: project areas, people to interview, and timetable.
37	Ethics	Six vignettes are given outlining ethical dilemmas. For each you are asked how you would deal with the situation, mentioning alternatives and reasons.

(*Continued*)

Table 34.2 (Continued)

Case	Subject	Description of Case Study or Exercise
38	Negotiation	Your project needs intranet development done to communicate with stakeholders. Several difficulties are apparent. Do the preparation for a negotiation with the head of the Intranet department.
39	Prevent failure	TRSA have initiated an important records management project. Work has started but problems have arisen. Identify what is satisfactory, and what areas need to be addressed to turn a likely failure into a success.

34.2 Enhancing Your Own Understanding

The starting point would be the self-assessment in Chapter 2 where the topics listed correspond to most of the chapters. You are invited to assess (i) your current skill or knowledge level in the topic and (ii) the level that you need or wish to have. By comparing your assessments you will quickly see which chapters will give you the most benefit. For any chapter that you choose to study, you can decide on the level of depth. To gain a thorough understanding of a chapter, I suggest that you do any quiz and cases that are referred to in Table 34.1. Answers are provided in Chapter 37. If only an overview is desired, then the cases may be omitted or else just skimmed through to get an idea of the kinds of situations encountered.

34.3 Giving Yourself an Advanced Program

I refer to it as a program rather than a course, because for people in busy careers there is too much to cover in one stretch. It would be better to do one or a few chapters a week for 3 to 8 months while sometimes referring back to topics already covered. Besides, learning is more effective if done over a longer period. Your learning will be enhanced if you put some of the techniques into practice in your everyday career; many apply to any professional or management work. You may need to adapt them to your environment, but that is part of the learning. If more than one of you do this concurrently, you could hold regular discussions, leading to higher motivation and better understanding.

34.4 Facilitating an Advanced Business Project Management Program

'Advanced' does not mean complex. It just means that you would cover aspects that even experienced PMs and management might not be familiar with. I have already used much of the chapter content, in a business school environment, for both classroom and fully online programs.

For online, I distinguish between synchronous (SYNC) and asynchronous (ASYNC) activities. For SYNC, the class is online at the same time and collaborates with the facilitator and with each other, using video conferencing tools. For ASYNC, the participant can download all material and do everything in their own time and in their own environment. Both have pros and cons. Generally, the best results are obtained with a combination of SYNC and ASYNC learning, or with classroom interaction supported by ASYNC preparation.

No doubt, you will have your own teaching techniques and preferences, so what follows are just some suggestions as to how the book might be used.

- The chapter content could be used to create slides (referencing the source) which supports your teaching. In my experience, discussion sessions around the slides produce better learning than a 'one-way' lecture.
- Similarly, the chapter content could be used as input to videos or audios for ASYNC learning (referencing the source). I have used slides that participants watch while they listen to audios, to good effect. They would download the slides and audios and do them as preparation (ASYNC), possibly going through new concepts more than once. However, because such preparation is one way, each module would be supplemented with a class discussion session held online (SYNC) or in the classroom. In class sessions, participants could ask questions or put forward ideas. Should the discussion peter out, you could use the right-hand column of Table 34.1 to pose questions or ask for explanations.
- Where each participant has a copy of this book, chapters can be assigned for pre-reading. Participants could be asked to check their understanding via quizzes, and to read the cases in advance while doing preliminary analysis on them. Once again, the class sessions could be in the classroom or online via video conference. The chapter content could be discussed using the questions in Table 34.1. The cases would be done in syndicates because most conference tools allow for 'breakout rooms'. Although it seldom happens, it will not matter if some participants have already glanced at 'possible' answers to the cases; the discussion should always raise new ideas.

Here are some related thoughts: Some chapters are best covered in several sessions, depending on the participants. Examples are Chapters 9 on scheduling and 12 on progress and cost tracking, each of which has a number of cases that are exercises. In such situations, where an exercise involves scheduling or calculations, it is best done individually. Each participant should do the exercise beforehand and be prepared to share how they approached it or any difficulties experienced in their syndicate groups. Nevertheless, syndicates often find innovative ways of doing scheduling or calculations as a group, while updating shared screens. For cases where a situation is discussed, I suggest that one syndicate member takes notes and is prepared to share them when the class reconvenes. This should be done by rotation so that everyone gets the opportunity.

34.5 In Conclusion

Much of what is mentioned above you probably already know. Moreover, you will have your own preferred approach to learning or teaching. Whatever the case, I hope that what is covered in the book will be of value in your professional career.

Chapter 35

Quizzes and Answers

Answers to quizzes are at the end of the chapter on page 364.

Quiz for Chapter 5 on Engaging with Stakeholders

Q1	Which of the following are probably NOT a stakeholder of this project? The person or group:
A	is actively involved in the project as part of the team or via a business relationship.
B	has interests that are affected by the execution or outcome of the project.
C	works in the same organization as the sponsor but is unaware of the project.
D	influences people that supply key resources to the project and people that will benefit from the project's outcome.
Q2	Which of the following lists of people or groups are, most likely, all project stakeholders?
A	The project sponsor; the business partners that supply critical skills; government agencies that expect reports produced by the project.
B	Project teams that work in the same office building; contract project staff; corporate finance treasury staff.
C	Functional managers that provide part-time resources; office cleaning staff; the organization's intranet team.
D	The customers of the organization that owns the project; the building security guards; the steering committee.
Q3	Three of the following strategies for engaging with stakeholders are valid. Which is INVALID?
A	Stakeholders that have considerable power or influence and that have high interest in the project's outcome should be managed closely.
B	Groups of stakeholders that have little power and interest in the project should be monitored, but without spending unnecessary effort.

DOI: 10.1201/9781003321101-39

C	Powerful and influential stakeholders that show no interest in the project should be ignored because any information would irritate them.
D	Lower-level stakeholders that are very affected by the outcome of the project should be kept well informed on relevant aspects of the project.
Q4	Which of the following would probably NOT be part of a stakeholder register?
A	The name of the person or group, and how they might affect the project, positively or negatively.
B	A description of the needs and expectations of the person or group.
C	The strategy for engaging with the stakeholder to gain support and reduce risk.
D	The names of the family members of each stakeholder and their birthdays.
Q5	Three of the following are valid strategies for dealing with stakeholders. Which is INVALID?
A	Have the project manager prioritize engagement with the stakeholders.
B	Listen to and discuss stakeholder concerns. Seek solutions before they become major issues.
C	Being open and honest and giving any adverse news in good time.
D	Inform all stakeholders that any grievances that they might have should be put in writing and sent to the sponsor.

Quiz for Chapter 6 on Project Definition

Q1	Which of the following are NOT true for a PDD (project definition document)?
A	Stakeholder input may come from discussion or from a PDW (project definition workshop).
B	On completion, the PDD should align with the business case.
C	A purpose of the PDD is to ensure that stakeholders have a common understanding of what will be delivered.
D	The PDD consists of multiple documents, each of which needs sign-off from key stakeholders.
Q2	The PDD generally includes, amongst other things:
A	An executive summary, business goals, scope and exclusions, milestones, costs, and risks
B	The project scope, a detailed specification of deliverables with suitable technical detail, roles, and responsibilities.
C	The business goals, critical success factors which specify what the project must deliver, assumptions and risks.
D	An executive summary, a detailed schedule, responsibilities for each activity, a diagram where appropriate.

Q3	Which of the following are NOT true of a business case?
A	The business case justifies why we should proceed with a project.
B	It is frozen and archived after the project is approved by key stakeholders.
C	It is owned by the project sponsor who may also be the business owner.
D	It provides useful input to the PDD and to subsequent planning.
Q4	After the PDD has been approved which of the following statements is FALSE?
A	Planning continues with many of the PDD's elements feeding into separate documents which are updated as the project unfolds.
B	As the project progresses, the PDD continues to be updated in parallel with tracking documents like the schedule.
C	The PDD's risks are used to start the project's risk register and its issues go onto the issues log.
D	The scope from the PDD is expanded and usually becomes input to an activities schedule.
Q5	When planning a project it helps to know which of scope/quality, time, and cost are constrained, to be enhanced, or to be accepted. Choose the INCORRECT statement from the following:
A	If budget is limited, then cost is 'constrained'.
B	If there are desired additional features that will be approved if time and cost permit, then scope is 'enhanced'.
C	When organizing a business conference, time is 'accepted' because cost is usually to be 'enhanced'.
D	For a fixed-price contract, scope needs to be clearly defined and is 'constrained'.

Quiz for Chapter 7 on Scope Definition

Q1	Which of the following is NOT an important aspect of scope planning?
A	Getting clarity on what work is included in this project and what is excluded.
B	Engaging with potential suppliers to find out what skills they might contribute.
C	Documenting the expected deliverables and referring to any available specifications.
D	Checking for understanding with stakeholders and agreeing the requirements.
Q2	Which of the following statements, relating to scope, is INCORRECT?
A	Scope can refer to the work required to produce deliverables, but it can also refer to characteristics of the deliverables themselves.
B	A work breakdown structure is a formalization of the project work. If work is not in the WBS then it is not part of the project.

C	Defining scope is not important because if we have overlooked anything, it can be added later through the change control process.
D	During execution the 'change control' process allows scope changes to be managed, while validation of the deliverables is needed to confirm that they are of acceptable quality.
Q3	Which of the following is NOT a valid method for collecting project requirements?
A	Getting all the requirements directly from your project team members because they should know what the business stakeholders want.
B	Holding facilitated workshops or focus groups with business stakeholders, aimed at uncovering and documenting their requirements.
C	Holding interviews with business stakeholders, and possibly sending out a requirements survey if such stakeholders are geographically distributed.
D	Observing the existing processes which relate to the objectives of the project.
Q4	Which of the following statements relating to the WBS is NOT TRUE?
A	The work packages are at the lowest level in the WBS (work breakdown structure).
B	The 100% rule says that exclusions should be included in the WBS.
C	Each work package should produce a deliverable and should be assignable to a group or individual.
D	An internal work package produces a deliverable that is used within the project, while an external one might be delivered to the customer.
Q5	Only one of the following statements is correct. Which one?
A	Before moving activities to the schedule, the PM always creates a WBS in a hierarchical format because it's quick and flexible.
B	Control components of the WBS are always at the lowest level so that costs can be analyzed in detail.
C	Rolling wave planning, or 'progressive elaboration', allows planning packages to be better defined closer to their time of execution.
D	Whether you are managing a small business project or a $100 million engineering project, a WBS dictionary must be maintained throughout the project.

Quiz for Chapter 8 on Estimating

Q1	Which of the following is **NOT** a reason why estimates are essential?
A	Estimates are used in a business case to justify proceeding with the project.
B	Without time and cost estimates we do not have anything to track progress against.
C	Estimates give the opportunity to add 'fat' and get approval for more money and time.
D	Estimates of activity durations are used for scheduling the project.

Q2	Choose the valid statement:
A	A bottom-up estimate requires a work breakdown structure, and must therefore be done before the project starts.
B	A top-down estimate involves estimating each activity in the project and summing the costs to get a cost for the entire project.
C	A top-down estimate is often done by analogous estimating – comparing this project to one that was completed recently.
D	A bottom-up estimate is done by using parametric modeling.
Q3	Which of the following is true of an Order of Magnitude (OM) estimate? Note that it is sometimes also called a Rough Order of Magnitude (ROM) estimate.
A	The OM estimate should indicate the range of the estimate which will generally be plus or minus 5%.
B	An OM cost estimate should give as precise an answer as possible, e.g. $1 386 401-36, because executives require accuracy.
C	One will never be asked to explain how an OM estimate was arrived at.
D	On OM estimate is often done before the project starts using limited information. It gives a rounded figure with a range.
Q4	Which statement relating to validity and reliability of an estimate is most likely to be **FALSE**?
A	For IT projects it is relatively easy to provide a reliable estimate of time and cost because the business people know what they want.
B	The longer the project, the more difficult it is to provide a reliable estimate because many assumptions change over time.
C	If the organization has done similar projects before and has kept records, the estimate for a project is more likely to be valid and reliable.
D	If the people making the estimate have experience and if the people doing the project are skilled, estimates are more likely to be reliable.
Q5	Which statement relating to estimating is **FALSE**?
A	A common cause of invalid estimates is that important scope items have been overlooked.
B	Analogous estimating is usually done by experienced people using historical project records.
C	A parametric estimating model is best applied where no similar project has been done before.
D	Parametric estimating models need to be adjusted over time, as the assumptions on which they are based, change.

Quiz for Chapter 9 on Project Scheduling

Q1	The project manager decides that, as soon as activity A is complete, activity B can start. Which of the following is correct?
A	A is the predecessor of B and the relationship is FS (finish-start), so B depends on A.
B	B is the predecessor of A and the relationship is FS (finish-start), so B depends on A.
C	A is the predecessor of B and the relationship is SS (start-start), so B depends on A.
D	A is the predecessor of B and the relationship is SS (start-start), so A depends on B.
Q2	Three of the following statements are true. Which one is FALSE? Note that Float and Slack mean the same thing.
A	The critical path is the chain of activities where each activity has zero slack.
B	If an activity has a float of 2 days, the activity can be ignored by the project manager because it is not on the critical path.
C	If there is any delay in the start of a critical path activity, or if a critical path activity takes longer than planned, the target date is less likely to be met.
D	A forward pass through a network of activities indicates the earliest end date. A backward pass determines the float on each activity, and hence the critical path.
Q3	The project manager decides that, 5 project days after activity A starts, activity B can start. Which of the following is correct?
A	Activity A depends on activity B. There is a SS (start-start) relationship, with a lag of 5 days.
B	Activity B depends on activity A. There is a SS (start-start) relationship, with a lead of 5 days.
C	Activity B depends on activity A. There is an FS (finish-start) relationship, with a lag of 5 days.
D	Activity B depends on activity A. There is a SS (start-start) relationship, with a lag of 5 days.
Q4	Which of the following tells why, for normal projects, Gantt (bar) charts are more practical than Precedence charts?
A	With a Gantt chart, one can see at a glance, the expected status of several activities, on a particular day.
B	With a Gantt chart, one can fit more activities onto a page, and it is easy to show progress on any activity.
C	Gantt charts showing current activities can usually be imported into a single PowerPoint slide for distribution to stakeholders who don't have special software.
D	All of the above.
Q5	Three of the following statements about practical scheduling are true. Which one is FALSE?
A	Setting up the schedule in a scheduling tool is relatively quick if one works from the WBS (work breakdown structure).

B	Not having too many levels in the WBS has the advantage that there are fewer summary tasks and that less horizontal space is used by indenting activity descriptions.
C	Once the WBS is finalized, it dictates the schedule and a work package may never result in more than one activity (or task).
D	Avoiding fixed start dates for activities means that if anything (like a duration or dependency) changes, subsequent activities are rescheduled automatically.
Q6	Three of the following statements, about scheduling business projects, are true. Which one is FALSE?
A	The complexity of many business projects means that a schedule would be too cluttered if one attempted to insert the many subtle dependencies.
B	The planned duration of an activity cannot be adjusted when the skill level of the resources (people that do the work) becomes known.
C	Many dependencies between activities are not clear cut and the project manager needs to use discretion, possibly using leads and lags.
D	For a business project, changes in how a deliverable will be produced may result in activities being added or changed during execution.
Q7	Which of the following statements about applying resources to the schedule for a typical business project, is true?
A	An unconstrained schedule considers dependencies but assumes unlimited resources. When applying the limited resources available, the resulting schedule almost always takes longer.
B	Software that can automatically smooth resource usage and optimize your schedule, is easy to use because people from the same discipline are interchangeable.
C	If the schedule was drawn up assuming that one person would do an activity, then applying four people will usually get it done in a quarter of the time.
D	When assigning resources to activities, the most experienced people should work on activities with slack (float), so the inexperienced people can work on critical activities.
Q8	Three of the following statements, about compressing a schedule, are true. Which one is FALSE?
A	Three approaches to compressing a schedule are Fast Tracking, Crashing and De-scoping.
B	Insisting on people meeting tight deadlines and getting them to work overtime (a form of crashing) always gets the project done on time.
C	Fast Tracking means doing activities in parallel that would normally done one after the other. It requires sufficient resources and often has some risk.
D	De-scoping means critically examining remaining activities, and getting sponsor approval to defer selected activities or even not do them at all.

Quiz for Chapter 10 on Managing Project Quality

Q1	The project is to develop a new motor car accessory. Who is responsible for the quality of the developed product?
A	The project sponsor
B	The Quality Assurance department
C	The marketing department and project team
D	The project manager
Q2	Which of the following is NOT an accepted description of quality?
A	Quality involves meeting customer expectations of the project's outcome.
B	Quality means providing features that the user asks for, even if they are not in the specification.
C	Quality means conforming to documented requirements or specifications
D	Quality means that the project output must meet the intended purpose.
Q3	The total cost of quality for a project is:
A	The cost of conformance plus the cost of non-conformance.
B	The cost of rework when inspection finds defects plus the financial impact of late payments.
C	The cost of non-conformance minus the cost of conformance.
D	The cost of quality planning plus the charges from the Quality Assurance department.
Q4	Three of the following statements are true. Which one is FALSE?
A	The specification for deliverables is the only thing we need to consider to produce quality output.
B	Even if there is a specification, the expectations of stakeholders, that will benefit from the output, should be understood.
C	If user stakeholders raise an essential requirement that is not in the specifications, then negotiations on time and costs will be needed.
D	Sound design and processes are usually more important in achieving quality, than inspection of output.
Q5	The Pareto principle states that:
A	Quality is free, because the more you spend on quality, the lower the overall cost.
B	Project processes need to be documented, communicated, kept up-to-date, and put into practice.
C	Periodic project health checks help the project manager to run a quality project.
D	80% of quality problems result from 20% of the causes.

Quiz for Chapter 11 on Managing Project Risk

Q1	Which statement best describes a project risk?
A	A project risk is an uncertain event or condition that if it occurs has a negative (or positive) effect on the project's objectives.
B	A project risk and a project issue are much the same thing and something always needs to be done about it.
C	A project risk is the sum of the risk of doing business, involving opportunities for profit or loss, and the risk that can be transferred to another party.
D	A project risk is the basic reason for undertaking the project because without risks there can be no reward.
Q2	Which of the following are all project risk management processes (not necessarily in sequence)
A	Plan risk management; define the project scope; perform quantitative risk analysis; identify procurement risks.
B	Identify risks or opportunities; perform qualitative risk analysis; plan risk responses; review risks during execution.
C	Identify opportunities for risk events; plan risk management; control risks so that they cannot happen; create risk checklist.
D	Create risk checklist; identify opportunities for scope; define project scope; implement risk responses.
Q3	Three of the following statements about a Risk Register are true. Which one is FALSE?
A	A risk register has a short description of each risk which may state the current situation, the risk event that could occur, and the consequences of the event.
B	A risk register has a way of scoring or prioritizing the seriousness of the risk, often based on the probability of occurrence and the impact if the risk happens.
C	A risk register should have one or more planned response actions for each risk (unless the strategy is to accept the risk).
D	A risk register is a list drawn up after the project, to indicate all the problems that affected the project, and the actions that were taken.
Q4	If we are doing qualitative risk analysis on a scale of 1 (low) to 10 (high). For a particular risk, the probability is rated at 2 and the impact at 5. Which statement below is most valid?
A	The risk priority is 5, being the higher of the impact and the probability figures. So this risk can be ignored.
B	The risk priority, the probability multiplied by the impact would be 10, which means that the project should be stopped because it is not viable.
C	The risk priority is the impact minus the probability, giving a score of 3 which means that we should change our plans to avoid the risk altogether.
D	The risk priority, the probability multiplied by the impact would be 10, which means that some response action should be considered.

Q5	Three important schedule activities require the same specialist skill of which there is a shortage in our organization. We might not be able to get the skill when needed. Several companies offer services related to the skill. Which of the following is the likely response strategy?
A	Avoid
B	Transfer
C	Mitigate
D	Accept

Quiz for Chapter 12 on Progress and Cost Tracking

Q1	Three of the following statements, on cost management, are correct. Which one is FALSE?
A	A sunk cost is money that has already been spent and cannot be recovered. It should play no further role in project decision making.
B	For a project done for a fixed price, once the cost has been estimated, allowing contingency for risk, the price will depend on things like competitive pressures and the availability of resources.
C	The company offers project management services. The cost of its offices and its senior management would be a variable, direct cost to each project.
D	If our project shows a negative cost variance, it means that we have spent more money than we planned to, for the work done.
Q2	Our project has a total budget of $2 million, and the planned value (control figure) for end June is $875 000. Our project accounts indicate that our actual costs at end June are $870 000. Which of the following statements is most valid?
A	We have a positive variance of $5 000, so we can report to the sponsor that the project is on track.
B	There is still $1.13 million left in the budget, so the project manager can be confident of finishing on-time and within budget.
C	Because we have incurred costs of $870 000, we can assume that the earned value (the value of work done) is $870 000.
D	Without knowing what has been achieved, we can draw no meaningful conclusion from these numbers.
Q3	The project is planned to finish mid next year. On 28 September, PV (planned value) is $118 000, EV (earned value) is estimated at $120 000, and the adjusted AC (actual cost) is $131 000. Which statement is most correct on 28 September?
A	The schedule variance is +$2 000 and the cost variance is –$11 000. So the project is behind schedule but has spent less than planned for the work done.
B	The schedule variance is –$2 000 and the cost variance is +$11 000. So the project is behind schedule but has spent less than planned for the work done.

C	The SPI (schedule performance index) = 1.02 and the CPI (cost performance index) is 0.92, so we are ahead of schedule, but overspent for the work done.
D	The SPI (schedule performance index) of 0.98 indicates that the project is behind schedule, while the CPI (cost performance index) of 1.09 indicates that we are underspent for the work completed.
Q4	The total project budget, which is scheduled for completion end June next year, is $180 000. On 28 September, the EV (earned value) is estimated at $120 000, and the adjusted AC (actual cost) is $131 000. Which cost estimate at completion is most likely to be correct?
A	$165 000
B	$180 000
C	$197 000
D	The cost at completion cannot be estimated from the available information.
Q5	Three of the following statements on EVM (earned value management), are correct. Which one is FALSE?
A	When using EVM, if our SPI (schedule performance index) is 1 or above, then we can ignore the critical path because we are on track from a schedule point of view.
B	It is easiest to apply EVM on projects where the scope is well understood up-front, and can be reliably estimated. It is more difficult where the scope only becomes known as the project progresses.
C	EVM is very time-consuming when done at the activity level for a business project where there are regular changes.
D	The earned value, at a particular date, is usually determined by the project manager based on the estimated percentage completion and planned value of each work package or activity.
Q6	Three of the following statements on PPTR (project progress tracker), are correct. Which one is FALSE?
A	PPTR works with high-level packages, and each is assigned a points value by the project manager that reflects its size and importance.
B	PPTR does not allow for changes because the project manager cannot add a high-level package or change the points assigned to a package.
C	Target percentage-complete figures, for the project or major subproject, are assigned by the project manager for each reporting date. These are compared with percentages derived from the actual points achieved, to track progress at a reporting date.
D	Costs are tracked outside of the PPTR spreadsheet, but can be brought into PPTR to calculate the CPI or cost variance.

Quiz for Chapter 13 on Teams and Organization

Q1	Which best describes a team? A team is …
A	A group of people who are closely located in an office space and who report in to the same manager.
B	A group of people, who all have similar skills, and are assigned full- or part-time to different projects by their manager.
C	A small group, with complementary skills, who hold themselves mutually accountable to achieve a common purpose.
D	A group of over ten people, with diverse backgrounds, who are committed to achieving individual objectives set by their manager.
Q2	Three of the following help team building. Which one does NOT directly contribute to team building?
A	Plan and communicate team member roles and responsibilities.
B	Meet, one-on-one, with business stakeholders to discuss requirements.
C	Arrange for the project sponsor to engage with the team members as a group.
D	Involve team members in planning and problem-solving sessions.
Q3	Which of the following are all characteristics of a high-performance team?
A	Shared leadership, building on differences, having drinks at lunch time daily, open communication.
B	Open communication, trust and mutual respect, continuous learning, a sense of purpose.
C	Effective working procedures, maximizing use of sick-leave, flexibility and adaptability, shared leadership.
D	Continuous learning, attending outside seminars, discussing politics in management, open communication.
Q4	Which of the following is a self-oriented behavior and might be undesirable in a team environment?
A	Asserting personal dominance on the group and interrupting the contribution of others.
B	Sensing the mood of the team and reflecting it back for discussion while sharing their own feelings.
C	Offering facts and new ideas relating to the solution of team problems.
D	Establishing mutually acceptable ways of interacting and communicating within the team.
Q5	Three of the following statements, about project structures, are valid. Which is INVALID?
A	The matrix project structure gives considerable flexibility because scarce skills can be used on several projects concurrently.
B	With a projectized structure, toward the end of a project, there may be disruption and morale problems due to staff having to move to follow-on work.

C	In a matrix project, the 'two boss' syndrome refers to the situation where a team member's line manager and the project manager have different priorities.
D	With a matrix structure, it is easy to share skilled resources and each project manager gets the required contribution when they need it.
Q6	Which of the following describes only people-management responsibilities of the project manager?
A	Allowing team members to resolve their own differences; scope management; doing regular appraisals; socializing with other project managers.
B	Counseling on personal problems that affect the project; monitoring project quality; arranging drinks with stakeholders; regular reporting.
C	Listening to team members; coaching inexperienced staff; having regular career discussions; setting objectives related to the project.
D	Staying close to the sponsor; arranging for mentors for certain team members; monitoring the schedule in meetings; resolving issues.
Q7	Which of the following statements, about the project manager's use of power, is most likely to be true?
A	A project manager with a 'facilitating' style will rely almost entirely on reward power.
B	A project manager with a 'facilitating' style tends to use expert, referent, and persuasive power.
C	A project manager with a 'managing' style will rely on their formal power because they lack expert skills.
D	A project manager with a 'managing' style will coerce their staff far more than they will reward them.
Q8	Which of the following are all regarded as motivating factors as opposed to hygiene factors?
A	Challenging work that is recognized by management; working with an excellent team; opportunities to develop new skills.
B	Earning a high salary; working with a team of fun people; management who are aware of their role on the project.
C	Comfortable office and nearby refreshments; work that is not demanding; having a good relationship with management.
D	Being the best performer in the team; excellent employee benefits; the opportunity to take time off when needed.

Quiz for Chapter 14 on Managing Project Issues

Q1	Three of the following statements, about project issues, are true. Which one is FALSE?
A	A project issue and a project risk are the same thing as they both cause extra work for the project manager.
B	An issue is a problem that, if not resolved, threatens the project's success.

C	An issue might be within the project manager's control, but it might also need support from the sponsor or steering committee.
D	Issues often relate to other project management disciplines. For example, resolving an issue might require approval of a change request.
Q2	Three of the following statements, about raising and documenting project issues, are valid. Which one is INVALID?
A	An issues log, with one line per issue, including the issue number and title, gives a quick view on the status of issues at project level.
B	It is unnecessary to document issues because the project manager will remember all problems and ensure that they are resolved.
C	An issue form or record, allows for a more detailed description of the issue as well as alternative approaches to resolving it.
D	The issue form whose format is flexible is usually one page, but could be many pages. It links to the issues log via the issue number.
Q3	After documenting the issue, which of the following best gives some of the steps to be taken in resolving a typical issue?
A	Decide whom to involve; meet to discuss the issue; agree and track resulting actions; upon resolution, close the issue with comments.
B	Phone the sponsor; convene a steering committee meeting; list alternatives; get sponsor to decide on the resolution.
C	Add the issue to the risk register; hope that the issue will disappear; close the issue in the issues log; mention the issue in the next project report.
D	Create a new project to deal with the issue; close the issue because it is no longer part of the initial project; report the avoidance action.
Q4	Which of the following are NOT a benefit of effective issues management?
A	By documenting each important issue, no serious problem will be overlooked.
B	Managing issues helps the project manager to stay informed on important project matters.
C	Considering and documenting alternatives makes it less likely that the best solution will only surface later.
D	Customers and the sponsor do not worry about issues, because they never get to know about them.
Q5	Three of the following statements are generally valid. Which one is probably INVALID?
A	Unexpected crises are more likely to happen if issues management is not being practiced.
B	A risk event that happens despite risk response actions usually causes an issue that would be addressed via the issues management process.
C	Where a critical project is hampered by many issues, a daily meeting with senior stakeholders contributes to resolving them in time.
D	Many issues must be dealt with during planning, but after execution has started, it is rare for a project issue to arise.

Quiz for Chapter 15 on Project Change Control

Q1	Three of the following statements are true. Which one is FALSE?
A	Project change control, or simply 'change control' is mainly about scope changes but can also apply to schedule and budget.
B	OCM (organizational change management) is about preparing stakeholders, inside and outside the organization, for changes brought about by projects.
C	Project change control is straightforward and best done informally. There is no need for documentation because changes benefit the stakeholders.
D	For certain projects, OCM activities form an important part of the project's scope and are sometimes overlooked during planning.
Q2	Which of the following would NOT be regarded as a change that needs change control?
A	A modification to the detailed specification for a deliverable.
B	The decision that our approach to a certain activity needs to change, even if the output remains the same.
C	A small additional feature that your team assures you will not incur any additional time or cost.
D	The sponsor indicating that he is prepared to move the deadline date provided that you justify the reasons.
Q3	Which of the following are LEAST LIKELY to help you manage scope creep?
A	Showing the attitude that all stakeholder needs must be met to keep them satisfied.
B	Briefing the team on the dangers of scope creep and on the process to follow if the business users ask for changes.
C	Documenting every change whether it gets approved or not.
D	Defining the scope and deliverables as thoroughly as possible.
Q4	For a customer survey project, your specialist changed some of the survey questions after the customer had approved the questionnaire and then distributed the survey. Which of the following is LEAST LIKELY to happen?
A	The customer requests that you repeat the approved survey at your own cost.
B	The customer regards this as unprofessional and showing a lack of control.
C	The survey results do not address exactly what the customer wanted to investigate.
D	The customer agrees to pay for the extra hours your specialist spent changing the survey.
Q5	A senior business stakeholder indicates that they need something additional that was not specified or agreed. The following are steps to deal with this change request. Which gives the most likely sequence? (a change request form and a change record are similar).
A	Get full details of the requirement; seek sponsor approval; add an entry to the change log; complete the change request form.
B	Get full details of the requirement; add an entry to the change log; complete the change request form; seek sponsor approval.

C	Complete the change request form; get full details of the requirement; seek sponsor approval; add an entry to the change log.
D	Seek sponsor approval; get full details of the requirement; add an entry to the change log; complete the change request form.

Quiz for Chapter 16 on Project Monitoring, Control, and Communication

Q1	Three of the following statements, on project meetings, are valid. Which one is INVALID?
A	Project tracking meetings should be regular and preferably on the same day of the week and at the same time.
B	In a tracking meeting, some of the purposes are to update the schedule, follow up on action items, and keep the team informed.
C	If tracking meetings start a bit late it does not matter, because there will always be enough time to cover important matters.
D	When a concern or issue is raised, it should be discussed briefly and then minuted as an action after deciding who should be involved.
Q2	Three of the following statements on meeting minutes are valid. Which one is INVALID?
A	Items on the minutes should be either for information or for action where a due date and the name of the responsible person are recorded.
B	The person taking the minutes does not need to understand the project but must record everything that was said in the meeting.
C	Meeting minutes and who attended, form vital project records. Only incomplete action items are carried forward, with the rest being archived.
D	Minutes should be written up and distributed as soon as possible after the meeting so that people are notified of action items promptly.
Q3	Three of the following statements on things that need to happen between meetings are valid. Which one is INVALID?
A	Walking about and discussing project matters with the team and other stakeholders sometimes brings up risks and issues in good time.
B	When interacting with the team between meetings, the project manager must draw a balance between neglecting people and disturbing them too often.
C	Where there are dependencies on other groups, the project manager should check in good time that the dependency will be met.
D	If the project manager finds a team member that is not sure what to do next, it is clear that the person is not competent to do the job.

Q4	Three of the following statements on maintaining a productive environment are valid. Which one is INVALID?
A	All negotiations with stakeholders should be by email, and the rest of the team should be copied to keep everyone informed.
B	The project manager should encourage a balance between sociability and too much noise or disruption in the workplace
C	Ensuring that equipment is working properly and that the right software is available, supports productivity.
D	The project manager should delegate most things but sometimes needs to get something done themselves – like getting Maintenance to fix flickering lights.
Q5	Three of the following are effective approaches for the project manager to take when communicating with stakeholders on important matters. Which is NOT an effective approach?
A	Maintaining eye contact, and having a body position and tone of voice that shows interest.
B	Listening to the speaker and at suitable intervals summarising the understanding of what the speaker has said.
C	Asking relevant questions, and acknowledging the speaker's feelings when sensitive issues arise.
D	Making it very clear that you have limited time, and that anything said must be short and to the point.
Q6	Three of the following statements about project reporting are valid. Which one is INVALID?
A	Senior stakeholders have limited time, so for most projects a report that is more than one page is unlikely to be read.
B	Reports should only be sent to stakeholders when the project is going well. If there are problems they should not be in writing.
C	In a larger organization, a standard report format makes it easier for stakeholders to find relevant information.
D	Because the situation can change quickly on business projects, reports should usually go out weekly or fortnightly (every 2 weeks).
Q7	Where a business project report is sent fortnightly, which of the following best gives some of the main items to cover?
A	Main events of the past fortnight; focus items for the weeks ahead; the main issues and risks; a RAG indicator; relevant progress data.
B	The RAG indicator; the achievements on the project from inception; the list of closed issues; planned and earned values with actual costs.
C	Focus items from the past month; list of project minutes issued; list of change requests from stakeholders; Costs to date.
D	The names of the project manager and team; the progress achieved in the past fortnight; a green RAG indicator; the project budget.

Q8	Which of the following statements, about the RAG (red, amber, green) indicator, is valid?
A	A red RAG indicates that there are some major problems, but the project manager has them under control, and schedule or cost overruns are unlikely.
B	An amber RAG indicates that the project is on track. The project manager has the few minor problems under control.
C	A red RAG indicates that there are serious problems that are beyond the control of the project manager or that a critical target is likely to be missed.
D	A green RAG indicates that the sponsor needs to engage with the project manager to get a first-hand account of some serious problems.

Quiz for Chapter 17 on Governance of a Project

Q1	Three of the following statements on project governance are valid. Which one is INVALID?
A	Without governance, when things go wrong there is little support available and many things are beyond the project manager's control.
B	Project governance is something that is done at top management level and does not involve the project manager.
C	Governance is a set of principles and processes to guide and improve the management of projects.
D	Governance is like the organization wrapped around the project. The project interacts with the organization in various ways.
Q2	Which of the following lists the people or groups that are most likely to be involved in the governance of a project?
A	Subcontractors to the project; the PMO (project management office); the office of the CEO.
B	The PMO; subcontractors to the project; the sales force; the project team.
C	The project team; the business users; the PMO; the organization's supply chain.
D	The project sponsor; the steering committee; the project manager; portfolio management.
Q3	Three of the following statements on roles in the steering committee (or project board) are valid. Which one is INVALID?
A	If a steering committee has been set up, it is usually chaired by the sponsor or business owner, sometimes referred to as 'the executive'.
B	On a steering committee, the senior business person represents the business users while the senior supplier is involved in providing resources – usually people.
C	The project manager has no role on the steering committee because its members are fully informed via project reports.
D	The same person might play more than one role. For example, the sponsor might also play their role of the senior business person.

Q4	The following are some of the project lifetime phases in which the sponsor is typically involved. Which gives the correct sequence?
A	Project selection; project planning; project closeout; assessment of benefits achieved.
B	Project start-up (or initiation); assessment of benefits achieved; project closeout; project execution.
C	Project start-up; project proposal; project execution; project planning.
D	Assessment of benefits achieved; project selection; project closeout; project planning.
Q5	Which of the following statements about the project sponsor is most valid?
A	The main role of the project sponsor is to provide funding for the project, which usually comes from the sponsor's own budget.
B	The sponsor should expect the project manager to take whatever decisions are needed and to confirm when the project is complete.
C	The sponsor does not need to have an interest in the project's outcome, but must be at a high level in the organization.
D	The project sponsor is accountable for project's success but delegates the running of the project to the project manager, while providing support.
Q6	Three of the following statements, about Gate Reviews, are valid. Which one is INVALID?
A	A person, possibly from the PMO, would gain valuable insights, from a broad range of projects, while facilitating gate reviews.
B	A gate review at the end of planning is particularly valuable as many assumptions used in the business case may have changed.
C	After gate reviews, which consider the updated business case, a decision may be taken to proceed with or to stop, the project.
D	Gate reviews are a cumbersome process because each review might take many days and involve most of the project team.

Quiz for Chapter 18 on Closing the Project

Q1	Three of the statements below, regarding project termination scenarios are true. Which one is FALSE?
A	Normal project closure occurs after project objectives are met and the scope is substantially complete.
B	When a project's business case is no longer valid, the project might be terminated prematurely.
C	Some projects are terminated or placed on hold if higher priority projects are initiated that require the same resources.
D	Run-away or perpetual projects are of such great value to the organization that they should not be terminated.

Q2	Three of the statements below, regarding closeout considerations are true. Which one is FALSE?
A	Project completion depends entirely on the deliverables being ready, so project closeout requires no effort.
B	How closeout is done reflects on the professionalism of the project manager and may leave a lasting impression on stakeholders.
C	Closeout activities should be considered during project planning, and some start before the deliverables are complete.
D	Budget should be planned for closeout activities, for example, the handover of documentation.
Q3	In which of the following lists do all activities relate to financial closure of a project?
A	Finalize cost tracking; check that all timesheets are submitted; check supplier invoices and authorize payments.
B	Give bonuses to stakeholders; plan people moves considering their hourly rates; redeploy equipment used.
C	Complete timesheets for the team; archive project reports; produce the closeout report indicating scope changes.
D	Do the initial budget to request funding; report on the cost status regularly; highlight cost implications of scope changes.
Q4	Three of the statements below, regarding the project completion or closeout report, are true. Which one is FALSE?
A	Considering the initial project objectives, the degree to which each was achieved should be stated.
B	Approved project changes should be summarised as well as the main risks and issues that impacted the project.
C	A section of the report should contain all the project reports, from initiation, to give a complete project history.
D	Possible future activities should be listed for consideration, some of which might be change requests that were deferred.
Q5	In which of the following lists do all activities relate to project closeout?
A	Resolve open issues; get contracts signed with any suppliers; monitor ongoing execution taking care of quality.
B	Schedule a post-project review; check with the sponsor for agreement on closeout status; discuss and finalize lessons learned.
C	Hold a project definition workshop with stakeholders; arrange for part-time team members to return to their managers; thank the sponsor.
D	Publicize the project on the internet; produce fortnightly project reports; evaluate the business stakeholders.

Quiz for Chapter 21 on Project Selection – Financial and Non-financial Criteria

Q1	Three of the following statements, on project selection, are true. Which one is FALSE?
A	Projects in an organization typically arise from strategy, from business operations, or from external requirements like legislation.
B	All projects, that are proposed in the organization, need to be discussed, resourced, planned, and executed, without delay.
C	After approval and during planning, if assumptions change significantly, a project's justification should be re-looked at, and the project may even need to be terminated.
D	An aim of portfolio management in an organization is to select the optimum mix of projects. It is seldom possible to do all that are justified.
Q2	Three of the following statements, on financial techniques for project selection, are true. Which one is FALSE?
A	When stating the estimated breakeven point, one must be specific as to whether it is from the start or the end of the project.
B	The project payback period is often estimated using undiscounted amounts. However, there is merit in also considering the longer payback period using discounted amounts.
C	NPV (Net Present Value) discounts future cost or benefit money amounts, to state them in today's terms.
D	IRR (Internal Rate of Return) deals with money flows inside the project, and is of no interest to executives.
Q3	Which statement is true?
A	The estimated project NPV varies with the discounting percentage used, so one should state the percentage with the NPV.
B	One should always state estimates of NPV with as much precision as possible because executives want accuracy.
C	One can only calculate NPV and IRR if one is certain of the cost and benefit figures. Estimates are unacceptable.
D	The longer the payback period, the more likely executives are to support the project, because they are in it for the long term.
Q4	At a discounting rate of 12%, what are the NPVs of $100 000: (i) paid immediately? and (ii) paid after 2 years? (The discounting factors for 12% are after: 1 year: 0.8929; 2 years: 0.7972; 3 years: 0.7118).
A	$89 290 and $79 720
B	$100 000 and $71 180
C	$100 000 and $79 720
D	$71 180 and $100 000

Q5	The costs incurred by a project come earlier than the benefits, so when calculating NPV using estimates, what happens to the NPV as we increase the discounting percentage (or rate)?
A	The NPV will reduce as we increase the discounting rate.
B	The NPV will stay the same because it does not depend on the discounting rate.
C	The NPV will increase as we increase the discounting rate.
D	The NPV will reduce as we increase the discounting rate, but it can never become negative.
Q6	The project estimates show a cost of $2.2 million and returns over 5 years of $4.6 million. The NPV, at the company's minimum return of 22%, is $490 000. Which of the following is the most plausible outcome of a sensitivity analysis?
A	If the actual return is 10% lower at $4.14 million, the NPV drops to $480 000.
B	If the actual return is 10% lower at $4.14 million, the NPV increases to $560 000.
C	If the actual cost is 20% higher at $2.64 million, the NPV drops to $50 000.
D	If the actual cost is 20% higher at $2.64 million, the NPV increases to $620 000.
Q7	When selecting projects, the return on investment usually matters. But, which of the following best states some of the other factors that should be considered?
A	Improved product quality; fit with the corporate culture; opportunities for travel to exciting destinations; risks to the sponsor's career.
B	The project's urgency; the dependency on other projects; the effect on the sponsor's annual bonus; alignment with the core business.
C	Support from the local community; how the press will report the project; the effect on your salary; meets special corporate selection criteria.
D	The level of risk to the organization; alignment with corporate strategy; the availability of resources; longer-term strategic benefits.
Q8	Three of the following statements, regarding the use of scoring models for project selection, are true. Which one is FALSE?
A	Scoring models offer lists of useful considerations that may otherwise be overlooked and should be discussed.
B	Looking at the results of scoring models is useful, but ultimately decisions should be taken by informed stakeholders.
C	Scoring models are the ideal way to compare projects, and their results must be binding because they are unbiased.
D	Two questions which indicate some of the limitations of scoring models are: Is the factor weighting correct? Are the factors relevant to the project at hand?

Quiz for Chapter 22 on Project Procurement, Outsourcing, and Partnershipp

Q1	Identify the INVALID statement.
A	For projects involving a major supplier, the project manager could come from the buyer or supplier organization. There could even be a project manager from both organizations.
B	As a supplier, if you start work before the contract is signed, it is likely to weaken your position in subsequent contract negotiations.
C	As a buyer, allow enough time for the procurement process as certain elements should not be rushed.
D	The Procurement department should be avoided because their procedures will delay getting things done.
Q2	Which of the following are NOT normally part of 'Procurement Planning' process?
A	Involvement of consultants (external or internal) where necessary.
B	Taking 'make or buy' decisions to determine what needs to be procured.
C	Drawing up an initial schedule for procurement activities.
D	Holding bidder conferences to clarify queries about the requirements.
Q3	Which of the following are NOT normally part of the 'Conduct Procurements' process, aimed at getting seller responses to an RFP?
A	Doing screening to avoid involving suppliers that are unsuitable.
B	Practicing change control as laid down in the contract.
C	Sending out the RFP document to selected suppliers.
D	Drawing up or extracting lists of potential sellers.
Q4	Which of the following contract types places the greatest risk on the seller?
A	CPPC – Cost-plus-percentage-cost contract
B	CPIF – Cost-plus-incentive-fee contract
C	FFP – Firm-fixed-price contract
D	Back to back contract
Q5	Which of the following are NOT normally part of the selection and award part of the 'Conduct Procurements' process?
A	Draw up requirements specifications for an RFQ, after analyzing the requirements.
B	Do scoring of an RFP response, on a weighted basis.
C	Finalize contract negotiations with the successful bidder.
D	Invite short-listed bidders to give final presentations to support their RFP response.

Q6	Which factor or factors drive the move to outsourcing?
A	Increased specialization means that an organization cannot keep a full range of skills in-house.
B	Competitive pressure is driving organizations to produce products and services faster, better, and at lower cost.
C	High-bandwidth communication and affordable transport/shipping make outsourcing more attractive.
D	All of the above.
Q7	The following are pros and cons of outsourcing. Which one could be a serious problem for the buying organization at a future time?
A	Outsourcing can make specialized skills and equipment available relatively quickly.
B	Once a part of the operation is outsourced, it can be difficult to bring it back in-house, as the skills may have been lost.
C	Outsourcing gives an organization considerable flexibility, as it need no longer be constrained by lack of the right resources.
D	Outsourcing requires a thorough contract, and sometimes also an SLA (service level agreement).
Q8	Three of the following are things that build trust between two organizations and foster a spirit of partnership? Which one would NOT help toward partnership?
A	As far as possible, risk is shared and both parties benefit if project goals are met.
B	Senior executives in both buyer and seller organizations have worked together before and have a good working relationship.
C	Communication is guarded because the buyer organization wants to protect its intellectual property.
D	Requirements of the outsource company are well documented and discussions are held to check the understanding.

Quiz for Chapter 23 on OCM – Organizational Change Management

Q1	Three of the following statements on change are valid. Which one is INVALID?
A	Organizational change management is about helping the people that are affected, to adapt to the changes brought about by a project.
B	Project change control and organizational change management mean pretty much the same thing because they are both about change.
C	Many types of projects require people to change the way that they do things; without their support, the project is unlikely to be successful.
D	Most people naturally fear and resist change. Therefore, where a project requires people to change, additional activities are needed to communicate and to help people adapt to the change.

Q2	Three of the following statements about organizational change are valid. Which statement is INVALID?
A	Strong sponsorship and executive resolve are vitally important in bringing about major changes that involve or affect staff.
B	First-line managers can be ignored in the change process because it is their staff, rather than them, that need to work differently.
C	Change is unsettling for staff, partly because it takes extra effort while normal work still needs to be attended to.
D	In bringing about major change, open and honest communication is important. Facilitated workshops can enable two-way communication.
Q3	In the Prosci ADKAR model for organizational change, in what sequence must the phases take place?
A	Desire; Awareness; Ability; Knowledge; Reinforcement.
B	Reinforcement; Knowledge; Ability; Awareness; Desire.
C	Awareness; Desire; Knowledge; Ability; Reinforcement.
D	Awareness; Knowledge; Desire; Reinforcement; Ability.
Q4	Three of the following statements about use of the ADKAR approach are valid. Which statement is INVALID?
A	The ADKAR phases often align to project phases. Thus awareness of the need is created after need is established, and reinforcement is done post-implementation.
B	The change facilitator should rate the completeness of each phase out 5, and start by focusing on the first phase in the sequence that scores below 3.
C	Reinforcement from management is needed after people have successfully learned the new way of doing things, lest people slip back into old habits.
D	Even if staff are committed to the change and are busy developing skills on the new way of working, there must be regular briefings to explain the need for the change.
Q5	Which of the following best lists techniques are found to be effective in organizational change management?
A	Briefing of staff by management; facilitated workshops involving affected people; training on new processes; support during implementation from skilled people.
B	Detailed instructions from top management to staff; briefing managers because they must get their staff to comply; training on anger management.
C	Not telling people about changes that will affect them lest they complain; sending newsletters about project progress by email; putting posters on the wall outlining corporate strategy.
D	Doing surveys and keeping the results confidential; lectures after implementation, on why the changes are needed; expecting people to adapt to new processes on their own.

Quiz for Chapter 24 on Contracts for Business Projects

Q1	Three of the following statements about the existence of a contract, are valid. Which one is INVALID?
A	If an offer is accepted subject to minor modifications, there would not be a binding contract as the conditional acceptance would be regarded as a counter-offer.
B	After a contract has been signed, it is easy for one of the parties to declare it null and void by stating in writing that they had not read an important clause.
C	Even if a bid in response to an RFP (request for proposal) is accepted, it would be wise to enter into a signed contract to allow important elements, that were in neither the RFP nor the bid, to be articulated.
D	While a verbal agreement may be binding, it may lack important detail and be difficult to enforce.
Q2	Three of the following statements, about the structure of a contract, are valid. Which one is INVALID?
A	The main, or body, contract covers definitions and clauses that are not expected to change and will apply to most contracted jobs.
B	Supplements, which are sometimes called addenda or annexures, are used to detail specific work and would refer to, and be governed by, a main agreement.
C	A properly signed supplement can override clauses in the main agreement for that supplement.
D	If other documents are referred to in a contract, they can be ignored as they hold no legal status.
Q3	Three of the following statements about contracts are valid. Which one is INVALID?
A	It is important to keep a copy of signed contracts. The project manager needs them: to ensure that obligations are met, for reference in case of disputes, and as a project record.
B	For projects resulting from a contract, there are likely to be delays unless both parties fulfill their responsibilities in agreed timeframes. Therefore, the contract must fully state such responsibilities.
C	When issuing an RFP (request for proposal) the contract will probably be signed with less delay if the draft contract goes with the RFP.
D	Because the contract spells out the obligations of both parties, there is no need for goodwill or cooperation between them.
Q4	A dispute has arisen during execution of a marketing project for a buyer organization. Neither you (the seller) nor the buyer organization wish to go to court. In what sequence would you use ADR (alternative dispute resolution) approaches to try to resolve the dispute?
A	Negotiation; Mediation; Arbitration
B	Litigation; Adjudication; Mediation
C	Negotiation; Arbitration; Mediation
D	Arbitration; Negotiation; Mediation

Q5	Which of the following best expresses the characteristics of a contract that will facilitate sound practices and reduce the likelihood of disputes?
A	Legal wording; other documents referenced where necessary; ADR mandatory; all project knowledge areas included; job responsibilities defined.
B	Short sentences; use of words like 'promptly' to show urgency; legally water-tight wording; everything referenced to the project plan.
C	Plain language, short sentences; no cross-referencing; no words subject to interpretation; project management processes built in; ADR specified.
D	Collaboration between the parties not permitted; regular use of 'satisfactory' to define quality standards; project processes included.

Quiz for Chapter 25 on Project Review

Q1	Which of the following best describes the potential benefits of a project review (whether a review, an audit, a retrospective, or a health check)? A project review ...
A	indicates to the project manager that management see the project as important; ensures that no scope item has been overlooked; prevents project failure.
B	reduces overall project risk; supports adherence to project standards; helps to develop the project manager's skills.
C	develops the project managers through their involvement; keep people in the PMO (project management office) busy; enforces standards.
D	prevents any risks from affecting the project; indicates to the sponsor that the project is priority; shows the project team that they are being watched.
Q2	Which of the following best describes the people that might play a role as reviewers?
A	Quality assurance; the project manager; the business stakeholders; the PMO (project management office).
B	Internal audit; the project sponsor; any other executive that is independent of the project; the procurement manager.
C	The project sponsor; the project manager; a senior project team member; internal audit.
D	Internal audit; quality assurance, the PMO (project management office); an external consultant.
Q3	Which of the following gives the three recommended steps when conducting a major project review (in any sequence)?
A	Initiate the review and checking dates; collect information and analyze it; Produce and submit the review report.
B	Read the project definition document; meet with the sponsor; ask the project manager to interview selected team members.

C	Meet with the project manager; read all project documentation; request the business stakeholders to produce the review report.
D	Engage with internal audit; comment on the performance of the team; send the review report to the sponsor.
Q4	Three of the following statements, about approaches to project review, are true. Which one is FALSE?
A	A 'retrospective' is a review of the project, or a portion of the project, looking backward, to determine what might be improved upon.
B	A project audit must, by legislation, be done by the same people that audit the organization's financials.
C	A health check can be done by the project manager and another experienced person, by assessing the project against a list of project areas.
D	A project review might be done by a small team, lasting a few days, and producing a review report.
Q5	Three of the following guidelines for conducting a project review are valid. Which one is NOT VALID?
A	The leader of the review team must have access to the project sponsor, and should agree with representative interviewees with the project manager.
B	During interviews, the reviewers need to reduce any threat to the project team by being sensitive to their emotions.
C	The interview discussion should stick to project matters rather than encourage comments about individuals or groups.
D	Writing up the review report can be done in less than an hour, so interviews can continue almost up to the time the report is due.

Quiz for Chapter 27 on Project Negotiation

Q1	Three of the following statements, about negotiations relating to projects, are valid. Which one is INVALID?
A	In negotiations related to projects, it is likely that there will be an ongoing relationship with people that you negotiate with. Therefore, the process and outcome should be seen as fair.
B	Interest-based negotiating involves seeking out what is really important to both parties and looking for an outcome that both parties are happy with.
C	Project managers spend quite a bit of time negotiating about things like resources, requirements, priorities, and supplier agreements.
D	Everything should be negotiated, even if there are risks and some discomfort doing so. The sole aim must be to minimize that cost of your project.

Q2	You are negotiating to bring a technical specialist from a consulting firm onto your project. You believe that the person offered has the best skills, but you could find other specialists that would be adequate. The consulting firm is having some difficulty placing the specialist concerned. Which of the following statements about power base and BATNA is correct?
A	The availability of other specialists weakens your BATNA and power base and the fact that the consulting firm is having difficulty placing the specialist weakens their power base.
B	The availability of other specialists strengthens your BATNA and power base and the fact that the consulting firm has the most skilled specialist weakens their power base.
C	The availability of other specialists strengthens your BATNA and power base and the fact that the consulting firm is having difficulty placing the specialist weakens their power base.
D	The availability of other specialists strengthens your BATNA but weakens your power base and the fact that the consulting firm is having difficulty placing the specialist strengthens their power base.
Q3	As part of your plant upgrade, you want to buy a reconditioned machine which would cost $50 000 new. You believe that $25 000 would be a fair price, and you would pay up to $30 000, but would be delighted to get it for $18 000. Your take on the sellers position is: reservation $21 000, likely price $26 000 and they would ideally like to get $32 000 for it. What is your estimate of the ZOPA (zone of possible agreement)?
A	$21 000 to $30 000
B	$25 000 to $26 000
C	$18 000 to $32 000
D	$18 000 to $50 000
Q4	Three of the following statements, about how to negotiate, are valid. Which one is INVALID?
A	Your aim is to get the best deal for your project. So provided that it is not outright illegal, some deception is fine, and if you have the power, then use it to the full.
B	Getting to know the other party well and helping them to know you, is likely to build a relationship of trust that can streamline negotiations and reach a satisfactory agreement faster.
C	In an important negotiation, there are advantages to having at least one colleague with you, especially if the other party has a team. Seeking your colleague's input may give a second opinion and can buy you think-time.
D	Asking questions and listening, improves your understanding. The knowledge gained increases your power and ability to reach a good outcome.

Q5	Three of the following statements, about negotiating tools and traps, are valid. Which one is INVALID?
A	Anchoring is a way of setting the starting point around which negotiation takes place. It is therefore important to have done research and know what is reasonable.
B	Using the contrast principle, the other party may put forward a few unsatisfactory options, before presenting something that is mediocre but acceptable. By contrast, the mediocre option may look really good.
C	Reactive devaluation is knowing that whenever the other party proposes something, there is a catch and a hidden agenda. Therefore the proposal must be rejected.
D	Framing is a way of choosing how to say something in a way that is likely to sound attractive to the other party.

Answers to Quizzes

Chapter	*Q1*	*Q2*	*Q3*	*Q4*	*Q5*	*Q6*	*Q7*	*Q8*
5	C	A	C	D	D			
6	D	A	B	B	C			
7	B	C	A	B	C			
8	C	C	D	A	C			
9	A	C	D	D	C	B	A	B
10	D	B	A	A	D			
11	A	B	D	D	B			
12	C	D	C	C	A	B		
13	C	B	B	A	D	C	B	A
14	A	B	A	D	D			
15	C	B	A	D	B			
16	C	B	D	A	D	B	A	C
17	B	D	C	A	D	D		
18	D	A	A	C	B			
21	B	D	A	C	A	C	D	C
22	D	D	B	C	A	D	B	C
23	B	B	C	D	A			
24	B	D	D	A	C			
25	B	D	A	B	D			
27	D	C	A	A	C			

Chapter 36

Cases to Support Your Learning

The aim of this chapter is to give you practice in applying the concepts and techniques.

Most of the cases present scenarios where your recommendations are asked as to how to handle the situation. Some of the cases are exercises (for example, producing a schedule or calculating costs). A few of the cases are designed to give a theoretical grounding, but the majority are practical and require an understanding of several areas of project management. Answers are given in the next chapter. The exercises generally have only one right answer. The case study situations have a variety of answers and there is no 'one right answer'. Therefore, what is given is a 'possible answer'.

For optimum learning, I recommended that you do the case as far as possible, without looking at the answer. Pencil is best as it is easy to erase, and working in an exercise book will allow you to keep your answers together for later revision. While mental arithmetic skill is valuable, a calculator is necessary for some cases. When you have done the case to the best of your ability, only then compare it with what is in the answer chapter. Take note of anything that you missed, and if you disagree with the answer, or if the answer has overlooked something important, then please send me an email (**fdeinhorn@gmail.com**) and it will be considered as a future amendment. For each case, the heading indicates the main area that it addresses. Some of the cases are real situations, but most are contrived from what has been observed in real situations that could occur in any country. The names of organizations and people are all fictitious.

36.1 Case 1. Endura Holdings (project initiation and arriving at a charter)

Your company, which specializes in managing projects, has just been asked to manage a project for Endura Holdings, a large corporate. You have no idea what the

DOI: 10.1201/9781003321101-40

project is about, but you have set up a meeting with the Endura executive that made the request. You believe that she might be the sponsor for the project.

1. For this initial meeting, draw up a checklist of things that you would want to discuss, and questions that you need answers to. Questions can be open-ended or specific. Most important, you want to leave with a thorough understanding.
2. What homework might you do before the meeting?
3. How would you ensure that you still have access to the executive after the meeting? – should further thoughts arise.

36.2 Case 2. Waluma Hospital (stakeholder analysis)

The Waluma private hospital in Klerksdorp in North Western Province has a staff of 120 people at all levels. Waluma is part of the MediWorld group whose head office is in Johannesburg. The group owns or manages 30 hospitals throughout South Africa.

Patient records are central to the operation of the hospital as more than half of the patients have been to the hospital before, and some have been regularly. Until 3 years ago, all patient records were paper-based. Then the group purchased a patient record system from a software vendor. It was customized extensively to meet MediWorld's needs and has been rolled out in seven of the hospitals – with mixed results. It is referred to as HIS (Hospital Information System). Waluma is to be number eight. Reviews of the earlier projects indicated that effective stakeholder management was a critical success factor.

You have been appointed Project Manager, and report into the project office in Johannesburg. The sponsor, Dr. Gubane, the hospital director, is open-minded. However, you are already aware that some of the more senior doctors are apprehensive, and some outright negative – "we deal with patients, not computers". HIS will be used by almost all staff in the hospital, including nurses, administration staff, and the outsourced laboratory. The latter cannot wait for the problems of controlling large volumes of paper files to end.

HIS is supported, by a team in Johannesburg. They are proud of what the system has achieved in hospitals where the system has been in operation for a while and is well accepted. One or their staff has been seconded to your team. Your other team members include trainers and IT infrastructure staff from Johannesburg.

1. List the stakeholders involved (some are not mentioned above).
   For the main stakeholders, indicate:
   - What they stand to gain
   - What their fears might be.
2. Construct a Power – Interest grid, and position each stakeholder (or group of stakeholders).
3. What specific approaches might you use to engage with, and manage expectations of, the most influential stakeholders.

36.3 Case 3. The Triple Constraint (project priorities for planning)

Discuss each of the following projects in the light of the triple constraint. Comment on which of the scope/quality, time, and cost parameters might be constrained, enhanced, or accepted.

1. A wealthy family is planning a 21st birthday party for their eldest daughter.
2. A couple with limited funds is planning a home renovation.
3. The department of health needs to test the flu vaccine that will be widely distributed early in Autumn to cover the expected flu strains.

36.4 Case 4. Trandy Inc. Employee Scholarship Scheme (PDD – project definition document)

You are a PM in the Trandy Group, a medium-sized distributor of IT hardware products and accessories, which employs 10 000 people nationwide. You have been requested to meet with Jane Bunda, the HR executive, to discuss a new project that she will sponsor with you as the PM. She does most of the talking:

> "Trandy is going to launch an employee scholarship scheme. It will be open to our employees for post-high school further education. Clearly it will be on a merit basis – academic performance is important but not the only thing. We want the scheme to be equally accessible to all our employees in whichever city they are and at whatever level in the company – but, wait, maybe we need to think about whether execs will be eligible. We are looking at spending $2 million per year, which should cover about 100 scholarships. Not only do we want to improve our desirability as an employer, but we want the ability to publicize some of the success stories that arise, on our website and maybe in local newspapers too – and hence enhance our corporate image.
>
> "You will have the support of three of our HR people, who, between them have a fair understanding of our policies, and have access to confidential HR records. Our thinking is that candidates must apply through their employee parents roughly 3 months before the start of the academic year. The timing is critical, because there must be evidence of an acceptance from the educational institutions, and we also need school grades at least from mid-year. It is now 10 months from the start the next academic year for most colleges. To give our employees time to plan, we need to launch in 5 months' time.
>
> "We are aware of many fly-by-night training outfits that offer qualifications of questionable value. So, we shall need a list of eligible educators. Certainly we would like commercial and technical subjects, because that's where some of our future employees will come from. But we also need to include the arts, like philosophy and languages. Technical colleges must also be in there,

because practical people with artisan skills are in such short supply these days. We are aware of our 1 500 contractors, but at this stage they will not be eligible, maybe that will change in future, especially for those that have been with us for more than 5 years.

"Yes, there are lots of things to be ironed out, and my steering committee will review your recommendations and give direction. For example, should we pay the fees directly to the institution or to our employees through the payroll. I lean toward the latter, because then tax and other considerations can be managed better. But that will involve Payroll. How do we handle failures? Not sure, but I'm reluctant to try to recover any money – rather let's withhold funds for the next year – but we need criteria, like what if someone has passed 3 out of 4 subjects? Where do we draw the line? So one of the project's first milestones is to produce a presentation on the concept – but allow time after it, in case of changes.

"Hopefully we shall have more applicants than we can fund, but even if not, we must only fund those that are likely to perform well during their studies. I think we shall need a committee to take decisions on borderline cases, and they would need to come from the business. I don't want this to be a purely HR initiative. Their buy-in is vital and they must approve applications from their staff. We need to brief them well and have a documented process that we go through. There are bound to be appeals. Maybe they would like to select staff members to act as an advisory panel?

"Oh, and let's define what we mean by a child. Should children of a spouse from a previous marriage be eligible? And another thought … we can't fund residence fees as well. If people choose to study in other cities then that will be for their own account. But that must all be in the brochure, including what allowances will be given for books or equipment. Since we are distributors, should we provide laptops at cost in lieu of money?

"Let's not forget about costs. I need to know how much this has cost, and my staff will charge their time to the project. Legal will too, and I want a legal review before making any announcement. I believe that we can put this together and launch for $150 000, but let's see what you come up with – obviously the $2 million is not a project cost. I'll consider the project finished when we have launched, awarded the scholarships for next academic year, and paid the money to our employees.

"That's about it. You have permission to get started, but I'd like to see an outline of the project soonest, and run it by the divisional heads".

A PDD would normally take at least a week to assemble. So, in the time available, get some practice by writing:

- A sentence for the executive summary indicating what must happen, or be delivered, for the project to be complete;
- One business objective;
- One project objective;
- One critical success factor;

- Three scope items;
- One scope exclusion and one other exclusion;
- One benefit (other than the business objective);
- One project cost item with an estimated amount;
- One role and responsibility (other than sponsor and PM);
- One milestone (with date);
- One risk with a response action;
- One issue and one assumption;
- The purpose, timing, and attendees for one regular meeting to be held.

36.5 Case 5. Objective, Requirement, Scope, or Exclusion? (scope planning)

The statements in the table relate to a project which is to build an extension to a functioning private hospital and implement the Hospital Information System (HIS) that is already in use elsewhere in MediWorld. Classify the statements, by type, indicating whether they relate to:

- O = Objectives
- R = Requirements
- S = Scope
- E = Exclusions from the scope.

If any statements are vague, the put a 'V' in front of it. Thus 'VR' is a vague requirement.

No	Statement	Type
1	Nursing staff must be able to request laboratory tests	
2	Supply of servers and HIS software is a dependency, but not part of the project	
3	Improve access to our patient records	
4	Adjudicate bids for furnishing and fitting out the wards	
5	Every staff member must have their own computer Id and Password	
6	Construction of the building	
7	Streamline administration	
8	All operating theatres and IT equipment must be have standby power	
9	There must be a server room suitable for the new Hospital Information System	
10	Provide a more comprehensive service	
11	Architectural design of buildings	
12	The envisaged brain scan equipment will not be acquired in the project timeframe	

13	It must take no more than 3 seconds to call up a patient record from HIS	
14	Carpet the lounge areas.	
15	Photographs of the upgraded hospital to be supplied for MediWorld brochure	
16	Flow of people/trolleys in the hospital should improve	
17	Electrical wiring	
18	There must be a classroom of 40 square meters, with projection facilities.	
19	Plan RFP (Request for Proposal) for building extensions	
20	Only designated staff may access patient records	
21	Train doctors on review and update of patient records via the HIS	
22	Increase market share and profit in the Klerksdorp area	
23	No re-cabling of the existing building will be done	
24	There must be an additional 85 beds –45 in general wards, and 40 in semi-private.	
25	Sign off requirements	
26	Dig foundations	
27	Minimize the number of trees that must be removed	

36.6 Case 6. NMA Conference (WBS – work breakdown structure)

The National Medical Association (NMA) requires a 3-day conference to be held to bring specialized staff together to listen to papers and collaborate on certain new medical techniques.

Your organization has a reputation for the total management of events of all types and sizes. A contract with NMA to handle this event has been signed. You have been appointed to manage the project. It is now January, and the conference is to take place at a suitable venue, in or near Johannesburg, sometime during October of this year.

The NMA will supply member lists, but has indicated that they would welcome non-members for a higher attendance fee. It is important that this event should at least break even, and preferably make a small profit for the NMA. While there are many thousands of members, it is envisaged that there will be a maximum of 250 attendees and speakers. Members of the NMA will be invited to put forward papers for presentation, and a senior member of the NMA will be available to advise on selection. There are also a few prominent overseas specialists that NMA wishes to invite as speakers. It is desirable that delegates be accommodated within easy walking, or shuttle transport, distance of the venue.

There will be certain plenary sessions where all delegates attend. Other sessions may run in parallel with each other and use smaller lecture rooms. The highlight will be a gala dinner just before the final day. Within a week of the conference, each delegate will receive a transcript of the proceedings by download from the NMA website.

Create a high-level WBS for this project. Your approach may depend on whether it will be done individually or in a syndicate group. The following are possibilities:

- Use post-it notes on a suitable surface (such as a smooth wall or on a table).
- Write on sheets of paper, each expanding one of the high-level WBS components.
- Type it hierarchically in MS Word or Excel using suitable indenting for lower levels.

36.7 Case 7. SpeedWall (definitive estimating)

You are a PM at SpeedWall. Your company has been asked to quote for building a wall 2 meters high for a length of 400 meters. It must be plastered on both sides, but not painted. The following information is available from your recent records.

- Foundations, of the required cross-section, cost $20 per linear meter for concrete which is delivered by a mixing truck.
- The wall will require about 100 bricks per square meter of wall (which already allows for the fact that wall is two bricks thick).
- Bricks cost $400 for 1000 bricks.
- Other materials such as sand, plaster sand, and cement are estimated at $40 per linear meter of wall.
- Foundations are laid at a rate of 10 meters per laborer-day for digging and pouring concrete.
- The bricklayers each work with a laborer and together they average 2 000 bricks laid per day.
- The plasterers also work with a laborer each, and they average 25 square meters per day.
- Bricklayers and plasterers each cost your company $300 per day; laborers cost $200 per day. This includes benefits and other costs.
- Working with several teams, the duration is estimated at 20 working days.
- Your supervisor costs $400 per day and works full time on site.
- Office and management overheads are estimated at 10% of the construction costs (labor, supervision and material).
- In addition, on a straightforward job like this, you add 5% of the construction cost for risk of bad weather or other unforeseen events.

What you are required to do:

- Calculate the relevant quantities (such as the number of bricks, and person-days of effort). Hence provide management with an itemized estimate of the total cost.
- Name two factors that influence the profit uplift that a company will apply when it bids.
- For the above wall, if the profit uplift is 16% on the total cost (giving a gross margin of about 14%), what would the selling price be, excluding any taxes.

36.8 Case 8. Estimating for Different Situations (project estimating)

You are a consultant and have been asked to advise on the following upcoming projects. The initial order of magnitude estimates are given in brackets.

- Delivering training nationwide to employees of a retail clothing company, on process changes that will result from a new warehousing system due to be implemented shortly ($400 000).
- Move of a manufacturing company to a new factory ($2 million).
- Implementation of a new corporate accounting system using package software ($10 million).

For each of the above projects answer the following questions.

1. At what points in the project's lifetime should an estimate be done?
2. What estimating technique(s) should be used at these points?
3. What considerations would affect the estimates?

There is not enough information to give a 'right' answer, so use some imagination. The purpose is to think through the estimating scenarios.

36.9 Case 9. Market Survey (basic precedence and Gantt chart scheduling)

Your organization needs to do a market survey for a client which will result in a presentation to the client and handover of documentation. All relationships are FS – finish to start

Activity	*Description*	*Duration Weeks*	*Predecessors*
A	Sign contract	2	-
B	Design survey	4	A
C	Identify target market	3	A
D	Collect data	6	B, C
E	Plan presentation	2	B
F	Analyze results	3	D
G	Document market demographics	2	C
H	Practice and give presentation	1	E, F

1. If you have read Appendix 2, then produce a Precedence (network) diagram
   - Do forward and backward pass
   - Identify which activities are on the critical path.
   - Determine the float for non-critical path activities.
2. Produce a Gantt chart (allow for 8 rows and about 20 columns each being 1 week).
   - Moving backward from the final activity, work out which are on the critical path, and the float for non-critical path activities.

36.10 Case 10. Organize a Conference (Gantt chart scheduling – more complex)

This involves some of the key activities for organizing a conference.

'fs' is finish to start (default if not specifically stated). 'ss' is start to start +n means a lag of n weeks. –n means a lead of n weeks.

Activity	*Description*	*Duration Weeks*	*Predecessors*
A	Engage with key stakeholders	1	-
B	Arrange venue	4	A
C	Agree date	1	A
D	Invite speakers	2	B, C
E	Adjudicate papers	10	D fs+4
F	Create a conference speaker schedule	2	E
G	Confirm speakers	10	E fs-6
H	Print brochure	2	F, G
I	Invite members to conference	1	H
J	Advertise conference	3	H
K	Record enrolments	8	I
L	Book accommodation	6	K ss+2
M	Run Conference Event	1	J, K, L

Produce the Gantt chart for the above conference.

I suggest that you create your own template either printing from Excel or with pencil and ruler. You will need 13 rows for the activities, and around 40 columns each representing a week. Start in week 1 (end of week 0).

Assume that the conference date has not yet been set.

- Determine the earliest week for the conference.
- Calculate the float for each activity and hence determine the critical path.
- What happens to the float if a decision is taken to hold the conference in week 38?

36.11 Case 11. Precedence from Conversations (preparation for scheduling)

The PM sometimes needs to use judgment as to which activities come before which others. But often, the PM gets input from experienced staff, especially team members, by listening and questioning. From the comments below, where possible, work out the precedence for activity D. Note for which comments we cannot tell the precedence for D. Assume the schedule is in weeks.

1. "We can only do D when C is finished".
2. "B must be underway for about 2 weeks before we start on D".
3. "D is the very first activity that we must get on with".
4. "Activity C is urgent and should take 5 weeks. D is also urgent but we can only really start it when C is about 2 weeks from finished".
5. "It's really quite simple. A needs to finish, and half-way through A we can start B. But D needs both A and B to finish before we can start it".
6. "After C is finished, we had better allow a week before we start D, because the document from C will need approval".
7. "Activity F does have a dependency on D, and realistically we should also wait until E is finished before starting F".
8. "Activity D will be a problem, there are three things that it depends on – A, B and C. A will provide the specs. B will get the test facility ready. When our specialist has finished C, she will be available to work on D and we can't really start D without her. But best we assume that she will need a week to catch up on other work before starting on D".
9. "Activity C involves ordering the materials for D, but we know that there is a 2 week lead time before we shall have the materials on site".
10. "D can only start in the new financial year, and we've put in a milestone B (zero duration activity) at the start of the first business day of the financial year".
11. "Activity C is on the critical path, but activity D is urgent too".
12. "A is the review and approval activity. When A is done we can do B which is to order the new laptops. Laptops have a lead time of 1 week and the technicians may take another week to load the software. After A we can also do C to order the new printing machine which has a lead time of 3 weeks. Then we can start D which will use the laptop to control the machine".

Note that for most business projects we schedule in work-days, five per week. But the principles are the same.

36.12 Case 12. Hospital Project (Gantt manual and on a scheduling tool)

The project has both building and IT elements. A new hospital wing will be built, and concurrently the new HIS (hospital information system) will be implemented. The purpose is to give you practice, first manually, and then with a scheduling tool. The data is given in the table below.

Ref	*Activity*	*Weeks duration*	*Predecessors*	*Resource*
1	Construction	0		
2	Dig + cast foundations	2	-	Don Grobler
3	Build walls. Install doors + windows	6	2 fs+1	Don Grobler
4	Erect roof. Fit ceilings	5	3	Don Grobler
5	Plaster + paint	4	4 fs-2	Don Grobler
6	Plumbing	0		
7	Lay sewers + pipes	3	2	Thabo Malinga
8	Install bathroom + kitchen fittings	5	7, 13	Thabo Malinga
9	Electrical	0		
10	Install conduit	2	2	Steve Jones
11	Do electrical wiring. Install fittings	4	10, 13	Steve Jones
12	Fitting + Finishing	0		
13	Install floor coverings	4	5	Mo Naidoo
14	Fit out wards	5	13	Lindi Bhika
15	Fit out server room	3	13	Lindi Bhika
16	Fit out classroom	2	15	Lindi Bhika
17	IT infrastructure	0		
18	Install + test servers	4	15	Sam Radebe
19	Install network cabling	6	13	Sam Radebe
20	Install + test workstations	2	18, 19	Sam Radebe
21	HIS (Hospital Information System)	0		
22	Gather hospital-specific data	4	-	Megan Salie
23	Customise HIS + test function	7	15, 20, 22	Megan Salie

Ref	*Activity*	*Weeks duration*	*Predecessors*	*Resource*
24	Load data from old system	6	23 ss+2	Megan Salie
25	Do UAT (user acceptance test)	2	23, 24	Megan Salie
26	Train users. Start using new HIS	4	16, 25	Bianca Coe
27	End of project (event)	0	26	

The exercise has two parts:

Part 1. Draw a manual Gantt chart in weeks using a template with 27 rows and at least 43 columns. Schedule as though resources were unlimited (and do not show resources). The shaded rows are summary activities and have no duration. For dependencies, 'fs' (finish to start) is the default if no dependency type is stated; 'ss' (start to start) is used for some activities; +n means a lag (delay) of n weeks; –n means a lead (pull-forward) of n weeks. The answer is given in the next chapter.

Part 2. Create a schedule using a scheduling tool like MSP (Microsoft Project). This is for readers who have a scheduler, but have had limited experience using it. The aim is to get practice rather than to produce a perfect schedule. Set durations to weeks and the start date to Monday 31 January 2022. You could schedule in days, but it will mean multiplying the durations by 5 to get them in work days.

The instructions that follow for Part 2 cannot be very specific because scheduling tools vary considerably, but here they lean toward MSP (Microsoft Project). All scheduling tools should give the same answer. I suggest the following progression:

- Enter the activities manually, or by copying from the table. Enter the durations for the activities but not for the summary activities. Indent the activities under the summary activities, and the summary activities should show as summaries and take their start and end dates from the activities under them. Note that I have not used a summary task for the entire project because it saves a level of indenting.
- Activities are usually numbered sequentially and should correspond with the table.
- Experiment with zooming to make the bars longer or shorter (to fit more on the screen). Set the date format to at least show the day, month, and year, for example, 31 Jan 22 or 2022-01-31.
- Insert the dependencies (predecessors) from the table. The format given in the table would apply to MSP. The tasks should then automatically move to honor the dependencies. Activity 23 has a redundant dependency linking it back to activity 15. Remove the dependency and the schedule should not change.

- When finished entering tasks and dependencies, and assuming that the start date is 31 Jan 22, the schedule should end on 25 Nov 22. I suggest that you save the schedule with a new name in case you need to go back to it, and repeat this at various points.
- If there is a column for float or slack, have a look at it. A float of zero means that the activity is on the critical path. Some schedulers have the ability to highlight critical activities (red for MSP).
- So far we have not taken holidays into account. Let's slot in a few: 15 and 18 Apr 22 correspond with Easter and are holidays in most countries. Let us add another holiday on 27 Apr 22. Note that the project end-date moves to 30 Nov 22.
- Set up the resources given in the table so that the first name will appear on the Gantt chart. I prefer to use first names rather than initials because there could be many people with initials 'MS', whereas with 'Megan' I know exactly who it is. Apply the resources to the appropriate activities. In this situation, there is only one responsible person shown.
- Look at the detail of an activity. One of the attributes of an activity might be whether it is 'effort driven'. In MSP, there is a check-box. If checked, it means effort driven. In this exercise, the activities are *not* effort driven. That means, if we add more resources, the duration stays the same. If the effort-driven box is checked, adding resources will automatically reduce the duration – which we do not want here. In MSP, we would also see that all activities have the constraint type 'as soon as possible', meaning that the start dates are not fixed, but depend on predecessors.
- Assigning a start date: Activity 22 is 'gather data'. It has no dependencies so we could start immediately. Suppose that Megan will only become available in May, we can move the activity out to start on Monday, 30 May 22. The activity would now have a constraint type of 'start no earlier than' the date entered.
- Resource Usage: Most schedulers can show if there are over-allocated resources. In MSP, this is given in the resource usage view. In this situation:

  Lindi seems over-allocated. This is not a problem because she represents a company with many resources.

  Megan also seems over-allocated but her estimates allowed for parallel activities.

  Sam, our IT technician, is over-allocated from 11 Jul 22. You decide that he cannot supervise network cabling and install servers at the same time. Do elementary resource leveling by moving the server activity to after the cabling activity has ended. The project end date should move out to 21 Dec 22.

- Because it is unwise to have training during the festive season, move it out to the following year by giving training a dependency of '25fs+7 weeks'. Accordingly, the end date moves to 15 Feb 23.
- At this point, one could save a baseline. I prefer not to because I have my earlier schedules saved. Also, adding and removing activities make it difficult to maintain a baseline. If you wish to try it, MSP does it in the 'tracking Gantt' view.

- Add a task. This happens a lot. Here is an example. Steve, the electrician, says that he needs a new task 'order electrical fittings' immediately after 'install conduit' because of potential supply constraints. Do so, and relink the dependencies. Note that this has no effect on the critical path.
- Recording progress: Assume that it is now 26 May 22, and that we are running on time. Show all tasks finishing prior to 25 May as complete. Also, set 'Install floor coverings' to 50% complete. And set 'Gather hospital-specific data' to 30% complete.
- Changing dates. Megan needs an extra 2 weeks for 'gather hospital-specific data'. This has no impact on the end date. 'Install floor coverings' will need an extra week. Change it to 5 weeks. This does affect the critical path and the end date moves to 15 Feb 23. Note that the percentage complete may also change by extending the durations, in which case set them back to the reported percentages complete.
- Filter the schedule: Most schedulers allow you to only display tasks that are of interest. If you are using MSP, you could change 'No Filter' to 'Incomplete Tasks', in which case it would hide completed tasks.
- At this point, the schedule is useful for tracking the activities that are still to be completed. It can be printed, or copied to a PDF or PowerPoint file. In MSP, I prefer to say 'Legend – none' as few people need it. Having the output in a file allows you to distribute it to stakeholders that do not have the scheduling software.

There is no answer for Part 2. If you managed to complete it, you will have a sound grasp of scheduling. If you are new to the scheduler, it might have been difficult. There is no need to remember the details of the scheduling tool because when you use it regularly it will become familiar quite quickly.

36.13 Case 13. Market Survey Schedule Compression (crashing the schedule)

This case uses the same data as for Case 9 which is to conduct a market survey for an important client. Your initial schedule, shown below in Figure 36.1, indicates that the survey project will take 16 weeks. However, the client has indicated that they must have the output in just 14 weeks. You have noted certain activities where it is possible to save time by crashing, and you have estimated what various reductions in duration would cost (see 'cost of reduction'). Other activities cannot be reduced by crashing.

Find the lowest cost way to save 2 weeks and finish at the end of week 14. It is suggested that you consider various approaches, and estimate what each would cost. Then select the lowest cost approach. This situation is somewhat theoretical because, in practice, the cost of reducing duration is seldom clear-cut. Nevertheless, it illustrates important considerations.

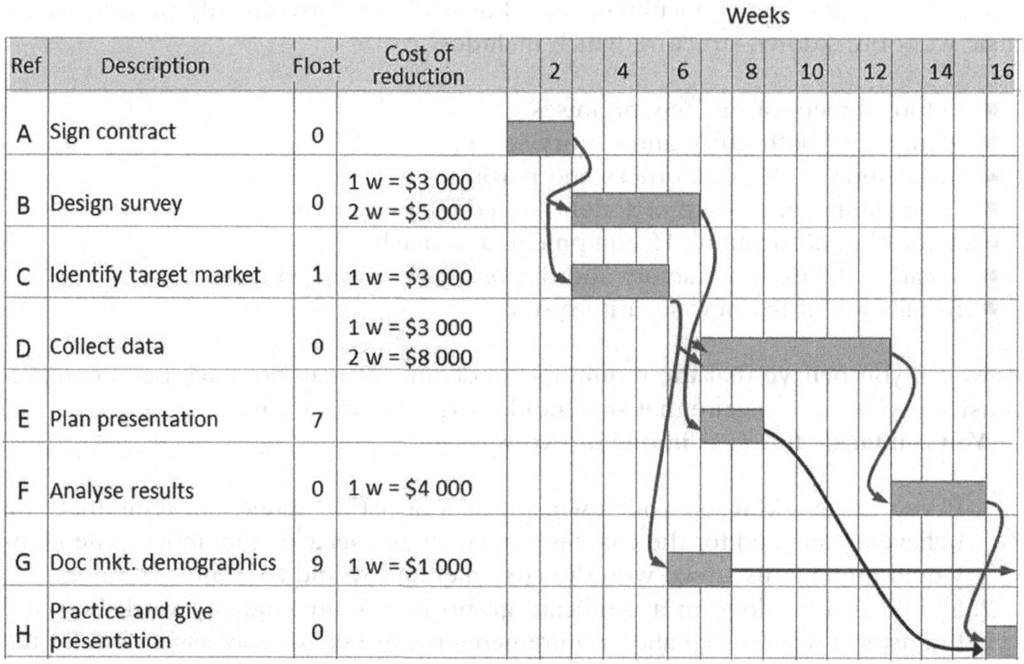

Figure 36.1 Survey schedule to be compressed.

36.14 Case 14. EduToy7 Factory Move (project quality)

EduToy7 is a manufacturer of educational toys. They are moving to larger premises about five kilometers from their existing factory. You have been appointed as project manager for the move. The move will be considered complete when: (i) all staff have moved, (ii) the factory is working normally, and (iii) all suppliers have been paid. Some aspects to consider:

- There is an office staff of about 20 people, including a design office.
- The factory employs 50 people, mainly setting up and operating a variety of machines.
- The new premises are being vacated by a packaging company that also had office space and a factory. They will remove all equipment including office partitioning.
- About half the staff drive to work. The remainder are given lifts or rely on public transport.
- There is a small IT server room and systems are available to staff in the building. Some systems are accessed by external toy distributors via a web front-end.
- A new card-operated security system will be installed in the new premises.
- The move will take place during October which is quite a busy period as the high-sales months are toward the end of the year. Factory downtime is of concern.

Based on a requirements document from EduToy7 you have already put together a basic work breakdown structure which includes:

- Refurbishment of the new premises.
- Planning of both office and factory space.
- Installation of dry-wall offices and partitions.
- Fiber cabling and setup of a cloud-based telephone system.
- Relocation of furniture, IT equipment, and machinery.
- Vacating the existing factory and disposing of unwanted items.
- Installation of the new security system.

However, you believe that the requirements document may not have been comprehensive and want to ensure that stakeholder expectations are met.

You can tackle this case in one of two ways:

1. If you are working on your own, produce a list of about ten items that you believe are needed for the customer to consider this a 'quality move'. The items would then be discussed with the customer and would feed into planning.
2. Should this be done in a syndicate group then hold a quality workshop and brainstorm what the quality requirements might be. Possibly assign one of the following roles to each syndicate member: sales manager, financial manager, factory representative, ordering clerk, toy designer, project manager (who would facilitate the discussion and draw up the list). Each is likely to bring a different perspective and have different quality needs.

36.15 Case 15. Nature Films (risk management)

You are a production project manager in Nature Films. The USA branch of the GWF (Global Wildlife Fund) wishes to raise awareness of the Cheetah's endangered status. They have commissioned Nature Films to produce a 40-minute film showing the habits of Cheetahs. This is Nature Films' first assignment from GWF. You have done similar work before and will take charge of the assignment. Nature Films has excellent contacts in the South Africa's Parks Board, and have decided that the Kruger National Park offers the best opportunities. While Nature Films has film material on Cheetahs, it is not comprehensive and some of it is not of suitable quality. The assignment will include taking a multi-disciplinary crew to the Kruger National Park, finding Cheetahs, and filming various aspects of their lives including mating, raising cubs, and hunting. You need to present Cheetahs in a positive light. You also need to show the dangers that affect their survival. The films will remain the property of Nature Films, but GWF will have exclusive and unlimited usage rights for 2 years from delivery date. Some of the constraints are a delivery date only 10 months away, and a budget of $1.2 million. What you are required to do:

- List at least five (negative) risks and at least one (positive) opportunity that you anticipate

- Do a qualitative analysis of the probability and impact of each risk.
- For the top three risks, indicate what strategy you would adopt (avoid, transfer, mitigate, accept), and some risk response actions that you might take.

36.16 Case 16. Budget for Project Math11 (cost budgeting and control figures)

You have been appointed PM for project Math11, which will be run, using contract staff, by the regional government department of education. It is to be a 7-month project to design and communicate improvements in the approach to teaching the Grade 11 Math syllabus at all schools in the region. Changes are to be effective next year. This is considered so important that the math department at each school will be briefed by specially trained communicators.

The project is planned to run from 01 May to 30 November. The main activities, which run end to end are:

- Initial design and prepare teaching changes. Estimated time: 2 months. Resources: 2 Specialists full time.
- Review proposed changes. Estimated time: 1 month. Resources: 2 Specialists full-time, 5 Reviewers 20% of their time.
- Brief Communications team. Estimated time: 1 month. Resources: 1 specialist 50% of time, 4 Communicators 50% of time.
- Communicate to staff at schools. Estimated time: 3 months. Resources: 4 Communicators full-time.

Project Management. As PM, you expect to spend roughly 1 day per week (20% of your time) throughout the project.

Travel, stationery, and printing costs are expected to be $3 000 per month during communication to staff at schools.

Rates per resource type (cost to Dept. Education)

Specialists and Reviewers:	$10 000 per month.
Communicators:	$8 000 per month.
Project Manager:	$10 000 per month.

Project costs are recorded by the project office based on resource allocated to the project and other costs incurred. Costs to date are notified to the PM a few days after the end of each calendar month.

Prepare a budget for Project Advantage.

- Create a template like the one below. Work in thousands (10 means $10 000)
- Label the columns for each planned month, and rows for each Activity.

- Enter the planned costs by month for each activity or cost type (like travel, etc.)
- Total the planned costs for each activity.
- Total the planned costs for each month.
- Calculate the cumulative planned cost at the end of each month. (These become the control figures against which the PM will track).

Activity cost items	May	Jun	Jul	Aug	Sep	Oct	Nov	Total

36.17 Case 17. Painting a Wall (Earned Value Management)

This simple exercise gives experience with tracking a project using EVM. For you to get value, the entire column must be filled in every day and commented on, before moving to the next day. Your project is to supply materials, prepare, and paint one side of a high wall that is 400 meters long, and must be done with brushes. You are using an experienced team and estimate that it can be done in 5 days and hence meet the customer's end-of-week deadline. You estimate that it will cost $10 000, and have agreed a price of $12 000 with the customer.

- How many meters do you plan to paint per day?
- What is the Earned Value/meter?
- What dollar amount do you expect to spend per day?
- You decide to monitor cost and schedule at the end of every day. Complete the figures for Day 1, then Day 2, then Day 3, etc. After each day, comment on what the figures are telling you.
- At the end of day 4, do the following estimates: ETC (estimate to complete) and EAC (estimate at completion).
- Given the Day 6 outcome, how much profit will you make on this contract?

End of →	Mon	Tue	Wed	Thu	Fri	Sat
Meters Planned	80	160	240	320	400	400
Planned Value ($)						
Meters Painted	60	132	212	300	380	400
Earned Value ($)						
Actual Cost ($) – money spent	1 400	3 300	5 500	8 000	10 200	10 700
Cost Variance ($)						
CPI (Cost Performance Index)						
Schedule Variance ($)						
SPI (Schedule Performance Index)						
ETC (Estimated To Complete) in $						
EAC (Estimate At Completion) in $						

36.18 Case 18. HR Job Description Project (Earned Value Management)

A small project involves writing 80 job descriptions. For simplicity, each is estimated to cost $1 000, although it is accepted that some will require a bit more effort and others a bit less. We plan to do them at a steady rate over a 4 month period. The Actual Cost will be measured by multiplying hours logged, by the dollars/hour rate for the people doing the work.

1. What is the Budgeted Cost for the project (excluding contingency)?
2. What is the Planned Value at completion?
3. What is the Planned Value after 1 month? After 3 months?

After 1 month we have completed 15 descriptions.

4. At that point what is the Earned Value?
5. Have we done more work than we planned, or less?
6. What is the Schedule Variance after 1 month?
7. What is the SPI or Schedule Performance Index?
8. Looking at the SPI, what tells you that we are behind schedule

After 1 month, based on the timesheets, the Actual Cost is $12 000

9. What is the Cost Variance?
10. What is the CPI (Cost Performance Index)?
11. For the amount of work done, have we spent too many dollars? What tells you that?

12. Give a possible reason why the Cost Variance is positive but the Schedule Variance is negative.
13. 6 days later we have completed 20 descriptions. Roughly how far are we behind schedule – from a time point of view?

After 3 months we have completed 54 job descriptions, and the Actual Cost is $50 000

14. What is the Earned Value?
15. Based on the Earned Value, what is the Percentage Completion?
16. What is the Cost Variance and the CPI?
17. What is the Schedule Variance and the SPI?
18. What is the EAC (Estimate at Completion) at this point?
19. Suppose that is was very important to complete all the job descriptions by the planned date, what would you do?

36.19 Case 19. Project Theta (Earned Value Management)

Project Theta has the following Planned Value cumulative control figures (k = thousands).

02 Jul	09 Jul	16 Jul	23 Jul	30 Jul	06 Aug	13 Aug
$110 k	$125 k	$140 k	$160 k	$180 k	$195 k	$215 k

As at 16 July, the Actual Cost provided by Project Accounting is $140 k.

1. From the information provided, can we conclude that the project is on track? Explain your answer.

On 30 July, the PM estimates that the Earned Value is $150 k and gets informed two days later that the Actual Cost at that date was $170 k.

2. What is the Schedule Variance and SPI at 30 July?
3. What is the Cost Variance and CPI at 30 July?
4. Roughly how many weeks are we ahead of, or behind, schedule?

Theta was planned to end on 15 October at a cost of $320 k

5. Based on the 30 July data calculate the EAC (Estimate at Completion) and the ETC (Estimate to Completion)
6. Based on Actual Cost, what is the estimated Percentage Completion of Theta at 30 July?

36.20 Case 20. Project Inter-World (Earned Value Management)

Inter-World is an IT software development project. It is divided into five phases which are conducted in the following rough sequence.

- Inception $200 000
- Design $400 000

- Program development $600 000
- Testing $600 000
- Go live and handover $200 000

Cost estimates for each phase are given. Costs relate to hours worked by team members, with overhead costs built into the rates.

The phases may overlap. For example, program development is planned to start before Design is complete. The critical path durations indicate that the project should be complete on 19 November.

1. What is the total Budgeted Cost for this project? The Planned Value at completion?

Three months into the project on 07 May, the Planned Value control figure is $680 000. The PM's estimate of the status of each phase is as follows:

- Inception complete
- Design 80% complete
- Program development 30% complete
- Remaining phases not started

2. Estimate the Earned Value for each phase, and the total.

Time is being captured at project level. I.e. it does not indicate to which phase it belongs. Costs are calculated directly from each person's time and rate. As at 07 May the Actual Cost to date is $730 000

3. Estimate the Schedule Variance and SPI.
4. Estimate the Cost Variance and CPI.
5. Comment on what these figures mean.
6. As at 07 May, most of the program development has been done on a non-critical part of the system. Explain why the SPI might be misleading.

As at 27 August: The Planned Value control figure is $1 450 000. The reported Actual Cost is $1 440 000. The PM estimates as follows:

- Design complete
- Program development 90% complete
- Testing 30% complete
- Go live and handover not started

7. Estimate the Earned Value for each phase, and the total at 27 August.
8. Estimate the Schedule Variance and SPI.
9. Estimate the Cost Variance and CPI.
10. Comment on what these figures mean.
11. Estimate the cost at completion.
12. Is the project likely to finish before year end?

36.21 Case 21. Hygiene Factors and Motivators (people management)

Here is a list of things that are generally beneficial for people working on the project:

1. Challenging work
2. A salary increase

3. Working with an excellent team
4. Positive attitude of management
5. Good physical working conditions
6. Learning opportunities.

For each, state whether you consider it a hygiene factor or a motivator, and give your reasons. Look at each from the point of view and feelings of the individual.

36.22 Case 22. HVD – Heavy Vehicle Distributors (team start-up)

Clement Sithole wished that building a team were as easy as the textbooks had suggested. His organization, HVD, was a distributor for a range of heavy vehicles with sales offices, service centers, and warehouses in 23 locations covering all provinces of South Africa. Clement and the IT Systems team were based in the head office near Johannesburg, and new CRM (customer relationship management) software package was being implemented as a cloud solution. Clement's project was to roll out the new business processes which would access the CRM system through a web interface. All the management, sales staff, and many of the maintenance and spares supply staff would be trained to use the system. However, the benefits of complete, and up-to-date, customer information, would only be realized if staff at all levels were willing and able to carry out the new processes effectively. Measurements were built into the system and could be monitored from head office. Because of the variety of customer demographics a few of the locations had unique requirements which affected the interfaces to other systems – hence the need for IT's involvement.

CRM was one of the initiatives arising from a top management strategy session where the need to know more about individual customers was emphasized. Responsibility had gone to Ron Clarke, the marketing director, who was the de facto project owner and sponsor. He had already been involved in selecting which software package would be used, and now wanted the rollout done without delay. In his initial meeting with Clement he had said "Exco want this fully operational by end October, in seven months' time. You're in charge, but keep me informed and let me know what support you need".

Clement, had struggled to assemble a team, but one by one he had managed to get the key team members on board in Johannesburg. The team consisted of Mohamed, a full-time change manager, two contract change specialists, Lindiwe, a part-time training manager, a developer of training material, Leela, an analyst from the IT department who had a good understanding of how to use the new system, Jennifer, an administrator, and part-time representatives from other departments including Johan from Sales. The training itself would be contracted out, and Isaac, a representative from the training organization would attend team meetings.

An early meeting had resulted in a modus operandi being agreed for the rollout of sites, which Jennifer had documented, and was starting to schedule. Immediately there were disagreements, with Mohamed insisting that his change managers needed time to familiarize, and with Lindiwe pointing out that training material would take at least 2 months to develop, followed by a month to teach the contract trainers. As a result, Jennifer made it very clear that the 7-month deadline was impossible, as these 'setup' activities would not leave enough time to do necessary work at the sites. She angrily suggested that Lindiwe take over the scheduling. Further disagreements arose between Johan and Leela, with Johan wanting all the new capabilities made available immediately with Leela recommending a more staged approach. Isaac was also not happy, because he had already lined up trainers and could not keep them waiting for 2 months.

Now, 3 weeks into this high-priority project, there seemed to be nothing but problems and disagreements. While Clement's approach had been to let the team get on with things, the result was unhappiness and a few unpleasant arguments.

1. From the information given, comment on how projects are handled at HVD.
2. Which aspects will make it easier, and which more difficult, for Clement to build a team?
3. What Tuckman stage is the project at? What might Clement have done differently?
4. What should Clement do now to deal with the situation and build an effective team?

Note: A change manager focuses on the people side of change by increasing employee adoption of a new situation, which might include business processes, systems and technology, job roles, and organization structures.

36.23 Case 23. The Wealth-Man Conversion (issues management)

You are a PM in a wealth management firm. Your project is to move your 'home-grown' IT investment administration system with its 120 000 clients, to the Wealth-Man package solution. Enormous benefits are expected owing to the robustness and flexibility of Wealth-Man. Besides you are already running new investments on Wealth-Man for over 10 000 clients.

Testing has gone well thus far, but now 6 weeks from the planned 'cutover', it has become apparent that the conversion process will take 70 hours. This means that unless something changes the conversion cannot be completed in a weekend. The longest process is the Wealth-man 'take-on' program that runs for 28 hours. Chen, the systems manager, seems quite worried, but has some ideas: maybe the suppliers can help? maybe the technical specialists can tune the database? maybe we can use a faster processor? Vanessa, the business manager is concerned that clients will be impacted if the conversion runs into Monday.

What you are required to do: Produce a simple issue document with necessary heading information and a summary of the problem. Also:

- State a number of alternative solutions (which may be used in combination).
- Indicate who should be involved in addressing the issue.

At this point, you do not have enough information to select a particular solution.

36.24 Case 24. Delia's Day (what it's like being a business PM)

"Oh, why am I always late?" wonders Delia as she pulls her car into the Tuesday morning traffic. Nevertheless she is at Yousure Insurance offices by 7:45, still thinking that she could have saved 20 minutes by leaving 10 minutes earlier. Delia is a PM from a consulting firm, assigned to Yousure for an important project to enhance their online business platform. She knows that the launch deadline is already tight. Her team of 14 are mainly Yousure employees with the most skilled and productive team members shared with other projects. She has managed to bring in two really excellent people from the consulting company, and realizes that they are critical to the project's success.

As she exits the elevator on the 4th floor and heads to the area where most of the team sit, she meets Zuko, the general manager of the online business division. He is the sponsor and, although very busy, has always been very supportive of the team. "How's it going?" he asks. "Great", she replies "the team are really committed and I'm sure they will bring this one home". They chat for a few minutes about a new member of the steering committee, and as Zuko turns toward the corridor he says "you will be sending me the project report, won't you – I've been looking out for it". "Sure" she replies, and goes to her more secluded desk in the corner. She's pleased to see that four of the team are there before her and all look busy.

Delia settles down to go through her mail. There are several messages because she was at a workshop the previous afternoon, and she makes a note on her pad to answer them. One of them is from Jacob, one of Zuko's staff, who is the business lead for the project. He's wondering when the demonstration of some of the customer screens will be ready. Delia knows that it was promised for a week earlier, but some unexpected technical hitches have caused a delay. She responds that it won't be long, and that she will give Jacob a time later today. Temba, one of her team members, comes across to discuss a problem. Delia listens intently, thinks briefly, and then makes a suggestion. "Thanks Delia, yes, that should work" says Temba as he hurries back to his desk.

Nine o'clock is the daily 'stand-up' meeting where the whole team gather in front of a whiteboard to discuss progress from the previous day, and to confirm plans for the day ahead. Just after nine, Delia finds a few team members chatting. "We should start in a moment, but I just want to wait for Mel because her input on those additional requirements will be critical". She goes back to her desk and phones Mel, who is in the middle of a discussion. Mel apologizes and promises to be across in a moment. By ten past nine, Mel arrives and most of the team are there. They spend the next twenty minutes discussing progress and how to overcome some persistent problems. The meeting ends on a positive note with the team convinced that they will have something to show Jacob on Friday. Delia makes a few adjustments to details on the whiteboard and returns to her desk. A team member is waiting for her and says "we urgently need David, he's the only person that can solve this technical problem, and we haven't seen him since last week". Delia knows that David has been pulled onto another project, but says that she will see what can be done. She moves quickly to the stairs taking her to the third floor where she finds David in a discussion with Seth, the other project manager. "I'll only be a moment" says David, and indeed two minutes later Delia has a somewhat heated, but useful, discussion with

Seth and David, getting an agreement that David will come across immediately to solve the problem. It's really fortunate, she thought, that I have helped Seth when he needed something from us. On her way back she meets Marcia, a financial manager who is on the project steering committee. Marcia: "will it be possible for us to sign-in and get an up to date status of the business concluded over the past month or two?" They discuss exactly what Marcia requires for financial forecasting. Delia is sure that it was not part of the specification, but says that she will ask one of the business analysts to look into it.

Back at her desk, Delia is relieved to see David working with two of her team. The looks on their faces suggest that David is onto something. She reflects on the situation and decides that she needs to update the schedule. She's a bit concerned about what it will tell, because they are already over a week behind schedule, and new requirements seem to be coming to light all the time. But, I guess they can't have everything, she thought, and still expect this to be on time. Suddenly her phone rings. It's her husband who tells her that he needs to attend a strategy session out of town, and wonders whether she can get their daughter to and from school tomorrow. She says that she will make a plan, but realized that her schedule does not allow for such disruptions.

At 12:30, she goes to the canteen with Thandi and Michael, her consulting firm team members. They express a view that the 'goalposts seem to be moving'. Delia agrees and suggests that they worry about it after lunch.

At 13.15, Delia gets back to the schedule, and realizes that it's more than a week out of date, and that she needs some details. She spends the next hour walking about and talking to members of the team. Her involvement is appreciated, and one or two team members even share some concerns about things that might cause problems. She reassures them that this is all in the nature of projects, and is nothing unusual. The schedule update confirms her worry. The project is over two weeks behind schedule. She updates the project report, noting that there is a slight delay, but still assigns a green RAG code because the launch is still 4 months away, and she believes that the team will catch up. At least, she thinks, we had not spent more money than was planned at the last month-end just over a week ago. She carefully checks the list of stakeholders, adds the new steering committee member, and sends the report. It's just over half a page, but it has all the necessary details. If we can't catch up, there is still time to brief the steering committee – we shall need to let them know about the delays gently.

The highlight of Delia's day happens just after 15:00 when two team members come to her desk, beaming, to tell her that a problem that had been holding them up for a week has now been solved. She congratulates them and walks about letting other team members know of the breakthrough. Around 16:00, Delia is discussing Marcia's financial requirements with a business analyst. It seems as though this will be quite a bit of work, and definitely cause a delay. The discussion is interrupted by a message on her smartphone, that Gerry, a junior member of the team, had a motor accident on the way to work, is injured, and will not be in for two days. She had wondered where he was but thought that maybe she had given him a day's leave. She plans to be in touch with Gerry next morning.

At 17:00 Delia realizes that she owes Jacob a time for the demonstration, and sends him a note suggesting 14:00 on Friday. Tomorrow, she will just have to persuade the team to produce the best they can by that time. At 17:45, most of the team have left, and Delia heads for the elevator thinking that there is just time to go to the gym, before going home for dinner. It's been a busy day, but hopefully tomorrow will bring some new breakthroughs on the project.

Answer the following:

1. What skills does Delia display as a PM?
2. In what weak areas might she improve?
3. What frustrations does she experience?
4. What are some of the positive aspects Delia experiences as a PM?

36.25 Case 25. Setting RAG Codes for Project Reports (communication)

You are the PM in the following project situations, and are preparing a routine project report. What RAG (red, amber, green) code would you assign? Would you communicate in any other way about the situation? Give brief reasons for your answers.

1. The project has CPI of 0.95 and SPI of 0.92. Management is aware that you are dealing with some serious issues.
2. The project is on time and CPI is 1.05. There are minor problems but you believe that you can handle them.
3. The project is on time and within budget. However, a problem has arisen that is beyond your control and is a show-stopper if it cannot be resolved.
4. It is mid-September and you have a hard year-end deadline. There are no major problems, but the project has slipped due to resource constraints, and there is now a 40% chance of missing the deadline.

36.26 Case 26. XP Insurance (project governance)

Six years ago, new management was appointed to XPI, and they comprehensively revamped the traditional product lines and methods. Now in 2010, XPI has a reputation for innovation, and provide a broad range of short-term insurance products covering, among others, vehicle, homes, household, and accident.

Six months ago, one of the actuaries, Ron Berman, proposed offering Home Value Protection insurance cover – or HVP as it became known. Conceptually it was to protect a homeowner from the consequences of being forced to sell the home at below the purchase price due to a list of adverse circumstances – loss of income being the main one. The issue was topical. In many countries, the sub-prime mortgage crisis and general economic slump were causing homeowners to lose their entire savings.

Thabo Dlamini, with 3 years' experience after his degree, reported into the project office. He had been appointed project manager and was to coordinate the wide variety of activities involved in bringing the new product to launch. Players included the product actuaries, IT, marketing, legal, training of business people. Henk Smit, a senior staff executive had agreed to play the role of sponsor. The project had been kept under close confidentiality wraps, but there had been considerable excitement among those who were selected as team members. It had taken little more than a month from the initial idea, to Henk having given the go-ahead to proceed. Apart from Samantha, the IT systems architect, Thabo was the only full-time person on the project.

Now, in mid-August, 5 months into the project everything seemed to be going wrong. The scheduled October date for launch to the broker community was fast approaching, and Thabo realized that the date could no longer be met. From the start, Henk's interest had waned rapidly, and 2 months ago he had moved into a new line position. Although he retained the sponsorship, he was just too busy to attend to HVP matters. The economy seemed to be improving, and there were early signs of the property market starting to recover. HVP was now common knowledge, and the corridor talk was that the product would have very low uptake from clients. The mood manifested itself in a number of ways:

- Ron Berman produced an early product specification, which Samantha had repeatedly said was incomplete. Promises of an update had not materialized.
- Marketing was never available, and told Thabo that they would get involved much closer to launch.
- Legal had made an experienced person available, but the main feedback given to Thabo was that there were far more legal issues than met the eye. A list had been produced, but the head of legal was not showing much urgency to get them resolved.
- Project meetings were poorly attended – most players apologized.

Costs – entirely related to people-hours – were below the plan, but Thabo knew that this was mainly because little work was being done.

Sending 'red' status reports did not attract much attention. The project office had not been party to approving the project, and Henk probably did not read the reports. The only aspect of the project that appeared close to schedule was the IT development, but Samantha warned that there could be 'surprises' when the product specification was finalized. Thabo had kept good records of the issues. Some he had managed to solve, but most seemed to be beyond his control. He did not want to resign, but realized that something drastic needed to be done.

1. Comment on the project governance process in XPI.
2. If you were a consultant, what improvements would you recommend?
3. If you were in Thabo's situation, what would you do next?

36.27 Case 27. Sponsor Situations (appreciating the sponsor's role)

You are a busy executive, and are responsible for a number of projects, either as sponsor, or as the supplier executive for customer projects. The following situations happen. What should you do? Make reasonable assumptions. Possibly consider more than one option.

1. The PM is not communicating:
   The 14-month project has been running for 8 months – much of it at remote locations. There have been regular monthly meetings. All the reports indicate

that things are on track. You have an uneasy feeling that this may not be the case. Questions raised were not fully answered, or were evaded. The PM is often difficult to reach – mobile phone taking messages, and patchy responses to emails. When you do reach the PM, you often get feedback in technical terms that are difficult to understand.

2. Customer staff are not playing their agreed roles:
   A project is underway for a key customer on the customer premises. In the last two reports, the top issue listed is that the customer is not fulfilling their responsibilities. The latest report shows that we are 2 weeks behind schedule. As per the standards, the project has moved from Green to Amber status.
3. Project dragging on and missing deadlines:
   The project is important, but it does not have a critical end date. It started in January and was scheduled to end in October. Now, in July, it is already 3 months behind schedule. Considering the achievement to date, the project is 10% overspent. The PM is cooperative and communicates regularly. There is always a reason for each delay. Initially, you accepted the reasons. Now you are becoming suspicious that the PM lacks commitment, and that a culture of making excuses and accepting delays has become a way of life with the team.
4. Inevitable budget cuts:
   Business has not been good due to an overall business slowdown. There are eight medium to large projects running in your area. You have engaged with each of the teams and reinforced the importance of their projects to the organization. You have nothing formal from either the CEO or Finance, but believe that budget cuts are inevitable.
5. PM resignation:
   The PM of one of your largest most critical projects has just resigned, having been made an exciting offer overseas. The PM had considerable knowledge of the technical processes required to achieve the objective, and regularly brought her knowledge to bear – which enhanced her effectiveness as the leader of the team. There is still over a year to go to planned completion.
6. Questionable business case:
   The business case for a new project has just been submitted. The engineers and business team, some of them your own staff, are all very keen. However, looking at the benefits in the business case you believe their value is overstated. While the costs look reasonable, this technical solution is new to your company, and no risks have even been mentioned.
7. Infrastructure revamp:
   The IT architect has impressed upon you that the current software infrastructure is out of date. She believes that it is becoming a limitation for new application development. Moreover, she has lost two of her team to competitors who are using the 'latest'. She has proposed a 3 year revamp the IT infrastructure – "it could be done in a year if we could stop everything". You are uncomfortable that it would certainly not be cheap, and that there will be little to show for it until it is all finished, not to mention the risks.
8. Resource issues:
   Several of the projects in your division are sharing resources in matrix mode. Some resources with specialist skills come from other areas. Things are not going well on two of the most critical projects, where there are regular holdups

due to resource constraints. It seems that other more assertive PMs, both in your division and others, seem to get more than their share.

36.28 Case 28. Rescon (closing and governance)

The Rescon division, employing nearly 2 000 people, is an autonomous part of a multinational organization. Their business focus is developing and manufacturing small electronic components that can be integrated into other manufactured products. The components provide wireless connectivity and intelligence that support IOT (internet of things) which Werner Gratz the division general manager believes has a big future in the emerging world of the 4th Industrial Revolution. Although most of his staff are employed in the manufacturing facility, his most technically skilled staff are involved in the development of new devices. Such technical development is done on a project basis, usually with a dedicated team augmented by a few specialists that work across projects.

Although there have been a number of huge successes, there have also been failures, usually where a key element of the technical solution could not be made to work, or where the resilience of the device did not meet Rescon's quality criteria. Recently, a very promising project had ended in failure. The device, aimed at the 'smart home' market had appeared exceptionally promising when it was proposed. Some of Rescon's top scientific and technical people had been assigned to work on the project which was planned to be complete in 10 months with a development cost estimate of $1.8 million. Eight months later the project manager reported technical issues, which she believed could be overcome, but would cost more and take longer. Reluctantly Werner had approved a further $700 000 despite the fact that some of the quality assurance staff believed that it would be very expensive to overcome one of the problems and that the additional amount was inadequate. After a further 5 months, it appeared that the problems would be solved, but another factor had arisen. A competitor had announced a similar product, at a price that would make Rescon's offering less attractive. After a heated debate between Finance, Strategic Marketing, and the research function, it had been decided to stop the project. It had been an unpleasant experience. The team felt that Rescon had let them down, and one outstanding researcher had resigned. The project manager, while accepting the decision, indicated that valuable lessons were being ignored.

Werner realized that this experience was in the nature of their business. Some projects with similar histories had ended successfully. Nevertheless, he had the feeling that the recent failure could have been managed far better – after all, the competitor's activities were actually known about, but had not been communicated by Marketing. Surely, he thought, there must be a way of stopping failing projects earlier? Werner was also concerned about the people. There must be some way of recognizing their excellent work, and keeping them motivated, even if the results had not been as expected.

What you are required to do: Outline an approach that Rescon might use in future to deal with high-risk development projects:

- What should the goals of such an approach be?
- Mention some specific steps in the approach.

The result should be a process that would leave Werner comfortable that, despite the risks, the portfolio of development projects was being governed in the best possible way.

36.29 Case 29. PM Situations (applying all core knowledge areas)

For each of the situations given, what approach would you take, what disciplines would come into play (for example, issues management), and what documentation would be produced? There is probably no single correct answer as you only have limited information to go on.

1. A key supplier has just phoned to say that they expect a 2-week delay filling a critical order.
2. Team member: "We are falling behind on the tender specification activity. Will it be a problem?"
3. Team member: "The solution that we agreed on doesn't work".
4. Stakeholder: "What you are producing for us will be inadequate. What we need is …"
5. Team member: "We knew that it might be a problem. Now it definitely is one".
6. Stakeholder: "Surely your new system must include giving special access to my audit team".
7. Stakeholder: "I have a feeling that we are spending a lot of money unnecessarily".
8. "When I was working on project X-ray, invalid addresses cost us a lot of time and money. I'm worried that it might happen here".
9. Sponsor: "Thought I should let you know, I've resigned, and Ms. Carley has been promoted into my position".
10. Start of project: Getting the project moving is proving difficult. Everyone seems to have a different view.
11. Sub-project manager: "At our meeting about two months ago, I'm sure that Marketing said forms and brochures would be ready by this week, and they are not".
12. Sponsor: "This is the first time I've heard about a delay. Why didn't I know a month ago?"
13. Stakeholder: "How can you tell me that there's no money for this. It was always part of the plan".
14. Team leader: "I know the deadline cannot be changed, but our team are too stretched to get all of this done".
15. Team member: "There is talk that department Y are dead against this project".
16. Team member: "I can't finish this on time because John does not have the ability to get his bit done".

36.30 Case 30. Delectable Confections (project selection)

Delectable Confections (DC) has been established for over 50 years and their core business is the manufacture and distribution of budget price sweets and chocolates. They have factories near several major cities. DC distribute with their own vehicle fleet throughout the South-Eastern states of the USA to convenience stores and supermarkets. Annual turnover is over $800 million. Corporate strategies include: Increasing market share, improvement of customer satisfaction, and reduction of operating costs. DC is weighing up the relative merits of two very different projects. You are the portfolio manager with responsibility for project selection, and are assisted by four functional managers on a part-time basis.

Project 1. Diversification into Ice Cream.
Recently DC were approached by a family-run ice cream manufacturer whose factory is close to your main sweet factory near Atlanta. Their sales have expanded rapidly and are now approaching $50 million per year. However, they lack management depth, and have no desire to run a larger company. They have offered their entire operation, including wholly-owned premises and machinery to DC for $12 million. Your team has done a due-diligence exercise and has come up with the following projections:

Up front cost: $15 million (which includes costs of integration into DC)
Profit contribution adjusted to reflect an amount at the end of each year:
Year 1: $5.0 m; year 2: $5.5 m, year 3: $6.1 m; year 4: $6.7 m; year 5: $7.4 m.

The Ice Cream company management has agreed to remain on as salaried employees for the first year after the purchase. Hiring and training have been included in the cost.

Project 2. Enhancement of Packaging Lines.
The packaging machinery in your plants is now over 15 years old, and has progressively been giving more trouble. The costs are felt in different ways:

- Increased downtime, which holds up the entire production process for a particular line. This can sometimes last for days.
- Faulty packaging which leads to rejects, or worse still, returns from supermarkets and other retailers – which has both financial and reputation consequences.
- Frustration throughout the distribution chain, from factory to retailers.

The project would involve the purchase and installation of new packaging machinery in all factories. It would be done on a prioritized basis, one line at a time. The project would last for almost a year, but benefits would be experienced as each line was installed. The new equipment has several additional advantages:

- More easily maintainable. Being current equipment, the supplier has a full range of parts, and trained technical support staff.
- It is quicker to setup for a new operation – saving many hours each month.

The proposal was initially submitted by the production executive, and supported by the senior distribution manager. The proposed cost of equipment and installation is $22 million toward the end of Year 1. Benefits would start immediately, but would be higher when all the equipment was in operation:

Year 1: $3 m; year 2: $6.5 m; year 3: $7.5 m; year 4: $8 m; year 5: $8.5 m.

The risks are low as DC has a long-standing relationship with the vendor, and the new equipment is in operation in several other organizations throughout the USA.

DC's financial executive indicated that 20% should be used as a discounting rate, as this was the minimum return that would be expected from any project requiring a capital outlay.

What you are required to do for each project:

Part 1: Use the data given, and assume, for amounts spread throughout the year, that the cost or benefit occurs at the end of the year. Estimate the:

- Payback period (the time to achieve break-even using undiscounted figures).
- NPV considering a 5-year period.
- IRR, possibly using a discounting rate of 30% as the 2nd fix.

Part 2: Mention other criteria that you should consider. Then, assuming that there are only enough funds to undertake one of the projects, what recommendation would you put to the board, and what reasons would you give to support it. Note that neither answer is right or wrong.

36.31 Case 31. Upview Investments (procurement – setting the scene)

This case is intended to create awareness of the differences in perspective between a potential buyer and seller. Here Upview Investments are the buyer, and M&P (Maseti & Pringle) a prospective seller. In a class situation different syndicates would be asked to consider Upview and M&P, followed by a discussion. Otherwise, consider both organizations.

Upview Investments

You are a small investment company with about 30 000 clients who are supported by just over 2000 financial advisors. You provide some of your service through a Contact Center (CC) which consists of 6 skilled people whom you have trained on your processes and investment offerings. There have always been problems in the CC area:

- Peaks and valleys in the call volumes, sometimes leading to long response times.
- Hiring the right people and providing a career path for them.
- Having the right technology in place to monitor, transfer, and follow-up on calls.

Matters have come to a head with one of your best CC operators resigning last week.

You have decided to outsource this function, but are not sure how to go about it. You have arranged an exploratory meeting with M&P, a company that specializes in offering CC services.

- What are your main concerns in selecting a company and entering into a contract?
- Mention some of the issues that you would wish to discuss in this initial meeting.

M&P (Maseti & Pringle) Contact Center Outsource Specialists

The CEO of Upview Investments has requested a meeting with representatives of your firm. It is clear that they are considering outsourcing, and you believe that you may be on their list as a possible supplier.

- What would be your main concerns about working with Upview?
- Mention some of the issues that you would wish to discuss with them.

How might this situation change if the buying company were a government department?

36.32 Case 32. Implications of Contract Types (procurement)

Here are three examples illustrating different contract types. Complete the missing dollar amounts. All figures are given in thousands of dollars and assume that the costs are auditable for the CPPC and CPIF contracts. Note that: 'Cost' is cost to seller; 'Price' is what buyer pays to seller. Profit = price – cost.

Firm Fixed Price (FFP).

FFP Scenario	Cost $000	Profit $000	Price $000
Budgeted	800		1000
Underrun	700		
Overrun	900		
Gross overrun	1200		

Cost plus Percentage Cost (CPPC). In this example, an uplift of 10% is agreed. So the seller would be paid the approved costs, plus 10%, which amounts to a profit of 10%.

CPPC Scenario	Cost $000	Profit $000	Price $000
Budgeted	1000		
Underrun	900		
Overrun	1100		

Cost Plus Incentive Fee (CPIF). Here a fee (or profit) of $100 000 is agreed, based on the actual cost being equal to the budgeted cost of $1.1 million. The risk sharing ratio is: Buyer 80% Seller 20%. Therefore, If the costs were $10 000 below budget, the seller would increase their profit by $2 000 (20% of the $10 000 saving), while the buyer would save $8 000 on what they budgeted to pay the seller.

CPIF Scenario	Cost $000	Saving $000	Profit $000	Price $000
Budgeted	1100	0	100	
Underrun	1000			
Overrun	1200			

36.33 Case 33. M&P Outsourcing Project (outsourcing and partnership)

Six months after signing the agreement to outsource their CC (contact center) function to M&P, Jake Moloi, the CEO of Upview Investments, was wondering whether he had taken the right decision. Upview is a niche investment company with about 30 000 clients who generally invest through financial advisors (over 2000 in total) who provide advice and sales roles. Some of Upview's service is provided through their CC. Prior to outsourcing, it consisted of 6 skilled people, who handled queries from both advisors and clients. There had always been problems with the CC: peaks and valleys in the call volumes, difficulty hiring good people and providing a career path for them, and having the right technology in place to monitor, transfer, and follow-up on calls. In November, the situation had become untenable when the best CC agent had resigned, leading to the decision to outsource.

Upview considered three local contact center outsource partners. One did not have experience with financial services and another firm was just too expensive. M&P appeared to be a reasonable fit, having financial experience and a recently implemented cloud-based technical solution which allowed for agents to work remotely. Due to CC staff loss at Upview, there was some urgency. Negotiations, though sometimes tense, had progressed swiftly with a contract being signed toward the end of February. While Lerato, Upview's client manager, had some concerns, she believed that M&P would make it all work.

Migrating the CC was handled as a project, managed by M&P, who assured Upview that they had appropriate experience. Caron Smith was M&P's project manager; she wasted no time setting up a project schedule. Thereafter things did not go quite as Lerato or Jake had expected. The plan was for the CC staff to move to M&P, but, although the staff knew that something was afoot, they knew little of the details. There had been some shock when they were confronted with unexpected job offers from M&P, which led to one of the team turning the offer down.

Training of M&P agents assigned to support Upview had been difficult. Lerato had expected them to have a basic knowledge of financial services, but three of the four had none. This hampered the training effort, which needed to be provided at short notice, due to some misunderstanding of the timeframe. Fortunately, special access to Upview's investment systems had been accomplished with few hitches.

The early-June cutover appeared to have gone smoothly, but it emerged that a block of client and broker notifications had not been sent, leading to the person monitoring the old phone number being swamped with calls. Caron claimed that she had passed the full list to the M&P admin office. Subsequent interaction between Lerato, Jakes, and Mr. Pringle the M&P sales executive had not been reassuring. "You must expect there to be some teething problems" summarized the outcome.

Things had settled down by August, but not to Lerato's satisfaction. M&P charges were based on logged call time, but in Lerato's view the charges were too high because the new agents were taking too long over simple queries. Moreover, escalations to Upview specialists were up from 12% to over 20% of calls. The monthly satisfaction survey sent to a random selection of clients and brokers supported her concerns: satisfaction was down from 78% to just over 60%. Although there was some reference to meeting existing service levels in the contract, it was not clear what would happen if they were not met.

By July, Caron had moved on, and Lerato's attempts, in August, to set up a meeting with Mr. Pringle to discuss the issues, were returned with an email alleging that Upview systems were not user-friendly. However, she did manage to get an appointment in two weeks' time. Jake shared her feelings that M&P's mission was to maximize their income at the lowest cost possible, while Upview's priority was satisfied advisors and clients, allowing them to develop their core investment business further.

- What problems do you observe with this partnering arrangement and the way the migration was handled?
- How might it have been handled better?
- Given the situation as it emerged, if you were brought in as a consultant, what would you recommend?

36.34 Case 34. Lorion (OCM – organizational change management)

Lorion is a non-unionized company with about 1 500 employees throughout South Africa. Many are highly skilled and provide consulting and technical services to a large client base. Times are difficult and business volumes and profit are under pressure. The average age of employees has risen and the executive committee wish to project a younger image. This resulted in the board deciding to reduce by roughly 100, to about 1 400 employees, starting with a voluntary retirement program for employees over the age of 50, who number almost 200 people. Most, but not all, of the over-50s, some in management positions, will be made attractive offers including cash and enhanced retirement benefits. The reason for *not* making the offer to a few over-50s would be their key positions or critical skills. For those who receive the offer, there will be deadlines for acceptance. For those that accept, the same last date employed will apply – just over 3 months away.

You have been appointed to manage the early retirement program, and to advise executive management. What you are required to do:

- List the categories of people who are, or might be, affected by this change.
- List the issues and concerns that the early retirement offer might raise.
- State what approach would you take to manage the change aspects, considering the tools and techniques at your disposal.

36.35 Case 35. BCT – Bowden Consulting & Training (contracts)

Your company, BCT, does consulting, training, and contract project management work for a variety of clients mostly medium and large. Services are generally provided on a cost plus or time and materials basis, but occasionally you do fixed price work. Up to now, you have relied on your clients to provide a services contract, some of which have been difficult to understand, with many clauses that do not apply to your type of work. You have decided to draw up your own contract which will be proposed to clients. There will be a body part with the clauses that apply to most situations. To this, supplements (also called annexures or addenda), each detailing one specific engagement, can be added when required.

1. Here is a list of things that might need to be included. Indicate in the columns to the right which should be put in the main agreement (M) and which should be in supplements (S). There could be more than one valid answer. Also, note any clauses or items that you would want to add.

Address for correspondence		Assignment of rights or obligations	
BCT responsibilities		Breach of agreement	
Change management process		Client responsibilities	
Confidentiality and non-disclosure		Conflict of interest	
Definitions (meanings) of terms used		Dispute resolution process	
Effective date		Force majeure	
Governing law		Identification of the parties	
Intellectual property rights		Liability	
Payment terms		Penalties (if applicable)	
Restraint of hiring		Restraint of trade	
Schedule of dates		Schedule of payments	
Scope of work		Termination	
Waiver		Warranties (guarantees)	

2. BCT has been asked by Beta Bank to run training on a new product in the low-income banking area. There are 4 000 staff to be trained of which over 70% are branch staff. Training will be done in six major cities in which Beta operates. Locations outside of the cities will send selected staff who will in turn conduct briefings on their sites. The core 1-hour lecture will be recorded and be available online. It is agreed that 2-hour interactive sessions involving 20 staff at a time should be sufficient. There may be slight differences in emphasis depending on whether staff are from branches or from other functions. It is now the end of February 2022 and the launch date is 30 June. The product details have been kept confidential, but you believe that they will be available to BCT by end of March.

Assume that the body contract with Beta bank, is in place. Draw up a proposed supplement, to cover the training assignment. Make any further assumptions that you wish, such as the type of contract (for example, fixed price), the venues, the charges. Ensure that the client's responsibilities are clearly stated.

36.36 Case 36. Warestar (project review)

You work for a national retailer of household goods with customers ordering online or from 130 stores countrywide. You have recently been appointed to their projects office. While waiting for your first project, you have been asked to conduct a review on project Warestar – a $5 million initiative to implement a new cloud-based warehouse package in the four main warehouses. The project involves interfaces to accounting and distribution systems, and changes to the business processes. Warestar has a dedicated team of 12 people, half of which come from the software vendor. The PM is from your organization and there are a number of business stakeholders involved, like the warehouse managers. The initiation stage was completed in 2 months. The first delivery stage, to implement the software in a pilot warehouse has been underway for a month. It is scheduled to finish in 10 months' time, ending next July. The PM is amenable to the review, but has indicated that her team are rather busy. The review is scheduled to start next Monday. You will work on your own, and are expected to deliver the report next Friday afternoon. Your new manager does not have any written guidance on how to conduct the review, and has suggested that you put something together. You have arranged to meet with some colleagues to gather ideas.

What you are required to do, working as a group (or individually):

1. List the main project areas on which you would want to gather information. For each area, note one or two questions that you would ask.
2. List which project documentation you would want to look at, some even before Monday.
3. Mention some of the role players that you would want to interview.
4. Draw up a timetable indicating how you would use the week. Allow time for a review with the PM prior to finalizing the report.

36.37 Case 37. Ethical Dilemmas (ethics and professional conduct)

The following vignettes illustrate the kinds of situations that a PM, or any other manager, might experience. For each of them, the question is "what should you do?"

They can be discussed in a syndicate group or you can consider the best approaches on your own. I suggest that for each, you identify a number of possible approaches and then think which will be best, taking into account the code of conduct, any legal requirements, and possible consequences of your actions. 'Model answers' are *not* given, because the best approach may depend on the assumptions that you make.

Bosango Metals

You are a PM working for a consulting company which offers project management as one of its core services. Bosango are a player in the scrap metal and beneficiation industry, and have asked your company to manage extensions to their main recycling plant. Your company has designated you to manage the project. You have some reservations because Bosango does not have a good reputation. There were court cases against them but you never heard the outcome. There were also rumors of corrupt dealings, but nothing was substantiated. You wonder whether you would be able to work ethically with them.

Mary Malaba

You are managing a medium-sized, but highly visible, 10-month project in your organization. It experienced some delays, but is expected to meet the revised date which is 3 months away. It requires people with both business knowledge and also some technical skills. Mary Malaba is one of your best business people. She is both thoroughly competent and is a positive influence on the rest of the team. She is fairly ambitious and has management aspirations. But, she believes that she will be rewarded if she performs to the best of her ability without 'looking around'. In a steering committee meeting, there is casual discussion of a management position becoming available in another department. Although Mary's name has not been mentioned, you realize that Mary would be a good fit. However, you know that she would leave a hole in your team, and that filling it might take time and even threaten your revised deadline. Also, Mary may never even hear of the opportunity.

IT System Deadline

You are the project manager for a new IT system and it is known that the critical launch deadline is tight. A month ago, management indicated that they would be sympathetic to special bonuses for the team if the deadline were met, and you conveyed this possibility to the team. Although your staff do not get paid for overtime, they have been working long hours and weekends. The six-week-out deadline now looks likely to be met, and the possible bonus may have had some influence. At this morning's steering committee meeting, you raised the subject, hoping to get clarity on the bonus budget. To your dismay, despite your strong justification, the consensus was that bonuses would be inappropriate because some overtime is expected. You are not sure whether to say anything, and, if you do, how your team will receive the news. It also occurs to you that the project outcome will affect your salary increase expected shortly after the project is complete.

Comp2 Stores

Comp2 stores is a medium-sized retail organization with over 500 stores and a small but growing online business. You are the project manager for their store refurbishment initiatives. One of your contractors, Shopfit5, who operates nationwide, do a considerable amount of work for Comp2. They are not cheap, but their work has been of excellent quality. However, over the past year, it appears that their standards have dropped. Some of the work has been unsatisfactory. You have discussed this with their management, and indicated that it will affect their vendor rating and their eligibility for future contracts. This morning your daughter, who has recently completed her studies, phoned to say that she has been offered an excellent job in Shopfit5's sales and contracting department. She is clearly very excited about the job and the salary offered. You wonder whether this results in a conflict of interests.

Crolex Chemicals

You work for ProjX4 and your management has asked you to manage extensions to expand the capacity of a chemical process for Crolex Chemicals, a customer organization. Times are tough. Crolex budgets are stripped to the minimum and they have retrenched staff in other areas. ProjX4 have under quoted, on a fixed price basis, just to keep their staff busy. For the expansion to last, the pipework would need to be of a certain specification. This was not clear in the contract documents, and to meet the cost budget you would need to use a lower specification which is a lot cheaper and would achieve a small profit. However, you know that the pipes might corrode in 3 to 5 years' time. Although unlikely to endanger staff, this would result in considerable expense and downtime. In discussion, your management has told you to use the cheaper spec saying that their lawyers could defend against legal action that far out.

Bettavap

Bettavap has been marketing e-cigarettes (cigarette substitutes) for nearly 5 years and are constantly developing lower-cost products in order to compete effectively. However, they need to convince both customers and regulators that their products are safe. You work for a reputable research organization. One of your projects is research for Bettavap on the customer experience of using their most promising new product, considering both enjoyment and possible medical impact. Over a year ago your team managed to assemble 115 smokers for the test and have been monitoring the experience ever since. You are due to present results in 3 months' time, and are very aware that Bettavap expects them to be positive. However, reviewing recent results with your lead statistician, there is an indication that some of heavier users of the e-cigarettes have been having unexplained breathing problems. Your statistician suggests that, if you reject three of the cases, the remainder would look pretty good, and offers to look for a justification to reject them.

36.38 Case 38. Getting Intranet Development Done (negotiation)

You are managing an important project in a large organization. As part of your project communications, you want to set up an intranet page, which will be updated for the project duration. To do this, you need intranet skills, and approach the manager of the intranet department. You know that they are busy and will charge costs to your project. You are reluctant to spend a lot of money, but you believe that, with the right skills, the work might be done in a week or two. One of your team members might even be able to help.

- What would your interests be? What might be the interests of the intranet manager?
- What is your power base and BATNA? What might those of the intranet manager be?
- Are there areas of mutual interest that can be discussed?

You are not given much information, so it's fine to use some imagination.

36.39 Case 39. TRSA Records Management (preventing failure)

Tradewin South Africa (or TRSA) is a retailer of household durable products including lines of furniture and white goods like dishwashers. They have grown rapidly, doubling in size over the past 3 years. There are now eight physical outlets and three warehouses, all located in or near cities. Each location has office staff, some of who are responsible for keeping records. Nevertheless, much of their business is done via web marketing, managed from Johannesburg, with local delivery. TRSA employs a total of 1200 staff throughout South Africa of which 150 are at the head office in Johannesburg. Head office functions include Marketing, Distribution, Finance, IT, Legal, Audit, and HR. Most of their sales are done via credit agreements, with customers paying off their purchases over a period. This has resulted in large amounts of documentation, both paper and electronic, that has mushroomed in recent years. Documentation is filed and managed in the departments where it arises – mostly in sales offices and warehouses.

After an adverse audit, relating to adherence to retention legislation, the decision was taken at board level to initiate a project to get the documentation records under control – including contracts, vendor, and customer information. It was to be overseen by Finance, and Joel, the head of internal audit agreed to play the role of sponsor. Ridwaan, the finance director, appointed Lucy, a senior administrator to manage the project. She had good experience in setting up filing systems at head office and storing critical records electronically. There was some urgency, as the board wanted the project completed in 10 months, in time for the next scheduled audit. Ridwaan assured Lucy that funding would not be a problem due to the importance of the project.

Ridwaan suggested that Lucy contact a friend of his who is sales manager at DocuRec, a commercial records-management company. After a meeting, a DocuRec representative put in a proposal which Lucy looked through. She realized that it would be advisable to go through the audit findings in detail, to check that the proposal would address the concerns.

Lucy decided that it was best to tackle a limited scope, and got the agreement from Joel to start with head office. She called a meeting of the HO staff responsible for capturing and filing records. She was happy about the way the meeting went. Several attendees were supportive of the initiative because they agreed that some of the filing was 'in a mess', and promised full cooperation. A start has already been made in getting the contracts under control. A few days later, Thabang, the manager of supply chain, suggested that while she was working with the records, it would be useful for his staff to have access to the list of supplier contracts. Lucy agreed with him, and said that she would do her best.

One of the legal people remarked that they had better comply with the new POPI (Protection of Personal Information) Act which would restrict holding and use of customer information. It was then that Lucy realized that she might be out of her depth, at which point she went to discuss her concerns with Joel.

Although a start has been made, there are a number of indicators that the project could be heading for failure. Identify:

- Any aspects of the project that are satisfactory.
- Aspects of concern that could result in failure of the project.

If you were brought in as a consultant:

- Give a few pointers as to what needs to be done to get the project onto a sound footing.

Work at a high level, as you are not given enough information to go into depth.

Chapter 37

Answers for Cases

All cases and exercises are labeled 'Case n'. The cases have a variety of answers and there is no 'one right answer'. Therefore, what is given is a 'possible answer'. The exercises generally have only one right answer. Should you find errors or have a different view on the answer given, then please let me know – **fdeinhorn@gmail.com**.

37.1 Case 1. Endura Holdings (project initiation and arriving at a charter)

1. Checklist of discussion items and questions:
    - Describe the project. Is it local or other countries as well?
    - What is the background? How did the project arise?
    - Who are the key stakeholders? Who needs to be involved?
    - What are the main goals and objectives?
    - What is the scope and what are the deliverables?
    - What role do you envisage for me, and my company? Would my role be full-time?
    - Will you be the project sponsor? If not who will be?
    - To whom would I report? Will there be a project steering committee or board?
    - How often would we meet? How do we handle urgent decisions?
    - Is there a business case? May I have a copy?
    - Has there been a feasibility study? May I have a copy?
    - Have you drawn up a project charter? (scope, responsibilities of PM)
    - To what extent is the project confidential?
    - Will resources be available internally, or do you expect me to source them?
    - When do you envisage the project starting? Any pre-requisites or dependencies?
    - Do you have dates in mind for key deliverables? and for the end of the project?
    - What is your financial year? How much money has been allocated for each year?

DOI: 10.1201/9781003321101-41

- Are there any other constraints or dependencies?
- Can we use our own project standards? Else, may I get details of your standards?
- What internal standards and procedures exist? What systems need to be updated?
- What reports are expected? how often?

2. Prior to the meeting:
   - Find out from the person in your organization that made the initial contact what they know about Endura and the executive that you will visit.
   - It would be wise to read about Endura on the web. Make a few notes and have a broad understanding of what they do and some of their terminology. This might take between 15 minutes and an hour.
3. At the end of the meeting (and depending on how the meeting goes):
   - Suggest that you send her a summary to check your understanding. Assuming that the project goes ahead, this could serve as a charter.
   - Ask whether you may contact her in case further questions arise. Get her email address and phone numbers.
   - Thank them for their time, the information shared (or whatever).

37.2 Case 2. Waluma Hospital (stakeholder analysis)

1. List of stakeholders. What do they stand to gain; what might their fears be?

Stakeholder	Stand to Gain	Possible Fears
MediWorld executives	Another step toward efficiency and reduced costs	How many doctors will resign?
Dr. Gubane (hospital director)	More efficient hospital.	Will my doctors accept it?
Doctors	No more lost patient files	Will we be able to enter things/find things in the system?
Patients	When I use a MediWorld hospital elsewhere, they have my record.	Will everyone in the hospital know what medical problems I suffer from?
Johannesburg project office		We had two hospitals go badly. Will this be another?
HIS support team	Another step forward for our brilliant system	There will be more demands for irrelevant changes to the system
Hospital administrators	No more chasing after files	A big part of our job has gone. What next?

Stakeholder	Stand to Gain	Possible Fears
Nurses		Will we have to enter every daily temperature reading?
IT infrastructure		
Laboratory staff	No more filing of lab result forms. No more lost forms	
HIS trainers	It's an opportunity to use our latest training material	Staff will resist the change. Can we convince them that this is an improvement? We shall have to travel to and from Klerksdorp.

2. Power/interest grid for HIS project at Waluma hospital – Figure 37.1.
3. Specific Approaches to engage and manage expectations:

- MediWorld Executives and PMO
  - Regular progress reports
- Hospital Director:
  - Regular progress reports
  - Review of approach, plan, and issues
- Doctors
  - Workshop on benefits and concerns
  - Training on effective use of system
  - Special support during early stages
  - Involve the hospital director

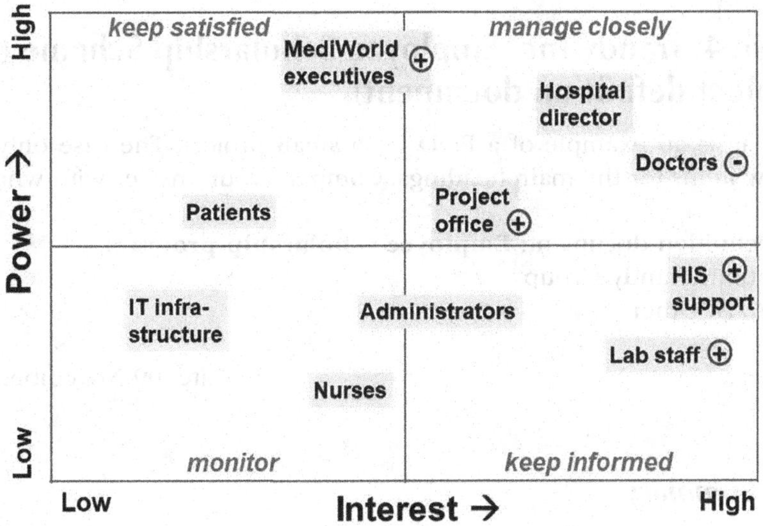

Figure 37.1 Stakeholder power/interest grid for Waluma hospital project.

- Patients
  - ♦ Brochure on benefits of new system, and allay fears
  - ♦ Brief admin staff on how to handle patient queries

37.3 Case 3. The Triple Constraint (project priorities for planning)

Answers should be reasonable and justified. The following are valid but other justified answers may be equally valid.

1. 21st birthday party.
   - Once the date has been set and invitations sent, the time is constrained.
   - The parents would want to enhance quality and possibly scope – to make the evening memorable.
   - Being wealthy, the parents will accept the fact that it may cost more than originally planned.
2. Home renovation
   - Cost will be constrained because of the limited funds
   - Quality or scope will be enhanced because the outcome is of long duration.
   - It is likely that some time overrun will be accepted.
3. Flu vaccine
   - Scope is constrained. The vaccine must be properly tested.
   - Time is enhanced, as it will enable more people to be vaccinated if distribution of the vaccine starts a few weeks before the flu season.
   - A cost overrun will be accepted because an effective vaccine, distributed in good time, is likely to save on health-care costs thereafter.

37.4 Case 4. Trandy Inc. Employee Scholarship Scheme (PDD – project definition document)

The following is an example of a PDD for a small project. The case only asked for one or a few items for the main headings. Compare your answer with what is below.

Project definition document: **Employee scholarship program**
Organization: Trandy Group
Author: A. N. Other

Date: 09 November 2022

Executive Summary

The project is to launch Trandy Group's employee scholarship scheme. The purpose is to provide an employee benefit that will enhance our reputation and our desirability as an employer. The project will be considered complete when applications for the 2023–24 academic year have been adjudicated, notified to successful employee parents, and paid to them through payroll. Because the scholarship is automatically renewed if the student passes, the new students each year should only get about one-third of the total annual funding. The budget for the September payout would therefore be about $700 000, and the amount would grow to $2 million in September 2025. The annual cost of administration and adjudication will be about $60 000 per annum. The cost of the project is estimated at $150 000.

Glossary

Term	*Description*
Academic year	Roughly September to June of the following year.
Colleges	Used in this PDD to cover universities, technical schools, and vocational training institutions.
Intranet	Company information available to all employees through the web.
PDF	Standard form of softcopy document that cannot easily be edited.
PMO	Project management office, which monitors all projects in Trandy.

Business Goals and Project Objectives

The main business goals are:

- Improved public image for Trandy.
- Be seen as an employer of choice.

The main project objectives are:

- New scholarship scheme announced by 17 March 2023
- 35 Trandy scholarship holders in educational institutions in September 2023.

Critical Success Factors (CSFs)

- Visible support from the organization through the divisional heads.
- Scheme launched to employees by 17 March 2023 to allow enough time for applications.

Scope

The main scope items identified to date are:

- Investigate scholarship schemes run by other organizations.

- List employees with children in the final school year.
- Determine educational institutions for which we shall accept applications.
- List processes required and document them, for example:
  - Submission and adjudication of applications
  - Request to consider a college that is not on the accepted list.
- Convene a representative group of employees to review documentation and provide input.
- Draft the scholarship scheme rules on eligibility, employee responsibilities (like reporting student results), and handling of situations that can arise.
- Develop and give presentations to divisional heads including what support is needed from them.
- Present the scheme to the steering committee and get approval.
- Make and test enhancements to the payroll system.
- Develop standard forms (manual initially).
- Develop employee scholarship brochure in PDF format.
- Convene candidate selection committee via a nomination process.
- Appoint scholarship administrator (within HR).
- Make provision on the intranet for the announcement and HR information.
- Announce scheme to employees via managers, email, and intranet.
- Handle employee queries.
- Receive applications, adjudicate according to rules.
- Committee review and recommend on borderline cases.
- Notify applicants of outcome for 2023–24 academic year. Send data to Payroll.
- Check that payments were successfully processed.

Approach

The project will not be broken into sub-projects. All team members will be involved with all aspects of the project. All project team members will be part-time on a basis to be agreed between PM and manager of the team member concerned.

Context Diagram

Not applicable.

Scope Exclusions

- Online application forms via the intranet. This is a likely future objective. The initial processes will use forms that can be signed and scanned.
- External publicity for the scheme.
- Monitoring of scholarship holders from September 2023. This will be the responsibility of the scholarship committee and carried out by the (part-time) scholarship administrator.

Other Exclusions

- Subsidies for anything beyond fees and an allowance for equipment and books. Therefore, costs like residence fees, travel, and clothing will not be covered.
- Applications from people other than Trandy employees, such as contractors.
- Only the first post-school qualification is eligible.

Benefits from the Project

Ref	*Benefit Description*	*$/Annum*
1	Improved public image. Being seen as employer of choice (goal)	1 500 000*
2	Reduced hiring costs owing to reduced staff attrition and promising people approaching Trandy (employer of choice goal)	1 000 000*
3	Trandy will have knowledge of outstanding students that could become future employees.	200 000*
4	Scholarship holders could become interns during their studies.	0
5	Ongoing administration	–60 000
6	Cost of scholarships: initially $0.7 m rising to $2 m	–2 000 000

* estimate supplied by sponsor

Costs of Doing the Project

Ref	*Cost Description*	*$*
1	PM time based on 50% full time for 10 months	52 000
2	Three HR specialists based on 25% full time on average	70 000
3	Changes to HR system	10 000
4	Changes to the intranet to cater to the new benefit	4 000
5	Legal review	4 000
6	Graphics and artwork for brochure	4 000
7	Miscellaneous costs (currently unknown)	6 000
	Total	150 000

Resources and Stakeholders

Name	*Role*	*Main Responsibilities*
Jane Bunda	Sponsor	■ Convene steering committee ■ Review project reports and respond
Name	Senior finance manager	■ Steering committee member
Name	Divisional manager	■ Represent the divisions on steering committee
Your name	Project manager	■ Normal PM responsibilities
Names when agreed	HR specialists	■ Conduct investigations ■ Design forms and document procedures ■ Facilitate meetings with Trandy employees at all levels

Name	*Role*	*Main Responsibilities*
Name	Legal	■ Legal review of scheme and brochures
Name	Payroll specialist	■ Implement changes to payroll system
Name	Intranet manager	■ Update intranet with scholarship information.
Name	Finance rep.	■ Advise on cash flow and tax matters.
Flowers Inc.	Artwork supplier	■ Presentation elements of employee brochure

Milestone Schedule

Date	*Milestone Description*
09 Dec 22	Meetings with divisional managers and employee representatives complete
06 Feb 23	Steering committee approve scholarship rules and processes in principle.
17 Mar 23	Announce the new scholarship scheme through managers and email.
12 May 23	At least 40 valid applications received
02 Jun 23	Employee applicants notified of outcome
24 Aug 23	All payments to successful applicants made by payroll.

Risks

Ref	*Risk*	*P*	*I*	*X*	*Response Action*
1	The scholarship money paid to the employee may not result in the academic institution being paid.	2	2	4	Recipients sign an acceptance and undertaking of responsibilities.
2	Employee representative group raise serious disagreements among themselves.	2	3	6	Notify the ground rules that the purpose is to gain input, but that in the event of disagreement the decision of HR head will be final.
3	There are very few qualifying applicants	1	3	3	Accept the risk. Survey eligible employees that did not apply, to determine the reasons.

Ref	*Risk*	*P*	*I*	*X*	*Response Action*
4	The administration is greater than expected, due to a high number of exceptional cases.	3	2	6	Accept the risk for 2023, but review all such cases and determine whether some could be eliminated in future by modifying the rules

P = Probability, I = Impact, X = Weighted risk or severity (P × I). Scale 1–10 for P and I

Assumptions, Issues, Dependencies

Ref	*Description*
E1	Handle a situation where school leaver has applied to several colleges but is still awaiting acceptance at application cut-off date.
E2	There is uncertainty about how payments will be treated from a tax point of view.
E3	Make early announcement of the intention to launch a scholarship scheme?
E4	Will executives be excluded from eligibility?
E5	Should part of the funding be in the form of hardware from Trandy?
A1	All procedures can be written by the HR team members
A2	Students that pass a year will automatically be funded for the next year until they achieve the planned qualification.
A3	Students will receive the scholarship for 3 years on average
A4	Students will not receive the scholarship the year after the parent employee leaves the company (except through normal retirement)
A5	Formally adopted children will be eligible.

E = Issue, A = Assumption, D = Dependency, C = constraint

Management System

- The steering committee will meet monthly and include the sponsor (representing HR), the PM, a divisional head, a senior finance manager, optionally a legal representative. The PM will take and circulate minutes.
- The project tracking meeting will take place weekly and last roughly 30 minutes. The schedule and action items will be monitored. Attendees are the PM, HR specialists, an employee representative, and a finance representative. Minutes will be circulated.
- A project report will be produced fortnightly and circulated to the project team, steering committee members, and divisional heads. Reports will also be lodged with the central PMO.

37.5 Case 5. Objective, Requirement, Scope, or Exclusion? (scope planning)

The following gives possible answers. Note that some statements could have more than one type. (O = Objectives, R = Requirements, S = Scope, E = Exclusions from the scope).

No	*Statement*	*Type*
1	Nursing staff must be able to request laboratory tests	R
2	Supply of servers and HIS software is a dependency, but not part of the project	E
3	Improve access to our patient records	O
4	Adjudicate bids for furnishing and fitting out the wards	S
5	Every staff member must have their own computer Id and Password	R
6	Construction of the building	S
7	Streamline administration	O
8	All operating theatres and IT equipment must have standby power	R
9	There must be a server room suitable for the new Hospital Information System	R
10	Provide a more comprehensive service	O
11	Architectural design of buildings	S
12	The envisaged brain scan equipment will not be acquired in the project timeframe	E
13	It must take no more than 3 seconds to call up a patient record from HIS	R
14	Carpet the lounge areas.	S
15	Photographs of the upgraded hospital to be supplied for MediWorld brochure	S/VR
16	Flow of people/trolleys in the hospital should improve	O/VR
17	Electrical wiring	S
18	There must be a classroom of 40 square meters, with projection facilities.	R
19	Plan RFP (Request for Proposal) for building extensions	S
20	Only designated staff may access patient records	R
21	Train doctors on review and update of patient records via the HIS	S
22	Increase market share and profit in the Klerksdorp area	O
23	No re-cabling of the existing building will be done	E
34	There must be an additional 85 beds – 45 in general wards, and 40 in semi-private.	R
25	Sign off requirements	S
26	Dig foundations	S
27	Minimize the number of trees that must be removed	VR

37.6 Case 6. NMA Conference (WBS – work breakdown structure)

The following answer uses two levels below the project level:

1. Manage stakeholders
   1.1 List stakeholders and contact details
   1.2 Draw up communication plan
2. Confirm venue
   2.1 List venue criteria (for example: size, location, accommodation, price)
   2.2 List possible venues
   2.3 Prioritize venues
   2.4 Select venue, notify venue management and get possible dates
3. Plan event with venue management
   3.1 Plan and cost meals and teas
   3.2 Document and agree staff responsibilities
   3.3 Plan gala dinner
4. Agree dates
   4.1 Review possible dates + fix date
5. Book accommodation
   5.1 List accommodation close to venue
   5.2 Negotiate discounts
6. Confirm speakers
   6.1 Invite NMA association members to submit papers
   6.2 Adjudicate papers
   6.3 Select papers and notify speakers
   6.4 Obtain paper/presentation in advance (member + guest)
7. Special guest speakers
   7.1 Get nominations
   7.2 Agree primary and backup invitees
   7.3 Send invitations and monitor responses
   7.4 Make travel and accommodation arrangements
   7.5 Agree a host per special guest speaker
8. Confirm delegates
   8.1 Plan strategy to advertise to members
   8.2 Post adverts in NMA journal
   8.3 Email detail to members + invite bookings
   8.4 Record bookings (by NMA staff)
9. Manage finances
   9.1 Produce a preliminary budget spreadsheet
   9.2 Decide on minimum number of delegates
   9.3 Plan pricing and discount structure, for full/partial attendance, speakers
   9.4 Receive deposits (or full fee)
   9.5 Record delegate bookings and payment status
   9.6 Plan partial refunds for non-attendance with advance notice

10. Advertise
    10.1 Confirm use of NMA's agency
    10.2 Agree advertising strategy and timing
    10.3 Run advertisements
11. Produce schedule for conference
    11.1 List papers to be presented
    11.2 Plan time schedule with available slots
    11.3 Allocate slots to papers.
12. Produce brochure
    12.1 Collate all information
    12.2 Design brochure
    12.3 Obtain graphics (pictures)
    12.4 Print brochures and make PDF available for emailing
13. Manage event
    13.1 Produce event packs – bags, binders, etc.
    13.2 Monitor guest speaker arrival
    13.3 List responsibilities for conference officials
    13.4 Assign responsibilities
    13.5 Produce briefing sheets for conference officials
    13.6 Management during event
14. Produce transcript
    14.1 Assemble papers in softcopy format
    14.2 Structure them into a suitable format for PDF
    14.3 Post to website and email link to delegates

37.7 Case 7. SpeedWall (definitive estimating)

The first step is to calculate the quantities. There are:

- 400 meters foundation
- 800 square meters of wall
- 1600 square meters of plastering
- 800 × 100 = 80 000 bricks

Then it is easier to calculate the material and effort costs:

- Material, Foundations 400 × $20 = $8 000
- Materials: Bricks 80 000 @ $400 per thousand $32 000
- Materials, Other 400 × $40 = $16 000
- Labor: Foundations $200 × 400/10 = $8 000
- Labor: Bricklaying 80 000 bricks/2000 × (300 + 200) = $20 000
- Labor: Plastering (1 600/25) × (300 + 200) =$32 000
- Supervisor: 20 days × $400 = $8 000
- Construction total = $124 000
- Office and management @ 10% = $12 400

- Contingency @ 5% = $6 200
- Total cost $142 600

Factors affecting bid price could be:

- Level of competition
- State of the economy and the market
- Degree to which the company's capacity is currently utilized.
- Risk level (although some is catered for via the contingency)

Price = Total cost × 1.16 (16% uplift) $165 416

37.8 Case 8. Estimating for Different Situations (project estimating)

There are no 'right' answers. The following answers involve making assumptions and are not comprehensive – for each of the projects, there are far more issues to debate. This underlines the fact that a meaningful estimate is best done after the main issues are resolved.

- Delivering training nationwide
  Given that the move to the new warehousing system has already been decided, the training must take place. So it is unlikely that an estimate would be requested up-front. However, management would probably want to know what training has cost as part of the larger program (to move to the new system). An estimate would be done during planning so that a budget could be given to the PM to track against and hence keep management informed. It would probably be a bottom-up estimate taking into account training venues, trainer costs, and travel.

  Considerations:
  - Does the training material already exist? If so, in what form? How much work is still needed, and is this part of the project?
  - Will all training be in classroom mode, or will some be online (for example, at remote locations)?
  - How long will the training take? Who will familiarize the trainers with the processes?
  - Will facilities be needed for 'hands-on' training on the new system?
  - Who will take responsibility for people that are enrolled, but do not show up?
- Move of a manufacturing company to a new factory
  An OM (order of magnitude) estimate should be done by people with experience before finalizing the decision to move. A bottom up estimate, based on the WBS, should be done during planning of the move. There might already be estimates (or quotes) from suppliers (for example, to move machinery).

  Considerations:
  - Which costs are part of the move, and which are not? For example:

  - ♦ Cost of a new machine purchased in preference to moving an outdated one.
  - ♦ Facilities in the new factory. Does the project pay for all, some, or none?
- Is lost production time included as a cost to the move?
- How much more will it cost if we shorten the move period? Should this be done if it reduces the lost production time?

■ New corporate accounting system
During investigation, and prior to project approval, an OM estimate of the software cost, and the implementation effort, duration and cost would be needed as input to the business case. The software supplier might contribute information on similar projects done elsewhere to enable analogous estimating. Preliminary tests might be done on a demonstration copy of the software to support estimates of effort.

After the decision is taken and the project started, a WBS would be created and bottom up time and cost estimates done for budgeting and tracking purposes. The estimates might be refined as more information becomes available.

Considerations:

- ■ Will the software vendor allow familiarizing with software prior to final commitment?
- ■ What interfaces need to be developed?
- ■ What costs are included in the project? – for example, training, business user hours, conversion from the existing system.
- ■ Who will resource and manage the project? Software supplier, our organization, or both?

37.9 Case 9. Market Survey (basic precedence and Gantt chart scheduling)

1. The precedence chart is shown in Figure 37.2.

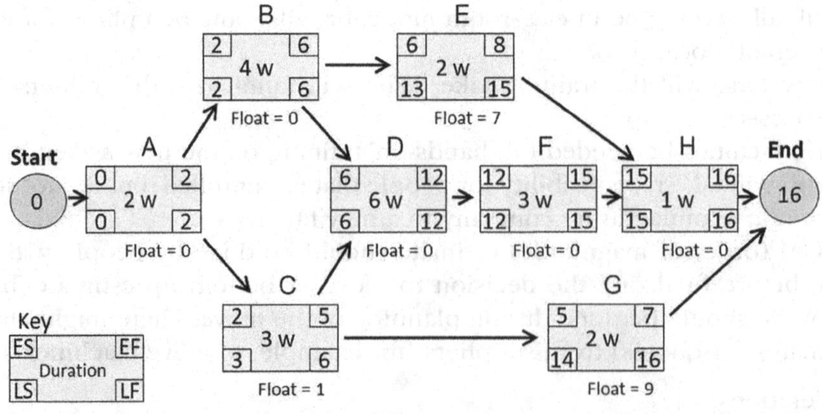

Figure 37.2 Market survey precedence (network) chart.

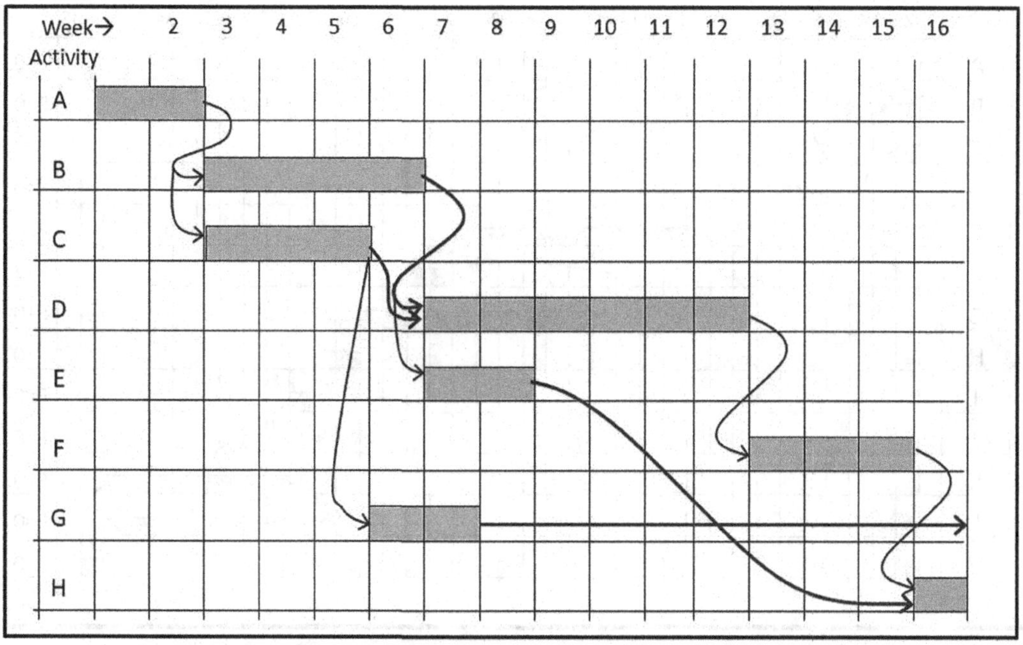

Figure 37.3 Market survey Gantt chart.

The critical path is A B D F H (the activities with zero float).

Activity C has a float of 1 week: E has a float of 7 weeks; G has a float of 9 weeks.

2. The Gantt chart is shown in Figure 37.3.

37.10 Case 10. Organize a Conference (Gantt chart scheduling – more complex)

Here is the Gantt chart for the schedule based on the estimates given.

- The earliest week for the conference is week 37.
- As shown on the right of the Gantt chart, only activities C, F, and J have float. All the others are on the critical path.
- If the conference were to be held in week 38 (a week after the earliest possible), then all activities except the conference itself would have an additional week of float. However, it would be best to complete the activities on or before the times given, and to keep the last week clear as a buffer. There will always be last-minute things to do, and having that week will reduce the stress levels (Figure 37.4).

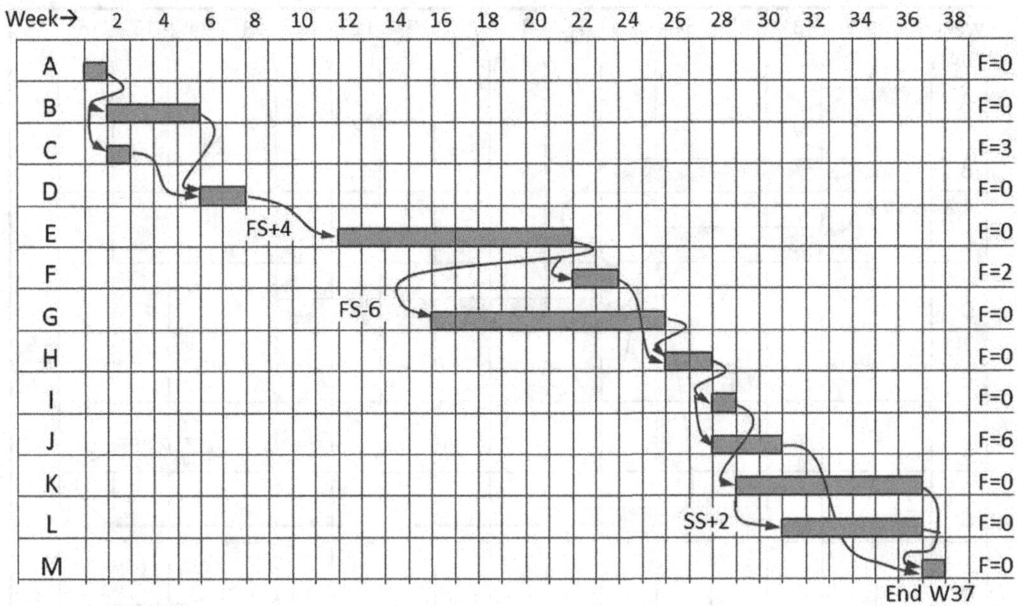

Figure 37.4 Organize conference Gantt chart.

37.11 Case 11. Precedence from Conversations (preparation for scheduling)

If we are scheduling in weeks, the fs+1 means lag of 1 week. Note that for business projects, scheduling is typically done in work-days in which case fs+1 means a lag of 1 day.

No	*Activity*	*Precedence*	*Comment*
1	D	C	which means C fs, as fs is the default
2	D	B ss+2	or B ss+2w
3	D	No predecessor	D can start immediately
4	D	C fs-2	
5	D	A, B	both are fs – the default
6	D	C fs+1	
7	D	We do not know	The comment gives the precedence for F not D
8	D	A, B, C fs+1	A and B are logical dependencies. C is a resource dependency.
9	D	C fs+2	The procurement 'lead time' results in a lag (+2)
10	D	Either B ss or B	D will start the same day (as the milestone is start of day)

No	Activity	Precedence	Comment
11	D	We do not know	No precedence is mentioned. D may not depend on C.
12	D	B fs+2, C fs+3	D has no direct dependency on A, and for the precedence we do not need to know any of the durations.

37.12 Case 12. Hospital Project (Gantt manual and on a scheduling tool)

The answer to Part 1 is given in Figure 37.5. No answer is given for Part 2; however, when the activities have been entered with their dependencies, it should look similar.

The answer to Part 2 should also look similar to Figure 9.7 in Chapter 9.

37.13 Case 13. Market Survey Schedule Compression (crashing the schedule)

The options given are to reduce time on B, C, D, F, or G. You can eliminate G because, even though the cost of compression is low, it has lots of slack and is not close to the critical path.

So looking at B, C, D, and F, your alternatives are.

- Cut 2 weeks on D. This is the most straightforward. Cost $8 000.
- Cut 1 week on D ($3 000). Cut 1 week on F ($4 000). Cost $7 000.
- Cut 1 week on B ($3 000) so that D can start a week earlier. Cut 1 week on D ($3 000). Cost $6 000.
- Cut 2 weeks on B ($5 000). This is not as good as it looks, as we also have to cut 1 week from C ($3 000) because D depends on both B and C. Cost $8 000.
- Cut 1 week on B ($3 000). Cut 1 week on F ($4 000). Cost $7 000.

So, the third bullet looks best with an additional cost of $6 000. It has the further advantage that if the actual time saving is not sufficient, you still have the option of reducing F. So, if a deadline is critical, it usually pays to save time earlier, rather than later. If one leaves the time savings too late, there is a risk that something else will go wrong, making the deadline almost impossible to meet.

It would be unwise to start anything before the contract is signed, so here, pulling the start of B or C forward is not an option. In practice, starting before the contract is signed would only be considered if there were no other options. Even then it would involve a negotiation with the client who might be prepared to sign a letter authorizing you to start on a rate per hour basis. Then, when the contract is signed, it would supersede the letter. However, if the contract is never signed, the cost of whatever hours were spent could be recovered.

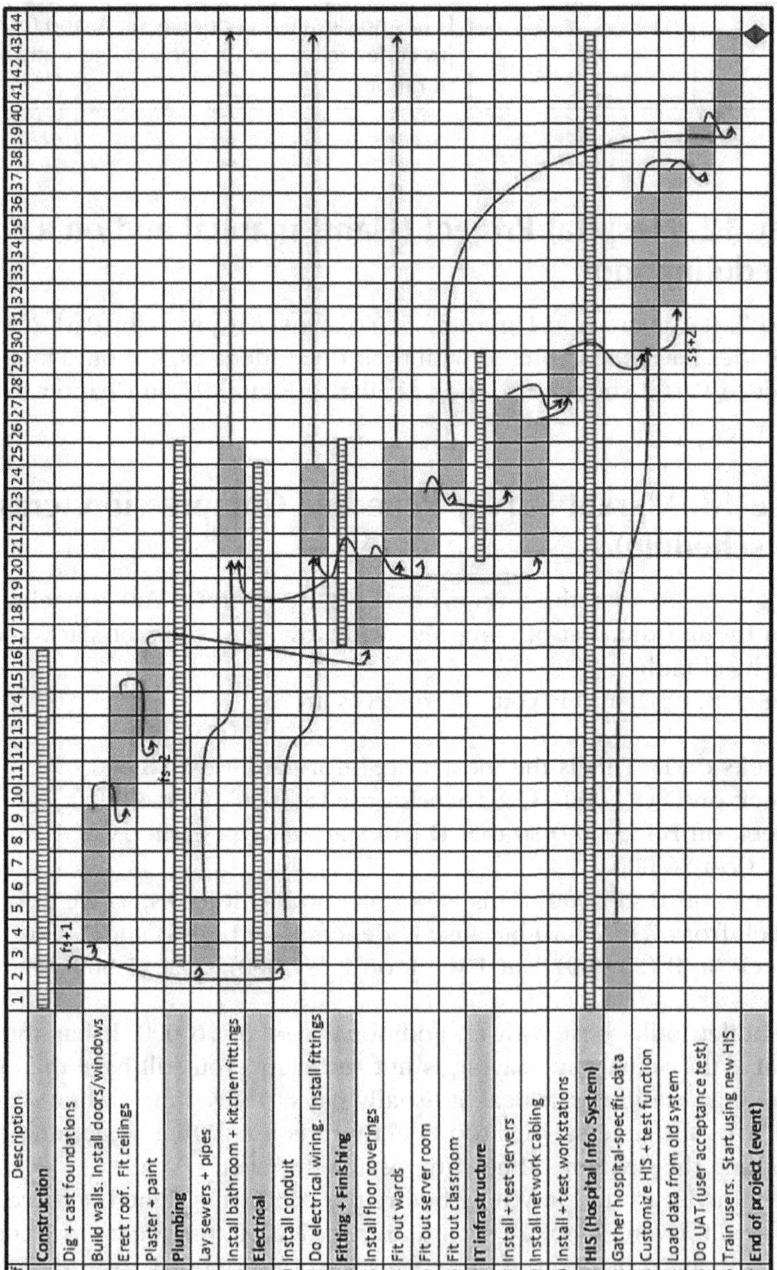

Figure 37.5 Hospital project Gantt chart done manually.

37.14 Case 14. EduToy7 Factory Move (project quality)

The following are possible quality requirements for the move. There may be more.

- Minimum staff productivity lost; minimum production time lost.
- Customers are kept informed and urgent orders are properly handled.
- Customer commitments are met. Negotiation should take place where there will be an unavoidable delay.
- Staff are kept informed and perceive that their welfare has been considered.
- Space plans are reviewed by departmental management in good time for essential adjustments to be made.
- Parking arrangements are decided on and communicated – including rules/procedures for visitor and general parking.
- Factory machine positioning is well planned. It should be easy to do maintenance and move work in progress between machines.
- Appearance of the building is pleasing, both exterior and interior.
- Nothing gets lost – including: stores, factory equipment, files, contents of desks and cupboards.
- Security is well handled throughout the move – no equipment or goods stolen.
- Security at the new premises is sound and requires no additional staff.
- All costs, related to the move are accounted for using codes allocated by Finance.
- IT systems and telephones are working prior to staff moving.
- Non-essential clutter in the offices is disposed of, with approval.

37.15 Case 15. Nature Films (risk management)

The risk register table below gives an illustrative answer. The register focuses on the negative risks, but also shows two positive opportunities.

- The strategy column would normally not be included in a risk register.
- Although dates are encouraged, a date is only shown for risk number 3 as an illustration.
- The priority (X) is not always exactly P × I. Judgment has been used for some of them.

P = Probability, I = Impact, both on 1 – 10 scale. X = Priority (P × I)

Rf	*Risk Description*	*P*	*I*	*X*	*Strategy*	*Response Actions*
1	Because Cheetahs are few in number, we cannot find enough Cheetahs, or are not able to get close enough, thus affecting the quality of our film footage.	4	3	12	Mitigate	■ Employ expert tracker/Cheetah expert ■ Use technology to dart and insert an identity chip ■ Study behavior of Cheetahs like seasonality, preferred environment.

Rf	*Risk Description*	*P*	*I*	*X*	*Strategy*	*Response Actions*
2	Because of the limited time, certain Cheetah behaviors may not be captured resulting in mediocre output	6	2	13	Mitigate	■ Classify and prioritize behaviors ■ Investigate cost of other sources for film material ■ Discuss the trade-off between time and content (scope) with GWF.
3	14 Aug 21. GWF are used to high standards, and may not be happy with the outcome	4	3	11	Mitigate	■ Review/document client expectations ■ Explain some of the challenges involved with Cheetahs ■ Include client involvement in contract ■ Regular reviews on progress
4	GWF depends on donations whose use they prioritize. So there may be payment delays or refusal to pay.	3	6	16	Avoid	■ Schedule of progress payments, possibly based on demonstrating planned content
5	A few members of the team are new, so the team may not work effectively together	2	4	8	Mitigate	■ Hold planning session (team building) to agree roles, team charter/ modus operandi, etc.
6	Because of the rough terrain, accidents or illness may delay work beyond the deadline	2	3	6	Mitigate	■ Identify backup person for each key role requiring certain people to have multiple skill sets
7	Permission to film in Kruger not granted	1	6	6	Mitigate	■ Apply early. Use contacts if necessary. ■ Involve Parks Board in planning and emphasize the benefits to them
8	Vehicle breakdown	2	1	2	Accept	
9	Film material is lost or damaged	2	4	8	Avoid	■ Adhere to standards ■ Back up film material regularly
10	Opportunity to harvest valuable film material	4	3	12	Share	■ Pay Parks Board for services like trackers.
11	Opportunity for more work from GWF if this is a success	3	4	13	Accept	

37.16 Case 16. Budget for Project Math11 (cost budgeting and control figures)

Figures in the table are in $ thousands (10 means $10 000)

Activity cost items	*May*	*Jun*	*Jul*	*Aug*	*Sep*	*Oct*	*Nov*	*Total*
Initial design, propose changes	20	20						40
Review proposed changes			20 10					30
Brief communications team				5 16				21
Communicate at schools					32	32	32	96
Project management	2	2	2	2	2	2	2	14
Travel, stationery, printing					3	3	3	9
Total per month	22	22	32	23	37	37	37	210
Cumulative total	22	44	76	99	136	173	210	

The table gives the plan. Some explanation:

- The shaded area is a bit like a crude Gantt chart showing when things will happen. The actual Gantt chart for tracking the work would have more detail.
- The PM working 20% of time on this project would be charged at 20% of $10 000 or $2 000 per month.
- The cost items are totaled in the right-hand column. Adding the line item totals downward gives the total cost 210 which means $210 000.
- The costs in each month are totaled downward. For example, August totals 5+16+2 = 23.
- The cumulative totals are calculated as follows:

    May is 22 as it is the first month.
    June is 22 (from May) + 22 = 44.
    July is 44 (from June) + 32 = 76.
    August is 76 (from July) + 23 = 99, and so on.

  Not surprisingly, the cumulative total at end November is 210 which should be the same as the total in the right-hand column. This serves as a check and balance because if they are not the same, then there is an error somewhere.

Typically this exercise would be done on an Excel spreadsheet. The cumulative figures would become the control figures at the end of each month. In EVM terms they are called 'planned values'. For example, if the project is on track schedule-wise, then the PM would expect to have spent about $99 000 at the end of August.

The people costs are the amounts that the contracting organization would charge to the department of education. The people themselves would be remunerated at lower rates.

Note that everything here is an estimate, the times, the costs, and even the activities.

37.17 Case 17. Painting a Wall (Earned Value Management)

Here are the answers. Remember that the value of the exercise is greatest if you work one day at a time and reflect on the day's results. Inserted figures in the table are bolded.

- You plan to paint 80 meters per day.
- The EV is $250 per meter, so you plan to spend $2 000 per day.

End of →	*Mon*	*Tue*	*Wed*	*Thu*	*Fri*	*Sat*
Meters Planned	80	160	240	320	400	400
Planned Value ($)	**2 000**	**4 000**	**6 000**	**8 000**	**10 000**	**10 000**
Meters Painted	60	132	212	300	380	400
Earned Value ($)	**1 500**	**3 300**	**5 300**	**7 500**	**9 500**	**10 000**
Actual Cost ($) - money spent	1 400	3 300	5 500	8 000	10 200	10 700
Cost Variance ($)	**+100**	**0**	**–200**	**–500**	**–700**	**–700**
CPI (Cost Performance Index)	**1.07**	**1.00**	**0.96**	**0.94**	**0.93**	**0.93**
Schedule Variance ($)	**–500**	**–700**	**–700**	**–500**	**–500**	**0**
SPI (Schedule Performance Index)	**0.75**	**0.83**	**0.88**	**0.94**	**0.95**	**n/a**
ETC (Estimated To Complete) – Cost in $				**2 667**		
EAC (Estimate At Completion) – Cost in $				**10 667**		

- End Monday: We are well behind schedule, but have spent slightly less than planned for the work done. We must step up our work rate to meet the customer's expectations.
- End Tuesday: We have increased the work rate but are still behind schedule. It did come at a cost, but to date, we have spent exactly what was planned for the amount of work done.
- End Wednesday: We achieved the daily plan of 80 meters. We are still behind schedule but the SPI has improved. Our costs are running slightly over plan but the CPI of 0.96 is still acceptable – it might still be possible to finish at the planned cost.

- End Thursday: We exceeded our daily plan and achieved 88 meters. We are still somewhat behind schedule. There should not be much left to paint at the end of Friday and we have discussed the situation with the customer. Our costs are still overrunning and based on the CPI of 0.94 we look like finishing nearly $700 overspent.
- End Friday. We achieved our daily work target but did not catch up further. We are still 20 meters short, which is not serious. The customer will accept that we go into Saturday morning. Costs were contained to what was planned for the day, but there will still be an overrun.
- Saturday. We finished the remaining 20 meters in a few hours. Although the SPI calculates to 1.00, it is really not applicable as we overran slightly. We manage to avoid further cost overruns. Our profit will be $1 300 – not what was planned, but better than a loss.

37.18 Case 18. HR Job Description Project (Earned Value Management)

1. BC = $80 000
2. PV at completion = $80 000
3. PV after 1 month: $20 000, 3 months: $60 000
4. EV = $15 000
5. We have done less work than planned.
6. SV after 1 month = – $5 000 (note it is measured in dollars)
7. SPI = EV/PV = $15 000/$20 000 = 0.75
8. We know that we are behind schedule because the SPI is less than 1.
9. CV after 1 month = + $3 000
10. CPI = EV/AC = $15 000/$12 000 = 1.25
11. No. The CPI is greater than 1, and the Cost Variance is positive.
12. There are various possibilities: One is that initially we could not get enough resources, but those that we got were more productive than expected or they started with the easiest job descriptions first.
13. We are 6 days behind schedule. We planned to achieve 20 descriptions after 1 month, and we actually achieved 20 six days later.
14. EV = $54 000
15. Percentage complete = 67.5% (100 × $54 000/$80 000)
16. Cost variance = EV – AC = + $4 000. CPI = 54/50 = 1.08
17. Schedule variance = EV – PV = $54 000 – $60 000 = – $6 000. SPI = 54/60 = 0.9
18. EAC = BC/CPI = $80 000/1.08 = $74 074. It would be rounded to $74 000 to avoid implying that the figure is exact.
19. There are several possibilities. Some are:
    - Bring in more resources even if their rate is higher.
    - Request the existing resources to work overtime at a higher overtime rate.
    - Offer an incentive payment to existing resources if they complete on time.

37.19 Case 19. Project Theta (Earned Value Management)

1. No, we cannot, because we don't know how much work has been done. Therefore, we do not have an estimate of the Earned Value.
2. SV = \$150 k – \$180 k = – \$30 k. SPI = 0.83
3. CV = \$150k – \$170 k = – \$20 k. CPI = 0.88
4. Roughly 1½ weeks behind schedule. At 30 July, the project is spending roughly \$20 k per week, so an SV of minus \$30 k equates to about a week and a half.
5. EAC = \$320 k/0.88 = \$360 k. ETC = \$360 k – \$170 k = \$190 k.
6. Since these are estimates, there is little value in calculating to a high level of precision.
7. Estimated percent complete, based on AC = 100 × 170/360 = 47% (rounded).
8. Estimate percent complete, based on EV = 100 × 150/320 = also rounds to 47%.

37.20 Case 20. Project Inter-World (Earned Value Management)

1. Both are \$2.0 m. They mean the same thing.
2. EV Inception = \$200 000

   EV Design = \$320 000

   EV Development = \$180 000

   Total EV at 21 May= \$700 000
3. SV = + \$20 000.SPI = 700/680 = 1.03
4. CV = –\$30 000. CPI = 700/730 = 0.96
5. The project is ahead of schedule. However, considering the amount of work done, we have spent more money than planned.
6. The SPI being greater than 1 indicates that we are ahead of schedule. However, progress on the critical path will determine whether we shall finish on time. So even if the SPI looks good, we may be behind schedule on critical path activities. Thus the PM must keep a close watch on critical path activities as well as monitoring the Earned Value figures.
7. EV Inception = \$200 000

   EV Design = \$400 000

   EV Development = \$540 000

   EV Test = \$180 000

   Total EV at 21 May = \$1 320 000
8. SV = –\$130 000. SPI = 0.91
9. CV = –\$120 000. CPI = 0.92
10. The project has now fallen well behind schedule, and is costing more than planned considering the work done.
11. EAC = \$2 000 000/0.92 = \$2 174 000

12. Probably not. This project was planned at about 10 months. The SPI indicates that it could take a further month. By then it would be well into the holiday season. Best to plan for completion late January.

37.21 Case 21. Hygiene Factors and Motivators (people management)

The following looks at each factor through the eyes of a team member. It expresses possible thoughts and feelings that a team member might have. The reasons given are not intended to be comprehensive because people's needs and emotions differ.

1. Challenging work is a motivator.
   Everyone knows that this work is difficult, and it will test my skills and ability. I like a challenge. The contribution to the project goal is likely to be appreciated and recognized when complete. The achievement will make me feel even better about my abilities (sense of self-worth) and will enhance my status in the team. It may result in further interesting work leading to expert status and possible promotion.
2. A salary increase is a hygiene factor.
   Yes, I felt good about the increase when I was notified on Monday, and it will certainly help to pay the bills. It was better than expected, but I always thought that I deserved a bit more. In fact, I would have been quite disappointed if it had not happened soon.
3. Working with an excellent team is a motivator.
   We really have good people in this team, and I'm proud to be part of it. Other people in the organization know that only excellent people get asked to join. What's more the team are a pleasure to work with. They help me, and I must never let them down. In fact, a lot of what I now know comes from working with them.
4. The positive attitude of management is a motivator.
   Management really needs this project to happen, and take a real interest. They know what I'm doing to contribute, and are quick to sort out problems that get in our way. They have confidence in the PM and our team, so we can't disappoint them.
5. Good physical working conditions are a hygiene factor.
   Yes, it's pleasant working here. There is enough light and it's not too noisy. The coffee is good, and there is a place where we can chat and not disturb people. Maybe it's too comfortable? Quite a few people around here seem to stay because they like the place, but they don't really do much work.
6. Learning opportunities are a motivator.
   I'm really excited. The PM asked me to do this job even though I don't really have all the skills. But, if I can get this right, I'll really be on top of some of the latest technologies – so it's worth putting in the extra effort. And what's more, if I get stuck Mary can help me, and she's an expert. This chance won't come along often.

37.22 Case 22. HVD – Heavy Vehicle Distributors (team start-up)

The following will indicate that building a team is difficult unless other things, like good sponsorship, sound project management, and realistic scope and timelines, are in place.

1. Project handling at HVD:
   - The concept of a project is understood, as well as the importance of having a project sponsor or owner.
   - The culture appears to be directive as there is no evidence that Exco had asked for a time or cost estimate. However, Ron Clarke shows some understanding of the sponsorship role.
   - There is no evidence of support structures like a PMO. Clement needed to determine what staff he needed and then negotiate to get them.
   - No project standards are mentioned, like project definition or formal reporting.
2. Things that will make team-building easier: The core team is mostly in one building; there are about eight members; the project is seen as important and has an executive as sponsor; the skill areas are covered.

   More difficult: Several members are part-time; members will not all be in Johannesburg when site implementation starts.
3. The project appears to be at the storming stage, probably aggravated because very little forming has taken place other than the meeting to discuss the site modus operandi for the rollout. Clement has done well to assemble a team with all the key players in 3 weeks, and get initial discussions underway. Some things that are missing are:
   - A definition workshop and document. Which might have started to address the points that follow.
   - The scope is not clear. There is debate about what the initial rollout should involve. Usually, it is not realistic to roll out all the processes initially and a pilot at one site is often desirable. Agreeing the site modus operandi might have been premature until the full scope was understood.
   - If the scope had been discussed, it would have been clearer what was needed before teams could go on site.
   - The roles are generally understood, but it seems there has been little discussion on how the team would work together.
4. What Clement should do now.
   - Several structured discussions are needed which might serve as on-the-job team building. Clement should use them to emphasize the roles, and the importance of each role. Maybe he should even accept some responsibility for the conflicts.
   - The first discussion might be a project definition workshop. This would clarify the full scope. It would also cover the roles and who would be responsible for each scope item. The issues would be listed but only debated briefly.
   - Several issues are unlikely to be resolved in the definition workshop and would need to be resolved very soon after. One issue would be the feasibility

of the deadline and the compromises that might be needed, such as longer duration and higher cost versus reduced initial business functionality. Some alternatives might be: a multi-stage rollout; a pilot site.

- After the team has been involved in coming up with recommendations, the sponsor needs to take decisions leading to a feasible plan.
- Having ironed out realistic scope, schedule, and cost with input from the team clashes within the team are less likely to occur.
- Then, having Ron meet with the team for 30 minutes (or less) would reinforce the sense of mission, and the importance of what the team are achieving. (Conversely, if the team were to perceive the schedule to be unrealistic, such a meeting might be counterproductive and tensions would persist).

37.23 Case 23. The Wealth-Man Conversion (issues management)

What follows is an example. It is not intended to be perfectly presented. An issue record is just short notes of all relevant information that is known. It will help the PM and team to resolve the problem – often only a page. It should be added to as events unfold.

Wealth-Man conversion Issue record Issue no: E07 20 July 2022
Title: Wealth-Man Conversion cannot be done in a weekend
Priority: A Owner: Chen

Description:
Testing of the planned Wealth-Man conversion indicates that it runs for 70 hours and cannot be done in a weekend. We must also allow additional time in case we need to abort the conversion and restore the existing system. The business has said that any overrun into Monday will be unacceptable due to client impact.

Alternative solutions:

- Faster server or tune database.
- Ask Wealth-Man vendor whether they have a solution.
- Can any sequential activities be done in parallel? Or done in advance?
- Move conversion date to a long weekend.
- Break conversion into pieces – do it over several weekends.
- Close business early on Friday or start up late on Monday – warn clients.
- Reconsider whether we can afford to convert.

Persons Involved (besides you, the PM)

- Systems Manager – Chen – give input on best people to involve
- Business Manager – Vanessa
- Database technical specialist

- Vendor technical representative
- Our own technical specialists.

Communication, how and to whom?

- Circulate issue doc and mention in weekly reports until resolved
- Project meeting – discussion and minute actions

Actions

- Identify suitable specialists and call urgent meeting.
- Agree on avenues to pursue, and meet twice a week to discuss progress.
- Add item to risk register. Discuss with sponsor.

Closing comments < to be completed when solution agreed, and issue resolved>.

37.24 Case 24. Delia's Day (what it's like being a business PM)

1. Skills
   - Maintains a network. Frequent contact with business, cooperative.
   - Good relationships with other PMs – help each-other attitude.
   - Universally respected.
   - Optimistic and shares the good news.
   - Assertive. Willing to confront.
   - Listens to her staff.
   - Sense of urgency. Responds promptly to issues.
   - Goes to people. Does not wait for them to come to her.
   - Good problem solver.
   - Hard worker.
2. Weak areas for improvement
   - Unwilling to give bad news early. It will be worse if it emerges later.
   - Raises expectations without realizing it (the financial requirement).
   - Not particularly good at time management – as seen from the status meeting. The attitude rubs off on her team.
   - Schedule used but not up to date. Reports go out late.
   - Un-structured. Does she know the basic PM techniques? (examples follow)
   - Makes follow-up notes, but does she use them?
   - Has she related the month-end costs to what was achieved at month-end?
   - Few records are kept, like meeting notes (maybe the whiteboard helps?)
   - Driven by issues but no evidence of issues documentation.
   - Ignored opportunities for managing risks (concerns expressed by team members)
   - No evidence of scope change management. This is affecting the project.
   - Was the scope ever agreed? There seems to have been a spec, but is it enough? Was there a PDD?

3. Frustrations
   - Business requirements are changing or were initially not thought of.
   - Not having control over all her resources.
   - Little time to deal with unforeseen events.
   - Difficult to balance project priorities against her family responsibilities.
4. Positive aspects
   - Responsible, interesting work.
   - Lots of variety. Contact with many people.
   - Freedom to manage time as she sees fit.
   - Learning opportunities related to the business and PM (does she consciously develop her PM skills or does she rely on her personality?)

37.25 Case 25. Setting RAG Codes for Project Reports (communication)

The RAG code is a matter of judgment and sometimes more than one RAG would be reasonable.

1. Amber. Although the performance indicators are not badly out of line, there are serious issues. No need to communicate further unless: (i) there has been a major change in a performance indicator since the last report or (ii) you decide that outside assistance is needed.
2. Green. This is about as good as it gets.
3. Amber. This problem needs attention and would certainly be reported as *the* top issue. Because it is beyond your control, it needs to be discussed with the sponsor to agree on who can best assist you to deal with the problem. If you were no closer to finding a solution a week later, then the next report would have a red RAG.
4. Amber. The sponsor and other stakeholders probably already know that resources are constrained, but they may not know that the end date is threatened. The amber RAG would be an early warning. The situation should be discussed with your team to confirm what would help to speed things up, and to indicate that leave may be at risk over the festive season. Next, the sponsor and other appropriate external stakeholders need to be told what resources you need, to ensure that the deadline can be met. Then if by early October, the situation has not improved, the RAG should move to red.

37.26 Case 26. XP Insurance (project governance)

Comment on the governance process in XPI.

- There appears to be no formal governance. The only evidence of some processes is that:
  - There is a project office,

  - A sponsor was appointed,
  - Thabo is getting input on costs, so there must be some sort of time recording system.
- The sponsor is not playing his role which suggests that no sponsor training has been given, and that the role is not properly understood.
- The fact that the project office was bypassed when the project was launched suggests that it has little power and is side-lined when something important comes up.
- The following disciplines seem to be missing:
  - A clearly communicated corporate strategy
  - A rigorous process of prioritizing projects
  - Producing and reviewing a business case,
  - Appointment of a project board – a lone sponsor is insufficient for a major project
  - Review of project reports, and taking action as a result
  - Any form of Phase Gate reviews
  - An escalation process for handling exceptions

If you were a consultant, what improvements would you recommend?

- I would recommend putting structures and process in place as follows
  - A documented process for initiating projects and governing them during their life span (until the project is terminated – complete or incomplete)
  - Appointment of a senior executive who owns the governance process. He needs the power to terminate projects based on input from a prioritization group. The project office might report to him.
  - The executive would chair a project selection and prioritization group.
  - Members would be selected from senior management.
  - The role of the project office would be more clearly defined. Some of their responsibilities might be:
    - ♦ Training and supplying PMs,
    - ♦ Creating project standards,
    - ♦ Managing feasibility studies and project initiation,
    - ♦ Reviewing reports and managing escalations
    - ♦ Tracking and reporting expenditure and progress across all projects

If you were in Thabo's situation, what would you do next?

- Produce a status report indicating the factors that suggest that the project be terminated. Prepare a 30 minutes presentation.
- Hold a discussion with my manager. Agree the way forward.
- Most importantly, agree which executives need to be involved with either getting the project onto a sound footing, or terminating it.
- A sound footing would mean a new sponsor whose success is affected by the project's outcome. The project office manager should be involved and be assigned at least dotted line responsibility.

- Request, via my manager, a formal review/audit of the project. Giving the presentation to the agreed executives might be the starting point.
- If nothing else works, I would request an interview with the CEO, and summarize the status for him in 5 minutes. Then request a decision.

37.27 Case 27. Sponsor Situations (appreciating the sponsor's role)

Not enough detail has been given to give a definite answer. The following are possibilities:

1. The PM is not communicating:
   This needs a face-to-face discussion. Maybe it can wait for after the next monthly meeting, but maybe it is more urgent. The outcome should be for the sponsor to get an honest and believable view of the project status (even if bad), and agreement on how communication should be conducted in future. Specifics should where possible be given. Mention the effect it has on you. Ask the PM how they are feeling about the project and where the difficulties lie. Maybe the PM is stressed by difficult team members or suppliers?
2. Customer staff are not playing their agreed roles:
   Once again a one-on-one discussion is needed. Ask the PM for a summary of the issue and the impact of the customer's neglect (which might affect more than time and cost). Check what was formally agreed in a contract or other documents. Does the customer understand their responsibilities? Ask what the PM plans to do. Ask whether support is needed. The next step might be for the sponsor to call on their opposite number at the customer. It might also be raised at the next steering committee meeting. The outcome should be that the customer understands the consequences of their inaction. They should agrees on improvements which would need to be monitored, and discussed at regular reviews.
3. Project dragging on and missing deadlines:
   This is difficult! Hold a face-to-face discussion where you share your concerns. The PM needs to know that you are unhappy with progress. Ask for the PM's perspective. There could be many reasons for the delays, like lack of skills or team members that are not committed. Ask whether there is an issues log? Have all issues been resolved? Ask what the PM thinks will make a difference. Ask what the PM can commit to? Discuss what is needed to make the commitments stick. A possibility is a 15 minute weekly checkpoint with yourself as sponsor, the PM, and the entire team. This would emphasize that the deadline is taken seriously. Maybe interim milestones will help?
4. Inevitable budget cuts:
   Pre-empt any cuts. Be proactive. Gather justification information for all the projects, and decide which should be put on hold first, second, third. There are many things to consider like reducing scope, rather than stopping, and what

resources might be released. Present your findings to top management. Agree the way forward (which may be to continue with all or to cut now) and agree at what points the situation will be reviewed again.

5. PM resignation:
Ask the PM for her suggestions, as she knows the people and the project. You will need a replacement, and may even need to bring in more than one person. Are any of the team members ready to take on more responsibility? Try to arrange that she still be contactable even after she has moved. The contact may never be used because often a newly constituted team will prefer to make their own way.
6. Questionable business case:
Request a risk identification with probability and impact (especially needed for new technology). Be aware that some of the staff may want to gain experience with new technology, but may not care about the consequences for the company. Ask for a specific person to be responsible for realizing each benefit, and ask for a way of measuring the outcome (which may mean measuring the current situation to enable comparison). If people are held accountable, and know the risks, they often scale down their estimate of the benefits. Then the justification can be re-assessed.
7. Infrastructure revamp:
This is also difficult. There needs to be a business case and maybe even a feasibility study. The 'stay as we are' scenario must be considered, and there may be more than one change scenario. People from different disciplines should be called upon to get a balanced perspective. When the way forward has been established, there needs to be a way of breaking it down into a program of projects so that no project lasts more than 8 months, and preferably each project should provide a benefit as soon as it is complete.
8. Resource issues:
Involve the executive group and get agreement as to which of your projects are critical to the organization. You may need their support when there is contention for resources. Determine which projects are less important and might be placed on hold. This would require prioritizing them and noting which use resources that are needed on the critical projects. Review priorities periodically, communicate the priorities, and encourage PMs to respect them. Also, list the skills that are not under your direct control and encourage the PMs to get agreements from the relevant managers which would include the estimated effort and timing.

37.28 Case 28. Rescon (closing and governance)

There is no perfect solution. This problem will always be a challenge in similar organizations. For Rescon, R&D and new product development are core parts of their business. Some risk is inevitable. Therefore the objectives are as follows:

- Achieve maximum benefit with minimum expenditure. The optimum solution requires early identification of projects that have an unacceptable probability of failure, and terminating them as early as possible, with as little expenditure as possible.

- Motivate staff to persevere toward the achievement of challenging goals. At the same time, minimize negative impact on them and their careers if their project is terminated for reasons that may be beyond their control.
- Achieve maximum learning from projects that fail or are terminated early.

A process along the following lines is recommended.

- Establish a project selection and prioritization (PSP) group, that will maintain a list of proposed R&D or development projects. PSP would comprise part-time people.
- Establish a rating scale for risk and potential reward. Classify projects as per Figure 19.2. Pearls are ideal, but some Oyster and Bread & Butter projects will also need to be undertaken. Avoid white elephants.
- For each, a team will be nominated to produce a proposal/business case. Some of the headings will be:
  - Benefits if the project succeeds and the technology is viable.
  - Expected cost of the project.
  - Assumptions, risks, and things that are unknown. The few key elements on which the success of the project depends should be mentioned.
- Where possible such projects should be staged. Ideally the early stages should indicate, at relatively low cost, whether the concept will succeed. Thus, the first project stage might be to build the prototype for a key element.
- In certain situations, stages could be time or cost 'boxed'. For example, the PM must produce the best results possible given a 6 month window and $500 000.
- Reviews should be held at the end of each stage, to recommend on whether and how the project should go forward. Members of the PSP group would form the core, and might invite specialists to join the review. While this has a cost, there is potential for building learning and skills in the process – along the lines of the phase gate approach explained in Chapter 17.
- If project stages are longer than 6 months, then a review should be done roughly halfway through the stage. Stages longer than a year should be avoided.
- Establish a budget annually for innovation type projects (as opposed to production type projects). I.e. consider innovation projects separately.
- Have two review cycles each year, where innovation projects are selected, for the coming 12 months, taking into account projects that are already underway.
- Maintain an inventory of project resources like people and their main skill areas. Take availability of key skills into account.
- Where a project is terminated, prematurely, the PM will produce a report of what was learned from the project, and what outputs might be used for other purposes.
- People should have quarterly discussions with their functional manager, and an annual 360 degree appraisal where input sources include co-workers on projects.
- Emphasize rewarding success, but not punishing failure – particularly when the risks were understood and the person had performed to the best of their ability

37.29 Case 29. PM Situations (applying all core knowledge areas)

For all situations:

- Ask questions and fully clarify the situation.
- Notify or consult appropriate stakeholders.
- Update relevant documentation, and, if significant, report on the situation.

The points below give actions that may be needed depending on what you find out. For example, in the first item, if you and the supplier can agree a suitable solution, then raising an issue should not be necessary. Where an issue does need to be raised, then the normal resolution process would follow. Some of the actions mentioned may be delegated.

1. Discuss it with the supplier. Can they send part of the order earlier? Does the supplier have an alternative solution? If necessary raise an issue (log and record) and note the schedule impact. Meet to discuss alternatives and find the best way forward.
2. Get reasons for the delay and a revised estimate. Assess the schedule impact. Find out who might help. Possibly raise an issue.
3. Raise an issue and consider alternatives. This may result in a change request.
4. Fully understand and document, what the inadequacy is, and what the stakeholder thinks is required. Possibly raise change request.
5. Raise an issue. Check risk register, to see whether it was there, else log a lesson learned.
6. Understand what is needed. Check: the scope statement, exclusions, and specifications. Possibly raise an issue and/or change request.
7. Understand the stakeholder's reasons and find out what they believe should change. Possibly revisit the business case, involving the sponsor.
8. Add the risk to the risk register and analyze it. Plan suitable response actions (which could be to: accept, avoid, transfer, or mitigate) and add any activities to your schedule.
9. Clarify who will be the new sponsor. Will it be Ms. Carley or someone else? Arrange a meeting with the existing and new sponsor, in which you would review the business case, the plan and the status.
10. Hold a PDW (project definition workshop). Resolve issues arising with the sponsor. Document the outcome as a PDD and have it approved by the sponsor and key stakeholders.
11. Get the meeting minutes (from the archive) and find out what was minuted. Meet with Marketing. Raise an issue if there will be a serious impact.
12. Check the last project report. Apologize if the delay was not reported and explain how it arose. Tell the sponsor what is being done to manage the delay.
13. Check: the scope statement, the exclusions, and specifications. If the item is in-scope, look at the estimates, and achievement versus expenditure status. If the item is out of scope, then discuss a change request.

14. Raise an issue. Look at the remaining scope. Discuss what deliverables might be de-scoped or deferred until after the deadline. Look at resource allocation and the possibility of getting assistance.
15. Engage with department Y and understand their thinking. If it is valid, discuss the situation with the sponsor. Update the stakeholder list and communication plan.
16. Meet with John and express the concern. Get his perspective and seek a solution. The next steps will depend on what you find and on the importance of the activity.

37.30 Case 30. Delectable Confections (project selection)

The financial estimates are tabulated and summarized for each project. The figures are rounded because they are based on estimates. The (simple) payback periods are estimated from the cumulative (undiscounted) figures and given from the start of the projects. The figures are followed by comments on the other factors that should be considered.

Project 1. Diversification into Ice Cream.
Note that the full cost will be incurred up front, and therefore at the end of year 0 with a discounting factor of 1.0.

End Year →	*0*	*1*	*2*	*3*	*4*	*5*	*NPV*
Return $m	–15.0	+5.0	+5.5	+6.1	+6.7	+7.4	
Cumulative	–15.0	–10.0	–4.5	+1.6	+8.3	+15.7	
Discount factor for 20%	1.0	0.8333	0.6944	0.5787	0.4823	0.4019	
Present values	–15.00	+4.17	+3.82	+3.53	+3.23	+2.97	+2.72
Discount factor for 30%	1.0	0.7692	0.5917	0.4552	0.3501	0.2693	
Present values	–15.00	+3.85	+3.25	+2.78	+2.35	+1.99	-0.78

The payback period is roughly 2 years and 9 months (going from –4.5 to +1.6).
The NPV at a 20% discounting rate is about $2.7 million.
The IRR is estimated at 27%

Other considerations:

- This project does not appear to align to any of the strategies. Revenue from ice cream does not add to their market share in their core business.
- This project implies a major diversification for Delectable. Ice cream is very different to confectionary. For example, distribution trucks would need refrigeration capability.
- There are significant risks with the project itself. For example, will the corporate cultures be compatible? Will the management integrate well? How subject are sales to seasonal factors and weather?

- It is doubtful whether the figures are reliable – hence the IRR may not materialize.
- Does Delectable have suitable managers who can be trained in the new business?
- Despite the good looking returns this project should only be undertaken if top management have good reasons for wanting to diversify into ice cream.

Project 2. Enhancement of Packaging Lines.

End Year →	*0*	*1*	*2*	*3*	*4*	*5*	*NPV*
Return $m		–19.0	+6.5	+7.5	+8.0	+8.5	
Cumulative		–19.0	–12.5	–5.0	+3.0	+11.5	
Discount factor for 20%		0.8333	0.6944	0.5787	0.4823	0.4019	
Present values		–15.83	4.51	4.34	3.86	3.42	+0.29
Discount factor for 30%		0.7692	0.5917	0.4552	0.3501	0.2693	
Present values		–14.62	3.85	3.41	2.80	2.29	–2.27

There is no up-front cost. The major costs and some benefits occur during year 1. The –$19 m is arrived at by offsetting the cost of –$22 m with the estimated benefit of +$3 m.

The payback period is roughly 3 years and 7 months (going from –5.0 to +3.0).
The NPV at a 20% discounting rate is about $0.3 million.
The IRR is estimated at 21% and only just meets the 20% criterion.

Other considerations:

- The project aligns to two of the strategies (customer satisfaction and reduced operating costs). It might also contribute to market share.
- The project is low risk – known suppliers with demonstrated experience.
- There is strong executive support for the project. It is likely to improve morale as the frustration resulting from downtime will be greatly reduced.
- Problems are likely to get worse if this project is deferred.

There may not be enough information to make a fully-informed recommendation. Over a number of years some syndicates have recommended the ice cream project, others the machinery project.

37.31 Case 31. Upview Investments (procurement – setting the scene)

Here are concerns that each party might have and issues that they might wish to discuss:

Upview Investments

- How long have M&P been in business? How stable are they?
- Where would outsourced CC people be located? In our building? M&P building? At home? Offshore?

- Will M&P take over our staff? Will remuneration packages be compatible?
- How should we approach our staff? What reaction can we expect?
- On what basis do M&P charge for the service?
- How can we measure an outsource company? Will there be a standard SLA (Service Level Agreement)?
- How will we know whether our clients are happy with the service?
- How would M&P staff be trained on our products and processes?
- How soon could this be put in place? Is there a process to follow?
- Who would be our contact at M&P? How often would we meet?
- If this doesn't work well, how can we get out of the arrangement?

M&P (Maseti & Pringle)

- How successful is Upview? How financially stable? How fast are they growing?
- Are they talking to any of our competitors?
- What are their criteria for selecting a firm? What process will they follow?
- Are Upview willing to pay for consulting services on how best to outsource? If not, we may put in considerable work and then lose the business to another company.
- What is important to Upview? What factors will win the business?
- If we win, do we have staff available? What type of skills are needed?
- What is the caliber of Upview CC staff? Will we want them?
- How much training is needed? Will Upview provide the training?
- What kind of user population will we be servicing?
- How soon will Upview need the service?

If the buyer were a government department, then, depending on the country, there might be strict rules as to how such an engagement could take place. If the buyer needed advice, they might need to follow a process to appoint a consultant. Then, to avoid a conflicts of interest, the consultant might not be able to bid, and would only be paid for their consultancy.

37.32 Case 32. Implications of Contract Types (procurement)

Firm Fixed Price (FFP).

Because it is fixed price, the price is always **$1 million.**

FFP Scenario	*Cost $000*	*Profit $000*	*Price $000*
Budgeted	800	**200**	1 000
Under run	700	**300**	**1 000**
Overrun	900	**100**	**1 000**
Gross overrun	1 200	**–200 (loss)**	**1 000**

Cost plus Percentage Cost (CPPC).

The uplift, or profit, is always 10% of the approved cost incurred.

CPPC Scenario	*Cost $000*	*Profit $000*	*Price $000*
Budgeted	1 000	**100**	**1 100**
Under run	900	**90**	**990**
Overrun	1 100	**110**	**1 210**

Cost Plus Incentive Fee (CPIF).

The profit is adjusted upward by 20% of a saving, or downward by 20% of an overrun.

CPIF Scenario	*Cost $000*	*Saving $000*	*Profit $000*	*Price $000*
Budgeted	1 100	0	100	**1 200**
Underrun	1 000	**100**	**120**	**1 120**
Overrun	1 200	**–100**	**80**	**1 280**

37.33 Case 33. M&P Outsourcing Project (outsourcing and partnership)

Problems with the partnering arrangement and the handling of the migration project:

- The transition was rushed, hence the agreement lacked detail in key areas.
- Upview signed the agreement from a weak power base. They were in a hurry.
- Upview's assumption was that M&P would take care of everything.
- There is no mention of M&P references having been checked.
- Any project definition done did not involving Upview.
- There was no governance structure for the migration project.
- The migration project was not handled sensitively:
  - Communication during the project was lacking, leading to misunderstandings and discomfort in Upview.
  - Organizational change management was not thorough: there was little or no engagement with the CC team, and client notifications were not checked.

Ways in which the partnering arrangement and migration might it have been handled better:

- A business case should have been created, comparing current costs and benefits with those expected with the outsourced arrangement, taking into account the risks.
- More thought should have been given to the risks and how to mitigate them.
- Bringing in an experienced independent consultant would have reduced the risk of overlooking something important.

- Upview might have hired and trained new agents before investigating the outsource, thus giving themselves time to do it properly. The possibility of a future outsource should then have been mentioned in new employee contracts.

A consultant brought in might do/recommend the following:

- Consider the most likely options:
  - Stay with M&P and fix the relationship,
  - Take the CC back in-house to Upview,
  - Find another outsource partner.
- The latter two will come at a cost, so start with the first option.
  - Meet with Upview and M&P separately to understand their perspectives/concerns.
  - Facilitate a meeting to discuss the concerns and try to agree a way forward.
  - Set up regular executive level reviews, and address the concerns raised. If trust and partnership cannot be built, then this outsource will not work.
  - In parallel, review the agreement, possibly getting legal advice, for the best way of terminating it, if necessary. This would be part of the preparation for negotiation. Termination might be done at the end of the initial agreement period, or earlier depending on the agreement. The estimated cost of the poorer service during the agreement would be a consideration.
  - Do a cost/benefit analysis, if it was not done before, to get an understanding of what it would be worth paying for a good service.
- Anticipate transition difficulties if the CC is brought back in-house or moved to another partner. M&P will not willingly give up their new business.

37.34 Case 34. Lorion (OCM – organizational change management)

Categories of people affected by the change:

- Those over 50 who receive the offer, and those that do not.
- Families and colleagues of those who may retire early.
- Managers who need to communicate. They include those who may lose valuable staff, and those that receive an offer themselves.
- Clients.
- Probably almost everyone else in the company.

Issues and concerns:

- Executives: Should we collaborate with employees before finalizing the offer?
- Executives: Should we indicate possible retrenchments if numbers are not met?
- Executives: How much should we offer? What if very few, or too many, employees take up the offer?

- Managers: Should I encourage people to accept, given that I will be short staffed?
- Over 50s: Why did I get the offer, am I not good enough? Or, why did I not get the offer?
- Over 50s: Will I have enough money to live if I can't find other employment?
- Other employees: How does Lorion treat older employees? Will it happen to me?
- What should we tell clients, especially where staff working with them have been made an offer?

Approach: (There are many ways of handling this. These are some elements)

- Briefing for managers, explaining the reasons and their roles.
- Executive letter to all those over 50, notifying the reasons and the process.
- Executive email to all staff.
- Managers personally deliver the offer to each nominated over-50 employee.
- Voluntary workshops with employees.
- Financial counselling for employees who have been made the offer.
- Review of targets for managers who lose staff.
- Farewell dinner for those leaving.
- Workshops after employees have left to discuss how best to adjust to the change.

37.35 Case 35. BCT – Bowden Consulting & Training (contracts)

Because contracts may vary between countries, your answer may differ from what is given below (which might apply in South Africa).

1. Classification of contract clauses into the main (body) contract, and supplements related to specific work under the main contract.

Address for correspondence	M	Assignment of rights or obligations	M
BCT responsibilities	S	Breach of agreement	M
Change management process	M	Client responsibilities	S
Confidentiality and non-disclosure	M	Conflict of interest	M
Definitions (meanings) of terms used	M,S	Dispute resolution process	M
Effective date	M,S	Force majeure	M
Governing law	M	Identification of the parties	M
Intellectual property rights	M	Liability	M
Payment terms	S	Penalties (if applicable)	S
Restraint of hiring	M	Restraint of trade	M

Schedule of dates	S	Schedule of payments	S
Scope of work	S	Termination	S
Waiver	M	Warranties (guarantees)	M,S

2. Proposed Supplement to Agreement between Beta Bank and BCT
   - Scope and BCT responsibilities:
     - Develop course material based on product details from Beta Bank.
     - Do three dry run sessions with facilitators and Beta observers.
     - Train the facilitators.
     - Make travel arrangements and do other course administration such as submitting class registers to the Beta Bank administrator.
     - Agree training dates with Beta.
     - Train 4 000 staff, in groups of about 20. Estimate 200 two hour sessions.
   - Beta Bank responsibilities
     - Make final product specification available by 31 March.
     - Provide training venues in following cities: <names of cities>. Cover transport costs of attendees from other locations.
     - Provide administrators who will enroll attendees and make them available. Provide registers per course slot.
   - Assumptions.
     - It will be acceptable for some classes to have up to 30 to compensate for situations where there are less than 20.
     - Three sessions can be scheduled at a venue per day. 08:30 – 10:30, 11:00–13:00, 14:00–16:00.
     - Thus there will be about 70 training days, with fairly even attendee spread.
     - All resources will be part time and charged for days worked.
     - Trainers will stay at venues throughout the week.
   - Timing
     - Training to start from 16 May 2022, and end on 24 June 2022.
   - Charges excluding taxes:
     - Basis will be Time & Material. Travel and living costs will be charged at actual, plus a 10% administrative fee.
     - Charges given in the table are estimates:

Resource	*$ daily rate*	*Days*	*$ Total*
Consultant and PM	700	40	28 000
Administrator	300	40	12 000
Course Developer	500	10	5 000
Session Facilitator	400	70	28 000
Travel and Living	300	70	21 000
Total			94 000

- Termination
  - This project will be complete when scheduled courses have been delivered or on 30 June 2022, whichever is earlier.

37.36 Case 36. Warestar (project review)

There are many valid ways that this could be planned and what follows is one way. The first question uses the health-check in Appendix 3, as input. The lists are illustrative rather than comprehensive and there are many items that might be added.

1. The main project areas and illustrative questions (there could be many more):
   - Project definition and change control:
     - Has a project definition workshop been held?
     - Are the project goals and objectives clear?
     - Are business requirements agreed with key stakeholders?
     - How are scope changes handled? How many have been logged?
   - Stakeholders and organization:
     - Are sub-projects defined? Who is heading-up each?
     - Are there sufficient resources, with adequate skills?
     - How effectively are the teams working together?
   - Work breakdown, estimating, schedule, and progress tracking:
     - What regular sponsor (or steering committee) meetings are held?
     - Is there a detailed schedule? How often tracked/updated?
     - Are the assumptions, that underpin estimates, stated?
     - Are progress tracking meetings held and minuted? Who attends?
     - Are progress reports being produced, circulated?
   - Risk management:
     - Is the risk register available and up to date?
     - Have actions been taken to respond to the main risks?
   - Issues management:
     - Are issues being logged, and resolved? How many open/closed?
     - Are decisions taken being recorded and circulated?
   - Quality management:
     - Are documents stored in a central repository? Easy to find?
     - Are all quality requirements agreed with warehouse management?
   - Performance management (cost and time):
     - Is the project budget with control figures agreed?
     - Are all project costs being tracked via time sheets or a cost ledger?
   - Contract and supplier management:
     - Is there a signed agreement with the software vendor?
     - Are vendor billing and payment mechanisms working effectively?
2. Project documentation for review:
   - Project management standards (is the project adhering to then?)
   - Business case (is it being reviewed and updated?)
   - Project Definition Document (or equivalent)

- Business requirements or functional specification
- Vendor contract
- Project organization chart. Roles and responsibilities
- Schedule and cost budget
- Project reports (for example, weekly)
- Minutes of project progress meetings
- Risk register; issues log and records; change log and records
- Quality plan and test plan (if ready).

3. Role players to be interviewed (besides the PM):
   - Sponsor (head of project steering committee)
   - Warehouse manager (preferably pilot site)
   - Financial manager most involved in warehousing
   - Manager from the vendor.
   - Solution architect and technical lead
   - Lead business analyst
   - Business process analyst and/or change manager (OCM).
4. Timetable for the review week:

Monday 08:00–09:00	Meet PM
Monday 09:00–10:00	Schedule appointments
Monday 10:00–13:00	Conduct interviews (business people, team, etc.)
Monday 13:30–17:00	Review interview notes. Note issues, further questions.
Tuesday 08:00–13:00	Conduct interviews
Tuesday 13:30–16:00	Review interview notes; note issues, further questions
Tuesday 16:00–17:00	Review preliminary findings with PMO manager
Wednesday 08:00–13:00	Conduct interviews
Wednesday 13:30–17:00	Work on report
Thursday 08:00–11:00	Work on report
Thursday 11:00–12:00	Review report with PM
Thursday 12:00 onward	Revise report, gather any missing data
Friday 08:00–12:00	Finalize report and submit.

37.37 Case 37. Ethical Dilemmas (ethics and professional conduct)

Answers are not given, due to the variety of assumptions that might be made.

37.38 Case 38. Getting Intranet Development Done (negotiation)

The outcome of the negotiation is uncertain, but here are the interests and power bases of the parties. It is likely that there is a ZOPA (zone of possible agreement).

- Your interests as project manager
  - Get onto the intranet as soon as possible (latest next Friday).
  - Make good impression: Intranet page must look attractive and be easy to get to.
  - You need advice on layout.
  - Two of your staff must be trained to update the intranet page.
  - You do not wish to spend more than $2 000 for the work.
- Your power base:
  - Your project is visible within the organization, and your page would be good for the image of the Intranet department.
  - You have an influential sponsor who would not be pleased if they are unhelpful.
  - BATNA: You might communicate by email or noticeboard.
- Intranet manager interests
  - She is short of staff, and can only spare a full time person in 3 weeks' time (unless a trainee can do the work with some help).
  - Recent similar jobs have charged out at $3 000 to $5 000.
  - She needs involvement from key persons in your project team.
  - She must charge standard rates, although a trainee is cheaper.
  - An important KPI (key performance indicator) is the opinion survey.
  - There is a location for project dashboards, but it's not very attractive. It will take effort to make it look better.
- Intranet manager power base:
  - She controls the skills.
  - It is not viable for PM to hire an outside contractor, so she is the only supplier.
  - Corporate standards support a tough position.
  - BATNA: She could remain uninvolved.
- Area of mutual interest for discussion:
  - If one of your technical resources can do the work under supervision, it will save cost, and also make it easier for you to maintain the intranet page.
  - Her trainee could be involved and learn from the experience.

37.39 Case 39. TRSA Records Management (preventing failure)

- Things that are going satisfactorily:
  - There appears to be executive agreement that the problem must be solved.
  - A sponsor has been appointed. However, the head of internal audit may not be a suitable person, as he is responsible for reviewing records management rather than putting records management in place.
  - Planning to pilot on a limited area. Acceptance that it cannot be done quickly.
- Aspects of concern:
  - Although Lucy has been appointed as PM, she may not have the project management experience. She might fit better as a key team member.
  - Limited in-house expertise exists. The size and complexity of the project are underestimated.

- Project start was rushed. There is no steering committee set up.
- No project definition was done, no definition workshop was held. Scope is unknown.
- Requirements are not fully understood. There is no plan to understand the as-is situation. TRSA is not ready to plan solutions and scope.
- The project went ahead without planning, and no risks have been identified
- The desired timescale is understood, but not whether it is realistic. A schedule cannot be done without knowing scope and resources.
- Stakeholders are not sufficiently involved – limited communication, limited input.
- Required resources are not understood. Roles are not clear. It is too early to engage with a team.
- Funds appear to be allocated, but no estimate is possible until scope is determined. Finance director assurance may not stick when true costs become apparent.
- Organizational change management aspects and training are not mentioned.
- Change control is lacking. A change request was verbally accepted from Thabang without the impact being assessed, and expectations were raised.
- A supplier proposal was given without requirements being given to the supplier. It is unwise to engage with a particular supplier until supplier criteria are established, and several possible suppliers have been considered. For example, can the supplier service all locations? Was SCM (supply chain management) involved?

■ Things that might be done now to get the project onto a sound footing:
  - This project could potentially be large. It might need to be run as a program as the solution might be phased. Therefore, appoint an experienced PM or alternatively a senior business person, with admin skills, to be in charge.
  - Start with a feasibility study. Identify key players involved. Gather information. Understand alternative solutions. Possibly engage with an impartial consultant that specializes in records management (rather than a supplier who is selling something).
  - Prioritize the audit issues (which may not give the full picture), and work out what could reasonably be delivered by the next audit.
  - Having agreed the broad scope, and done order-of-magnitude estimates, prepare a business case (no more than ten pages). When approved, confirm the PM, and start planning.

- Project isn't [illegible]. There is no steering committee [illegible] up.
- No project definition exists for [illegible] definition [illegible] was held. Scope is unknown.
- Requirements are not fully understood. There is no plan to understand these [illegible]. The team is not ready to plan without scope.
- The project team should [illegible] the defined timescale [illegible] realistic schedule [illegible] without [illegible] scope [illegible].
- Stakeholders are not sufficiently involved [illegible] limited input.
- Required resources are not understood [illegible]. It is the ability to manage [illegible].
- Funds approved [illegible] allocated [illegible] until scope [illegible] not [illegible] approved [illegible].
- Organizational change [illegible] formal change control is lacking. A change request was [illegible] (without [illegible] being assessed, and [illegible] were [illegible]).
- A supplier proposal was given without requirements [illegible] supplier [illegible] established [illegible] suppliers [illegible] considered. For example, can the supplier [illegible] management involved [illegible].
- Things that should be done [illegible] the project [illegible] meeting.
- This project could [illegible] a [illegible] solution [illegible] alternatively [illegible] to be [illegible] involved. Rather [illegible] an important [illegible] selling [illegible].
- [illegible] not give the [illegible] and work out what [illegible] delivered [illegible].
- Having [illegible] and that [illegible] of magnitude estimates [illegible] no more than [illegible] approved [illegible] PM, and [illegible].

Appendix 1

Glossary of Terms and Acronyms

When communicating, knowing the terminology is a great help to PMs. Most of the terminology used in this book is standard with a leaning toward the terms as they are defined in PMI's PMBOK. The aim of Table A1.1 is to avoid confusion by giving the meaning of terms or acronyms. The table is not intended to be comprehensive and focuses on terms that could be ambiguous. However, it must be noted that there are people, organizations, and literature that use some of the terms differently.

Table A1.1 Glossary of Terms and Acronyms

Term/Acronym	*Meaning*
AC	Actual cost. *See* EVM.
Activity	Work that must be done in a planned duration. It means the same as 'task'. The start and completion of an activity are events.
Agile	Approach to a project where scope is not fixed, but is decided during execution. Agile is particularly effective where the requirements unfold as the project progresses. Examples are certain IT projects and new product development. *See also* Scrum and Kanban.
Agile attitude	A mindset where there is willingness to understand problems or new requirements and where necessary, rapidly re-evaluate the project's plan.
Benefits realization	Achieving the planned benefits from a business project – often carried out by business people, to ensure that the deliverables of the project are used to produce business benefits as outlined in the business case. Realizing benefits may be within the project's scope, or may be done outside of the project – especially where the benefits take time to materialize. (Benefits realization may be lacking where the focus is on the deliverables with insufficient attention given to how they will be used).

(*Continued*)

Table A1.1 (Continued)

Term/Acronym	*Meaning*
Business case	Document justifying why the project should proceed. It must include the benefits, costs, and risks associated with the project. The business case needs to be revisited throughout the project's lifetime – for update and to confirm that the project remains justified or that planned benefits are being realized.
Business driver	A key business need that will be addressed by the project.
Business owner	The term is used in various ways. In this book, it has a similar meaning to the sponsor or project sponsor.
Challenged project	The project has completed or is likely to complete. However, there is stakeholder dissatisfaction possibly due to an unsatisfactory business outcome; cost overruns; or a significant schedule delay.
Closeout	Activities done to bring a project to an orderly close, including any reporting and archiving of documentation. Closeout can also refer to the event of the project ending.
Closeout report	Produced at or just after the end of the project. Amongst other items, it gives the extent of deliverables achievement, duration and costs. Also called an end-project or project completion report.
Cloud software	Software that is external to the organization and is available via the internet. Where it is charged on a rental basis, the charges may vary according to functionality, usage, or number of users.
Compliance	Things (including projects) done to ensure that an organization complies with legislation. Also, the department with responsibility for compliance. New laws inevitably result in projects in many organizations.
Constrained schedule	When unlimited resources are assumed, we have an 'unconstrained' schedule. The schedule is determined only by the logical dependencies between the activities and their estimated durations. When limited resources are then applied, the schedule almost always needs to change to avoid overloading the resources. It invariably takes longer and is called a 'constrained' schedule or a 'resource-constrained' schedule.
Contingency	Money or time put aside for the PM to use if risks materialize. Management reserve is similar, but the PM needs to request it from the sponsor.
Controlling	Controlling a project uses information gathered in monitoring, makes comparisons with what was planned, and then makes required adjustments to the project, or recommendations to the sponsor.
CSF	Critical success factor. Things that must be in place for the project to succeed.

(*Continued*)

Table A1.1 (Continued)

Term/Acronym	*Meaning*
Customer	The internal person(s) or external organization for whom the project is being done. The term 'client' means something similar but is used when a service is being provided. In this book, we generally refer to 'the customer' who is represented by a project sponsor.
CYA	Cover your 'assets'. This is done by having sufficient evidence (preferably written) to justify your actions. While protecting yourself should never be the primary objective, documenting situations with reasoning helps to make better choices and enables you to defend those choices later.
Decision rights matrix	Used on projects with stakeholders from different disciplines. It might be authorized by the sponsor near the start of the project to delegate decision areas to designated stakeholders (which might include the PM).
Decisions log	A log of business decisions taken that affect stakeholders, particularly those outside of the project team. It would state who took the decision and the date. It might have a section at the bottom for superseded decisions. Its purpose is to keep stakeholders informed.
Deliverable	Output of the project. Something that can be checked or measured. A business project may produce several deliverables. Often the deliverables are used by business people post-project to derive business value (benefits realization).
DevOps	DevOps brings the IT development and operations support teams together. The focus is on delivering regular and maintainable new functionality to the customer while supporting what is in production. Although the practices existed earlier, DevOps started to become formalized around 2007.
De-scope	Remove project scope by agreement with the sponsor. The aim may be to meet a critical deadline by eliminating or deferring non-urgent items.
Documentation	The relevant documents produced during the projects lifetime. Typically, they would be Word, Excel, scheduler, of Slide documents.
Event	The completion of one or more activities (or tasks). An event may be a Milestone. An event may also refer to a risk happening (risk event)
EVM	Earned value management. Method of assessing whether the project is on schedule and on track with budget. It is encouraged in most methodologies. The parameters EV (earned value), PV (planned value), and AC (actual cost) are used. 'Classical' EVM (as found in most textbooks) is sound, but usually needs to be applied differently for business projects (*see* PPTR).

(Continued)

Table A1.1 (Continued)

Term/Acronym	*Meaning*
Failed project	Considerable resources have been applied but the project is never completed or fails to meet the most important objectives. A project may not be considered failed where: (i) new evidence shows the business case to be unsound and the project is terminated promptly or (ii) the project is put on hold when an even higher priority project arises.
Float (*also called* 'slack')	The amount of time a scheduled activity can be delayed without affecting the end date of the project. *Also known as* 'total float'. 'Free float' is not used in this book. It is the delay to an activity before it affects any following activity.
Gantt chart	A bar chart presentation of a project schedule or timeline.
Governance	A set of principles and processes to guide and improve the management of projects in the organization. It is done at the level of multiple projects where project selection is needed, and at the level of a single project where the focus is on ensuring that the business case remains sound and that benefits are realized.
In writing	Documented confirmation of what is agreed. It might be signed or it might be from a confirmable source, like an email. Seldom would it be written with a pen.
IT	Information Technology.
Kanban (Agile)	Work is delivered continuously. A new work item may be defined, but it is only authorized for execution when an earlier one is completed. *See* Agile.
Kanban board	A whiteboard, which may be electronic, used for Agile projects, to track the status of activities (for example: not started; in progress). It may be referred to as a 'scrum board'.
Lifetime	*See* 'project lifetime'.
Living document	A document that is updated and versioned during the project's lifetime.
Matrix management	Many project team members are not dedicated, but work on more than one initiative.
Methodology	Set of standard processes and techniques used.
Milestone	A significant and measurable event in a project.
Monitoring	Monitoring the project involves observing and measuring certain aspects. It also includes noting things that may not have been planned such as new risks, issues that arise, and change requests.
MS	Abbreviation for Microsoft. For example, MS Word = Microsoft Word
MSP	Abbreviation for Microsoft Project, a scheduling tool which is sometimes referred to.

(*Continued*)

Table A1.1 (Continued)

Term/Acronym	*Meaning*
OCM	Organizational change management. Activities to engage with the many stakeholders that need to adapt what they do to realize the benefits.
On track	The project or activity is proceeding according to plan.
Package	The lowest level of the WBS. All packages define the work needed for the project. It is either a work package (if well defined), or a planning package (if more detail needs to be gathered closer to execution). Each work package results in a deliverable and can be assigned to a person or group.
Parking lot	In the project context, it is a list of items to be considered later or when the project is complete. I sometimes call it a 'futures list'.
PDD	Project definition document. Done close to the start of the project. It gives an overview of key areas like goals, scope, milestones, role-players, benefits, costs, and risks. Typically 3 – 12 pages. An aim is to ensure that the sponsor and stakeholders have common expectations. Also known as 'project charter', 'project brief', and 'terms of reference'.
PDW	Project definition workshop, used to gather and agree information that should be in the PDD.
Phase	It is used in many ways. Examples: part of a project's life cycle, like the 'planning phase'; an entire project where there are a series of related projects (usually large); part of the ADKAR progression in OCM.
PM	Project manager, who might have many responsibilities similar to those of a program manager.
PMI	Project Management Institute based in the USA but represented worldwide
PMBOK	PMI's guide to the Project Management Body of Knowledge. Up to version 6, it covers processes and knowledge areas. From version 7, it covers project management principles and project performance domains.
PMO	Project management office. A group of people whose mission is to support effective project management in an organization. A PMO's responsibilities vary widely by organization and over time.
Portfolio	A group of projects and programs that support all or a significant part of the organization.
PPM software	Project portfolio management software. It can provide the functionality to manage a portfolio of projects. It would cater for storage of project documentation in a structured way, with the ability to access the information to provide useful reports for both PMs and management. Increasingly PPM software is cloud-based.

(Continued)

Table A1.1 (Continued)

Term/Acronym	*Meaning*
PPTR	Project progress tracker. A method to track project progress against a plan. It honors EVM principles but unlike 'classical' EVM, it is easy to apply and provides meaningful results quickly.
Precedence	Used in scheduling to indicate which activity comes before (precedes) which other activity.
PRINCE2	A methodology used in many countries. PRINCE stands for 'projects in a controlled environment'.
Program	A set of related projects, managed in a coordinated way to achieve a broadly defined goal.
Progressive elaboration	An iterative approach to refine the scope of a project as more information becomes available. *See* rolling wave planning.
Project charter	Mandate given to the PM, with some guidelines, to start the project and apply resources. In some organizations, the charter has a similar meaning to a PDD (but this conflicts with PMI's definition of the term).
Project failure	The term is subjective. It is likely to be used where one or more of the following lead to significant stakeholder dissatisfaction: Planned benefits are not realized; key requirements are not met; the costs exceed the value of the benefits; benefits are negated by a schedule overrun.
Project issue	A problem that, if not resolved, threatens the success of the project.
Project life cycle	The phases done during the project – from start to end.
Project lifetime	Starts when the project is first envisaged and ends when all business benefits have been substantially realized. It starts earlier than the life cycle and ends later.
Project mandate	Used by PRINCE2 and having a similar meaning to 'project charter'.
Project plan or simply 'the plan'	Consists of many project documents such as: WBS, schedule, cost spreadsheet, resource plan. Some are monitored and updated regularly.
Project risk	An uncertain event or condition, that if it happens, has a negative (or positive) effect on the project or the organization
Project selection	Deciding which projects should proceed and when they should start.
Project sponsor	*See* sponsor.
PV	Planned value. *See* EVM.
QA	Quality Assurance. It could describe a review that is held to check quality. It could also be the designation of a person or department.
Realize benefits	*See* benefits realization.

(*Continued*)

Table A1.1 (Continued)

Term/Acronym	*Meaning*
Requirements	What the project must produce or enable, from a business point of view (*see also* specifications).
Resource(s)	Any valuable input to the project. Often it refers to the people that work on the project, but it could relate to money, machinery, equipment, or materials.
RFP; RFQ	Request for price; request for quotation (sent by buyer to potential sellers).
Risk register	List of anticipated risks, with a rating and planned response actions. It is indicated which risks have happened or can no longer occur.
Rolling wave planning	The schedule is detailed for the near-term activities. Activities further out are included at a high level and detailed closer to the time. It uses the approach of 'progressive elaboration'.
Scheduling tool	Or 'scheduler'. Software that allows the PM to enter activities, dependencies and resources, and then calculates and displays the schedule. MSP is referred to in this book, but it is just one of many schedulers on the market.
Scope (two uses)	Project scope: work that must be done to produce specified deliverables (*see* WBS). Product scope: features or functions of a product or service.
Scope creep	Uncontrolled additions to the approved project scope (which usually lead to time and cost overruns).
Scrum (Agile)	Work is delivered in sprints lasting between 2 and 6 weeks. The content of the next sprint is only finalized at the end of the earlier sprint. *See* Agile.
Specifications	Requirements stated with technical detail (*see* requirements)
Sponsor	Executive or senior manager who is accountable for the project meeting its objectives. The sponsor has decision-making authority regarding the project, but may delegate certain aspects of it. The sponsor owns the business case and should be affected positively or negatively depending on the project outcomes.
Stage	Often synonymous with Phase (*see* Phase)
Stakeholder	Any person or group that is directly or indirectly affected by the project or its outcomes. The sponsor, PM, and the project team are also stakeholders.
Steercom	Short for 'steering committee' – group that advises on major project decisions. Usually headed by the sponsor and attended by the PM. Similar to 'project board'.
Subproject	Part of a project that is executed by a defined team with a leader (or subproject manager). Sometimes also called a 'work stream'.
Task	Work that must be done. Means the same as 'activity'. (*see also* event)

(Continued)

Table A1.1 (Continued)

Term/Acronym	*Meaning*
Template	A project management template is a skeleton document with a name and purpose. Typically templates have headings and blocks to be filled in with text or numbers. Examples might be for a risk register or a resource plan. Some may be mandatory in a particular organization.
Track	In this book, 'tracking' covers both monitoring and controlling. Hence, 'tracking meetings' are used to monitor progress and agree actions that arise. *See also* on track.
Triple constraint	Scope/quality, time, and cost. There are trade-offs between the three.
User	Stakeholder that will use the deliverables of your project.
WBS	Work breakdown structure. A hierarchical structure where all the packages at the lowest level are needed to produce the project deliverables.

Appendix 2

Scheduling Theory – Precedence Diagrams

A2.1 Introduction

The aim of this appendix is to give a sound grasp of the theory behind scheduling. You can skip this if you are already familiar with precedence (network) scheduling with forward and backward passes. The explanation makes use of precedence diagrams which are seldom used for business projects but which are found in most textbooks. It should therefore be read in conjunction with Chapter 9 which gives a more practical perspective of scheduling.

A2.2 Precedence Scheduling – Useful for Grasping the Theory

The explanation that follows uses the AON (activity on node) network representation. It gives the theory underlying Microsoft Project (MSP) and many other schedulers. The 'precedence' for an activity (or task) indicates which other activities precede (come before) this activity, or, on which other activities this activity depends. We shall walk through a simple example which will illustrate the concepts. The example assumes that we have a piece of land and want to build a shed on it and also a perimeter wall. The four activities are given in Table A2.1 where all dependencies are FS (finish-start). The example shows scheduling in weeks. In practice, I normally

Table A2.1 Precedence for Our Scheduling Exercise

Ref.	Description	Duration	Precedence
A	Design shed	2 weeks	-
B	Build shed	6 weeks	A, C
C	Build wall	5 weeks	-
D	Paint wall	4 weeks	C

schedule in work days, with 5 work days to the week, but the principles are identical. Note that the durations are planned durations – the best estimates of the PM and team. The actual durations will only be known later and depend on many things, like who does the work and issues that arise.

The table shows that designing the shed and building the wall can start immediately (no precedence activities). There are a number of decisions that the PM has taken:

- Building the shed (B) will only start when the design (A) is complete.
  Also, building will only start when the wall has been built (C) to reduce the risk of materials for the shed being stolen.
  So 'A, C' means that both A and C must be complete for B to start.
- Painting the wall (D) will only start when the wall is fully built (C).

The sequence of the table rows does not matter. B is above C, but depends on C finishing. The table can be translated into a precedence diagram as shown in Figure A2.1.

At the start and end of the schedule are circles. Each activity, like A, is a node. The arrows show the dependencies. For example, from Start, which is also a node, there is an arrow to A, showing that A depends on project start. B has arrows from A and C showing that B can only start when both A and C are complete. Each node has four parameters in the corners as indicated in the key:

- ES (early start) is the earliest that the activity can start.
- EF (early finish) is the earliest that the activity can finish.
- LS (late start) is the latest that the activity can start for the overall project to meet its early finish date.
- LF (late finish) is the latest that the activity can finish for the overall project to meet its early finish date.

Clearly, the parameters assume that our duration estimates are valid.

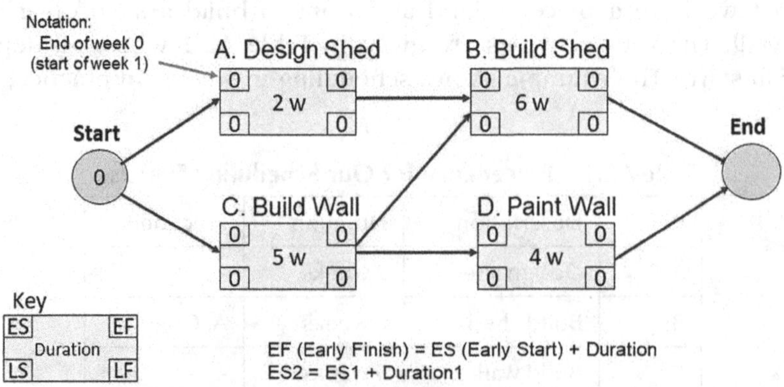

Figure A2.1 Starting precedence diagram for building a shed.

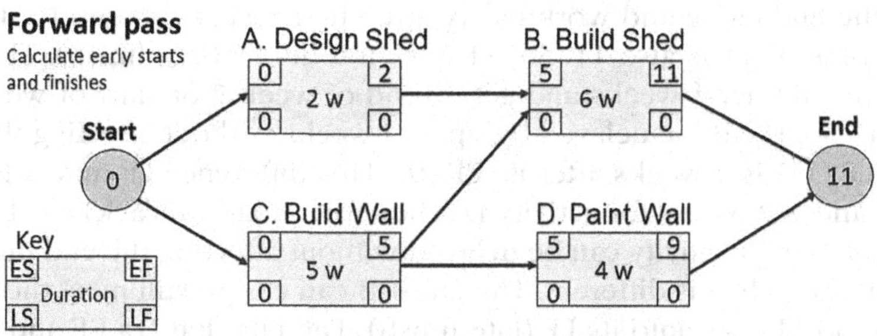

Figure A2.2 Forward pass (with ES and EF for all activities).

A2.2.1 Forward Pass

First we want to know the earliest times that each activity can start and end (ES and EF). This will give us the estimated early end time for the whole project. To make the arithmetic easy, we adopt a simple convention: the numbers always refer to the *end* of a week. The end of week 0 is exactly the same as the start of week 1. So in Figure A2.2, the project starts at the end of week 0. Activities A and C which can start immediately also start at 0. The EF of A is therefore 0 + 2 (weeks duration) = 2, meaning that the earliest that A (design shed) can finish is at the end of week 2. Likewise, the earliest that C can finish is at the end of week 5.

If we continue like this, we get the early starts and early finishes for all activities. This is known as doing a 'forward pass'. Each activity must wait for all its preceding activities to finish before it can start, so B starts at the end of week 5 because it must wait for C to finish. Activity B has an EF of 11 which is the highest EF and hence determines the end of the project. So 11 goes into the end circle indicating that the earliest that the project can finish, is at the end of week 11. Note that, here we use week numbers for convenience; in practice, most schedulers give dates – the start and end date for activities, and the end date for the project.

A2.2.2 Backward Pass

However, we do not yet know which activities can be delayed without affecting the end date of 11. We find this out by doing a backward pass as shown in Figure A2.3.

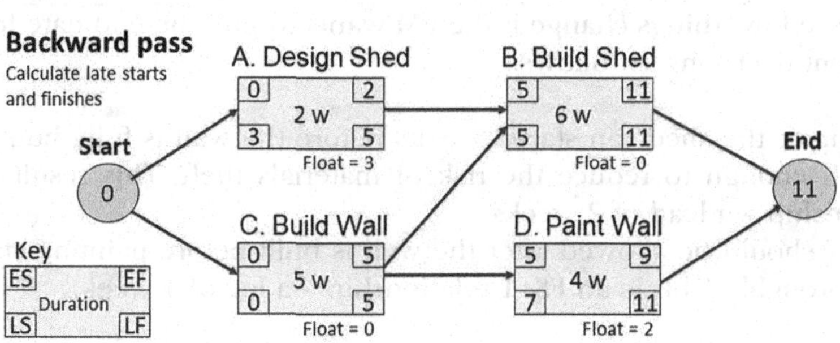

Figure A2.3 Backward pass (with LS and LF for all activities).

We start at the end circle and work backward. The latest D can end to still meet the project end time of 11 is also 11. So, 11 goes into its LF (late finish). Then working backward, we subtract 4 weeks and get 7 (end of week 7 or start of week 8) as the LS (late start). So, D can be delayed by up to 2 weeks without affecting the end time, because its LF (11) is 2 weeks after its EF (9). This difference LF minus EF is known as the 'float' and is 2 weeks for activity D. Therefore, float (or slack) can be described as the amount that an activity can be delayed without affecting the end time (or date).

The situation with B is different. The latest B can end to still meet the project end time also 11. So 11 goes into its LF (late finish). The fact that B's EF and LF are both 11 means that there is no flexibility, and any delay in B will push out the end time. The difference LF minus EF is zero for activity B (11 – 11). Working backward, we see that A has a float of 3 (5 – 2), while C has a float of zero (5 – 5). Why is C's LF 5 and not 7? The reason is that if it were 7 (from D) then B would be delayed. So when working backward, one must take the *lowest* LS of succeeding (following) activities.

A2.2.3 Critical Path

The activities with zero float are known as critical activities. Any delay in starting them or any delay during the activity is likely to delay the end time. On the other hand, A can be delayed 3 weeks and D can be delayed 2 weeks before they become critical and threaten the end time. The path traced by the critical (float zero) activities is known as the 'critical path', in this case, activities C and B form the critical path.

A2.2.4 Constrained and Unconstrained Schedules

What we have produced is an 'unconstrained' schedule. It assumes that we have all the resources (people and materials) that we need to do the work. The PM might have one team to design and build the shed, and another team to build and paint the wall. If the PM only had one team that could do either sheds or walls, the figure would look different. If activities were still done in parallel, the durations would almost certainly be longer. But alternatively, activities could be planned end on end to avoid overloading the team. The result would be a resource-constrained schedule, or simply a 'constrained' schedule. A constrained schedule invariably takes longer!

A2.2.5 Handling Lags and Leads

Now let us see how things change if the PM wants to pull the end date forward, and takes different decisions as follows:

- Building of the shed can start 2 weeks before the wall is fully built – it should be high enough to reduce the risk of materials theft. This results in an FS-2 relationship – a lead of 2 weeks.
- A week should be allowed after the wall is built before painting starts to let it dry thoroughly. This is an FS+1 relationship – a lag of 1 week.

This changes the picture. The forward pass given in Figure A2.4 shows that the project can finish at the end of week 10.

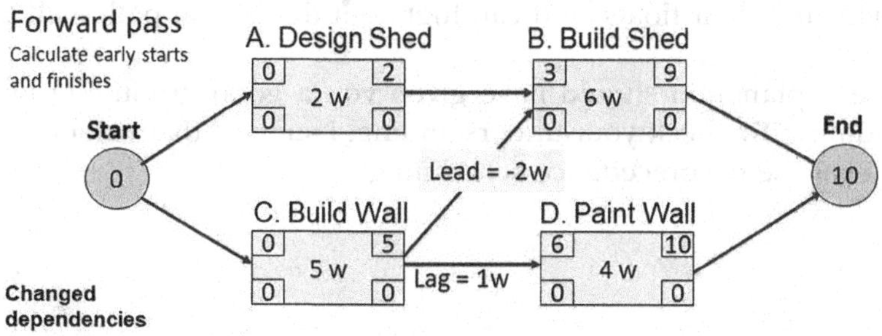

Figure A2.4 Forward pass for the changed dependencies.

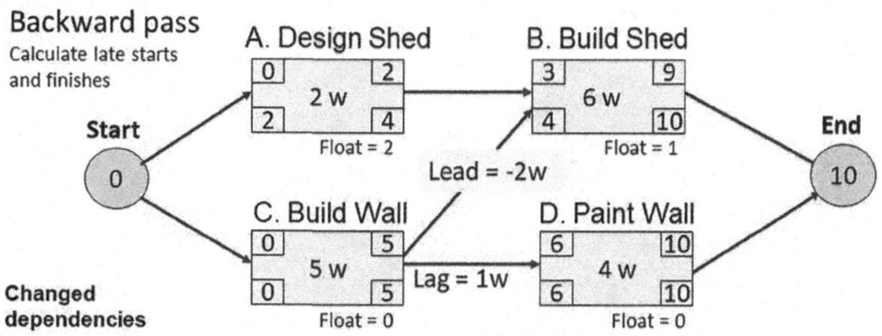

Figure A2.5 Backward pass for the changed dependencies.

The backward pass is given in Figure A2.5. Once again, we work backward from the end time of 10 along the lower path of LF and subtract the duration to get LS.

Even going backward, the lags and leads must be taken into account. So going from D to C, the lag of 1 must be subtracted from D's LS of 6 to give C's LF of 5. We also need to consider the path of B back to C. Now we add back the lead of 2 weeks to B's LS of 4, and get 6. But we cannot use the 6 because the 5 from D is lower, and going backward, we use the lower number. Upon recalculating the floats, we see that the floats for A, B, and D change, and only C remains with a float of 0. The critical path also changes. D now has a float of 0 and moves onto the critical path, whereas B with a float of 1 is no longer on the critical path. Nevertheless, the PM cannot become complacent. A float of 1 week is still close to the critical path, and delays in designing the shed or late delivery of materials could push B back onto the critical path.

A2.3 Summary

Doing these calculations is a lot of work, especially when a schedule becomes complex. Fortunately, when using a scheduler, like MSP, the PM enters the project start date, the activities, their durations, and the dependencies. Then, the scheduler in a split-second does what we manually did above. It calculates the start and end date of each activity and their floats, and can highlight the critical path – all the activities with zero float.

The above explanation should have given you a good grounding on the theory behind scheduling To check your understanding, I suggest that you do Case 9 part 1, which is an exercise on precedence scheduling.

Appendix 3

Two Useful Templates

Many templates are needed in project management and your organization may have standards that require them. If not, you can create your own templates from diagrams in the chapters or from examples on the web. Nevertheless, two useful templates are given below. They are not in any final form. They merely give suggested headings and possible table structures. Because of the variety of business projects, there should be flexibility as to how any template is used. Sometimes headings will be added, removed, or re-sequenced. Also, the table structures will often need to be changed. In the templates that follow, comments or illustrative examples are given in italics which should be removed before use.

PDD (Project Definition Document)

First page: project name, author name, date, organization name (optional). Circulation list (optional). There is no need for a table of contents if the PDD is less than eight pages. The executive summary could start on the first page.

1. **Executive summary**
2. **Glossary**

Term	Description
CPI	*Consumer price index*
Beneficiation	*Used in mining industry and relates to extractive metallurgy. Any process that improves the economic value of the ore.*

3. **Business goals**
   The main business goals are:
   - *Goals should be given at high level, as benefits come later.*
4. **Project objectives**
   The main project objectives are:
   - *These would cover the main deliverables with target dates.*

5. **Critical success factors (CSFs)**
   - *These describe the few things that must be in place for the project to succeed.*
6. **Scope**
   Provide enough information to get a good idea of what work must be done, and what deliverables must be produced. Bullet or table form is easiest to grasp. Avoid excessive technical detail. If the project will be broken into subprojects, these could be sub-headings. Volume data can be included where it puts activities into perspective.
7. **Approach** (optional)
   If the general approach is not clear from the scope, then give a brief description of how the project might be executed.
8. **Context diagram**(s) *(if applicable)*
   Simple diagram, map, or photograph that will clarify the project. It could show the relationship between various parties or systems.
9. **Scope and other exclusions**
   State scope that does not form part of this project. Bullet form is best. Indicate where exclusions might be done as separate initiatives. State anything relevant that will be excluded from a deliverable.
10. **Benefits from the project**
    Monetary figures are estimates.
    Modify the table and column headings to suit your situation. E.g. some benefits may be one-off, or benefits may vary by year. It is valid to list benefits even if no monetary amounts are given.

Ref	Benefit description		
1			

11. **Costs of doing the project**
    Most costs will be incurred during the life of the project. Operational costs, may continue after project completion and could be shown as costs or negative benefits. Costs might be separated according to whether they are internal or from procurement. Check which stakeholders (other than the team) will charge their time to the project.

Ref	Cost description		
1			
	Total		

Only mention net present value or return on investment if they apply.

12. **Resources and stakeholders**
    This must cover the project team. It should also include stakeholders or key members of the steering committee, e.g. sponsor, senior business people, key suppliers.

Name	Role	Main responsibilities
John Malaba	*Sponsor*	o *Convene steering committee* o *Review project reports and respond*

13. **Milestone schedule**
List of Milestones with target dates. A milestone is an event, not an activity.

Date	Milestone description
31 May 2022	*New premises fitted out and ready for staff to move in*

14. **Risks**
Things that could affect the project's objectives or impact the net value of benefits
P = Probability, I = Impact, X = Weighted risk or severity (P – I). Scale 1 – 10

Ref	Risk	P	I	X	Response action
1	*Business people may not understand purpose of project*	*3*	*2*	*6*	*Convene business workshop*

15. **Assumptions, Issues, Dependencies, and Constraints**
A = Assumption, E = Issue, D = Dependency, C = constraint

Ref	Description
A1	*Business staff responsible for the process changes will not charge costs to project*

16. **Management system**
Covers meetings, regular communications, reports, etc., and their frequency, attendance, and circulation.
17. **Documents for reference**
List any relevant contracts, specifications, feasibility reports, or a business case.

Business Project Health-Check

The items in the table below are not comprehensive and need review before their use in your project environment. Any scoring system could apply, but we used a 0 to 3 scale, where: 0 means not applicable or thoroughly satisfactory, and 3 means that the item needs urgent attention. Use of the template is covered in Chapter 25 on project review.

Project Code:	Project name:	
PM name:	Reviewer name:	Review date:

1	**Project definition**	**Score**	**Comments**
1.1	Is the business case documented and up to date?		
1.2	Has a Project Definition Workshop been conducted?		
1.3	Has a Project Definition Document (PDD) been produced, covering all headings in the template?		
1.4	Has the PDD been circulated, commented on, and approved by the sponsor and key stakeholders.		
1.5	Are the project goals and objectives clear?		
1.6	Do the goals align with the corporate strategy?		
1.7	Have the goals been communicated to team members?		
1.8	Is the scope of the project defined in terms of items to be included or excluded?		
1.9	Have the scope and objectives of any subprojects been defined, documented and agreed? Are their interdependencies with the total project documented?		
1.10	Has the PM listed the standard templates that will be used to manage the project?		
1.11	Have all assumptions been documented? (e.g. dependencies on other groups or projects).		
2	**Change control** (mainly scope changes)	**Score**	**Comments**
2.1	Has a documented change control procedure been agreed with key stakeholders? (e.g. the sponsor)		
2.2	Have changes to date been documented accordingly?		
2.3	Have agreed changes been approved by the sponsor?		
2.4	Have project schedules and financial plans been updated to reflect approved changes to date?		

2.5	Is there a record of proposed changes that will be considered after the project is complete?		
3	**People and organisation**	**Score**	**Comments**
3.1	Are the project manager, sponsor, and key subproject managers in place for the project?		
3.2	Has an appropriate organization structure for the project been defined and agreed?		
3.3	Are stakeholder responsibilities agreed / documented?		
3.4	Are adequately skilled people and other resources assigned?		
3.5	Are roles and responsibilities, for project team members, agreed and documented?		
3.6	Are agreements in place with managers of involved resources? (e.g. part-time team members).		
3.7	Have current activities been assigned to team members?		
3.8	Is there a training plan for team members?		
3.9	Have any health and safety concerns been addressed?		
3.10	Is any Internal Audit involvement agreed?		
4	**Stakeholder communications**	**Score**	**Comments**
4.1	Has a communications plan been drawn up? Is it being adhered to?		
4.2	Is a contact list available with mobile numbers and email addresses?		
4.3	Is a list of all stakeholders being maintained which outlines their interests relating to the project?		
5	**Work breakdown and deliverables**	**Score**	**Comments**
5.1	Has a WBS (work breakdown structure) been produced?		
5.2	Have milestones with dates been defined?		
5.3	Have deliverables been specified?		
5.4	Have acceptance criteria for deliverables been agreed?		
6	**Estimating and pricing**	**Score**	**Comments**
6.1	Have people and other costs been estimated, documented, and agreed?		

6.2	Do estimates include all project scope items?		
6.3	Are assumptions stated which underpin the estimates?		
6.4	Has appropriate contingency for risk been included?		
6.5	Has any pricing (to customers) been approved?		
7	**Schedule and progress management**	**Score**	**Comments**
7.1	Are regular sponsor and/or steering committee meetings being held? Are minutes available?		
7.2	Is the business case (including benefits, costs, and risks) being maintained and reviewed periodically? Are decisions taken to continue, make changes, or stop?		
7.3	Has a schedule with activities and dates been produced, with sufficient detail for the coming months?		
7.4	Has responsibility for each near-term project activities been assigned? (including subprojects and suppliers)		
7.5	Are schedule deadlines for major deliverables clear?		
7.6	Is the schedule being tracked regularly (e.g. weekly)?		
7.7	Are tracking meetings held regularly? (e.g. weekly)		
7.8	Are tracking meetings minuted via a standard template with an attendance register, and being archived?		
7.9	Are project reports using an agreed template being sent to stakeholders? (if not weekly, how regularly?)		
7.10	Are stakeholders comfortable that they are being kept informed, especially of out-of-line situations?		
8	**Risk Management**	**Score**	**Comments**
8.1	Has a Risk Register with identified risks been created?		
8.2	Have risks been assessed for likelihood (probability) and impact? (includes risks to all stakeholders)		
8.3	Are risks being assessed and updated periodically?		
8.4	Are risk response actions being decided and tracked?		
8.5	Has adequate money and time contingency, for risks, been allocated?		
9	**Management of issues and decisions**	**Score**	**Comments**
9.1	Are issues being logged via the Issues Log and Issue Records?		
9.2	Are open issues prioritized and tracked to completion?		

9.3	Is the escalation route clear for issues that are beyond the PM's control?		
9.4	Are decisions taken being recorded and circulated?		
9.5	Is the issues management process working effectively?		
10	**Quality management**	**Score**	**Comments**
10.1	Has a backed-up repository for documentation been set up which is appropriately accessible to stakeholders?		
10.2	Are the title, date, author, and security classification stated on all documents?		
10.3	Has a workshop been held to list quality requirements?		
10.4	Is there a quality management plan for the deliverables?		
10.5	Will the deliverables have adequate documentation?		
10.6	For a project with IT content, is there a test plan?		
10.7	Are stakeholder satisfaction surveys being conducted?		
10.8	Is a lesson learned log being maintained?		
11	**Tracking and reporting (cost and time)**	**Score**	**Comments**
11.1	Are documented budgets agreed with the stakeholders?		
11.2	Where peoples' hours are charged to the project, are the hours being recorded, and the actual costs tracked?		
11.3	Is a tracking spreadsheet being used to estimate the percentage completion?		
11.4	Are reports given to key stakeholders, at least monthly, covering the status, with schedule and cost indices?		
12	**Contract management and approvals**	**Score**	**Comments**
12.1	Is there a signed contract (agreement) between key stakeholders? (e.g. between buyer and seller)		
12.2	If a contract is still due, has a letter of authorisation been signed allowing work to continue and be paid for?		
12.3	Does the contract spell out the responsibilities of all parties, and do they fully understand them?		
12.4	Are stakeholder expectations clearly defined? Are they likely to be met?		
12.5	Is ownership of all assets (equipment, hardware, software, etc.) documented and agreed?		
12.6	Is the process for checking and approving deliverables agreed?		

13	Supplier / subcontractor management	Score	Comments
13.1	Does a contract or document-of-understanding exist with all sub-contractors or suppliers? (in certain cases an accepted quotation might suffice)		
13.2	Have their track record / financial status been validated?		
13.3	Have any proposed solutions been validated?		
13.4	Are billing and payment processes agreed, and in place?		
14	**OCM (organisational change management)**	**Score**	**Comments**
14.1	If the project or its output affects many stakeholders, has scope for communications/workshops/training been planned?		

Index

Q

S

Printed in the United States
by Baker & Taylor Publisher Services